Mizan Series 5

MUSLIMS IN THE MOVIES

The Mizan Series

The Mizan Series is published by the Ilex Foundation in partnership with the Center for Hellenic Studies. The series supports the central mission of the Mizan digital initiative to encourage informed public discourse and interdisciplinary scholarship on the history, culture, and religion of Muslim societies and civilizations.

www.mizanproject.org

Also in the Mizan Series

Muslim Superheroes: Comics, Islam, and Representation,
edited by A. David Lewis and Martin Lund

Muslims and US Politics Today: A Defining Moment
edited by Mohammad Hassan Khalil

The End of Middle East History and Other Conjectures
by Richard W. Bulliet

Deconstructing Islamic Studies
edited by Majid Daneshgar and Aaron W. Hughes

MUSLIMS IN THE MOVIES

A Global Anthology

Edited by
Kristian Petersen

Ilex Foundation
Boston, Massachusetts

Center for Hellenic Studies
Trustees for Harvard University
Washington, D. C.

Distributed by Harvard University Press
Cambridge, Massachusetts and London, England

Muslims in the Movies: A Global Anthology
Edited by Kristian Petersen

Published by the Ilex Foundation, Boston, Massachusetts and The Center for Hellenic Studies, Trustees for Harvard University, Washington, D.C.

Distributed by Harvard University Press, Cambridge, Massachusetts and London, England

Production editor: Christopher Dadian
Cover design: Joni Godlove
Printed in the United States of America

Cover Image: Still photo from Musa Syeed's *Valley of Saints* (2012), by Yoni Brook.

Library of Congress Cataloging-in-Publication Data

Names: Petersen, Kristian, 1979- editor.
Title: Muslims in the movies : a global anthology / edited by Kristian
  Petersen
Description: Boston, Massachusetts : Ilex Foundation ; Washington, D.C. :
  Center for Hellenic Studies, Trustees for Harvard University, 2021. |
  Series: Mizan series; 5 | Includes bibliographical references. |
  Summary: "Muslims in the Movies provides a series of essays that explore
  the portrayal and reception of Muslims in Euro-American film,
  transnational productions, and global national cinemas. The volume
  brings together a group of internationally recognized experts to
  introduce Muslims in the films of Europe, North America, Australia,
  Iran, Egypt, North Africa, Saudi Arabia, Nigeria, India, Indonesia, and
  the Philippines. The interdisciplinary collection explores issues of
  identity, cultural production, and representation through the depiction
  of Muslims on screen and how audiences respond to these images.
  Together, the essays operate as an introduction to the subject of
  Muslims and film for new readers while also serving as new works of
  critical analysis for scholars of cinema"-- Provided by publisher.
Identifiers: LCCN 2021009321 | ISBN 9780674257788 (paperback)
Subjects: LCSH: Muslims in motion pictures.
Classification: LCC PN1995.9.I697 M88 2021 | DDC 791.43/68297--dc23
LC record available at https://lccn.loc.gov/2021009321

CONTENTS

Contributors

Abdalla Uba Adamu, Prof. Dr., is a lecturer in the Department of Information and Media Studies, Faculty of Communication, Bayero University Kano, Nigeria. His main research focus is on transnational media flows and their impact on the transformation of Muslim Hausa popular culture, especially in literature, film, music, and performing arts. He is an ethnographic filmmaker and also an ethnomusicologist. Prof. Dr. Adamu was a visiting professor of the European Union at the University of Warsaw in 2012; as well as visiting professor at Universität zu Köln, State University of New Jersey, Columbia University, University of Florida, SOAS and University of Basel. His website is www.auadamu.com

Vivienne SM. Angeles is associate professor at the Department of Religion and Theology at La Salle University in Philadelphia. She has published on the areas of Islam in the Philippines and Southeast Asia, Islam and gender, visual expressions of religion, and religion and migration. Angeles was a Fulbright scholar at the Center for Civilizational Dialogue at the University of Malaya and was president of the American Council for the Study of Islamic Societies. She was co-chair of the Religion in Southeast Asia unit and currently a member of the International Connections Committee of the American Academy of Religion.

Michela Ardizzoni is an associate professor at the University of Colorado at Boulder. Her research focuses on global media, connected media practices, and media activism, and marginality. Her study of Italian television, *North/South, East/West: Mapping Italianness on Television*, was published in 2007. She is the co-editor of *Beyond Monopoly: Globalization and Contemporary Italian Media* (2010) and *Mediterranean Encounters in the City* (2015). Her research has also appeared in several media journals, such as *Journalism, Jump Cut, Journal of Communication Inquiry, Journal of Italian Cinema and Media Studies, International Journal of Communication*, and *Communication, Culture and Critique*. Her most recent book, *Matrix Activism: Global Practices of Resistance* (2017), examines contemporary forms of media activism in Italy, North Africa, Senegal, and the United States. She's currently working on a book-length project on the politics and economies of expendability and superfluity of vulnerable bodies as they are represented in contemporary media.

Elliott Bazzano is associate professor in the Department of Religious Studies at Le Moyne College, where he teaches courses on Islam and comparative religion. His research focuses on the interplay of Qur'anic interpretation, polemics, and mysticism, as well as pedagogy in religious studies scholarship. His articles have appeared in *The Journal of the American Academy of Religion*, *Teaching Theology and Religion*, and *Religion Compass*. He writes for the Wabash Center blog *Teaching Islam*, and hosts podcasts for New Books in Islamic Studies. He also serves as co-chair for the Study of Islam unit of the American Academy of Religion.

Thomas Barker is the head of the School of Media, Languages and Cultures at the University of Nottingham Malaysia and associate professor of film and television. He is the author of *Indonesian Cinema after the New Order: Going Mainstream* (HKU Press, 2019) and has written for *The Jakarta Post*, *The Handbook of Diasporas, Media, and Culture*, *Routledge Handbook of Cultural and Creative Industries in Asia*, *TRaNS: Trans-Regional and -National Studies of Southeast Asia*, and *The Conversation* on topics in the sociology of culture. He has held visiting positions at National Chengchi University, UCLA, Universitas Indonesia, and the National Library of Australia.

Claire Chambers is a senior lecturer in global literature at the University of York. She is the author of *British Muslim Fictions* (2011), *Britain Through Muslim Eyes* (2015), and *Making Sense of Contemporary British Muslim Novels* (2019). She has also published a collection of her essays entitled *Rivers of Ink* (2017). Finally, she co-edited *Imagining Muslims in South Asia and the Diaspora* (2015) and *A Match Made in Heaven* (2020). Her research has been supported by funding from HEFCE, the British Academy, the Leverhulme Trust, and the AHRC. Claire is editor-in-chief (with Rachael Gilmour) of the *Journal of Commonwealth Literature*.

Nancy Demerdash-Fatemi is an assistant professor of art history in the Department of Art and Art History at Albion College (Michigan, USA), where she teaches a range of courses in visual culture and art and architectural history. She holds graduate and doctoral degrees from the Massachusetts Institute of Technology and Princeton University, respectively, and publishes widely on modern and contemporary art and architecture of the Middle East and North Africa. Her current book project examines architectural and urban interventions in late French colonial Tunisia, amidst the backdrop of decolonization and nationalism. Additionally, she serves as an assistant editor for the *International Journal of Islamic Architecture*.

Alberto Fernández Carbajal is senior lecturer in English literature at the University of Roehampton (London). His research is placed at the intersection of colonial, postcolonial, queer, diaspora, and Islamic studies. He is the author of *Queer Muslim Diasporas in Contemporary Literature and Film* (Manchester University Press, 2019). He is a former recipient of a Leverhulme Early Career Fellowship, article editor of the open-access online journal *Postcolonial Text*, and he is the exiting vice-chair of the Postcolonial Studies Association (UK).

Mohannad Ghawanmeh's expertise centers on Arab cinema, but extends into silent cinema, nonfiction cinema, transnational cinema, and religious cinema. Mohannad holds a PhD in Cinema and Media Studies from UCLA. He is recipient of the Teshome Gabriel Memorial Award, the Dr. Jack Shaheen Memorial Scholarship, the Otis Ferguson Memorial Award for Critical Writing, the Kemp R. Niver Scholarship in Film History, and a special mention from Domitor, the international society for the study of early cinema. Mohannad is engaged in two book projects, a cultural history by way of political economy of silent and early sound cinemas in Egypt, 1896–1934, and a monograph tentatively titled *The Harem on the Screen*.

M. Cooper Harriss is an associate professor in the Department of Religious Studies at Indiana University, in Bloomington, where his research and teaching focus on religion, literature, and culture in the Americas and beyond. He is a founding co-editor of the journal *American Religion* (Indiana University Press), the author of *Ralph Ellison's Invisible Theology* (NYU 2017), and is presently working on a book about Muhammad Ali and American religion.

Syed Haider is head of academic subjects for the International Study Centre at Royal Holloway, University of London. He is currently working on a monograph on Muslim modernities on the Hindi screen and has published most recently an essay on the media coverage of the shootings in Orlando in the journal *Men and Masculinities*. Syed has contributed chapters to a volume on *Postcolonialism and Islam*, edited by Geoffery Nash et. al and Om Dwivedi's *The Other India*. He is a member of Challenging Precarity: A Global Network and his research interests lie in the expression of historical and contemporary Islamicates.

Alicia Izharuddin is a research associate at the Women's Studies in Religion Program at the Harvard Divinity School where she is currently writing her second book on negative emotions. She has published in *Signs: Journal* of *Women in Culture and Society*, *Indonesia and the Malay World*, *Asian Cinema*, *Feminist Media Studies*, among other journals. Her first book, *Gender and Islam in Indonesian Cinema* (2017) was published by Palgrave Macmillan.

Michael Muhammad Knight is the author of fourteen books, most recently *Metaphysical Africa: Truth and Blackness in the Ansaru Allah Community* and *Muhammad's Body: Baraka Networks and the Prophetic Assemblage*. He is assistant professor of religion and cultural studies at the University of Central Florida.

Mehal Krayem has a PhD from the University of Technology Sydney. Her book *Heroes, Villains and the Muslim Exception* explores the representation of Arab and Muslim masculinities in Australian film and television. After teaching for nearly a decade, Mehal now works at the Centre for Social Justice and Inclusion.

Rebecca Moody is an assistant teaching professor of religion at Worcester Polytechnic Institute in Worcester, MA. Her research interests include religion in North Africa and the Middle East with a focus on Islam and its representation in visual culture; she situates her theoretical scaffolding at the intersection of cultural studies, feminist theory, film theory, and affect theory. Moody's current book project, *Synaesthetic Shock: Gender, Politics and the Varieties of Islamic Experience in Moroccan Film by Moroccan Women Filmmakers*, considers recent fiction film by women filmmakers as oblique forms of resistance to dominant narratives about Islam and Muslim women in Morocco.

Nacim Pak-Shiraz is professor of cinema and Iran, and head of Islamic and Middle Eastern Studies at the University of Edinburgh. She has published in the fields of visual cultures, constructions of masculinity, and the engagement of religion and film. She has authored *Shi'i Islam in Iranian Cinema: Religion and Spirituality in Film* (2011 and 2018), and edited *Visualizing Iran: From Antiquity to Present* (2017). Pak-Shiraz has also curated five annual film festivals in Edinburgh and been a jury member and presenter at a number of international film festivals in Europe and Asia.

Kristian Petersen is an assistant professor at Old Dominion University. He is the author of *Interpreting Islam in China: Pilgrimage, Scripture, and Language in the Han Kitab*, published with Oxford University Press. He is co-editor, with Christopher Cantwell, of *Digital Humanities and Research Methods in Religious Studies: An Introduction*, published with De Gruyter. He is the design architect and curator of the Women of Islamic Studies project, a crowdsourced database of women scholars who work on Muslims and Islam. Finally, he is the co-host of the New Books in Islamic Studies and New Books in Religion podcasts on the New Book Network.

Hussein Rashid, PhD, is a contingent faculty member, currently associated with The New School. He was teaching at Barnard College while working on his chapter for this volume. He has published on cultural contributions of American Muslims, intra-Muslim racism, Muslims and music, Muslims and comics, Shi'i theology, and digital humanities and study of religion. He also served as the content lead for the Children's Museum of Manhattan's *America to Zanzibar: Muslim Cultures Near and Far* exhibit. He also has a consultancy, islamicate, L3C, that works on representations of Muslims.

Sofia Sjö is adjunct professor at the Department of Study of Religions at Åbo Akademi University, Finland. Her research areas include religion and film, digital religion, religion and gender, and religion and young adults. In the area of religion and film research, she has particularly focused on science fiction and contemporary Nordic films. Her research has been published in a number of journals and edited volumes, among them *Journal of Religion and Film*, *Journal of Religion and Popular Culture*, and *Religion, Media and Social Change*.

Samhita Sunya is an assistant professor of cinema in the Department of Middle Eastern and South Asian Languages and Cultures at the University of Virginia. Since 2018, she has been an associate programmer for the Virginia Film Festival. Her research, teaching, and curatorial interests span world film history, intersections of audio-visual media and literature, and sound studies. Supported by a Mellon Humanities Fellowship and residence at Yale University's MacMillan Center, she is completing a monograph titled *Sirens of Modernity: World Cinema Via Bombay*.

Approaching Muslims in the Movies

Kristian Petersen

MUSLIMS IN THE MOVIES are often caricatures of life – sensational and incomplete – relying on worn representational formulas, which reproduce stereotypes about Muslims. We find this pattern across global film industries, such as in Britain,[1] France,[2] India,[3] and China.[4] American film is the worst offender historically.[5] Recent Hollywood films continue to fail in expanding the recognizable characteristics of Muslims on screen, often reifying a dichotomy between "good" and "bad" Muslims and limiting the narrative domain to issues of national security, war, and terrorism.[6] The resultant vilification of Muslims in the United States is indebted to the cinematic production of "Islam," often understood as the static tra-

1. See for example Jameela 2018. For a broader introduction to Muslims and media patterns in Britain see Poole 2002, and de Rooij 2020.

2. The social anxiety about France's minority Muslim population is often filtered through a fixation on the veil. This subject is compellingly explored in Handyside 2019, and Davies Hayon 2019. Mack 2017 (especially Chapter 4) explores the counterpart through the representation of Muslim men's deviant sexuality. A good deal of scholarship also addresses how filmmakers of Muslim heritage are producing counter narratives that disrupt the dominant French visual and ideological patterns. See Higbee 2000, Kealhofer-Kemp 2016, Rosello 1998, and Tarr 2005.

3. As a large minority population Muslims are often framed as a threat to national unity and a population that is wholly "other" than the Hindu majority. See for example Chadha and Kavoori 2008, Haider 2013, Hussein and Hussain 2015, Kabir 2010, Khatun 2016, Khatun 2018, Kumar H. M. 2013, Kumar H. M. 2016, and Raghuvanshi and Kumar H.M. 2017.

4. China is the world's second-highest grossing movie market after North America and has a long history of film production. While Muslims have been largely absent from most Chinese productions, recent big budget Hollywood style action films have relied on American stereotypical imagery. *Operation Red Sea* (*Honghai xingdong* 红海行动) (Dante Lam, 2018), which focuses on a mission to rescue Chinese citizens in Yemen during the 2015 civil unrest, is one of the highest-grossing films ever in China and won the Best Picture award at the 34th Hundred Flowers Awards (*Dazhong Dianying Baihua Jiang* 大众电影百花奖), one of the country's highest cinematic honors. This film reproduces many of the "terrorist" tropes about Muslims that are found in American cinema and its enormous success demonstrates that Chinese audiences tolerate, at best, or even at worst enjoy anti-Muslim cinematic imagery and narratives.

5. For the long history of Muslims in Hollywood pictures see Shaheen 2001, Shaheen 2008. For more recent developments see Alhassen 2018.

6. Alsultany calls this dichotomy "simplified complex representations." See Alsultany 2012.

dition that organizes followers' actions and thoughts. This mediation is the closest site of proximity of a Muslim encounter for many Americans.[7] The structural framework of these portrayals and the socio-political consequences of representations have been mapped out in preliminary terms in previous scholarship.[8] *Muslims in the Movies: A Global Anthology* extends this work by expanding the boundaries of our investigation, asking new questions of the filmic archive, and magnifying our analysis of particular cultural productions.

These essays set "Islam" as the visual, narrative, social, political, or historical horizon within which they analyze cinematic cultures. We do not put forth a normative category of Islam and try to defend it but rather examine the multitude of ways Islam is deployed in the production of films. Islam is a rich and diverse archive of practices, expectations, ideas, and assumptions that Muslims interpret and draw upon to fashion everyday life. We probe the affective operations that filmic interpretations of Islam produce, the dispositional locations from which they are assembled, and try to discern the public sentiments they were meant to elicit. This approach ends with competing images of what the tradition is, how Muslim identity is formulated around it, and the manners in which it structures aspects of social life.[9] Collectively, we investigate the variety of definitional accounts of Islam that inform articulations of Muslim identity within various global contexts.

Muslim identity is necessarily central to our project. While we are interested in how Muslim identities are represented and deployed in filmic cultures, we seek to understand the constructive assumptions and social consequences of these portrayals rather than police the boundaries of what is acceptable. For example, being Muslim in Hollywood films is demarcated by a limited set of recognizable features (dress, accent, race, etc.) that make the individual "legible" to viewers because their representation meets structured audience expectations.[10] For other viewing publics, subjects will be judged by a different set of local socially defined

---

7. One survey found that only about half of Americans say they personally know someone who is Muslim. Those who do, generally have much more sympathetic feelings towards them. Pew Research Center 2017.

8. Key scholarship on representations of Muslims include Bayraktaroğlu 2018, Hussain 2009, Khatib 2006, Mahdi 2020, McAlister 2005, Morey and Yaqin 2011, Ramji 2013, Ramji 2016, Rashid 2014, Semmerling 2006.

9. Very few studies actually use Islam as a guiding analytical framework. Dönmez-Colin 2004, Izharuddin 2016, and Pak-Shiraz 2011 are the only book-length projects that center the tradition as an exploratory field for investigation. Cheema 2018, and Rakhmani 2016 use Islam to frame their investigation of television screen cultures.

10. Petersen 2017.

criteria of what signifies Muslim by spectators. Hollywood's long history of negative images of Muslims is still within our analytical terrain but we hope to think about Muslim identity outside of this limited archive. We also move beyond scholarship that is focused on Western representation by investigating national and regional cinemas in Muslim majority societies. These perspectives provide new domains of Muslim identity formation and construction situated within drastically different social, linguistic, and cultural contexts. Multiple international designations of who is a Muslim, their distinctive characteristics, and how they express their personalities, generate a cinematic catalog of greater depth, nuance, and diversity. While religious minorities exist in places like Iran, Indonesian, or Egypt, religious subjectivity can often be assumed on the part of the producers and the audiences in these locations. Social nuance will shape the particular shade of Islamic practice or language whereby a cinematic assemblage of Muslimness can be constructed in radically different ways compared to Muslim minority filmic contexts.[11] Overall, the essays explore depictions of Muslims as minorities and their ideological function in film, as well as retrieve how Muslim identities and the tradition are imagined and represented in cinematic cultures with large Muslim audiences.

WHAT DOES THIS BOOK DO?

Muslims in the Movies: A Global Anthology brings international breadth and analytical depth together through a series of complementary essays that explore Euro-American film, transnational productions, as well as Muslim national cinemas. Our studies use films as a platform for asking questions about various dimensions of Islam and Muslims in modern society. Conversely, we place images, stories, and production settings within perspectives found in a wide spectrum of locally interpreted Islamic discourses and practices to delineate the multiple layers and elements visually and audibly portrayed on screen. Each essay is designed for an intelligent novice audience in the immediate subject matter but will conjure broader debates and theories for students and scholars of religion, film, or both. They are written in a concise and accessible manner in order to outline a strong analysis but will also stimulate future investigation by the reader. Through critical theoretical approaches, we examine how Islam, as variously defined, pervades the global history of classical and modern cinema. Altogether, we explore issues of identity, cultural production, and

11. A more thorough illustration of this interpretive strategy that understands "Muslim" cultural representations as contested domains emerging from the dialogue between producers, industries, and audiences can be found in Petersen 2020.

representation though the depiction of Islam and Muslims on screen and how audiences respond to these portrayals. The interdisciplinary collection provides a global examination of the multiple roles Islam plays in film.

One aim of the collection is to bring together analytical patterns and themes from scholarship on national cinemas, representation, transnational film, and religion and film. Scholarship on national cinema of Muslim majority populations is well-established in contexts like Iran,[12] Egypt,[13] Turkey,[14] Palestine,[15] or the Maghreb.[16] Yet several substantial Muslim majority cinematic cultures have yet to be thoroughly researched, such as Southeast Asia[17] or Nigeria.[18] However, even in many of these germinal studies Islam as a subject rarely serves as organizing domain for analysis. However, it seems Islam often lurks in the background for some of the existing studies and a clear inquiry into its definitional articulation and its structuring capacity on national cinemas is frequently absent. Similarly, the terrain of scholarship on Religion and Film is well developed

12. Some key texts are Atwood 2016, Dabashi 2011, Ginsberg and Lippard 2020, Ghorbankarimi 2015, Langford 2019, Leaman 2001, Mottahedeh 2008, Naficy 2011a, Naficy 2011b, Naficy 2012a, Naficy 2012b, Pak-Shiraz 2011, Partovi 2017, Rekabtalaei 2019, Sheibani 2011, Tapper 2002, and Zeydabadi-Nejad 2009.

13. Some key texts are Armes 2010, Armes 2015, Armes 2018, Bisschoff and van de Peer 2019, El-Shammaa 2020, Ghazal 2020, Ginsberg and Lippard 2020, Gugler 2015, Hillauer 2006, Khouri 2010, Shafik 2007, and Shafik 2017.

14. Some key texts are Arslan 2010, Atakav 2013, Dönmez-Colin 2008, Dönmez-Colin 2013, Dönmez-Colin 2019, Ginsberg and Lippard 2020, Leaman 2001, Suner 2010, and Thwaites Diken 2018.

15. Some key texts are Armes 2015, Armes 2018, Ball 2012, Brittain 2020, Burris 2019, Dabashi 2006, Dickinson 2016, Ginsberg 2016, Ginsberg and Lippard 2020, Gugler 2015, Hillauer 2006, Leaman 2001, and Yaqub 2018.

16. Some key texts are Armes 2005, Armes 2006, Armes 2010, Armes 2015, Armes 2018, Austin 2012, Bisschoff and van de Peer 2019, Bedjaoui 2020, Davies Hayon 2018, Dwyer 2004, Gauch 2016, Ginsberg and Lippard 2020, Gugler 2015, Higbee, Martin, and Bahmad 2020, Hillauer 2006, Lang 2014, Leaman 2001, Limbrick 202, Martin 2011, O'Riley 2010, Orlando 2009, Orlando 2011, Orlando 2017, and Shafik 2017.

17. Some foundational texts include Barker 2019, Hanan 2017, Ingawanij and McKay 2011, Izharuddin 2017, Khoo 2006, Lim and Yamamoto 2011, Muhammad 2009, Muhammad 2010, and van der Heide 2002.

18. There is a good deal of scholarship on the Nigerian film industry (dubbed "Nollywood"), focused primarily on English-language production even though Nigerian-language films are more numerous, including the relevant texts Haynes 2016, Krings and Okome 2013, and Saul and Austen 2010. However, exploration of the Hausa language videos industry based in the predominantly Muslim northern Nigeria has garnered lesser attention. Some stimulating scholarship includes Abubakar and Dauda 2019, A. U. Adamu 2010, A. U. Adamu 2013, A. U. Adamu 2017a, A. U. Adamu 2017b, Y. Adamu 2002, Ibrahim and Yusuf 2020, M. Ibrahim 2017, M. Ibrahim 2020, M. M. Ibrahim 2013, M. M. Ibrahim 2019, Krings 2007, Krings 2008, Krings 2015, Larkin 2000, Larkin 2004, Larkin 2008, and McCain 2013.

in many ways but still lacking in terms of the diversity of traditions that are examined under this rubric. Islam is one such lacuna. One reason for this is the lack of dynamic sources for further study in non-Christian traditions and films that are not limited to Euro-American cinemas. Therefore, these essays are written in a manner to appeal to readers with interests adjacent to Islam in film who would like to explore the topic in new contexts and at greater theoretical complexity. The volume is structured in a way that makes it useful for teaching and the text can be utilized in classes, either read in tandem with other texts or as a focused reader for use on its own. Altogether, we seek to add complexity and depth to this literature by situating Islam as the central component in the analytical rubric of Religion and Film with the inclusion of various national cinematic cultures.

APPROACHING MUSLIMS IN THE MOVIES

The essays within explore this relationship in a variety of ways and span a wide range of geographies, cultures, and thematic approaches. Several examine a national cinematic context to plot the trajectory of representations of Muslims within contemporary film. Michela Ardizzoni maps out the Italian cinematic terrain, focusing on the function of Muslims in several mainstream comedic films. She demonstrates that through a number of sensory signals – speech, dress, food, etc. – Muslims are generally deemed culturally foreign to the national body for mass audiences. We find this general tendency to depict Muslims as "other" in the Australian context as well. However, Mehal Krayem shows how Muslim-Australians have used the romantic comedy (rom-com) genre, as a means to engage mainstream audiences and participate in a form of "listening across difference." This mediated approach supports the decentering of "whiteness" in Australian storytelling and enables the disruption of inequitable social hierarchies in the national context. Vivienne Angeles also tackles communal difference and the conditions of being a minority, but in the Philippines. She illustrates how Muslim filmmakers counter dominant stereotypical representations of Muslims by telling a wide range of stories about Philippine Muslim women and their own local struggles, hopes, and victories.

Other authors in the volume zoom into a specific frame of cinema, such as screenwriters, directors, or even a single film. Claire Chambers examines how two British film writers of South Asian heritage, Hanif Kureishi and Ayub Khan-Din, shift their depictions of Muslim characters in their stories over time. She pinpoints the 1989 Rushdie affair as a pivotal moment that dramatically altered public attitudes and assumptions about

British Muslims. Alberto Fernandez-Carbajal presents Canadian poet and filmmaker Ian Iqbal Rashid's archive of cinematic portrayals of queer Ismaili diaspora life. Rashid's early filmwork disrupts rom-com genre conventions and also public understandings of Islam by narrating a same-sex Muslim romance in a post-colonial modernity. Nacim Pak-Shiraz uses films by the Iranian director Asghar Farhadi as an avenue for understanding the concepts of "truth" and "justice" in the Shi'a context of the Islamic Republic of Iran. We find that Farhadi's Iranian citizens find themselves in tension between the promise of social justice and the pragmatic exercise of Islamic governance. Elliott Bazzano introduces readers to Saudi Arabian writer and director Haifaa Al-Mansour's feature film directorial debut, *Wadjda* (2012). He examines the multiple ways the film disrupts assumptions about the Kingdom's religious rigidity – narrated through notions of girlhood, motivations for religious observance, and knowledge of scripture – but also critiques practices justified by Islamic discourses, including gendered social norms or inequitable marriage practices. Rebecca Moody evaluates Moroccan filmmaker Farida Benlyazid's *Bab al-Sama Maftuh* (1989) and how she portrays Moroccan women shaping the local gendered spatial logic that informs the Islam of everyday life. The characters' religious practice inhabits a space between secular feminism and conservative Islam, which causes a visual rupture for both North African and Euro-American audiences.

Two essays treat the relationship between Muslims and cinema through a brief social history of the film industry. Mohannad Ghawanmeh looks at the development of mid-twentieth century Egyptian cinema, especially those depicting Islamic history, and the role of religious professionals and institutions in approving their production. The centuries old al-Azhar University and mosque served as a clearinghouse for vetting popular entertainment before public consumption. Ghawanmeh's essay both introduces us to Egypt's golden era of "religious film" but also the institutional censorship practices that filmmakers had to navigate in order to get their films made. Similarly, Abdalla Uba Adamu examines the institutional setting for filmmaking in Nigeria and public concerns that film promotes immorality among Muslim youth. He provides an analysis of a recent proposal to create a "film village," or soundstage, as the center of the Hausa language video film industry in Kano, dubbed Kanywood. Public debate swirled on social media, including the opinions of local Islamic religious professionals, with the circulation of memes critiquing film's perceived promotion of lax piety, such as the mixing of genders or encouraging Western style dress. This type of social analysis of film industry adds a great deal to what we can learn from the visual, discursive, and formal investigation of films that are provided throughout the remainder of the book.

Another approach taken by many of the authors is a thematic strategy that ties several films together around a single conceptual thread. Syed Haider, for example, explores what he dubs as "Sufi aesthetics" in two Bollywood films. These artistic visual and sonic techniques are rooted in a vernacular sensibility of spiritual praxis. But instead of being fixed in actual ritual practice they become signifiers of a common public culture of Muslim modernity. Samhita Sunya explores "terror comedies" from Morocco and India as satirical critiques of the logics undergirding the global "War on Terror." By using conventions for the comedic genre and inverting stereotypes from Hollywood cinema these films focus our attention on the dramatic scripting of US global intervention and its effects on Muslims. Nancy Demerdash-Fatemi looks at French cinema through the lens of conversion – both to Islam, and away from it. Her analysis places these films within debates on *laïcité*, anxieties about immigration, and public attitudes towards Muslims in France. Sofia Sjö tackles similar terrain through representations of growing up Muslim in a Nordic context through Danish, Norwegian, and Swedish productions. She finds that some Nordic films employ Muslim youth as a narrative juncture mediating public struggles around issues of belonging, identity, religion, and tolerance. Alicia Izharuddin tracks corresponding troubles in Southeast Asia where "Islamic films" are responding to transnational media circuits of terrorism and Islamist extremism. She shows how Indonesian filmmakers' and audiences' own vision of Muslims are produced through a reconfiguration and refraction of global encounters with public discourses. Thomas Barker explores the deepening archive of Indonesian cinema as an avenue to public debates about Muslim practices. He focuses on recent films dealing with polygamy, including both advocates and detractors, and shows how contemporary filmmakers imagine the role of marriage, romance, and family in society. Finally, Hussein Rashid filters out secondary characters that are marked as Muslim in contemporary science fiction films but where their religious identity does not advance the plot of the story. There is no necessary relationship between being Muslim and the character's role in the story. For these "incidental Muslims" religious belonging can be used to strengthen a character's disposition but it is not determinative to their actions. Rashid offers a useful new theoretical paradigm that allows audiences to imagine religious interaction that is non-confrontational and observe nuanced Muslims characters.

A final strategy presented in the volume is a cinematic genealogy of a single character. These essays examine two of the most important US Muslims, Muhammad Ali and Malcolm X, and present their various mediated forms. Both figures serve as frameworks to understand race, religion, and public assumptions about the role of Islam in America. M. Cooper Harris looks at three films that provide snapshots of Ali's life in motion – his refusal to be drafted by the military in the 1960s, the 1974 global spectacle dubbed "The Rumble in the Jungle," and the narrative feature, *Ali* (Michael Mann, 2001), which recounts this whole period of his life. He plots the representational shifts of Ali's religious identity and places the films in the context of decolonization, US imperialism, and American racism. Overall, Harris considers the cultural management of African American Muslims through media and the resurrection of Ali as a secular America hero. In a similar fashion, Michael Muhammad Knight uses depictions of Malcolm X as an arena to explore American myths about the civil rights movement, the subject of the "Black Muslim" and the Nation of Islam, and the boundaries of the global Muslim community. Films most often reinvent Malcolm for contemporary purposes and fail to attend to the complexity of his religious and political trajectories. Taken together, these films repeatedly advance a demonization of the Nation of Islam, a reification of Islamic "orthodoxy" as race inclusive and universalistic, and present Malcolm X as a violent foil to a neutered vision of an imaginary Martin Luther King, Jr..

While *Muslims in the Movies: A Global Anthology* attempts to present a broad introduction to various cinematic geographies and novel methodological approaches to the study of Islam and film that is accessible to a novice audience it can only do so much. As with any volume, there are many areas we have not been able to explore in great depth, or even at all. It is hoped that the collection will both deepen scholarship on Muslims and cinema but also open up the subject for new publics. If we have done our job well many more questions will arise for the reader and more exploration on the subject will be warranted. So what are some of the avenues to explore in the future? The volume serves only as the most recent guide for scholarship on the subject and aspires to prompt new horizons for the study of Muslims in the movies.

Works Cited

Abubakar, A. A. and S. Dauda. 2019. "Socio-Economic Psychology of Nigeria's Nollywood and Kannywood Film Industries." In *Nollywood in Glocal Perspective*, edited by Bala Musa, 163–86. New York.

Adamu, A. U. 2010. "Islam, Hausa Culture, and Censorship in Northern Nigerian video film." In *Viewing African Cinema in the Twenty-First Century: Art Films and the Nollywood Video Revolution*, edited by M. Saul and R. A. Austen, 63–73. Athens, OH.

———. 2013. "Transgressing Boundaries: Reinterpretation of Nollywood Films in Muslim Northern Nigeria." In *Global Nollywood: The Transnational Dimensions of an African Video Film Industry*, edited by M. Krings and O. Okome, 287–305. Bloomington, IN.

———. 2017a. "Transcultural Connections: Hindi Films, Transborder Fandom and Muslim Hausa Audiences in Northern Nigeria." *African and Asian Studies* 16 (1–2): 103–27.

———. 2017b. "Controversies and Restrictions of Visual Representation of Prophets in Northern Nigerian Popular Culture." *Journal of African Media Studies* 9 (1): 17–31.

Adamu, Y. M. 2002. "Between the Word and the Screen: A Historical Perspective on the Hausa Literary Movement and the Home Video Invasion." *Journal of African Cultural Studies* 15 (2): 203–13.

Alhassen, M. 2018. "Haqq and Hollywood: Illuminating 100 Years of Muslim Tropes and How to Transform Them." Pop Culture Collaborative.

Alsultany, E. 2012. *Arabs and Muslims in the Media: Race and Representation after 9/11.* New York.

Atwood, B. 2016. *Reform Cinema in Iran: Film and Political Change in the Islamic Republic.* New York.

Armes, R. 2005. *Postcolonial Images: Studies in North African Film.* Bloomington, IN.

———. 2006. *African Filmmaking: North and South of the Sahara.* Bloomington, IN.

———. 2010. *Arab Filmmakers of the Middle East: A Dictionary.* Bloomington, IN.

———. 2015. *New Voices in Arab Cinema.* Bloomington, IN.

———. 2018. *Roots of the Arab Cinema.* Bloomington, IN.

Arslan, S. 2010. *Cinema in Turkey: A New Critical History.* New York.

Atakav, E. 2013. *Women and Turkish Cinema: Gender Politics, Cultural Identity and Representation.* London.

Austin, G. 2012. *Algerian National Cinema.* Manchester, UK.

Ball, A. 2012. *Palestinian Literature and Film in Postcolonial Feminist Perspective.* New York.

Barker, T. 2019. *Indonesian Cinema after the New Order: Going Mainstream.* Hong Kong.

Bayraktaroğlu, K. 2018. *The Muslim World in Post-9/11 American Cinema: A Critical Study, 2001-2011.* Jefferson, NC.

Bedjaoui, A. 2020. *Cinema and the Algerian War of Independence.* New York.

Bisschoff, L. and S. van de Peer. 2019. *Women in African Cinema.* New York.

Brittain, V. 2020. *Love and Resistance in the Films of Mai Masri.* New York.

Burris, G. 2019. *The Palestinian Idea: Film, Media, and the Radical Imagination.* Philadelphia, PA.

Chadha, K. and A. P. Kavoori. 2008. "Exoticized, Marginalized, Demonized: The Muslim 'Other' in Indian Cinema." In *Global Bollywood*, edited by Anandam P. Kavoori and Aswin Punathambekar, 131–45. New York.

Cheema, M. 2018. *Women and TV Culture in Pakistan: Gender, Islam and National Identity.* London.

Dabashi, H. 2006. *Dreams of a Nation: On Palestinian Cinema.* London.

———. 2011. *Close Up: Iranian Cinema, Past, Present, and Future.* London.

Davies Hayon, K. 2018. *Sensuous Cinema: The Body in Contemporary Maghrebi Film.* New York.

Davies Hayon, K. 2019. "Faiza Ambah's *Mariam* and the Embodied Politics of Veiling in France." *Paragraph* 24 (3): 333–350.

de Rooij, L. 2020. *Islam in British Media Discourses: Understanding Perceptions of Muslims in the News.* Manchester, UK.

Dickinson, K. 2016. *Arab Cinema Travels: Transnational Syria, Palestine, Dubai and Beyond.* London.

Dönmez-Colin, G. 2004. *Women, Islam and Cinema.* London.

———. 2008. *Turkish Cinema: Identity, Distance and Belonging.* London.

———. 2013. *Routledge Dictionary of Turkish Cinema.* London.

———. 2019. *Women as Images and as Image-makers in the Cinemas of Iran and Turkey.* London.

Dwyer, K. 2004. *Beyond Casablanca: M. A. Tazi and the Adventure of Moroccan Cinema.* Bloomington, IN.

El-Shammaa, M. 2020. *The National Imaginarium: A History of Egyptian Filmmaking.* Cairo.

Gauch, S. 2016. *Maghrebs in Motion: North African Cinema in Nine Movements.* New York.

Ghazal, A. 2020. *Egyptian Cinema and the 2011 Revolution: Production, Censorship and Political Economy.* London.

Ghorbankarimi, M. 2015. *A Colourful Presence: The Evolution of Women's Representation in Iranian Cinema.* Newcastle upon Tyne, UK.

Ginsberg, T. 2016. *Visualizing the Palestinian Struggle: Towards a Critical Analytic of Palestine Solidarity Film.* New York.

Ginsberg, T. and C. Lippard. 2020. *Historical Dictionary of Middle Eastern Cinema*. Second Edition. Lanham, MD.

Gugler, J. 2015. *Ten Arab Filmmakers: Political Dissent and Social Critique*. Bloomington, IN.

Haider, S. 2013. "Shooting Muslims: Looking at Islam in Bollywood through a Postcolonial Lens." In *Postcolonialism and Islam: Theory, Literature, Culture, Society and Film*, edited by G. Nash, K. Kerr-Koch, and S. Hackett, 208–16.

Hanan, D. 2017. *Cultural Specificity in Indonesian Film: Diversity in Unity*. New York.

Handyside, F. 2019. "The Politics of Hair: Girls, Secularism and (Not) The Veil in *Mustang* (Ergüven) and Other Recent French films." *Paragraph* 24 (3): 351–69.

Haynes, J. 2016. *Nollywood: The Creation of Nigerian Film Genres*. Chicago.

Higbee, W. 2013. *Post-beur Cinema: North African Émigré and Maghrebi-French Filmmaking in France since 2000*. Edinburgh.

Higbee, W., F. Martin, and J. Bahmad. 2020. *Moroccan Cinema Uncut: Decentred Voices, Transnational Perspectives*. Edinburgh.

Hillauer, R. 2006. *Encyclopedia of Arab Women Filmmakers*. Cairo.

Hussain, A. 2009. "Islam." In *The Routledge Companion to Religion and Film*, edited by John Lyden, 131–40. London.

Hussein, N. and S. Hussain. 2015. "Interrogating Practices of Gender, Religion and Nationalism in the Representation of Muslim Women in Bollywood-Contexts of Change, Sites of Continuity." *Exchanges: The Interdisciplinary Research Journal* 2 (2): 284–304.

Ibrahim, M. M. 2013. "Hausa Film: Compatible or Incompatible with Islam?" *Performing Islam* 2 (2): 165–79.

———. 2019. "Kannywood: Creating a New Film Industry." *Journal of African Films and Diaspora Studies* 2 (1) :81–94.

Ibrahim, M. 2017. "Conflict and Violence at the Crossroad of Religion and 'New' Media: Periscoping Faith-based Crisis through the Eyes of Camera in the Sharia-age of Northern Nigeria." *Journal for the Study of the Religions of Africa and its Diaspora* 3:91–109.

Ibrahim, M. 2020. "Islam and Visual Culture: Sharia Implementation and Cinema as Visual Management in Nigeria." *African Studies Review*, 1–24.

Ibrahim, M. and A.Y. Yusuf. 2020. "'Don't Say It in Public': Contestations and Negotiations in Northern Nigerian Muslim Cyberspace." In *Swearing and Cursing: Contexts and Practices in a Critical Linguistic Perspective*, edited by N. Nassenstein and A. Storch, 165–84. Berlin.

Ingawanij, M. A. and B. McKay. 2012. *Glimpses of Freedom: Independent Cinema in Southeast Asia*. Ithaca, NY.

Izharuddin, A. 2016. *Gender and Islam in Indonesian Cinema*. New York.

Jameela, M. 2018. "Britain's Muslims as the Enemy Within in Contemporary British Cinema." In *The Enemy in Contemporary Film*, edited by M. Löschnigg and M. Sokołowska-Paryż, 91–104. Berlin.

Kabir, A. J. 2010. "The Kashmiri as Muslim in Bollywood's New Kashmir Films." *Contemporary South Asia* 18 (4): 373–385.

Kealhofer-Kemp, L. 2016. *Muslim Women in French Cinema: Voices of Maghrebi Migrants in France*. Liverpool.

Khatib, K. 2006. *Filming the Modern Middle East: Politics in the Cinemas of Hollywood and the Arab World*. London.

Khatun, N. 2016. "Imagining Muslims as the 'Other' in Muslim Political Films." *Journal of Arab and Muslim Media Research* 9 (1): 41–60.

———. "Love Jihad and Bollywood: Constructing Muslims as Other." *Journal of Religion & Film* 22 (3).

Khoo, G. C. 2006. *Reclaiming Adat: Contemporary Malaysian Film and Literature*. Vancouver, BC.

Khouri, M. 2010. *The Arab National Project in Youssef Chahine's Cinema*. Cairo.

Krings, M. 2007. "Muslim Martyrs and Pagan Vampires: Popular Video Films and the Propagation of Religion in Northern Nigeria" *Postscripts* 1 (2–3): 183–205.

———. 2008. "Conversion on Screen: A Glimpse at Popular Islamic Imaginations in Northern Nigeria" *Africa Today* 54 (4): 45–68.

———. 2015. *African Appropriations: Cultural Difference, Mimesis, and Media*. Bloomington, IN.

Krings, M. and O. Okome, eds. 2013. *Global Nollywood: The Transnational Dimensions of an African Video Film Industry*. Bloomington, IN.

Kumar H. M., S. 2013. "Constructing the Nation's Enemy: Hindutva Popular Culture and the Muslim Other in Bollywood Cinema." *Third World Quarterly* 34 (3): 458–69.

———. 2016. "Metonymies of Fear: Islamophobia and the Making of Muslim Identity in Hindi Cinema." *Society and Culture in South Asia* 2 (2): 233–55.

Lang, R. 2014. *New Tunisian Cinema: Allegories of Resistance*. New York.

Langford, M. 2019. *Allegory in Iranian Cinema: The Aesthetics of Poetry and Resistance*. London.

Larkin, B. 2000. "Hausa Dramas and the Rise of Video Culture in Nigeria." In *Nigerian Video Films*, edited by J. Haynes, 209–41. Athens, OH.

———. 2004. "From Majigi to Hausa Video Films: Cinema and Society in Northern Nigeria" In Hausa Home Videos: Technology, Economy and Society, edited by A. U. Adamu, Y. M. Adamu, and U. F. Jibril, 46–53. Kano, NG.

———. 2008. *Signal and Noise: Media, Infrastructure, and Urban Culture in Nigeria.* Durham, NC.

Leaman, O. 2001. *Companion Encyclopedia of Middle Eastern and North African Film.* New York.

Lim D. and H. Yamamoto. 2011. *Film in Contemporary Southeast Asia: Cultural Interpretation and Social Intervention.* New York.

Limbrick, P. 2020. *Arab Modernism as World Cinema: The Films of Moumen Smihi.* Oakland, CA.

McAlister, M. 2005. *Epic Encounters: Culture, Media, and U.S. Interests in the Middle East since 1945.* Berkeley, CA.

McCain, C. 2013. "Nollywood, Kannywood, and a Decade of Hausa Film Censorship in Nigeria." In *Silencing Cinema: Film Censorship Around the World*, edited by D. Biltereyst and R. Vande Winkel, 223–40. New York.

Mahdi, W. F. 2020. *Arab Americans in Film: From Hollywood and Egyptian Stereotypes to Self-Representation.* Syracuse, NY.

Mack, M. A. 2017. *Sexagon: Muslims, France, and the Sexualization of National Culture.* Fordham.

Martin, F. 2011. *Screens and Veils: Maghrebi Women's Cinema.* Bloomington, IN.

Morey, P. and A. Yaqin. 2011. *Framing Muslims: Stereotyping and Representation after 9/11.* Cambridge, MA.

Mottahedeh, N. 2008. *Displaced Allegories: Post-Revolutionary Iranian Cinema.* Durham, NC.

Muhammad, A. 2009. *Yasmin Ahmad's Films.* Petaling Jaya, MY.

———. 2010. *120 Malay Movies.* Petaling Jaya, MY.

Naficy, H. 2011. *A Social History of Iranian Cinema, Volume 1: The Artisanal Era, 1897-1941.* Durham, NC.

———. 2011. *A Social History of Iranian Cinema, Volume 2: The Industrializing Years, 1941-1978.* Durham, NC.

———. 2012. *A Social History of Iranian Cinema, Volume 3: The Islamicate Period, 1978-1984.* Durham, NC.

———. 2012. *A Social History of Iranian Cinema, Volume 4: The Globalizing Era, 1984-2010.* Durham, NC.

O'Riley, M. 2010. *Cinema in an Age of Terror: North Africa, Victimization, and Colonial History.* Lincoln, NE.

Orlando, V. 2009. *Francophone Voices of the "New" Morocco in Film and Print: (Re)presenting a Society in Transition.* New York.

———. 2011. *Screening Morocco: Contemporary Film in a Changing Society.* Athens, OH.

———. 2017. *New African Cinema.* Rutgers, NJ.

Pak-Shiraz, N. 2011. *Shi'i Islam in Iranian Cinema: Religion and Spirituality in Film.* London.

Partovi, P. 2017. *Popular Iranian Cinema before the Revolution: Family and Nation in Fīlmfārsī*. London.

Petersen, K. 2017. "Hollywood Muslims in Iraq." *Journal of Religion and Popular Culture* 29 (2): 87–103.

———. 2020. "Female Filmmakers and Muslim Women in Cinema." In *The Routledge Handbook of Islam and Gender*, edited by Justine Howe. New York.

Pew Research Center. 2017. "US Muslims Concerned about Their Place in Society, but Continue to Believe in the American Dream." Pew Research Center, July 26. https://www.pewforum.org/2017/07/26/findings-from-pew-research-centers-2017-survey-of-us-muslims/.

Poole, E. 2002. *Reporting Islam: Media Representations of British Muslims*. London.

Raghuvanshi, V. and S. Kumar H. M. 2017. "Cinematic Construction of Other: Performing Pakistan in Hindi Cinema" In *Culture and Politics in South Asia Performative Communication*, edited by D. Nath Pathak and S. Perera, 222–35. London.

Rakhmani, I. 2016. *Mainstreaming Islam in Indonesia: Television, Identity, and the Middle Class*. New York.

Ramji, R. 2013. "Muslims in the Movies." In *The Bloomsbury. Companion to Religion and Film*, edited by William Blizek, 177–87. London.

———. 2016. "Examining the Critical Role American Popular Film Continues to Play in Maintaining the Muslim Terrorist Image, Post 9/11," *Journal of Religion and Film* 20 (1).

Rashid, H. 2014. "Muslims in Film and Muslim Filmmaking in the United States." In *The Oxford Handbook of American Islam*, edited by Yvonne Yazbeck Haddad and Jane I. Smith, 459–73. Oxford.

Rekabtalaei, G. 2019. *Iranian Cosmopolitanism: A Cinematic History*. Cambridge.

Rosello, M. 1998. *Declining the Stereotype: Ethnicity and Representation in French Cultures*. Hanover.

Saul, M. and R. A. Austen, eds. 2010. *Viewing African Cinema in the Twenty-First Century: Art Films and the Nollywood Video Revolution*. Athens, OH.

Semmerling, T. 2006. *Evil Arabs in American Popular Film: Orientalist Fear*. Austin.

Shafik, V. 2007. *Popular Egyptian Cinema: Gender, Class, and Nation*. Cairo.

———. 2017. *Arab Cinema: History and Cultural Identity*. Cairo.

Shaheen, J. 2001. *Reel Bad Arabs: How Hollywood Vilifies a People*. Northampton, MA.

———. 2008. *Guilty: Hollywood's Verdict on Arabs After 9/11*. Northampton, MA.

Sheibani, K. 2011. *The Poetics of Iranian Cinema: Aesthetics, Modernity and Film after the Revolution*. London.

Suner, A. 2010. *New Turkish Cinema: Belonging, Identity and Memory*. London.

Tapper, R. 2002. *The New Iranian Cinema: Politics, Representation and Identity*. London.

Tarr, C. 2005. *Reframing Difference: Beur and Banlieue Filmmaking in France*. Manchester, UK.

Thwaites Diken, E. 2018. *The Spectacle of Politics and Religion in the Contemporary Turkish Cinema*. New York.

van der Heide, W. 2002. *Malaysian Cinema, Asian Film: Border Crossings and National Cultures*. Amsterdam, NL.

Yaqub, N. 2018. *Palestinian Cinema in the Days of Revolution*. Austin, TX.

Zeydabadi-Nejad, S. 2009. *The Politics of Iranian Cinema: Film and Society in the Islamic Republic*. London.

The Cinematic Secularization of Muhammad Ali

M. Cooper Harriss
Indiana University

THE STORY REMAINS FAMILIAR: In February, 1964, Cassius Clay defeated Sonny Liston for the world's heavyweight boxing championship. The next morning he confirmed rumors that he was a Muslim, no longer Christian but a convert to the Nation of Islam (NOI) and a close friend of Malcolm X. Clay soon became "Muhammad Ali."[1] His conversion signaled a broader transformation for the boxer called "the Louisville Lip," who became a political activist for social change in the US and emerging postcolonial world. Ali, who fought for his country as a boxer in the 1960 Rome Olympics, refused military induction in 1967, near the height of the Vietnam War: "I ain't got no quarrel with them Vietcong," he told reporters. "No Vietcong ever called me 'nigger.'"[2] His status as a "minister of the religion of Islam" forbade such military involvement, he explained, so Ali deployed his First Amendment rights, invoking religious liberty against government mandate.[3]

Often absent from this chestnut of Ali lore is the theology that undergirds the boxer's Islamic complaint: To be authentically black like God, the NOI preached, is to be Muslim. Only by recognizing and buying into this identity may one become free – spiritually, to be sure, but free moreover from the oppression created by Christian America and its European backgrounds. US military action abroad depends upon poor and marginalized Americans to fight overseas in support of the same exceptionalist gospel of white supremacy and economic domination that oppresses them at home. Ali – this fighter who wouldn't fight – took exception to such exceptionalism on religious grounds and found himself arrested, stripped of his championship and boxing credentials – effectively banished from his livelihood for three years of his prime while his case worked its way to the US Supreme Court.

Ali's defense hinged on his qualifications as a Conscientious Objector. There is no small irony in the claim of a prizefighter, who earns his livelihood by beating other men to the brink of consciousness and beyond, claiming

---

1. Roberts and Smith 2016.
2. Eig 2017 suggests that Ali never made the second pronouncement (about the Vietcong) "until years later on a movie set" (213–14).
3. Remnick 1999, 291.

religious exemption from military service on nonviolent grounds. This proves doubly so when one considers that a majority of Ali's opponents were black men whom he fought even as he refused to fight a foreign war against other people of color. Exonerated (on a technicality) by the high court, Ali returned to action in 1970, regaining and losing the heavyweight title twice more before retiring from boxing in 1981. During this second period of his career, Ali found a level of popularity that he never knew in the 1960s, when his brash behavior and political resistance cast him outside of accepted public conduct for a black man. In retirement, as he contended with the effects of Parkinson's Syndrome, Ali took on the mantle of "Great American," became (officially and unofficially) an emissary for US interests abroad in Africa and the so-called Middle East, and converted once again – this time into a beloved figure of Americana.

No ceremony exhibits this transformation more vividly than Ali's "surprise" appearance as ceremonial torch lighter at the 1996 Olympic Games in Atlanta, marking him (as he often called himself more generally) "the Greatest" among a distinguished cohort of former US Olympians. The fighter who fought for his country in Rome before refusing to fight for his country in Vietnam was welcomed back into the fold – an American hero because this act of protest became transformed from "draft dodging" to a patriotic struggle for religious conscience. By taking exception, he became exceptional. It can also be no coincidence that the tremor in his hand that coursed through his body, a symptom of Parkinson's Syndrome almost certainly triggered by decades of blows to the head, also cast Ali in a new light. No longer a physically imposing and defiant black man, his celebrity and disability disarmed his most threatening aspects (words, personality, and bodily power). This revision of Ali rendered him "safe," neutralizing his former danger as a black man and a Muslim.

In this way Ali-the-Muslim has been secularized. Vincent Lloyd argues that "the careful management of race and religion are the prerequisite for accepting the public significance of a fundamentally raced religious figure."[4] By becoming more "American," Ali becomes less black – an organizing principle of his Islamic conversion. He also becomes less Muslim. Consider the paradox of a man named "Muhammad" becoming an icon of American exceptionalism in an age characterized by rampant US Islamophobia. Accordingly, even as Ali remained insistent about the importance of his Islamic identity and what Islam might mean as an American religion in the world, other narratives have sought to package and sell him in defiance of this religious identity. Making Ali's Islam into an expression of US religious

4. Kahn and Lloyd 2016, 1.

freedom sublimates it to powerful narratives of American exceptionalism. Ali's Muslim-ness no longer challenges "America" but becomes part of an American story about diversity, social conscience, and civil rights in a sanitized account of the black freedom struggles of the 1960s and 1970s.

Much like the story that opens this chapter – Ali as NOI mascot of US exceptionalism and religious freedom – popular narratives about Muhammad Ali tend to organize his career in a way that secularizes (by smoothing over or explaining away) complicated or inconvenient aspects of his Islamic identity. They do so at the expense of recognizing the NOI as Islam, or they otherwise avoid the fullness of Ali's Islamic belief and practice beyond a story of redemption that feeds his elevation to American icon. Despite ongoing tensions with the NOI, including his suspension from the organization and their withdrawal of professional support during his exile from boxing (1967–70), Ali willingly remained affiliated until its dissolution in 1975, following the death of its long-time leader Elijah Muhammad. Ali followed Elijah Muhammad's son (and successor) Warith Deen Muhammad's subsequent move toward Sunni Islam through the World Community of Al-Islam in the West (later the American Society of Muslims) in 1976, an organization that understood itself to be part of a Muslim international (a vision very much in keeping with Ali's erstwhile friend Malcolm X's own post-NOI vision, cut short by his assassination in 1965).[5] The relative seamlessness of this transition for Ali supports Edward Curtis's claim in defiance of the common misunderstanding that the NOI was "neither legitimately religious nor authentically Islamic." Indeed, "religious life in the NOI can be understood and analyzed as a subtle process of Islamization in which members of the NOI debated the meaning of their religion, accepting and rejecting various elements of *other* Islamic traditions as they struggled to practice a form of Islam that was relevant to their historical circumstances."[6]

In the 1980s and beyond, Ali maintained close relationships with immigrant Muslim communities that proliferated following the 1965 Hart-Cellar Act, which reformed US immigration quotas and transformed US religious, racial, and ethnic demographics. In the process he supported these immigrants' own "conversion" to and innovation of Islam as American religion.[7] The final years of Ali's life also witnessed a turn to Sufism, evident

---

5. Marable 2011's discussion of Malcolm's "free agent" period (297–301). See also Curtis 2002 98–104, 107–08, 113–17.

6. Curtis 2006, 5, 13–14. Similarly, Grewal 2013 writes that "the NOI define[d] itself in terms of a global Muslim majority" (109).

7. GhaneaBassiri 2010, 292–93. See Wheeler 2020, also, Grewal 2013, 131–34 and Howe 2018's description of Ali's participation in a *mawlid* held in suburban Chicago in 1994 (124).

in the aphoristic cadences of his final autobiography.[8] The foregoing biographical sketch provides a provisional sense of the richness and variety of Ali's more than half-century as a Muslim – many aspects of which remain unknown or unrecognized by broader publics in the US and abroad. The unfamiliarity of these aspects shows evidence of ongoing attempts to manage and shift the terms of Ali's Islamic identity away from the challenge it poses to conceptions of American religion, offered in lieu of more general and unremarkable expressions of religious freedom and diversity.

This chapter locates evidence of such management (and considers an antidote) in three representative films about Muhammad Ali, probing a cinematic archive of his secularization as American Muslim over the course of two decades around the turn of the twenty-first century. The films include *The Trials of Muhammad Ali* (Bill Siegel, 2013) – a documentary focusing on Ali's refusal of military induction in the 1960s; *When We Were Kings* (Leon Gast, 1996) – Leon Gast's observational documentary account of the 1974 "Rumble in the Jungle" fight against George Foreman in Zaire; and Michael Mann's feature film *Ali* (Michael Mann, 2001), starring Will Smith and highlighting the span from the first fight against Sonny Liston in 1964 to his retaking of the title from Foreman in Kinshasa a decade later. Of particular interest is the way filmmakers treat Ali's "Islam," packaging a digestible, secularized vision of Ali as champion for religious freedom. Following Curtis, these films focus especially upon Ali's involvement in the NOI, often at the expense of his later emergence as a globally inflected US Muslim – an argument then assumed by viewers, both fabricating and fabricated by the enduring myth of American exceptionalism that renders him not just "good," but "the Greatest."

In service of these points I focus on two provisional aspects of the problematic use of Islam in these films, aspects that drive Muhammad Ali's cinematic secularization and its effect on public understanding of Ali as a Muslim: 1) their depiction of the relationship of the NOI to global and other US Islamic contexts (especially Sunni) as they work through the "validity" of Ali's Islamic identity, and 2) the way that temporal framing (the timeframe) of Ali's life and career in these films (and, indeed, most every film) secularizes Ali's identity as a Muslim and therefore an American religious figure. A more fulsome understanding of Ali's Islam, matched with careful attention to the power of film to generate myth (as well as its ability to shore up these same myths) may help come to terms with both Ali's complicated relationship with American exceptionalism while also clearing ground for understanding Ali's remarkable career as a globally inflected American Muslim beyond the

8. Ali with Ali 2004.

limited scope of religious freedom and the relative "legitimacy" of his NOI Islamic identity.

RELATIONSHIP BETWEEN NOI AND GLOBAL ISLAM

New religious movements like the NOI frequently face questions about their fidelity to purely conceived or canonically rendered versions of more established traditions.[9] Recall Curtis's point that the NOI is often understood as "neither legitimately religious nor authentically Islamic."[10] The three films considered here take up, obliquely and head-on, the related burdens of the NOI's religious legitimacy and Islamic purity – despite the fact that no "pure" form of any religious tradition exists. Indeed, the protectiveness that more established groups register against what they take to be a bowdlerized expression of their own tradition attests specifically to the threat of presumed legitimacy that these new movements can present. In this way a primary reason why Muhammad Ali (despite his name) does not register as "fully" Muslim in many public contexts owes to the broader sense that the NOI is not "real" or "good" Islam.[11]

One may argue that Ali *never* practiced "good" or "real" Islam. Salim Muwakkil notes in *The Trials of Muhammad Ali*:

> Since 9/11 Islam has acquired so many layers and dimensions and textures. When the Nation of Islam was considered a threatening religion, traditional Islam was seen as a gentle alternative. And now, quite the contrary. The Nation of Islam is seen as a tamed, domestic version and traditional Islam is seen as a threatening thing. Muhammad Ali occupies a weird place in that shifting interpretation of Islam.

Muwakkil's changing dynamics render Ali's Islamic identity always a contested one. Historically speaking, if "legitimate" Islam is "good" Islam, then he is never *really* Muslim. In this way his Islamic illegitimacy proves useful for limiting the prophetic power of his activism in the 1960s, making it political, not religious. Similarly, after September 11, 2001 (in particular) his status as "not a real Muslim" both places Ali-the-US-exceptionalist outside of the Muslim-as-terrorist stereotype while offering a vehicle to rehabilitate his 1960s dissent into benign civil-rights activism.[12]

9. Hammer and Rothstein 2012, 3.
10. Curtis 2006, 5.
11. See Hussain 2016, 4–5.
12. Ali also deployed an implied version of this construction of "real" Islam. Standing among the rubble of the World Trade Center on September 21, 2001, he claimed: "Islam is not a killing religion.... Islam is peace" (Eig 2017, 529).

In other ways the NOI pulls double duty in popular accounts of Ali's life, divided along a borderline of "respectability." A strident political black nationalism usually embodied by Malcolm X (who, though to a lesser extent than Martin Luther King, now finds himself rehabilitated and coopted in similar terms as a civil rights leader) stands at odds with the group's more outlandish cosmologies and the hypocrisies of NOI leadership.[13] Elijah Muhammad ordinarily provides Malcolm's foil of lust and avarice in these morality plays, with a second son – Ali's longtime manager Herbert Muhammad (shown by the 1970s to be in cahoots with the even slicker, though no less mendacious Don King) – serving as his father's more proximate surrogate. Still, the NOI provided Ali's justification for refusing military induction, necessitating this popular paradox: Ali is not *really* Muslim because he belonged to the NOI; at the same time he was a "true believer" in it, willing to stake his reputation and livelihood for the sake of his sincerely held, if misbegotten, religious beliefs. The specter of Elijah Muhammad (as Malcolm's nemesis) becomes a point of cinematic justification for the "sincerity" of such beliefs.

Michael Mann's *Ali* pits a corrupt, complicated Elijah Muhammad against charismatic Malcolm X.[14] Ali's betrayal of Malcolm, and Malcolm's subsequent assassination, establish a contrast between the true believer and the shady figure. Ali, the film suggests, chose wrong and continues to live with the consequences of his decision, but the motivation behind his conversion and the hindsight it affords over time purify his NOI-membership as not related to spaceships or criminality but, rather, to a secularizing civil rights legacy of strident black protest. *Ali* highlights Ali's suspension from the NOI during his professional exile, depicting a further black eye for the organization. Being of limited use to the Nation, potentially ever again, Ali becomes taboo in Mann's depiction – a status conveniently reversed upon his legal exoneration and professional reinstatement, when Herbert Muhammad rematerializes as business manager in Ali's dressing room as if nothing ever went wrong between them. Money wins the day.

In lieu of Herbert Muhammad, *The Trials of Muhammad Ali* deploys Louis Farrakhan (the present-day leader of a re-formed NOI) as Elijah's adjunct, a devil's advocate in its narration of Ali's rise and fall in the 1960s and beyond.

13. Graham 2014.

14. I do not claim the legitimacy of this view, which overlooks (among other things) the fact that Elijah Muhammad was imprisoned for five years for refusing military service during World War II – the same sentence that Ali faced had his conviction been upheld by the Supreme Court (Clegg 2014, 83). My point here is that this understanding of Ali vis-à-vis Malcolm X and Elijah Muhammad remains pervasive – indeed both proffered and supported by the didactic function of these films. (See also Chapter 2 of this volume, Michael Muhammad Knight, "'Beware of Them Cameras:' Film Representations of Malcolm X.")

In one sense Farrakhan disrupts easy conclusions. Consider the film's opening sequence, which begins with 1968 footage of Ali joining Eamonn Andrews's UK talk program via satellite. Andrews say to Ali, "you are a professional fighter, right?" Ali replies, "I am a minister of the religion of Islam, also...." Andrews then gauges the reaction of his guest, US producer and talk show host David Susskind, who reminds viewers that Ali is not merely a felon – likely bound for prison – but also a "simplistic fool and pawn." The film then cuts to 2005 footage of Ali receiving the US Presidential Medal of Freedom from President George W. Bush. This abrupt transition certainly signals Ali's transformation in the court of public opinion.

But then a voice chimes in – a voice of slow deliberation that effectively mocks the scene: "He was given the Medal of Freedom by the president of the United States," it begins, with Bush speaking through the voice's affective caesura, claiming ownership over Ali as "one of our own." The voice, which a cut to his talking head only now reveals to be that of Farrakhan, continues:

> What does it mean, the Medal of Freedom? We bring you up, oh yes! This is Muhammad Ali the great fighter, the great humanitarian, the great *Muslim*! [Pause] Years ago [however], Ali sat right here, and Ali looked at me. He said, quote, "Still a nigger." I said, "Oh Ali! Don't talk like that!" He said "Still a nigger." What did my brother mean?

A strange tension emerges here. On the one hand, a viewer may find it plausible that Ali made such an observation to Farrakhan in a private moment. On the other hand, Farrakhan's statement, its sardonic tone and placement in this orientational montage, cast Ali's exceptionalist redemption into question. How a viewer interprets this anecdote depends entirely upon their impression of Farrakhan and the NOI. In this way Farrakhan takes on the role Elijah Muhammad plays in the *Ali* biopic as profiled above, casting Malcolm X in a favorable, sincere light. Farrakhan's presence stands in for the outlandish and morally tenuous characterization of his predecessor in a way that, by virtue of its very claim, encourages viewers to eschew Ali's religious particularity in favor of his secularization via the exceptionalist myth.

When We Were Kings dwells on the question of the NOI's Islamic viability differently, partly because of issues surrounding its release but also because it operates on different narrative terms. Legal battles over rights to the footage delayed the film's production for two decades.[15] As a consequence, an observational documentary from the mid-1970s becomes unavoidably retrospective – all the more formidably through mid-1990s pronouncements

15. Joyner 1997.

by talking heads Norman Mailer, George Plimpton, and Spike Lee. Islamic dimensions are certainly present, from Drew "Bundini" Brown calling Ali a "prophet of Islam" to Ali's repetitions of the phrase "I am God," which aligns with NOI theologies of the Blackman as God.[16] Further implicit is the film's setting – in, en route to, or in preparation for the fight in Zaire as part of the NOI Afroasiatic cradle of civilization and home of the original man. Ali's Muslim-ness is fully in place, yet it becomes more ambient, literally emergent from the landscape and encoded in his interactions with the people of Zaire, who shout "*Ali Bomaye!*" ("Ali, kill him!") in adoration as he trains and moves about in public.

Nevertheless, whereas *Ali* and *Trials* contend extensively with Ali's Islam, *When We Were Kings* largely elides it. In fact, the relative stability of Ali's implicit (NOI) Islamic identity in *When We Were Kings* seems odd when one considers the intrigue afoot in the NOI at the time of its production. Any sense of Elijah Muhammad's severely compromised position in 1974 is absent from the film. The leader was sick (he would die less than four months after the fight in Kinshasa) and power struggles within the NOI for who might assume control after Elijah Muhammad's death were ongoing.[17] Thus, even amid the NOI's demise (Farrakhan would resurrect a second edition, but not before the dissolution of the original NOI), *When We Were Kings* steers clear of the specific question of its relationship to other global Islams, even as it situates Ali as (by default) a still-NOI Muslim, feeling and framing himself as a figure of global significance, capable of swaying crowds fed up with colonial power (though also suffering under the regime of President for Life Mobutu Sese Seko). Indeed, Ali's astonishing popularity in and around Kinshasa also owes at least in part to George Foreman's arrival from the US in aviator sunglasses, attended by a German shepherd dog – the costume and accessory of Belgian colonial rule.

Primarily these films prove uncertain of how to handle any relationship between the NOI and other Islams (such as the Sunni Islam to which Ali would migrate after 1975). Therefore they essentially avoid the question at the expense of greater clarification. Accordingly, the NOI is not Islamic insofar as it is demonstrably "religious," but it also fails as a political movement because the group loses traction over time. Its "bad" religious politics cannot measure up to the sincerety of Ali's "good" political stand for religious freedom. Thus, it becomes secularized in order to promote Ali's agency for civil rights and his status as an international celebrity and

16. Muhammad 1973.

17. See especially Clegg 2014's Chapter 10, "In the Last Days" (269–84) for an account of these maneuvers.

humanitarian. Such generalization suggests that the religious terms of his generative act of refusing military induction belong to a former era; it is not "authentically Muslim" but derives from this sectarian aberration, calling into question the necessity for these films to pursue the Islamic "growth" that Farrakhan describes taking place in later decades of Ali's life.

THE TEMPORAL FRAME

This leads to our second category of engagement with these three films: their temporal frame – the way they organize and thus secularize the terms of Ali's Islamic identity through periodization. The question of periodization remains problematic in any attempt to study Ali, partly because his boxing career may be so neatly drawn into pre- and post-exilic timeframes, which were later inflected through the reality that his public engagement waned as he became more profoundly disabled by Parkinson's Syndrome. He remained a public figure, just not in the same provocative way he maintained from the early 1960s to the mid-1980s. His charismatic affect diminished. Some found him pitiful or even pathetic, perhaps recoiling from their own fear of frailty and demise. Ali biographer Jonathan Eig, whose own contribution places outsized emphasis on the earlier parts of Ali's career (Ali retires in 1981 on page 498 and dies, thirty-five years later, on page 534) notes the tighter management of access to Ali and reliable information about his later life. Ali's prime (meaning the 1960s through the mid-1970s) *sells* in a way that his long demise does not, but it does so specifically because this long demise renders Ali's prime safe, historical, a closed case, domesticated and secular instead of wild and holy. The quibble here concerns not only *why* Ali's life finds subdivision but, also, demands reflection concerning how such periodization informs and reinforces the way viewers understand Ali-the-Muslim as a direct result of watching these films.[18]

The first point to address is the template of the story they chart: Ali's rise to the heavyweight championship, his fall as he is stripped of his title (for remaining true to his code), and the resurrection of his greatness through reinstatement, eventually recapturing the title. This template

18. I should acknowledge here that *conveniently* finding problems of periodization in three selected films risks charges of a selection bias. Readers should survey the available archive of films, to be sure, but also of other media, which reflect an overwhelming preference for Ali's career through the mid-1970s. There are exceptions, yet their limitations often prove the rule. Consider *Muhammad Ali: The Unauthorized Story* (Chip Taylor, 2009), a 52-minute made-for-television hagiography that rehashes Ali's entire life – a work most notable for its thorough unremarkability. Conversely, *Ali: The Mission* (Amani Martin, 2013), an ESPN 30 for 30 short film (13 minutes long) is quite good, yet it is too short to warrant comparison with these other films.

represents a classic archetype for mythic hero tales ranging from Christian scripture and Anakin Skywalker to Mircea Eliade's rendition of the "eternal return."[19] Historically speaking, Ali wins the title in early 1964, loses it in 1967, finds reinstatement in 1970, and regains his title in 1974. The primary subject matter of *Ali*, *Trials*, and *Kings* aligns precisely along this decade-span, though the template does find variety in its adaptations of this timeframe. *Ali*, as a "biopic," charts this decade (with flashbacks) from Ali's preparations in Miami for the first Liston fight to his celebration over the felled Foreman upon recapturing the title in Kinshasa. *Trials* and *Kings* dive deeply into specific moments – Ali's fall and resurrection, respectively. This is not to say that these depictions lack for broader context. *Ali*'s flashbacks take the viewer to childhood memories of young Cassius Clay watching his father paint a white Jesus in a Louisville church sanctuary (resonant for Ali's eventual conversion to the NOI). *Trials* also visits these church paintings. *Trials* and *Kings* incorporate considerable backstory and all three films turn to montage of later moments in Ali's life – his post-boxing career, the effects of his illness and disability, his awards and eventual coronation as "great American."

Significantly, though, these films' most substantive cinematic engagement with Ali coincides with his membership in the NOI. In this way they endorse this specific mode of Islamic identity while at the same time appealing to background materials that reinforce it (*Ali*'s white Jesus, Cassius Clay fighting for his country at the Olympics in Rome before he refuses to do so in Vietnam). The later montages, however, deemphasize the real transitions in Ali-as-Muslim that characterize his post-1974 career and post-retirement life. Indeed, by venerating Ali as freedom fighter and standard-bearer for conscience, these later gestures (as byproducts of periodization) reinforce Ali's ostensible NOI-Islamic identity – one that, as the previous section reflects, remains tenuous and complicated as an expression of "real" Islam. This NOI identity then becomes secularized for its contributions through Ali's fall and resurrection as a champion of religious freedom and civil rights, then reinforces – even naturalizes – this understanding for public consumption.

RETRYING ALI

What, then, might a film look like that does justice to Muhammad Ali as a Muslim in the movies? In one sense it would need to understand itself as

19. See Wax 2011's idea of the "grand narrative" of Christian scripture; "The Rise, Fall, and Redemption of Anakin Skywalker," http://www.starwars.com/video/the-rise-fall-and-redemption-of-anakin-skywalker; and Eliade 1971.

an "independent" venture. The terms of Ali's secularization have become so intertwined with his popularity and emergence as exceptional American that any attempt to avoid such exceptionalism would risk alienating a broader audience. Such a film could still focus on Ali and the NOI, yet returning to Lloyd's point that secularism manages race and religion alike, it ought to take seriously Judith Weisenfeld's focus on "religio-racial" dimensions of black identities in the NOI and beyond in order to fracture these expectations. Weisenfeld avoids charismatic leaders, engaging instead with the frameworks these leaders and their traditions "provided ... for understanding black history and identity that reoriented members in space and time."[20] Like Curtis's focus on the rank and file, Weisenfeld's reorientations take place as individual members and communities confront myriad processes of living: filling out forms, marrying, negotiating religious responsibilities and social obligations.

In one sense *Trials* and *Ali* achieve a version of this. Given the impossibility of depicting Ali as simply one of the rank and file, we do see evidence of his wrangling with professional obligations (in *Trials*) and family life (in *Ali* – where he remarks to Veronica Porche, later his third wife, that because of his eye for women he should have waited to become a Muslim). The problem becomes one of time. By framing these quandaries within the limited purview of roughly 1964–1974, it becomes impossible for the narrative to escape any sense of inevitability. These problems, the very conflicts that drive cinematic action, will surely find resolution in, or shall at least be ironed out by, Ali's success – his legal victory and reinstatement and, of course, his resurrection as heavyweight champion.

I want to offer two possible solutions to the problem of time in representing Ali and Islam. The first would be simply to engage with different decade spans. Rather than 1964–74, what would it mean to look at 1974–84, which includes his recapturing the title, the death of Elijah Muhammad, his duties as an emissary for the US government in 1980, his retirement, and his Parkinson's diagnosis? How might 1991–2001 (from his negotiations with Saddam Hussein, his 1996 Olympic appearance, and on to the aftermath of September 11) offer new insight to a beloved *uber*-American named Muhammad? Beyond the exceptionalist identity that has been foisted upon him (and that he certainly enjoyed and willingly capitalized on), how might the way he occupied – post-NOI – the vanguard of Islam's emergence as American religion drive a cinematic narrative?

A second possibility collapses time, drawing it to a smaller scale. In one sense *Kings* achieves this, limiting itself to 1974 and the events surrounding the Rumble in the Jungle. To a lesser degree *Trials* does this as well. What

20. Weisenfeld 2016.

both lack (despite their considerable merits) is interiority. The viewer engages fully with Ali as persona of his own (and others') creation. Thus, in *Kings*, the dynamic changes that were afoot in Elijah Muhammad's final days as leader of the NOI simply do not register. We witness Ali's discovery of himself as Blackman in Africa, yet the observational genre does not provide a didactic element (at least not one that would prove useful for the otherwise uninitiated in NOI belief, thought, and practice). Deep dives into moments of representative interiority in Ali's life might prove useful for breaking out of the temporal secularization of race and religion.

One extant dramatic text that might work especially well on film is Will Power's *Fetch Clay, Make Man* (2012), a stage play that focuses on a couple of days just before Ali's second Liston fight in May, 1965. What proves notable about the play is Powers's willingness to puncture uncritical presumptions of inevitability. In training, uncertain that he was not just "lucky" the first time he beat Liston, Ali summons Lincoln Perry – the actor who depicted Stepin' Fetchit on screen in the 1930s – to join his entourage. Ali wants Perry to teach him the "Anchor Punch" that Perry reportedly learned from Jack Johnson (and that historically, if controversially, would fell Liston in the second fight). Again, though limited to the NOI era, *Fetch Clay, Make Man* does offer key elements of Weisenfeld's solution for breaking out of religio-racial secularization: 1) it focuses on a limited scope of time, 2) it reflects the absence of leaders (Elijah Muhammad is mentioned, but Ali deals with petty authorities like Brother Rashid, a former criminal who now represents a local sense of NOI obligation), and 3) it focuses, if not on the rank and file, on more quotidian issues than the grander narratives tend to depict. Malcolm X has been dead just under three months and there are rumors that his followers will come after Ali and the NOI representatives at the arena. What does it mean to be afraid? Ali battles with his wife Sonji Roi, who bristles at NOI requirements of dress for women and her husband's attempts to enforce these requirements. Finally, the play grapples with a racial dilemma drawing Ali (the freedom fighter) and Stepin' Fetchit (the ostensible movie-minstrel) parallel. What does it mean for Ali, as an authentic NOI Blackman, to perform in exaggerated modes that border on minstrelsy? What does it mean for this NOI Muslim to learn as a boxer, performer, and black man from the likes of Stepin' Fetchit? As Power puts it in his preface to the play, "If these two seemingly opposite iconic figures were partners, what did that say about race politics and the complexities of American culture?"[21] What, indeed, might it contribute to Ali's Islamic political theology?

By limiting the temporal scope, Power avoids the trappings of Whiggish exceptionalism that often accompany depictions of Ali in this time, and

21. Power 2016, 11.

that contribute to his secularization as a black man and a Muslim through recourse to civil rights and religious freedom. The curtain falls on Lincoln Perry, left behind at the NOI's insistence, watching Ali's victory (in the first round, via Anchor Punch) on a portable television whose screen the audience cannot see. This dramatic choice forecloses much indulgence in these excesses. Instead the audience witnesses an Ali who is scared and compromised, complicit in the death of Malcolm, and possibly in danger not only from Malcolm's followers but his own co-religionists if he cannot retain the title. He cannot negotiate a proper relationship with his wife according to what he understands marriage's religious obligations to entail. In Stepin' Fetchit he consorts with and draws pugilistic and performative inspiration from a figure of pure anathema to NOI ideology. In short, Ali is in a tight spot and everything hangs in the balance. Things could still go very differently from the narrative we know to anticipate. Triumph is not assured. In this way Ali's religio-racial negotiations concern a set of ordinary problems borne out of living in the world as a Muslim, not his status as "Great American" or standard bearer for religious freedom and racial authenticity. As religions do, these matters point to and invest such quotidian concerns with larger, more ultimate significance. Still, any attempt to clarify Ali's Muslim-ness requires willingness to challenge the pieties that also secularize him. Any success delineating questions of NOI legitimacy and fracturing the ordinary temporal organization of his life will yield a cinematic Muhammad Ali more worthy of the name.

WORKS CITED

Ali, Muhammad with Hana Ali. 2004. *Soul of a Butterfly: Reflections on Life's Journey*. New York: Simon & Schuster.

Clegg, Claude Andrew, III. 2014. *The Life and Times of Elijah Muhammad*. Chapel Hill, NC: UNC Press.

Curtis, Edward E., IV. 2002. *Islam in Black America: Identity, Liberation, and Difference in African-American Islamic Thought*. Albany, NY: SUNY Press.

———. 2006. *Black Muslim Religion in the Nation of Islam, 1960–1975*. Chapel Hill, NC: UNC Press.

Eig, Jonathan. 2017. *Ali: A Life*. New York: Houghton Mifflin Harcourt.

Eliade, Mircea. 1971. *The Myth of the Eternal Return: Cosmos and History*. Princeton, NJ: Princeton University Press.

GhaneaBassiri, Kambiz. 2010. *A History of Islam in America: From the New World to the New World Order*. Cambridge, UK: Cambridge University Press.

Graham, David A. 2014. "White-Washing Malcolm X: *The Atlantic*'s View in 1965." *The Atlantic* (21 February).

Grewal, Zareena. 2013. *Islam Is a Foreign Country: American Muslims and the Global Crisis of Authority.* New York: NYU Press.

Hammer, Olav and Mikael Rothstein, eds. 2012. *The Cambridge Companion to New Religious Movements.* Cambridge, UK: Cambridge University Press.

Howe, Justine. 2018. *Suburban Islam.* New York: Oxford University Press.

Hussain, Amir. 2016. *Muslims and the Making of America.* Waco, TX: Baylor University Press.

Joyner, Will. 1997. "The Fight Took 8 Rounds, the Film 22 Years," *New York Times* (16 February).

Kahn, Jonathon and Vincent Lloyd, eds. 2016. *Race and Secularism in America.* New York: Columbia University Press.

Marable, Manning. 2011. *Malcolm X: A Life of Reinvention.* New York: Penguin.

Muhammad, Elijah. 1973 (1965). *Message to the Blackman in America.* Phoenix, AZ: MEMPS.

Power, Will. 2016. *Fetch Clay, Make Man.* New York: Overlook.

Remnick, David. 1999. *King of the World: Muhammad Ali and the Rise of an American Hero.* New York: Vintage.

Roberts, Randy and Johnny Smith. 2016. *Blood Brothers: The Fatal Friendship between Muhammad Ali and Malcolm X.* New York: Basic Books.

Wax, Trevin. 2011. *Counterfeit Gospels: Rediscovering the Good News in a World of False Hope.* Chicago: Moody.

Weisenfeld, Judith. 2016. *New World a-Coming: Black Religion and Racial Identity during the Great Migration.* New York: NYU Press.

Wheeler, Kayla Renée, ed. 2020. "Roundtable: Is Islam American Religion?" American Religion 2, no. 1 (Fall): 5-40.

"Beware of Them Cameras":
Film Representations of Malcolm X

Michael Muhammad Knight

You will be in the public eye. Beware of them cameras. Oh, them cameras are bad as any narcotic.

– Elijah Muhammad, in Spike Lee's *Malcolm X* (1992)[1]

Never accept images that have been created for you by someone else.

– Malcolm X[2]

In her analysis of Spike Lee's *Malcolm X*, bell hooks argues that in order to translate Malcolm's life into an epic Hollywood biography, bending Malcolm to fit within the genre's most commercially viable template, Lee constructed a "fictive Malcolm" more acceptable to the broadest audience possible – including not only conservative Black consumers, but a market that remained predominantly white.[3] This chapter extends hooks's insights to consider Malcolm's Muslim identities as they undergo translation into film.

Cinematic portrayals of Malcolm X's life, message, and legacy adhere to recurring tropes of ongoing change and reinvention, consistently characterizing Malcolm's journey as one that takes him out of the Nation of Islam's "militancy" and "heresy" into a more mature, globally connected, and universal spirituality. In this treatment, Malcolm's pilgrimage to Mecca creates an impermeable border between these two phases of his life. Malcolm's cinematic interpreters ask that we understand his career in the Nation as one marked by inauthentic and "cultish" religiosity, extreme politics, and even advocacy of violence. Only by leaving the Nation can Malcolm reach Mecca to find "true" Islam, disavow extremism, and become newly global in his outlook. Cinematic retellings of Malcolm's life present the end of his Nation ministry as *the* definitive component of his legacy.

The films examined here collaborate in a production of master narratives to write Malcolm's life as an anti-Nation polemic. These depictions of Malcolm betray the full complexity of his religious and political trajectories

1. *Malcolm X*. Dir. Spike Lee. Warner Bros., 1992. Film.
2. Quoted in hooks 1994, 181.
3. hooks 1994, 180–92.

both within and beyond the Nation. They erase Malcolm's relationship to the broader "Muslim world"[4] during his Nation tenure, utilize Malcolm's acceptance of white Muslims in Mecca to soften his critiques of American whites, and edit Malcolm's politics to enable his rehabilitation within "Civil Rights" imaginaries of the Black freedom struggle. This chapter argues that cinematic depictions of Malcolm X, in their shared tropes and narrative priorities, enforce past demonizations of Nation-era Malcolm as the violent antithesis to Dr. Martin Luther King, Jr., while also rewriting post-Nation Malcolm for greater compatibility with their fictive reconstruction of King.

THE TEMPLATE: *THE AUTOBIOGRAPHY OF MALCOLM X*, AS TOLD TO ALEX HALEY

Public conversation in the immediate aftermath of Malcolm's 1965 assassination produced the image of an extremist demagogue whose rhetoric led him to his fate. While Elijah Muhammad explicitly proclaimed that Malcolm "got what he was preaching," King and the NAACP also responded to Malcolm's assassination with vague commentaries on violence that also seemed to subtly indict Malcolm for his own murder. The *New York Times* asserted that Malcolm's "ruthless and fanatical belief in violence" had "marked him for notoriety, and for a violent end."[5] These postmortem reflections took place without the mitigating presence of Malcolm's *Autobiography*, which was released after the assassination and would produce a new master narrative of Malcolm's journey, one that prioritizes Malcolm's rehabilitation as a potential moderate.

The *Autobiography of Malcolm X* does not provide an "autobiography" in the popular assumption of a subject's unmediated reflection on his or her own life. Rather, the *Autobiography* filters Malcolm's voice through the mediation of Alex Haley, a twenty-year veteran of the Coast Guard who dismissed the Nation as a "racist cult" and denounced its positions.[6] Though Malcolm read chapter drafts and gave feedback, Haley would exercise increasing editorial sovereignty over the text, particularly as Malcolm's changing life circumstances detracted from his attention to the work and caused Haley to reimagine the chapter outline.[7] Even before Malcolm's break from the Nation, Haley intended for the book's conclusion to reject the Nation's platform of racial separatism. With the expectation that Malcolm's journey would conclude with him still serving as Elijah Muhammad's national

---

4. Aydin 2017.
5. Marable 2011, 454–57.
6. Marable 2011, 219–20.
7. Marable 2011, 352.

representative, Haley planned to write an afterword in his own voice that would critique Malcolm and argue that most African Americans favored integration. Even when Malcolm left the Nation, Haley did not immediately anticipate that the break was permanent.[8] As Malcolm reinvented himself via travels that included his transformative pilgrimage to Mecca, however, Haley found Malcolm moving in a direction more compatible with his own views. Malcolm's account of his pilgrimage, expressed in his famous statement of praying with "fellow Muslims whose skin was the whitest of white, whose eyes were the bluest of blue,"[9] provided Haley with what he had already planned for the *Autobiography*'s hopeful conclusion, now in Malcolm's voice. Haley also wrote to his publisher with hope that Malcolm's newfound Sunnī "orthodoxy" would lead to the *Autobiography* becoming internationally marketable, given "intense interest in the Moslem countries where he is viewed as the most famous Orthodox brother in America."[10] The *Autobiography* still includes an epilogue from Haley, who recalls his experiences collaborating with Malcolm and chronicles Malcolm's assassination.

As evident with a survey of its chapter titles, *The Autobiography of Malcolm X* organizes Malcolm's life into a series of dramatic ruptures and reconstructions of identity. Haley titles several chapters in the *Autobiography* with Malcolm's personas and nicknames at various stages: "Mascot," "Homeboy", "Harlemite," "Detroit Red," "Hustler," "Satan," "Minister Malcolm X," and finally "El-Hajj Malik El-Shabazz." The *Autobiography* thus presents El-Hajj Malik El-Shabazz as Malcolm's final reinvention, marking him with a distinct name to signify the concluding stage of his journey. In popular Sunnī imaginaries today, "El-Hajj Malik El-Shabazz" appears as Malcolm's true name, reflecting his Sunnī identity; in contrast, "Malcolm X" signifies the "heretical" Nation that he had abandoned. As much as Minister Malcolm X had abrogated Detroit Red, El-Hajj Malik El-Shabazz abrogates Minister Malcolm X. The *Autobiography* contributes to this perception by erasing the complexity of Malcolm's "Sunnī" name. Malcolm had used the name Malik Shabazz for years while a minister in the Nation, and had used the name Malachi Shabazz even before receiving his X.[11] Though "El-Hajj" signified Malcolm's post-Mecca ḥajjī status, the surname Shabazz referred to an ancient Black tribe in the Nation's sacred history; according to Elijah Muhammad, the tribe of Shabazz first established civilization on earth 66

8. Marable 2011, 330–31.
9. X and Haley 1965, 346–48.
10. Marable 2011, 402.
11. Lincoln 1994, 106.

trillion years ago.[12] Rather than consider Malcolm's final name as a site of possible continuities, the *Autobiography* emphasizes El-Hajj Malik El-Shabazz as an absolute break from Minister Malcolm X.

Haley further concretizes the border between Malcolm X and El-Hajj Malik El-Shabazz by minimizing the Nation's engagement of the broader "Muslim world." The *Autobiography* encourages readers to assume that Malcolm's pilgrimage to Mecca reflects his first meaningful encounter with global Muslim contexts or "orthodox" Sunnī tradition. Further enforcing the image of Nation-era Malcolm as entirely isolated from non-Nation Muslims, the *Autobiography* gives no acknowledgement of Elijah Muhammad's travels in Muslim-majority countries such as Egypt, Turkey, Pakistan, and the Sudan or his reception in those countries, let alone his pilgrimage to Mecca years before Malcolm.[13] Elijah had performed the pilgrimage in 1959 in part as an assertion of his own Muslim authenticity, answering charges from Sunnī opponents that he would not be allowed into the city.[14] In the account of his 1964 *ḥajj* in the *Autobiography*, Malcolm appears unequipped to pass the Saudi state's vetting process and secure his legitimacy as a Muslim pilgrim, and struggles to learn basic ritual practices during his pilgrimage; Malcolm thus implicates Elijah for having failed to properly educate his ministers in Islam, let alone the Nation's rank-and-file members. Contrary to the depiction of Malcolm having no significant access to "orthodox" Islam prior to his *ḥajj*, however, Malcolm had already traveled to Saudi Arabia in 1958 to secure Elijah's pilgrimage visa. During these travels, Malcolm used the name Malik Shabazz "so that my brothers in the East would recognize me as one of them."[15] While the *Autobiography* portrays Malcolm's 1964 pilgrimage to Mecca as a signifier of his exodus from the Nation, Malcolm had intended to perform pilgrimage during his 1958 travels, canceling for unclear reasons[16] The Malcolm-Haley authorial voice denies Elijah's Islamic transnationalism and legitimacy as a pilgrim to Mecca, producing an artificial binary in which El-Hajj Malik El-Shabazz appears as the orthodox, global, and universal Muslim that stands in absolute distinction against an illegitimate, local, and sectarian Nation.

This binary informs film depictions of Malcolm X and Elijah Muhammad. In this privileging of Malcolm over Elijah as an authentic Muslim, Malcolm's Islamic credentials remain contingent upon his disavowing his former

---

12. Muhammad 1973, 31.
13. Clegg 1997, 141.
14. Clegg 1997, 131–134.
15. Lincoln 1994, 106.
16. Marable 2015.

teacher, encountering the "Muslim world" presumably for the first time, and maturing beyond the provincial limits of the Nation.

ROOTS: THE NEXT GENERATIONS

As a sequel to *Roots* (1979), 1979 television miniseries *Roots: The Next Generations* follows the Haley family history into the twentieth century and covers Alex Haley's own life, including his experiences interviewing Malcolm for *Playboy* and collaborating with him on the *Autobiography*. Incidentally, Malcolm is portrayed here by Al Freeman, Jr., who later plays Elijah Muhammad in Spike Lee's film. Haley first meets Malcolm at a Nation mosque, finding discomfort with the Fruit of Islam's rigid protocol and hostile demeanor as well as the stern Elijah Muhammad portrait looming over him. Malcolm expresses skepticism that the media of "the white man" would accurately tell his story. Haley later attends a Nation event, observing Malcolm's repeated damnations of "white devils" (particularly Malcolm's own white grandfather) and "Uncle Tom" integrationists. Malcolm turns the audience against a white journalist seated in the front row, unintentionally provoking a man to leap out of his seat and attack the reporter. Though Malcolm then attempts to act as a calming voice, the scene establishes Malcolm's power to provoke violence with his words.

The episode also shows Haley's visit to George Lincoln Rockwell's Nazi compound. In his stiff interactions with Rockwell's swastika-banded paratroopers, the scene rhymes with Haley's earlier visit to the Nation of Islam, suggesting a degree of symmetry between the groups. Rockwell's assessment of Haley's multiracial ancestry mirrors Malcolm's self-loathing over his white grandfather, and Rockwell even insists that he's "saying the same thing that Malcolm X is saying." Haley later rejects their comparison: the problem that Malcolm addresses is real, even if Malcolm offers only a "distorted reaction."

We next see Malcolm with a goatee, signifying his post-Mecca stage. Recalling his experience of Mecca, an energized Malcolm marvels at the pilgrims' racial diversity and declares a transformation in both his theology and anthropology: "I realized if we could accept the oneness of God ... maybe we could accept the oneness of man." He tells Haley of his discovery that "not all whites are racists. Some are sincere. Some are even capable of brotherly love toward a Black man. *That* should be in the book." Haley shows Malcolm pages of the *Autobiography* and receives Malcolm's approval. Discussing the inevitability of his assassination, Malcolm asks for Betty Shabazz to be named the recepient of his royalties, rather than the Nation of Islam.

The episode depicts Malcolm's assassination in the Audubon Ballroom, starting with Malcolm's approach to the podium and greeting of *As-salāmu alaikum* (which Malcolm also provides in English translation, highlighting its mention of peace). Haley's reflection on Malcolm's "X" later in the episode inspires Haley to embark on the search for his own "original name" and the history of his family, which leads to his writing *Roots*.[17]

As another chapter in the continuing Haley family odyssey, the seventh installment of *Roots: the Next Generations* does not place Malcolm at the center of its narrative, but rather as a plot device within Alex Haley's journey. With little screen time, Malcolm does not become a developed character, but moves between polar opposites. We first see him as a militant demagogue, seducing audiences into violent rage; when he next appears, he has been transformed by his pilgrimage to Mecca into a moderate who advocates color-blind universalism and anticipates his own murder by the fanaticism from which he had graduated. Post-Mecca Malcolm exhibits neither the anger with which the episode characterizes Nation-era Malcolm, nor the urgency in Nation-era Malcolm's call for justice. Post-Mecca Malcolm appears merely as a born-again man of religion who has surrendered his rage and embraced hope.

DEATH OF A PROPHET

The 1981 docudrama *Death of a Prophet* (Woodie King, Jr.) tells the story of a fictional "Prophet Minister" portrayed by Morgan Freeman, while providing an introduction that explicitly frames the fiction as inspired by Malcolm's assassination. The film opens with footage of 1960s activism and voiceover narration describing "turbulence" and various unnamed "leaders," followed by a clip of Ossie Davis, activist (and witness to the assassination) Yuri Kochiyama, and Amiri Baraka recalling the assassination. This opening documentary sequence prepares viewers to engage Prophet Minister as a stand-in for Malcolm.[18]

The narrative begins with members of an unnamed organization attempting to locate Prophet Minister at a hotel in New York, asking for room numbers of a "Mr. Shabazz" and "Mr. Garvey," among other names. These men address each other as "Comrade"; one bearded member resembles post-Mecca Malcolm while wearing a bowtie that recalls the Nation. Unidentified arsonists set fire to Prophet Minister's house, causing him to flee with his wife and small daughters. Prophet Minister's opponents plot his assassination and make harassing phone calls to his hotel room,

17. "Episode 7." *Roots: the Next Generations*. ABC. 1979.
18. *Death of a Prophet*. Dir. Woodie King, Jr. 1981. Film.

while Prophet Minister is shown performing *sujda* (the prostration portion of Muslim prayer). Prophet Minister reveals his awareness of the plot against him, even identifying the planned date for his assassination as February 26 (the Nation's annual holiday, Savior's Day; Malcolm was assassinated on February 21). As he travels throughout the city, Prophet Minister appears as a friend of white hippies and Black bookstore owners; he identifies himself as "only ... a minister in a religion that most people in this country haven't heard about," and names his mission as simply starting a "storefront church." At his organization's headquarters, he receives visits from FBI agents as well as dignitaries from Ghana and Mecca. The FBI blames Prophet Minister's rhetoric for having inspired men who destroyed the Liberty Bell and Statue of Liberty; Prophet Minister answers that no member of his "church" would perform such actions, and rejects the FBI's attempt to buy his cooperation. Prophet Minister's Ghanian and Meccan visitors speak to his dual commitments both as a pan-Africanist and the minister of a "church." The visitor from Ghana, head of the Organization of African Unity (OAU), reveals that Prophet Minister's speeches have turned people away from religion altogether; the Meccan states that Islam has achieved world riches for its adherents and invites Malcolm to come "learn the ways of Allah," adding, "You could be the imam." The OAU leader gives Prophet Minister a competing offer, inviting him to head Ghana's national university. Prophet Minister declines them both.

Prophet Minister refers to the unnamed organization that wants him dead, as well as its leader, in ways that echo the *Autobiography*. When asked, "Why do they hate you?" Prophet Minister answers, "I must have hurt someone very badly. He and I understand each other very well. He looks on me as his son, but I made the mistake of growing up." The film also depicts Malcolm's friendship with Elijah Muhammad's son, Wallace D. Muhammad (later Warith Deen Mohammed), who would lead the Nation after Elijah's death towards Sunnī reorientation. During their meeting outside, Prophet Minister offers sagacious advice: "You are your own man ... Read *everything*, but only believe what you can see and feel." The unnamed young man, wearing pseudo-military dress that recalls Fruit of Islam uniforms, tells Prophet Minister, "I wish you were my father ... One day, I will be head of this organization, and I will always honor you...I understand your teachings and I will teach as you are teaching."

Death of a Prophet ends with Prophet Minister's assassination, which echoes Malcolm's death in details such as its setting (Harlem's Audubon Ballroom) and the conspirators' cue ("Get your hand out of my pocket"). Though the film maintains a fictional universe that does not provide a straightforward examination of the Nation or Malcolm's journey within and beyond it, *Death of a Prophet* repeats what would become the master narrative, presenting the Nation of Islam as an assemblage of pathological cultists who murder Malcolm for having outgrown them.

MALCOLM X

The canonical cinematic representation of Malcolm X remains Spike Lee's 1992 biopic, which authorizes itself in part through connection to the *Autobiography* (for his screenplay, Lee revised the Baldwin-Perl script that had been explicitly based on the *Autobiography*). Though Lee does engage in liberties with the creation of fictitious characters and the erasures of important women from Malcolm's life,[19] the film presents itself as a faithful reproduction of the *Autobiography*. Malcolm (portrayed by Denzel Washington) offers voiceover reflections throughout the film with quotes taken from the *Autobiography*, presenting a simulation of the film as Malcolm's firsthand account, and promotion for the book appears in the film's closing credits.[20]

Malcolm X presents the Nation as critical to Malcolm's awakening to the destructive forces of white supremacy. Nonetheless, Malcolm shows that he has outgrown the Nation chiefly in his willingness to accept white allyship and pursuit of United Nations intervention in the Black freedom struggle. While critiquing the film for its deradicalization of Malcolm, hooks notes that Lee took care with his representation of Elijah Muhammad, "preserving the integrity of his spirit and work."[21] Nonetheless, Lee presents Elijah Muhammad as bereft of religious legitimacy beyond his mystique as the Messenger, never showing him to have any meaningful grasp of Islam or connections to transnational Muslim networks. In this sense, it follows the *Autobiography* in portraying Malcolm's pilgrimage as his first access to a greater Muslim world. As in the *Autobiography*, Lee erases Elijah's travels through Muslim-majority countries and Elijah's own pilgrimage to Mecca, not to mention Malcolm's earlier travels in the Middle East.

ALI

Less than a decade after Lee's biopic, Malcolm would appear in Michael Mann's Muhammad Ali biopic, *Ali* (2001), portrayed by Mario Van Peebles. The film follows Ali from his 1964 fight with Sonny Liston through his 1974 travel to Zaire for the "Rumble in the Jungle" against George Foreman. While

19. hooks 1994, 180–92.
20. hooks 1994, 180–92.
21. hooks 1994, 180–92.

Ali's Malcolm corresponds to the Haley/Lee treatment, the film also depicts Ali's conversion and changing relationship to the Nation in ways that echo Malcolm's trajectory.

Ali calls attention to the intellectual gulf between Ali and Malcolm with a scene in which Malcolm stares out a hotel room window, mentioning an invitation to speak in Nigeria and attempting to engage Ali in conversation while Ali remains fascinated by images of termites on the television. The scene then provides *Ali*'s treatment of Malcolm's break from the Nation, attributing the split to Malcolm's revolutionary spirit and the Nation's refusal to take part in the Civil Rights movement. Malcolm confesses his frustration with the Nation's conservatism:

> When I heard about those four little girls who got bombed in that
> Birmingham church, the prohibitions of the Honorable Elijah
> Muhammad prevented me from speaking my thoughts in action –
> because Birmingham was part of the Civil Rights struggle. You know,
> begging for our place at the white man's table. But dead children are
> dead children.[22]

Without giving a clear reason, mentioning only a struggle to contain his anger, Malcolm reveals that he has been suspended as a minister of the Nation. *Ali* gives no account of the historical circumstances surrounding Malcolm's suspension, namely Elijah Muhammad's offense at his remarks on President Kennedy's assassination. Instead, *Ali* invokes Birmingham, renaming the key issues as Elijah Muhammad's hostility to the Civil Rights movement and Malcolm's uncompromising moral conscience. This scene renders Malcolm simultaneously more revolutionary than the Nation (highlighting the burning urgency in his heart's call to action) and more compatible with dominant Civil Rights narratives (recentering Birmingham and erasing Malcolm's declaration of "chickens coming home to roost"). Malcolm remains too committed to justice to ever be contained within the Nation, but not so unacceptably radical that he might gloat at the death of a president.

The next scene contrasts Malcolm's imminent exodus against Ali's meeting with Elijah Muhammad, during which Elijah grants Ali his "original name." He is not Cassius Clay or even Cassius X, but now Muhammad Ali. Elijah's son Herbert then becomes Ali's manager, and Malcolm learns both that Ali will no longer be traveling with him to Africa and that his suspension has been "extended indefinitely."

Malcolm and Ali later bump into each other during their separate travels

22. *Ali.* Dir. Michael Mann. Columbia Pictures, 2001. Film.

through Africa. Malcolm introduces Ali to his companions: Maya Angelou, Chinese ambassor Huang Hua, and Algerian ambassador Taher Kaid. Ali has no idea where to go or what to see and defers to Malcolm's authority: "Oh, man. Where should I go? I want to go all over this place." Malcolm instantly answers, "Go to Algeria. See Ben Bella. Then go to see Mecca and Medina. I just came from there." Malcolm proceeds to recount his experiences of the pilgrimage, running through the key points and details made famous in his letter from Saudi Arabia and the *Autobiography*: performing seven circumambulations around the Ka'ba, drinking from the well of Zamzam, praying on Mount Arafat, and sharing in his *ḥajj* with millions of pilgrims from all over the world, including "blond-haired, blue-eyed Muslims, Arabs, Africans, Indonesians. Seeing brothers just like us, praying together, it was beautiful." In his dropping of names and experiences, Malcolm establishes himself as both a spiritually mature Muslim and confident citizen of the world in ways that elude Ali, who remains limited within the Nation's parochial vision and can only respond with a cultist's memorized defense: "You shouldn't have quarreled with the Honorable Elijah Muhammad." As Malcolm tries to connect with Ali on an uneven field, Ali repeats his answer twice more. The two part ways, Ali returning to his Nation handlers and Malcolm rejoining his traveling party of poets and diplomats.

Ali later depicts an FBI agent concerned that Malcolm's new openness and global cosmopolitanism has rendered him an even greater menace to the state. The agent complains that Malcolm, formerly a divisive personality in the Black freedom struggle, now shakes hands with King, suggesting the possibility of a united effort; moreover, Malcolm now travels abroad and engages figures such as Bella and Nasser. If the FBI had hoped to turn Malcolm and Elijah Muhammad against each other, the plan has backfired, at least in the case of the former: "We were better off before, with Malcolm inside the Nation."

Amidst Ali's own navigations of the complexities between his marital life and his life in the Nation, the film depicts Malcolm's assassination. Ali learns of the news while driving his car in a scene that resonates with a scene in Spike Lee's biopic of Malcolm driving to his fated Audubon Ballroom appearance (adding to the rhyme between films, versions of Sam Cooke's "A Change is Gonna Come" accompany both scenes). Ali later repeats steps in Malcolm's journey, experiencing his own suspension and disillusionment. Unlike Malcolm (and the film's implication), however, Ali never leaves the Nation; he remains a faithful member through the passing of Elijah Muhammad in 1975 and joins in its "orthodox" reforms led by Elijah's son Warith Deen Mohammed. Concluding in 1974, *Ali* does not follow this part of

Ali's Muslim trajectory, but instead suggests that his relationship with the Nation has deteriorated beyond repair. With the Nation having quietly faded out of the plot, Ali appears at the film's end as a solitary seeker across the world, broadening his perspective beyond the Nation and finding himself in travel as Malcolm had.[23]

BETTY AND CORETTA

The 2013 Lifetime movie *Betty and Coretta* (Yves Simoneau) covers the friendship that developed between Dr. Betty Shabazz and Coretta Scott King in the years after their husbands' assassinations. The film opens with references to President Obama's dedication of the Dr. Martin Luther King, Jr. memorial in Washington. The narrative begins with Malcolm (Lindsay Owen Pierre) – sporting a goatee, signifying his post-Nation stage – addressing an audience at a church in Selma, during which Malcolm proclaims that he does not advocate violence beyond self-defense. "I believe in nonviolence," he tells the audience, "if a person is nonviolent with me." Continuing to adhere to nonviolence when confronted with violence, however, remains "a waste of time."[24] This middle position between violence and nonviolence, the film implies in subsequent scenes, represents a liminal Malcolm-in-progress, having departed from the radical Nation of Islam but not yet a responsible participant within the Civil Rights movement. Coretta approaches Malcolm after his talk, prompting Malcolm to introduce himself as Malik (which Pierre pronounces "Maleek"). Coretta remarks, "I know you as Malcolm." He answers, "Well, you didn't know I changed it, then." Coretta condemns Malcolm's presence in Alabama as destructive to her husband's struggle: "It's irresponsible to talk the way that you do." Malcolm asserts that her husband should be thanking him; his presence will scare the white establishment into working with King. Malcolm and Coretta then engage in a brief debate over the merits of bringing the Black freedom struggle to an international stage; Coretta objects on the grounds that it would endanger Lyndon B. Johnson's reelection.

Coretta then visits her husband in jail and informs him of Malcolm's arrival. Dr. King accuses Malcolm of crass self-promotion and giving the struggle a bad name. Coretta counters that Malcolm "seems different" and had "even changed his name." According to Coretta, Malcolm is "softening" and "could come around, given time." Dr. King, adamant that Malcolm refuses to disavow violence, hopes that she's right.

Dr. King later blames Malcolm for his own assassination in a "chickens

23. *Ali.* Dir. Michael Mann. Columbia Pictures, 2001. Film.
24. *Betty and Coretta.* Dir. Yves Simoneau. Lifetime. 2013.

coming home to roost" moment, lamenting, "Nothing good can ever come from preaching violence." In the next scene, Betty's friend attributes the firebombing of the NOI's Harlem mosque to "Malcolm's supporters" as they watch media coverage that provides fiery rhetoric from Louis Farrakhan (named here as Louis Farrakhan, though he was still Louis X at the time). Farrakhan's celebration of Malcolm's death provokes Betty's friend to declare, "Talk like *that's* what got brother Malcolm killed," echoing King's verdict.[25]

SELMA

Malcolm appears only briefly in *Selma* (Ava DuVernay, 2014), his presence serving chiefly to represent one of the challenges facing King as he navigates a volatile and treacherous landscape that includes not only various factions of white people, but also a Black radicalism that threatens to detonate his vulnerable alliances. President Lyndon B. Johnson tells King that he's happy to see King as the leader of the movement, rather than one of "those militant Malcolm X types." Malcolm (portrayed by Nigel Thatch) becomes the embodiment of an imminent threat to King's careful tightrope walk.

Rumors of Malcolm's presence in Alabama cause panic among the responsible movement leaders: Esther Williams remarks, "The Negro cannot be talking that 'By any means necessary' madness to these people! They 'bout ready to bust as it is." Williams fears that when Malcolm's followers "pick up their guns and start shooting white folk," the National Guard will come in and murder everyone. When Malcolm arrives at the chapel, confirming their worst nightmare, their faces transform. James Bevel simply exclaims, "Holy shit." However, this might not be the Malcolm that they had expected. James Forman introduces him as Malcolm X, but Malcolm corrects him: "Actually, El-Hajj Malik El-Shabazz." This firm break between names, again resonating more with the chapter outline of the *Autobiography* than Malcolm's historical use of them, enforces the film's portrayal of Malcolm's newfound political openness corresponding to a more legitimate religiosity.

In *Selma*, as in *Betty and Coretta*, Malcolm finds himself confronted by Coretta Scott King at Brown Chapel. Bevel suggests that Coretta "ask our Muslim party-crasher here not to speak, out of respect for her husband being in jail at the moment and all." During their exchange, Malcolm pleads that he means no disrespect by his appearance, to which Coretta objects that Malcolm had said disrespectful things about her husband in the past. Malcolm accepts that he has been "piercing" in his critique of nonviolence,

25. *Selma*. Dir. Ava DuVernay. Paramount Pictures, 2014. Film.

but assures her that a religious transformation has matured his perspective: "Mrs. King, I have recently traveled to Mecca, the holy land. And I've learned more than I ever previously knew. During the hajj, several million people of different nationalities worship in unison." Malcolm then suggests that because the local sheriff does not know that Malcolm has changed, Malcolm can disguise himself as a radical to scare whites into working with Dr. King: "Let my being here represent the factions that *will* come if they don't give the good Reverend what he's asking for, and soon." Malcolm pleads that he no longer has an "army behind me," but only himself and "the truth."

Again echoing *Betty and Coretta*, Coretta reports of her exchange with Malcolm to her husband. "He spoke well but with less, um, *fire*, I guess is the word." She recalls Malcolm talking about petitioning the United Nations and making reference to the "field Negro and the house Negro." Dr. King smirks, "I wonder which one I am in his scenario? Not hard to figure out." Coretta answers, "It wasn't like that this time." King objects to his wife's defenses of Malcolm and resents the suggestion that Malcolm could meaningfully support the struggle: "This movement, *our* movement has been the one that's moved the needle ...We lay down our lives against those dogs and those bombers and those billy clubs, while people like him talk and shout about it. But what has he changed?"[26]

Malcolm appears in *Selma* entirely as a problem, serving to embody the extremist fringes that threaten King's responsible leadership and delicate diplomacy. Malcolm complicates King's vision only when King refuses to accept the "new Malcolm," El-Hajj Malik El-Shabazz, as a changed man. At no point does *Selma* challenge the reputation of the "old Malcolm" that had provoked such alarm among King's collaborators. Anything of value that Malcolm X might offer remains locatable exclusively on the post-Nation side of his life, in which Malcolm X has been abrogated by El-Hajj Malik El-Shabazz.

CONCLUSIONS

In his Haley-mediated *Autobiography*, Malcolm X's life of changes becomes immediately compatible with a cinematic plot structure that would organize his story as three acts: 1) the troubled youth whose family was destroyed by the Ku Klux Klan and a racist state system, and who struggles to find his way within a white supremacist society; 2) the prisoner who finds redemption in the Nation and rises to become its most prominent minister; 3) the disillusioned seeker who experiences rebirth in Mecca and returns home with a new vision for a better world. In its various reiterations, the narrative

26. *Selma*. Dir. Ava DuVernay. Paramount Pictures, 2014. Film.

triangle frames Malcolm's life in such a way that the Nation represents an immature state from which Malcolm must evolve. This also happens to be the vision of Malcolm's life that would satisfy a mass consumer audience comprised mostly of white viewers.

To the extent that these films make arguments for Malcolm's legitimacy, they do so by distancing him from the Nation of Islam. They also soften and whitewash Malcolm's post-Mecca politics, highlighting his faith in the United Nations but marginalizing his continued commitment to the struggle for Black liberation. Rendered invisible is the Malcolm who affirmed at one of his post-Mecca rallies that he had *not* changed in regard to his feelings about white Americans.[27] The truest Malcolm, in this recurring template, can be found exclusively in the less than one calendar year that he spent as a Sunnī Muslim, rather than the seventeen years that he spent in the Nation.

To this end, the Nation consistently appears to possess no genuine connections to transnational Muslim communities. Malcolm cannot achieve a meaningful linkage with the global *umma* or even grasp that there are white Muslims until he can escape and transcend the Nation. These retellings of Malcolm's life, adhering to the *Autobiography*, leave out details such as Malcolm first traveling to Saudi Arabia in the 1950s, Malcolm embarking on his 1964 *ḥajj* while still self-identifying as a follower of Elijah Muhammad (though outside the Nation as an organization), or Elijah giving Malcolm what many assume to have been his "Sunnī name," Malik Shabazz. Portraying the Nation as entirely isolated from the broader "Muslim world," they also erase the Nation's transnational engagements, including Elijah's own pilgrimage to Mecca and visits to Muslim-majority countries, Elijah's friendliness with Egypt's president Gamal Abdel Nasser, or even seemingly mundane details such as the Nation obtaining its copies of the Qur'ān through a Pakistani importer in New Jersey.[28]

Reports that Manning Marable's *Malcolm X: A Life of Reinvention* would undergo adaptation as a television miniseries raise concerns for the ahistorical tropes that have informed cinematic retellings of Malcolm's life. While Marable's scholarship masterfully resists those tropes, Marable himself is sadly not here to oversee the adaptation. Media discussions of the upcoming series have already performed a critical error in identifying Malcolm as a "civil rights activist" – a mold in which film portrayals of Malcolm frequently attempt to recast him, and one that Malcolm himself had rejected. It remains to be seen whether Marable's scholarly challenge to master narratives of Malcolm's life will inform a challenge to Hollywood's fictive Malcolm.

27. X and Breitman 1994, 213.
28. *Ali* 2015.

Works Cited

Ali, K. 2015. *The Lives of Muhammad.* Cambridge.

Aydin, C. 2016. *The Idea of the Muslim World.* Cambridge.

Clegg, C. 1997. *An Original Man: The Life and Times of Elijah Muhammad.* New York.

hooks, b. 1994. *Outlaw Culture.* London.

Lincoln, C. 1994. *The Black Muslims in America.* 3rd edition. Grand Rapids, Michigan.

Marable, M. 2011. *Malcolm X: A Life of Reinvention.* New York.

Muhammad, E. 1973. *Message to the Black Man in America.* Chicago.

X, M., and Alex Haley. 1965. *The Autobiography of Malcolm X.* New York.

X, M., with George Breitman, ed. 1994. *Malcolm X Speaks.* New York.

The Incidental Muslim:
The Characters We Overlook

Hussein Rashid

INTRODUCTION

The "incidental Muslim" is a character in a film who is integral to the story, but does not need to be Muslim. Her religious identification does provide depth to the story, because it provides depth to the character. The role of the incidental Muslim is to move the story arc forward, but may or not may not invoke her religion in doing so.

Unlike a main character, such as might be found in a "Muslim Cosby Show," the incidental Muslim empowers the re-centering of narratives of Americanness by embedding the Muslim character in a web of relationships not defined by religion. We can see this process unfold through characters from the films *Pitch Black* (David Twohy, 2000), *Ender's Game* (Gavin Hood, 2013), and the *Book of Eli* (The Hughes Brothers, 2010), where each individual is marked as Muslim in different ways.

The first figure is Imam from the Chronicles of Riddick films, particularly his appearance in *Pitch Black*. Imam is a character, whose existence is defined by his religiosity. The second character is Alai (pronounced "ally" in the film), a friend and confidante to the lead character of *Ender's Game*, Ender Wiggin. Only one line in the entire movie marks him as Muslim, but his interactions with Ender define his character and make him an instrumental part of the cohort of heroes. Finally, by expanding the definition of who could be a hero in a movie, to someone who may be Muslim, but without necessarily being defined by their religion, we will read the ways in which there may be Muslim characters in the *Book of Eli*.

The first two characters are clearly marked as Muslim, but to different degrees. We may think of them as "legible Muslims," those who are presented to viewers through imagery and discourses but disrupt public assumptions about Islam. These characters are not legible in a stereotypical way, but are still visibly Muslim.[1] This difference allows us to examine the different work each character does in the film to portray Muslims as part of a larger society. The third example is a counter-factual. The character is not

---

1. Petersen 2017, 88.

marked as Muslim, nor is he a legible member of any religious tradition. If we treat him as a Muslim character, we can hypothesize as to how he would be read by the viewing audience.

From a viewer's perspective, the incidental Muslim serves to normalize Islam and Muslims. Traditional parasocial contact hypothesis (PCH) looks at main characters to normalize a marginal group into an American dominant culture.[2] Colloquially, this process is known as the "Will and Grace Effect," for the sitcom which originally ran from 1998 to 2006, and is credited with making LGBT individuals more visible, and thus more familiar, to the dominant viewing audience. As a result, it is believed that marriage equality became more acceptable as a political proposition in the United States.[3] The same process should apply to other marginalized groups, such as Muslims, in the American context.

PARASOCIAL CONTACT THEORY

The primary theory of transformation that integrates Muslims into narratives of being American in these case studies is parasocial contact hypothesis (PCH). PCH argues that media can serve as a way to reduce negative attitudes of specific groups by creating a sense of dissonance that results in an attitude change.[4] This work is informed by two earlier theories, Contact Hypothesis and Para-Social Interaction.

The basic premise of Contact Hypothesis, or Intergroup Contact Theory, is that intergroup interaction will reduce prejudice between the groups.[5] This contact is not simply introducing different people, but that the engagement must be structured in some way.[6] In addition, groups should have similar status, interests, and tasks; the contact fosters close relationships; the groups do not reinforce stereotypes of themselves; and, activities encourage the groups to work together.[7]

Parasocial Interaction is "intimacy at a distance."[8] Focusing on television, the theory states the viewer and actor are in a type of face-to-face relationship. Parasocial Contact seems to work because the viewer's brain engages with TV characters much as it does real life interactions.[9]

There are two considerations that we must account for in taking this

2. Tukachinsky et al. 2015, 18.
3 Schiappa et al. 2006.
4. Schiappa et al. 2005, 94.
5. Schiappa et al. 2005, 94.
6. Allport 1979, 261.
7. Pettigrew and Tropp 2005, 263.
8. Horton and Wohl 1956.
9. Schiappa et al. 2006, 20. See also Bell 2014, 133.

theory to the study of movie narratives. The first consideration is that barriers are more easily broken down when there appears to be some sort of authority that encourages constructive engagement, so that the participants believe they have permission to cross divides.[10] Yet, constant negative news portrayal of Islam and Muslims suggests both an official approbation of attempting to understand Muslims, and creates a situation of negative parasocial contact.[11] Narrative media, more so than news media, is the basis of parasocial contact hypothesis. In fact, the negative news cycle may actually set up the necessary environment to create the dissonance with the viewer that PCH suggests is needed to be effective.[12]

The second consideration of adapting PCH to the space of movies is the single presentation of the story. In TV, a series may offer an ongoing narrative that reinforces certain representations of Muslims. This ongoing engagement helps to create the dissonance in the viewer's world view.[13] Without such engagement, there is a risk of stereotypical or idiosyncratic associations with Muslims[14].

Films may offer the ability for more complex identifications, in part through shared environments, which create a visual community. More importantly, turning to psychological processes, the viewer integrates their change of state in the movie and takes it into the world outside of the theater.[15]

From this basis, I argue that we can apply PCH to a cinematic context, although perhaps not with the same magnitude of results we see with TV viewers. What is apparent from TV research is that intergroup identity is important, differences should be marked, but at a certain point, the emphasis on difference becomes counter-productive.[16] The greatest success in effecting change is amongst shows that have a diverse, organically integrated cast, who deal with salient issues of difference as part of a larger storyline, rather than as *the* storyline. This type of indirect discussion of difference allows for greater audience participation and recognition, echoing Allport's initial premises.[17] Each of the three movies functions with different elements of theoretically successful parasocial contact. What they share

10. Pettigrew and Tropp 2005, 265, 271.
11. Pickel and Yendell 2016, 285. For further discussion of likeability and acceptability, see Tukachinsky et al. 2015, 23. See also Gottschalk and Greenberg 2008; Nacos and Torres-Reyna 2007; Pennington and Kahn 2018.
12. Schiappa et al. 2005, 94.
13. Schiappa et al. 2005, 94.
14. Plate 2003, 7. cf. Semmerling 2006; Shaheen 2001.
15. Plate 2003, 2–3. See also hooks 2009, 4.
16. Bell 2014, 145; Pettigrew and Tropp 2005, 272.
17. Bell 2014, 134, 138, 149.

in common is not the obviousness of the characters' Islam, but the ways in which those religious identifications are integrated into the narratives.

RIDDICK SERIES

The *Chronicles of Riddick* franchise crosses multiple media and focuses on the eponymous character, Richard B. Riddick. *Pitch Black* (2000), the first film of the universe, introduces us to Imam Abu al-Walid, a character marked as Muslim, through his dress, speech, and actions. Officially, he belongs to a religion that is an intentional combination of Christianity and Islam. However, for all practical purposes, the religion is presented, and can reasonably be read, as Islam. Imam – his title is used in a familiar way as a name in the films – offers viewers an opportunity to understand how an "incidental Muslim" functions to normalize the presentation of Muslims in a larger narrative.

Imam is taking three young men with him on pilgrimage to New Mecca aboard the ship Hunter Gratzner, which crashes on a planet. This planet has photophobic predators, which proceed to attack the survivors of the crash as the planet enters an extended period of darkness caused by an eclipse. Riddick is the antihero, imprisoned on the ship by a bounty hunter and freed in the crash, who helps the other characters survive attacks by the creatures.

The characters struggle for survival, and the differences amongst them are made secondary to that desire to survive. However, each of the characters is provided with significant motivation to be on the ship, and a basis for their moral decision making in their various struggles. For Imam, he is guided by his faith. He does not need to be Muslim for his arc. He could be any person of faith, belonging to any religion, including a religion that does not exist outside of Riddick's cinematic universe. To make the character Muslim ties him to the reality viewers live in, and allows them to carry their sympathetic response with them out of the theater. The character is also significant because when the film was released major films were not dealing with religion in a meaningful way.[18]

Imam's title and reason for being on the ship, a religious pilgrimage to New Mecca, indicate clearly to the viewer that he is Muslim. It is his style of dress that continues to remind viewers of his religion. His clothing is reminiscent of nomadic desert dwellers, akin to the Tuareg. It allows him to be legibly Muslim, using dress and title in stereotypical ways. However, once Imam's religious identification is established, the film seeks to subvert expectations of that identification, creating a necessary dissonance for transformation to take hold.

18. Walliss and Aston 2011, 55–58.

In the film industry in the United States, Arabs and Muslims are conflated through stereotyping and presented in one of four broad categories: villains, sheikhs, maidens, and cameos.[19] Imam fits none of these basic categories. His role is more as a spiritual caretaker. If the point of creating stereotypes is to craft an identity of the Other that we can easily define our Self against, then Imam makes that construction of Self through opposition difficult.[20] Imam is honorable, caring, selfless, and is grounded in a deep belief that is approachable to the viewer. Racially, Imam is Black, further subverting the conflation between Arab and Muslim. While there are Black Arabs, in the American imaginary, the Arab figure is constructed along anti-Semitic lines, with a dark, or swarthy, but not Black, complexion.

As the boys in Imam's care are killed by the creatures, Riddick engages Imam on his faith. First, Riddick responds to Imam's assumption that Riddick does not believe in God, as Imam prays over Riddick:

RIDDICK: What're you doin'?

IMAM: Blessing you like the others. It's painless.

RIDDICK: And pointless.

IMAM: I see. Well, even if you don't believe in God, it doesn't mean He won't be --

RIDDICK: You don't see. 'Cuz you don't spend half your life in lock-down with a horse-bit in your mouth and not believe. And you surely don't start out in a liquor store trash bin with an umbilical cord wrapped around your neck and not believe. Oh, absolutely I believe in God. And I absolutely hate the fucker.

IMAM: He will be with us. Nonetheless.

Riddick sees suffering as proof of God's existence. While it is not explicit, one can read Riddick's declaration as stating that the suffering he has experienced can only come from powerful being. Riddick's faith is one of antagonism, but not rejection; Imam is steeped in devotion, regardless of what happens to him. That difference in engagement represents broad possible responses to questions of theodicy. Their responses are broad enough that parts of the viewing audience who have participated in similar questioning may be able to identify with at least one of the figures, if not both.

At another point, it begins to rain, extinguishing the torches the

19. Shaheen 2001, 20–34.;Shaheen 2008, 25–33. See also, Blizek 2009, 177.
20. Semmerling 2006, 81.; Hall 1991, 15–17. Cf. Rashid 2014.

survivors made to keep the predators away. Riddick says to Imam, "So where the hell's God now, huh? I'll tell you where! He's up there pissing on me!" Riddick, once more, defines his relationship with God as antagonistic. Imam, seems conflicted about the rain. He recognizes that it is decimating the group's defenses, but he also seems to consider it a blessing, especially as earlier in the film the group was looking for water. At that earlier point in the film, Imam even says that God will lead them to water.

Much like the character of Azeem, played by Morgan Freeman, in *Robin Hood: Prince of Thieves* (Kevin Reynolds, 1991), Imam is a figure of honor, and that honor flows from his faith.[21] He is protective of the young men with him; he fights for them; he mourns them. A viewer sees him as a fighter by circumstance, not by choice. Violence is not an intrinsic part of his nature. While his religion may be distinct, the issues he struggles with as a believer are shared across monotheistic traditions, and his interactions with Riddick on the question of God's justice demonstrate this commonality. Over the course of the movie, Riddick and Imam develop a genuine friendship, one that causes Riddick to visit Imam in the second movie and defend Imam and his family from a new menace. Viewers who identify with the protagonist have made a connection with Imam as well.

ENDER'S GAME

In the movie *Ender's Game*, we see a different approach to the faith of Alai, the explicit Muslim character of the film. Much like *Pitch Black*, there is an external stressor that brings together a disparate group of individuals. In this situation, it is an ongoing conflict with an alien race known as the Formics. In order to meet the perceived threat of this race, humanity has come together create a training environment known as Battle School, to train young men and women for combat. This system is based on the belief that children have the adaptability to meet the threat of the aliens and win.

The military commanders in charge of recruitment and training believe that Andrew "Ender" Wiggin is the most gifted individual they could find to defeat the Formics. He is described as being both a strategic and a tactical genius, and these qualities emerge from his intense empathy for others, including his enemies. He is able to fully understand another person and give them what they want.

In Battle School, he is put through a variety of formal and informal trainings, designed to sharpen his skills and isolate him socially, in order to make him more aggressive. As he takes on more of a command role, he is

21. Ramji 2005.

able to choose who his team will be. The people he chooses are those he is able trust, and with whom he has made deep connections over the course of his training. One of these individuals is Alai.

Like many of the characters in the film, Alai's national origins are unclear. However, he is part of a visually diverse ethnic group that appears to mirror the source material from the novel upon which the movie is based.[22] Alai is introduced early in the film, and he is a target for some of the more aggressive students in his cohort. Ender steps in to defend him, creating the friendship that lasts throughout the movie.

When Ender is being moved from one training unit to another, leaving Alai in the old group, we discover Alai is Muslim. Ender is summoned to his new group in the middle of night. His commanders instruct him to leave his belongings and move to new quarters, and he is walking down a long corridor when Alai calls out to him. In wishing him success, Alai shakes Ender's right hand with his own right hand, places his left hand on Ender's right shoulder, and says, "as-salam alaykum. Peace to you." A look is exchanged between the two characters, but the meaning of the look is ambiguous. It could be a look of friends saying farewell, "until we meet again," or a more regretful, long-term goodbye. That the two figures have a strong relationship is undeniable. The physical contact and steady, prolonged gaze, indicate that there is a mutual affection between these two boys.

The scene is striking because of the voluntary intimacy that is conveyed through their proximity. In *Pitch Black*, the characters are near each other out of necessity. They must defend themselves against unknown predators. They enter into intense conversation because of the situation. In *Ender's Game*, in this sequence, everything is driven by voluntary choice. Alai *chooses* to follow Ender into a long hallway and call out to Ender. Ender *chooses* to stop and turn around. Alai *chooses* to walk to Ender and offer his hand. Ender *chooses* to accept the hand. The result is that when Alai greets Ender with the traditional Muslim greeting of "as-salam alaykum," there is a sense of release in that action. The tension that preceded this moment with Ender's training, and the call to move quarters is dissipated.

In this scene, no words are expressed after Alai presents Ender "as-salam alaykum. Peace to you." Ender is not shocked, nor does he question why Alai is offering that phrase to him. It is taken as part of the world in which Ender and Alai occupy: racially and religiously diverse.

As in *Pitch Black*, we see an organically integrated cast working towards a common goal. Differences are salient, but are not explicitly addressed. Instead, difference is expected and contributes to the strength of the group.

22. Doyle and Stewart 2004, 188.

Alai's friendship gives Ender strength. Another cadet, one of the few female characters in the film, Petra, trains Ender in combat skills. Throughout the film, phenotypic difference is obvious, whether race or gender. Religion is a hidden difference that did not need to be addressed in the film. Regardless of why Alai's faith is introduced, the result is the same: Islam is normalized in the filmic universe. As viewers who identify with Ender, we can then identify Alai as "one of us," as part of the in-group, rather than as an Other.

Ender's empathetic nature indicates to us that Alai can be trusted. Ender serves as an external validation to Alai's humanity, and for those viewers who doubt the humanity of Muslims, it creates a sense of dissonance. This dissonance is amplified by virtue of the setting in a military academy. In an American context, the symbolism of serving in the military has traditionally served as a marker of belonging to the nation, of Americanness.[23]

BOOK OF ELI

Unlike *Pitch Black* or *Ender's Game*, there is no "team" that comes together in *The Book of Eli*. The film is set in a post-apocalyptic period, and suggests that unspecified religions had a role in the conflict. The main character, Eli, is on a quest to deliver a text of great power to a library of human civilization in a location the viewer would recognize as Alcatraz. He is aided in his quest by a young woman named Solara.

We discover that the book that Eli has, and which his antagonist, Carnegie, wants, is a King James Bible. We also discover that Eli is blind, and his version of the Bible is in braille. He ultimately has to give the Bible to Carnegie in order to save Solara's life. He is still able to "deliver" the book, as he has memorized it and can dictate it to the scribes at the library.

On the surface, *The Book of Eli* seems to violate many of the premises outlined by PCH. It is does not include an organically integrated team, where differences are explicit and engaged with as part of a larger story line.

The object that drives the story is a religious object, but the religion of the characters is never addressed. Carnegie wants the Bible as a means of control over his subjects. He does not appear to have any faith whatsoever. Eli does appear to be faithful, but his religion is never explicitly mentioned. The fact that he is carrying a Bible, and is reverential to it, may lead viewers to think he is Christian, but there is enough ambiguity in his actions that we cannot definitively say that he is a Christian.

It is this ambiguity that makes this film rich for a discussion of the role of

---

23. For examples of how this connection between the military and American-ness functions with respect to Muslims in the United States, see Curtis 2016, 6–7.

the "incidental Muslim" in film. The movie is symbolically rich with shared religious idioms across Christianity and Islam, and certain instances favor a Muslim reading of the film. While the average viewer may miss some of the symbolic reading, the film offers a way to think about integration of Muslims not through external validation of their presence, but by constructing a world where their presence is a given. The engagement with difference is so natural that it is invisible to the average viewer. In the film we explicitly see different races and abilities, and so we can posit that in a film about a religious object, we should also be able to see different religions, even if only implicitly.

Some scholars have posited that *The Book of Eli* is an optimistic film, "where America can start over unencumbered by the past."[24] If we start from this premise, it is easier to accept that Muslims are normalized in a post-Apocalyptic America, and could potentially contribute to saving human cultures. One can make a phenomenological argument that Eli may be presented as Muslim during Eli's burial, when Eli is wrapped in white cloth, similar to Muslim funerary practices.[25] Whilst not any more definitive about Eli's religious identity than his care for the Bible, it does allow us to think about how new social structures are constructed in a new environment[26] This post-apocalyptic space is about creating a new world, but the new cannot be born absent the old. The configurations of difference may change, but the fact that differences exist have to be acknowledged. Islam and Muslims are still part of this world, although perhaps in ways that are no longer readily familiar.

We can continue with a phenomenological approach to Eli's actions indicating he's a Muslim. For Muslims, the Bible is a scripture, one that they believe to have been corrupted, but still sacred and worthy of preservation. Eli is blind and cannot see the words to read them, paralleling the prophet of Islam, Muhammad, whom Muslims consider to have been illiterate. Muhammad delivers the message orally, much like Eli does in the film. In both instances, scribes write down the words to help preserve them. Eli says that a voice guided him to the scripture and promised him protection until the message had been delivered. This moment echoes a moment in the Qur'an, when God speaks to Muhammad and offers him similar protection:

> O Apostle! Communicate that which has been sent down to you from your Lord, and if you do not, you will not have communicated His

24. Walliss and Aston 2011, 62.
25. Lacy 2014, 32. See also, Hussain 2017.
26. Moya and López 2017.

message, and Allah shall protect you from the people. Indeed Allah does not guide the faithless lot. (5:67)[27]

Scholar of religion Conrad Ostwalt offers a description of Eli's delivery of the Bible through a Christian lens, but one that could equally apply to a Muslim perspective. He states, "Eli has ingested 'the word,' sacramentally, and it is literally part of him, his thought processes, his motivations, and his actions. Eli is the embodiment and preservation of 'the word....'"[28]While the idea of ingesting the word as sacrament is clearly Christian, the embodiment of the word, through internalization, is common in Muslim traditions as well.[29]

A final note on a Muslim reading of Eli has to do with the imagery of the West. Eli is taking the Bible to the West, which may stand for a type of colonial expansion in the American imaginary, as well as a "movement toward the change of consciousness, identity, nation – or "becoming" something different."[30]In addition to this understanding of the role of the West, the idea of the sun rising in the West is a common image in Muslim apocalyptic literature.[31]

A goal of the film may be to destabilize "Christian absolutism, supremacy, and hegemony."[32] Once the Bible is dictated, typed, and bound, it is shelved next to the Tanakh and the Qur'an. In this reading, the Qur'an also serves as a character, in a cameo, and as an important signifier.

The *Book of Eli* does not function within the parameters of a traditional PCH research. However, I would suggest that because culture is defined dialogically, the ways in which PCH is effective will change. This film offers a potential next iteration of how parasocial interaction may happen. When difference is so accepted, either out of a societal transformation or post-apocalyptic necessity, and in the case of *The Book of Eli* perhaps both, then common symbols and language become normalized. Muslims may consider Christians and Jews as People of the Book, having received similar revelations, but reading Eli as a Muslim bears witness to what that means in practice.

CONCLUSION

If film is a medium that expresses a nation's sense of self, then we have to ask how it presents marginalized communities such as Muslims and if Mus-

27. Qara'i 2005.
28. Ostwalt 2013, 43.
29. For an understanding of the embodiment of the Qur'an, see Ware 2014.
30. Lacy 2014, 29.
31. Cook 2002, 14.
32. Lacy 2014, 32.

lims can be more than diaspora subjects.[33] In a space where there is only one way of being, differences are effaced and disciplined, leaving little room for variations from a dominant norm. As a result, Muslims lose the right to be culturally different from that hegemony.[34] At the same time, the power of media to dominate a community also offers a way to change dominant perceptions of the Other. Cultural critic and pedagogical scholar bell hooks offers a reflection of what that potential may be, when she says:

> For those of us who dare to desire differently, who seek to look away from the conventional ways of seeing blackness and ourselves, the issue of race and representation is not just a question of critiquing the status quo. It is also about transforming the image, creating alternatives, asking ourselves questions about what types of images subvert, pose critical alternatives, and transform our worldviews and move us away from dualistic thinking about good and bad. Making a space for the transgressive image, the outlaw rebel vision, is essential to any effort to create a context for transformation. And even then little progress is made if we transform images without shifting paradigms, changing perspectives, ways of looking.[35]

It is this transformative aspect of media that concerns me in this essay. I focus on the change that happens through indirect contact and non-stereotypical characterizations. It is this emphasis which leads me to look at "incidental Muslims" in film and the ways in which they normalize the presence of Muslims in society. It is no coincidence that all of the films are speculative fiction. It is in this space of imagination, of what could be, that artists can "solve" society's concerns.[36] Inadvertently, they are also providing the vehicles to make their solutions real.

WORKS CITED

Allport, G. W. 1979. *The Nature of Prejudice*. Reading, MA.

Bell, C. V. 2014. "Talking Racial Politics Online." In *Parasocial Politics: Audiences, Pop Culture, and Politics*, edited by J. Zenor, 133-52. Lanham.

Blizek, W. L. 2009. *The Continuum Companion to Religion and Film*. London; New York.

Cook, D. 2002. *Studies in Muslim Apocalyptic*. Studies in Late Antiquity and Early Islam 21. Princeton, NJ.

---

33. Wright 2007, 107.
34. Müller and Hermes 2010, 194.
35. hooks 2015, 20.
36. Leonard 2003, 253; Saldívar 2011, 574.

Curtis, E. E. 2016. *Muslim Americans in the Military: Centuries of Service.* Bloomington.

Doyle, C. and S. L. Stewart. 2004. "Ender's Game and Ender's Shadow: Orson Scott Card's Postmodern School Stories." *The Lion and the Unicorn* 28 (1): 186-202.

Gottschalk, P. and G. Greenberg. 2008. *Islamophobia: Making Muslims the Enemy.* Lanham.

Hall, S. 1991. "Ethnicity: Identity and Difference." *Radical America* 23 (4): 9-20.

hooks, b. 2009. *Reel to Real: Race, Class and Sex At the Movies.* New York.

———. 2015. *Black Looks: Race and Representation.* New York.

Horton, D. and R. R. Wohl 1956. "Mass Communication and Para-Social Interaction: Observations on Intimacy At a Distance." *Psychiatry: Journal for the Study of Interpersonal Processes* 19:215-29.

Hussain, A. 2017. "Funerals and Death Rites: Honoring the Departed." In *The Practice of Islam in America: An Introduction*, edited by E. E. Curtis, 188-208. New York.

Lacy, M. G. 2014. "Racial Shadows, Threat, Neoliberalism, and Trauma: Reading the Book of Eli." In *Race and Hegemonic Struggle in the United States: Pop Culture, Politics, and Protest*, edited by M. G. Lacy and M. E. Triece, 19-41. Madison.

Leonard, E. A. 2003. "Race and Ethnicity in Science Fiction." In *The Cambridge Companion to Science Fiction*, edited by E. James. and F. Mendlesohn, 253-63. Cambridge.

Moya, A. and G. López 2017. "Looking Back: Versions of the Post-Apocalypse in Contemporary North-American Cinema." *Film Criticism* 41, no. 1.

Müller, F. and J. Hermes 2010. "The Performance of Cultural Citizenship: Audiences and the Politics of Multicultural Television Drama." *Critical Studies in Media Communication* 27 (2): 193-208.

Nacos, B. L. and O. Torres-Reyna. 2007. *Fueling Our Fears: Stereotyping, Media Coverage, and Public Opinion of Muslim Americans.* Lanham, MD.

Ostwalt, C. E. 2013. "The Bible, Religion, and Film in the Twenty-First Century." *Currents in Biblical Research* 12 (1): 39-57.

Pennington, R. and H. E. Kahn, eds. 2018. *On Islam: Muslims and the Media.* Bloomington, Indiana.

Petersen, K. 2017. "Hollywood Muslims in Iraq." *Journal of Religion and Popular Culture* 29 (2) :87-103.

Pettigrew, T. F. and L. R. Tropp 2005. "Allport's Intergroup Contact Hypothesis: Its History and Influence." In *On the Nature of Prejudice: Fifty Years After Allport*, edited by J. F. Dovidio, P. S. Glick, and L. A. Rudman,

262-77. Malden, MA.

Pickel, G. and A. Yendell. 2016. "Islam als Bedrohung?: Beschreibung und Erklärung von Einstellungen zum Islam im Ländervergleich." *Zeitschrift für vergleichende Politikwissenschaft* 10 (3-4): 273-309.

Plate, S. B. 2003. *Representing Religion in World Cinema: Filmmaking, Mythmaking, Culture Making*. Religion/Culture/Critique 2. New York.

The Qur'an. 2005. Translated by. A. Q. Qara'i. Elmhurst, NY.

Ramji, R. 2005. "From 'Navy SEALs' to 'The Siege': Getting to Know the Muslim Terrorist, Hollywood Style." *Journal of Religion and Film* 9, no. 2.

Rashid, H. 2014. "Muslims in Film and Muslim Filmmaking in the United States." In *The Oxford Handbook of American Islam*, edited by Y. Y. Haddad and J. I. Smith, 259-73. Oxford.

Saldívar, R. 2011. "Historical Fantasy, Speculative Realism, and Postrace Aesthetics in Contemporary American Fiction." American Literary History 23, no. 33 (The Twenty-First-Century American Novel): 574-99.

Schiappa, E., P. B. Gregg, and D. E. Hewes. 2005. "The Parasocial Contact Hypothesis." *Communication Monographs* 72 (1): 92-115.

———. 2006. "Can One TV Show Make a Difference? Will & Grace and the Parasocial Contact Hypothesis." *Journal of Homosexuality* 51 (4): 15-37.

Semmerling, T. J. 2006. *"Evil" Arabs in American Popular Film: Orientalist Fear*. Austin.

Shaheen, J. G. 2001. *Reel Bad Arabs: How Hollywood Vilifies a People*. New York.

———. 2008. *Guilty: Hollywood's Verdict on Arabs after 9/11*. Northampton, MA.

Tukachinsky, R., D. Mastro, and M. Yarchi. 2015. "Documenting Portrayals of Race/ethnicity on Primetime Television Over a 20-Year Span and Their Association With National-Level Racial/Ethnic Attitudes: TV Portrayals and National-Level Attitudes." *Journal of Social Issues* 71 (1): 17-38.

Walliss, J. and J. Aston. 2011. "Doomsday America: The Pessimistic Turn of Post-9/11 Apocalyptic Cinema." *The Journal of Religion and Popular Culture* 23 (1): 53-64.

Ware, R. T. 2014. *The Walking Qur'an: Islamic Education, Embodied Knowledge, and History in West Africa*. Chapel Hill.

Wright, M. J. 2007. *Religion and Film: An Introduction*. London and New York.

"Then It Was 1989, the Year the World Changed": Shifting Representations of British Muslims Before 9/11

Claire Chambers

University of York

OVER THE LAST THREE DECADES there has been a spate of films, plays, and TV programs in which mostly non-Muslim directors have represented British Muslims. To take only the film dramas, they range from Udayan Prasad's *Brothers in Trouble* (1995) and Ken Loach's *Ae Fond Kiss* (2004), to Sarah Gavron's cinematic adaptation of Monica Ali's novel *Brick Lane* (2007). I argue that the increase in attention paid to Islam and to characters of Muslim heritage in British films is due to a turning point which is not solely – as is commonly assumed – 9/11 and its aftermath, but owes more to the Rushdie affair of late 1988 onward.

Crowds of angry Muslim protestors burned Salman Rushdie's allegedly blasphemous novel *The Satanic Verses* in two poor and ethnically divided northern cities, Bolton and Bradford. Soon afterward, on February 14, 1989, the Ayatollah Khomeini's fatwa against Rushdie and his publishers had dramatic impact in the UK as well as on global geopolitics, shining the spotlight onto Muslims who had hitherto constituted an invisible minority group subsumed within the broader category of "British Asians." The fatwa was abhorrent and indefensible, but the dominant liberal reaction to the protests was also questionable. Rushdie was positioned by commentators such as Fay Weldon and Malise Ruthven as one of their own, a pale-skinned, Cambridge-educated voice for freedom of speech, whose apparent Voltairean upholding of debate and democracy was juxtaposed in a favorable light with the supposedly barbaric, "alien" values of the protestors.[1]

The Rushdie affair marked a tipping point after which British Muslims were more likely to self-identify as belonging to a separate community, as well as being perceived by outsiders as a distinct, regressive, and perhaps threatening group. As Rushdie himself puts it in this article's titular quotation from his 2012 memoir, *Joseph Anton*, 1989 was "the year the world changed."[2] Whereas national origins and race had previously been interpreted as the dominant attributes of particular migrant groups, it was after

1. *Ruthven* 1990, 1. See also Weldon 1989, 6–8.
2. Rushdie 1989, 126.

58

the Rushdie affair rather than 9/11 that religion came to the forefront in British debates about multiculturalism. This is evidenced by the fact that it was four years before the World Trade Center attacks in 1997 that the Runnymede Trust published its influential report *Islamophobia: A Challenge for Us All*. The report identifies the Rushdie affair as "one of the formative, defining events in the stories not only of nations and communities but also of countless individuals."[3] To this list of nations, communities, and individuals, I would add that 1988–1989 was also a pivotal moment for cultural production. Specifically, the protests against *The Satanic Verses* and their repercussions had significant impact on film outputs. Not only did the sheer volume of cinematic depictions of British Muslims increase, but there were also discernible changes in relation, first, to the genres employed and, second, to the way Muslims were portrayed. Somewhat surprisingly in light of the seriousness of the death threats against Rushdie and his publishers, comedy emerged as a particularly popular medium through which auteurs examined British Muslims and Islam. And "Muslim" moved from being an identity marker that was worn relatively lightly in films (with class, gender, and ethnicity being more important to film-makers and writers), to a post-Rushdiean fascination with Islam, especially what was then termed its "fundamentalist" tendencies. To construct this argument I focus on one pre-Rushdie affair film, *My Beautiful Laundrette* (Stephen Frears, 1985), and two post-1989 but pre-9/11 texts, *My Son the Fanatic* (Udayan Prasad, 1997) and *East Is East* (Damien O'Donnell, 1999).

My Beautiful Laundrette was directed by Stephen Frears based on Hanif Kureishi's screenplay. Kureishi would become a celebrated comic novelist and short story writer. His breakthrough novel *The Buddha of Suburbia* (1990) was set in the 1970s, and was turned into a BBC drama serial (Roger Michell, 1993) with a soundtrack by David Bowie. Like *My Beautiful Laundrette* the novel probes Englishness, an identity which was in crisis after the loss of Empire. Frears went on to direct other films dealing with sexuality and migration, such as *Prick Up Your Ears* (1987), *Dirty Pretty Things* (2002), and the problematic recent Raj revival film *Victoria and Abdul* (2017).

My Beautiful Laundrette is set in south London in the 1980s and focuses on a variety of social issues at the time, including Thatcherism, violence toward post-war migrants and their children, same-sex love, unemployment, and the British class system. This was one of the first films to bring South Asians in Britain into the mainstream. Gay kisses too were a rarity on screen in the 1980s. The remarkable thing about *My Beautiful Laundrette* is the understated way in which these issues are presented – they are normalized.

3. Runnymede 1997, 7.

Like Kureishi, Omar is bicultural and British-born. His British mother Mary died a year before the film starts,[4] having taken her life by jumping onto the railway line that passes very close to the family's dismal flat. Omar's downwardly-mobile Pakistani migrant father, known as Papa, is from upper-class stock, and worked as a socialist journalist before he descended into alcoholism and ill health. Against this backdrop it would have been easy for Kureishi to portray Omar in stereotypical terms as a culturally confused biracial individual. Indeed, a Pakistani-born character, Cherry, dismisses Omar as an "in-between," while her wide-boy husband Salim tells Omar he has "too much white blood." But the film tilts away from such doxa, for the most part positioning Omar's mixed heritage as an enabling springboard propelling him towards flexible cultural identities.

Also in flux and mutable is Omar's sexuality. The film portrays a relationship between two men from different ethnicities and social classes. The man who becomes Omar's lover, Johnny, is a working-class white Briton who lives a precarious life as a squatter at the start of the film, ending the narrative as Omar's business partner – bloodied but unbowed from an attack by the racist gang he formerly belonged to. At its ceremonial opening, Omar's uncle's mistress, Rachel, comments that the new laundrette is "like an incredible ship," while later a rival laundrette-owner, Zaki, continues the nautical metaphor by asking Omar: "So you're planning an armada of laundrettes?" Yet viewers are never allowed to forget that this Thatcherite image of entrepreneurialism as smooth sailing belies the laundrette's name, "Powders," and the seamy world of drugs and violence which enabled its inauguration. As a member of the "lower class,"[5] and with his gangland connections, Johnny is integral to the business endeavour's shady side. For example, Omar's uncle Nasser gets a reluctant Johnny to evict a Pakistani poet from one of the houses he rents out, commenting that he cannot be expected to hold loyalties to his countrymen: "[W]e're professional businessmen. Not professional Pakistanis." And it is Johnny's contacts who sell the cocaine that Omar finds stashed in a false beard.

Although homosexuality had been decriminalized in Britain in 1967, by the 1980s same-sex relationships was still stigmatized. From 1988 to 2003, the contentious and discriminatory Section 28 of the Local Government Act passed by Margaret Thatcher's government made it illegal to "promote homosexuality." However, Johnny and Omar flout society's prohibitions, the gang's heteronormativity, and Omar's family pressures. The movie famously juxtaposes the gay sex scene with a vignette in which Nasser and his mis-

---

4. Kureishi 1986, 52.
5. Kureishi 1986, 76.

tress are openly dancing in the laundrette. The laundrette is bright, whereas Johnny turns off the light in the back room, indicating that having a mistress can be openly displayed and is more accepted than same-sex desire. The adroit use of a two-way mirror in this scene demonstrates that lovers may differ in age, ethnicity, or class but such differences are superficial.

Early on Omar's father expresses concerns about his son's sexual orientation, asking his brother, Nasser, to "fix him with a nice girl. I'm not sure if his penis is in full working order." Papa's ideal fiancée for Omar would be Nasser's daughter, Tania, and for a while Tania idiosyncratically plays along. She startles Omar by baring her breasts to him through a window he gazes from during a drinking session with Nasser and his mostly Pakistani friends. A few scenes later, though, Johnny and Omar start their sexual relationship. Before long, Omar behaves arrogantly and dismissively toward Johnny, suggesting that he is still unsure of his sexuality. He goes as far as drunkenly proposing to Tania, though it seems that neither character takes this seriously. By the film's end, the audience assumes that Omar has accepted his preferences and feels comfortable admitting his fluid sexuality to himself.

One of the striking things about this 1980s film is that it contains no explicit references to Islam or Muslims. Pakistan and Pakistanis are often referred to, Urdu is spoken, and Omar makes dal (lentil curry) for his father. However, religion is only mentioned three times and in highly tangential ways. The first instance comes when a *"middle-aged Pakistani [...] wearing salwar kamiz"*[6] removes his long white beard to reveal its use as a container for smuggling drugs. Neither the film nor its screenplay explicitly state this, but in appearance there is little doubt that the man looks like a *maulvi*, a pious Muslim leader, intimating a sly swipe at religion as a mask for hypocrisy. The second indirect allusion to Islam comes in Nasser's ironic claim that Pakistan "has been sodomized by religion" such that "it is beginning to interfere with the making of money." Nasser's homophobic diction collocates incongruously with Omar and Johnny's love, and his unfavorable comparison of religious Pakistan with "heaven[ly]," secular Britain markedly contrasts with his earlier sexualization of the European country ("I believe in England. You just have to know how to squeeze the tits of the system.") Finally, when she learns about her husband's affair, Nasser's wife Bilquis uses black magic (*kala jaddu*) against his mistress, Rachel. In the film *kala jaddu* is connected to culture rather than religion; Islam is never once evoked as Bilquis "*mix-[es] various ingredients in a big bowl*."[7] Instead, the wronged wife dictates an airmail letter and speaks heatedly about going home to Pakistan, suggest-

6. Kureishi 1986, 71; emphasis in original.
7. Kureishi 1986, 95; emphasis in original.

ing that her use of black magic messily intermixes South Asian folk culture with religion. It is left to Rachel to bring in a Christian vicar to exorcise the spell Bilquis has cast, leaving painful wheals on the mistress's stomach and causing her to fearfully terminate her relationship with Nasser. In his introduction to the film Kureishi acknowledges that he only brought in the black magic plot strand to give Shirley Anne Field a meatier role as Rachel.[8]

As such, in *My Beautiful Laundrette* Kureishi, like many other Muslim-identified authors writing in Britain during the 1970s and 1980s, largely took Muslimness for granted as an identity component, placing much greater emphasis on national origins, ethnicity, and sexual orientation than religion. All this would change after Khomeini issued his fatwa against Rushdie, a close friend whom Kureishi had thanked in his introduction to the film's screenplay.[9] The unprecedented threat against Rushdie from the government of Iran and from some British Muslims left an indelible mark on Kureishi, who would speak out publicly on his mentor's behalf,[10] and would at least mention the fatwa in most of the essays he wrote after 1989.[11] Kureishi also became the first British writer with Muslim heritage to accord serious attention in his creative writing to the issue of violent extremism in the name of Islam – using the vehicle of comedy. In 1995 he published *The Black Album* (1995), a novel set in 1989 which takes the controversy around Rushdie as its point of departure, although he is known as "the writer" and is never explicitly referred to by name.[12] The novel was also staged at the National Theatre and other playhouses in 2009 and again in 2019, to mark anniversaries of the Rushdie affair. Kureishi sheds light on how racism (but Islamophobia less so) causes young second-generation migrant Muslims to become more religious than their parents. However, *The Black Album* provides few clues as to how the dogmatic, puritanical group of Muslim extremists attracts the intelligent protagonist for as long as it does.

The same might also be said of "My Son the Fanatic," Kureishi's short story written in 1997, which was adapted into a film directed by Udayan Prasad the same year. For both Prasad and Kureishi the film represented a shift from portraying cultural Muslims to religious Muslims, even if their sympathies mostly lay with these characters' secular antagonists. Prasad's previous (debut) film was an adaptation of Urdu writer Abdullah Hussein's

---

8. Kureishi 1986, 43.

9. Kureishi 1986, 44.

10. See, for example, Rushdie 2012, 218.

11. Kureishi 2011.

12. Instead, he is twice alluded to as the author of *Midnight's Children*; see Kureishi 1995, 9, 169.

1981 novella "The Journey Back," titled *Brothers in Trouble* (1995). Barely touching on religious identity, in *Brothers in Trouble* Prasad, a Hindu-background socialist director, zeroed in on the precarity[13] of South Asians eking out a living in the factories of 1960s northern England, sleeping in shifts with several men occupying a single room, and dealing with workplace aggression and vicious racism. For Kureishi, not only was *My Son the Fanatic* a celluloid first in that he trained his imaginative gaze on religion rather than culture, but unlike Prasad this was also his first movie set outside of London,[14] in the north of England. The setting was intended to be Bradford, site of the most notorious burning of *The Satanic Verses* in January 1989. Indeed, Phil Hubbard observes that the film was "[b]ased loosely" on real-life campaigning to get prostitutes off the streets of Bradford's Muslim-majority district of Manningham during the 1990s.[15] Moreover, early in the script, taxi-driver protagonist Parvez gives a newly-arrived German named Schitz a car-tour around the unnamed locale, and a screen direction explains in terms that resonate with Bradford's history: "*This is an opportunity for Parvez to show off his knowledge of his adopted city, its geography and history. He talks about the mills, the great nineteenth-century entrepreneurs, the first Pakistani immigrants, and he points out their shops.*"[16] The film tethers the location even more closely to Bradford in viewers' minds as Parvez tells Schitz that the Ayatollah Khomeini had a robe made in one of the now-demolished garment factories, a point repeated by his Islamist son with greater pride later on. However, protests in West Yorkshire prevented *My Son the Fanatic* from being filmed in the city,[17] so the production company relocated to nearby (and predominantly white) Halifax.

There is a scene early on in which a northern working-men's club comedian singles out the visibly-minoritized Parvez as the target for his brand of racist, Islamophobic "humour." Kureishi's script adumbrates that "*the Comedian is telling Paki, Rushdie and Muslim jokes.*"[18] In the film the comedian says more specifically, and using highly offensive language of which I have omitted the most triggering sentences:

---

13. Butler 2004.

14. After *My Beautiful Laundrette*, Kureishi wrote the screenplays for *Sammy and Rosie Get Laid* (Frears, 1987) and *London Kills Me*, which he also directed (Kureishi, 1991), both of which also had London settings.

15. Hubbard 2006: 67.

16. Kureishi 1997b, 9; emphasis in original.

17. Ramesh 1998, np.

18. Kureishi 1997b, 46; emphasis in original.

> Hey! Somebody farted. I can smell shit somewhere. Hey, it's Salman
> Rushdie himself. What you're smelling here, folks, is a satanic
> arsehole. If there's any of Rafsanjohnny's mates in here, slip me a
> tenner and I'll shoot the bastard for you.

Here the name "Rushdie" is used as a talisman under which to bait the only
ethnic minority audience member in the comedy club. That well-worn color
racism trope of malodorous people and their food is allied with cultural racism and Islamophobia, manifested through a provocative reference to the
protests against the novel, *The Satanic Verses*. This chimes with events from
David Caute's contemporaneous novel, *Fatima's Scarf*, in which the name
of the fictional Rushdie figure is evoked in graffiti that appears alongside
swastikas on the walls of mosques in "Bruddersford" (an amalgamation of
Bolton, Bradford, and other northern towns).[19]

My Son the Fanatic's opening credits play out over pastoral images of
Yorkshire. These contrast with the ebulliently hybrid and urban song "Little
Britain," by electro-dub band Dreadzone, which contains the lyrics "In this
green and pleasant land | We have a dream to understand | [...] Ancient cross
and Zion star | Eastern ways and praise to Jah." Just as Dreadzone destabilizes
Elgar's and Blake's quintessentially English hymn "Jerusalem," the film's
opening scene is an inversion of the British-Asian movie's set piece in which
two prospective families-in-law meet over tea and samosas to explore the
feasibility of an arranged marriage. Parvez's commitment to integration
and secularism means that the young couple – Parvez's son Farid and his
white girlfriend, Madelaine Fingerhut – are already well acquainted, tea is
replaced by un-Islamic champagne, and the only discernible resistance to
their marriage comes from the snobby and racist police chief, Fingerhut,
and his wife.

Yet as the film unfolds, Parvez's Anglophilia and belief in cultural
mixing is undermined by his stereotypically repressed South Asian wife,
Minoo, who tells him: "I hate this dirty place [England]! The men brought
us here and then left us alone!" Minoo's rage is unsurprising, given that she
has discovered Parvez's close relationship with a prostitute named Bettina.
More significant and from left-field is the resounding challenge Farid makes
to his father's value system by breaking off his engagement to Madelaine,
giving away his possessions, extoling purity, and renouncing bacon and
booze in favor of mullahs and the mosque. Whereas *My Beautiful Laundrette*
merely contained hints of the Islamic faith, in *My Son the Fanatic* the presence
of a *maulvi* is spelled out when Farid invites his religious teacher to stay
in the family home. Although Parvez longs to see what is concealed in his

19. Caute 1998, 102.

beard, unlike the 1980s film this is no drug-smuggling prosthetic. The *maulvi* wreaks havoc in their domestic sphere, borrowing a fan heater to replicate South Asia's warm climate, commandeering the television for the watching of cartoons, and supporting the intimidation of local prostitutes including Bettina. The film builds to a climax after Parvez's taxi, bound for the airport to carry Schitz home, gets caught up in a violent demonstration against the sex-workers. Parvez abandons the frightened and abusive Schitz in the crowd, and this galvanizes him to return home, evict the *maulvi*, beat up Farid (who responds with the line: "Who's the fanatic now?" before escaping with his zealot friends), and despondently watch Minoo's departure for the subcontinent. The film comes full circle with a rural scene in which Bettina and Parvez walk in the woods, talking of traveling together in India. In the post-credits scene, Parvez returns alone to his suddenly deserted house, listens to his favorite jazz music, which Minoo had previously called "too trumpety," and turns on lights, creating a chiaroscuro effect, to drink a glass of whiskey.

One of the 1990s' and early-2000s' most well-known British-Asian comedies, *East Is East*, was written by Ayub Khan-Din, who began his acting career as Sammy in Kureishi's 1987 film, *Sammy and Rosie Get Laid* (Stephen Frears, 1987). *East Is East* started as a play, first staged in 1996. Mainly comic in tone, it is set in the north of England against the backdrop of Enoch Powell's racist repatriation policies and the 1971 War that led to Bangladesh's independence from Pakistan. As with the fictional Khan family (1999), Khan-Din's family owned a chip shop in Salford and lived in substandard housing. Yet despite its vintage 1970s setting and autobiographical elements, *East Is East* is shaped by the Rushdie affair, focusing some two years before 9/11 on an intractable version of Islam being practiced in northern England. The film does not merely depict such well-worn "Asian" topics as arranged marriage, but also examines specifically Muslim practices such as circumcision, polygamy, halal dietary requirements, and mosque attendance.

Despite the titular reference to Rudyard Kipling,[20] Khan-Din eschews portrayals of East and West as entirely discrete and opposed. For example, he depicts Ella Khan as inhabiting a no-man's land between her (Eastern) husband's intransigence and (Westernized) children's rebellion. Ella's best friend Annie tells her: "You're in the middle, [...] you have to keep your head down." Even Tariq and Saleem, the most skeptical of George's children who still live at home, realize that they are caught between two antagonistic groups, recognizing the truth in their father's comment, "You no English, English people no accepting you." Racism is an everyday reality for them all,

20. Kipling 1889/2001, 245–47.

meted out by characters such as their right-wing neighbour Mr. Moorhouse and a colleague who launches another Kipling reference by giving Abdul the derogatory nickname "Gunga Din."[21] However, most of the siblings simultaneously reject George's belief that culture and religion are solutions to their hostile environment. When the patriarch asseverates that "in Islam, everyone equal see, no black man, or white man," it rings hollow given the context of the murderous war being fought between Muslims in West and East Pakistan.

George believes that good Muslim children should marry whomever their father chooses: "Is my decision no yours." Yet the children, to varying degrees, rebel against arranged marriage, discerning hypocrisy in the fact that George married their mother, a white Catholic woman, against the wishes of his family, especially his Pakistani first wife. His children call George "Genghis," denoting Genghis Khan, a bloodthirsty thirteenth-century Mongol warrior. This reflects George's often violent temperament: he is prone to swearing, hits the children, and shockingly beats up Ella. However, he is not solely what Ali Nobil describes as a "one-dimensional" bully;[22] he has a gentle side despite his domineering attitudes. Viewers witness tender scenes between him and Ella, such as when he buys her a hairdresser's chair and makes endearing requests for a "half-cup" of tea. George's vulnerability is apparent when his attempts to control his family prove futile. Alone and insecure, he *"paces back and forth"* before *"put[ting] his head in his hands."*[23] Another humanizing moment comes when George buys a watch for Sajid to assuage his guilt for the latter's late circumcision. However, the timepiece has its figures in Arabic, even though Sajid can neither read Arabic nor tell the time. There is also an irony at work here, since as a Pakistani George cannot understand the Arabic language, highly valued in Islam, any better than his son. This is one way in which the film signals its interest in Muslim, as opposed to broader nationalist, themes.

Critics have tended to approach *East Is East* as a "British-Asian" or "British-Pakistani" film.[24] There is some justification for a focus on nationality, especially in the light of *East Is East*'s 1971 War backdrop. Khan-Din explains that in his childhood, "the disintegration of Pakistan mirrored in some way what was going on with us."[25] George idealizes Pakistan and finds it hard to accept that the country is breaking up, just as he struggles with his grow-

21. Kipling 1889/2001, 418–20.
22. Nobil 2009, 105.
23. Khan-Din 1999, 97; emphasis in original.
24. See, for example, Buonanno, Sams, and Schlote 2011, np; Sharma 2009, *passim*; and Hingorani 2010, 95–100.
25. Khan-Din 2009, np.

ing children's demands for their own independence. In the play, Ella bluntly points out that George had always seen the Bengalis as not being true Pakistanis.[26] Yet since George romanticizes Pakistan as a place of order, he takes the loss of Bangladesh personally, its secession reflecting his own loss of control over his children.

As important as national and cultural paradigms are to readings of *East Is East*, these often occlude the important topic of religion. Khan-Din's film not only depicts the well-worn trope of arranged marriage, common to various Asian cultures (Hindu, Sikh, and Muslim), but also examines specifically Muslim practices. For example, one of the film's crises involves circumcision, as it transpires that Sajid's foreskin is still intact. Pronouncing "this tickle-tackle very embarrassing," George worries that the religious transgression means that he will be unable to arrange the marriages for his sons that he craves. Another issue explored is polygyny, a practice that is permissible in Islam, though not in other South Asian religions such as Sikhism and Hinduism. It should be noted that although Muslim men are allowed up to four wives this occurs infrequently in Pakistan, and the practice is being transformed in the diasporic context.[27] George has "Mrs. Khan number one" back in Pakistan, but for all intents and purposes they are separated. Apart from George sending home money and clothing, his first wife is an absent present, with George pretending he will bring her to England or return to her embrace in order to tease Mrs. Khan number two: Ella. All this changes in the sequel, *West is West* (Andy De Emmony, 2010), wherein George takes Sajid home to be introduced to his first wife, the extended family, and Pakistani mores.

Another important Islamic reference is found in discussion of halal dietary requirements amidst the pressures of running a chip shop. The children hide from their father the fact they have been cooking pork products by spraying air-freshener around the room. The film's strapline accordingly quips: "This is a battle of bacon butties over onion bhajis!" If "battle" seems strong, one has only to recall that George beats Ella after she calls him "pig bloody ignoran[t]"; as Sara Ahmed notes, "his violence is a response to a speech act that is offensive to Muslims."[28]

Mosque attendance is a final bone of contention between George and his offspring. The mosque bus is a malign presence in the film, as it forcibly transports the children to the madrassa, where they fail to understand Qur'anic verses learned by rote. In a sparsely furnished room, a grim-faced cleric wearing shalwar kameez, turban, and black jacket paces in front of his

26. Khan-Din 1996/1997, 14.
27. Charsley and Liversage 2013.
28. Ahmed 2010, 146.

cowed pupils. Twice he gets them to evoke God's graciousness and mercy –
"Bismillah ar-Rahman ar-Raheem" – before leading them in a recitation of
the *shahada*, the testimony of faith. The camera pans along wooden benches,
and viewers see the most religious of the brothers, Maneer, rocking earnestly
in his glasses and skullcap as he asserts God's singularity and Muhammad's
prophet status via the Arabic words "lā ʾilāha ʾillā llāh muḥammadun rasūlu
llāh." As the camera travels down the line, viewers see a bored-looking Tariq
nattily clad in leather jacket and sideburns reciting the surah uncompre-
hendingly. Slouching Saleem fans himself lethargically, and with an eyeroll
declares "rasoo la la" in his broad Mancunian accent. This irreverent depiction of religious performance notwithstanding, Abdul delivers a poignant
speech in the theatrical version of *East Is East*, in which he describes fleeing
home from the pub having been subjected to a string of "wog jokes, chink
jokes, Paki jokes" not unlike the barbs hurled at Parvez in *My Son the Fanatic*'s
horrendous nightclub scene. He relates his subsequent epiphany:

> When I got home, me dad was here praying, I watched him Tariq,
> and it was right, to be here, to be a part of this place, to belong to
> something. It's what I want. I know me dad'll always be a problem, but
> I can handle that now, perhaps I might make him change; but I don't
> want that out there, it's not who I am, it's as alien to me as me dad's
> world is to you.[29]

Alienated by macho drinking banter, Abdul takes comfort from his father's
unselfconscious prostrations before God and feels that advantages are to be
found in "belong[ing] to something," just as Islam offers its faithful membership of the global ummah, or Muslim community. This scene did not make it
into the screenplay, and even Abdul's quiet tears as he witnesses the "*gentle
and poetic*"[30] movements of George at prayer are cut from the final wrap.
As James Procter notes, *East Is East*'s director, Damien O'Donnell, "seek[s] to
capitalise on the elusive capacities of the everyday – its presumed universality – for mainstream global consumption." Not only does he do this by
de-emphasizing the younger Khans' ethnicity and the film's "local politics,"[31]
but also, I submit, by effacing Islam's positive effects from the film.

    To conclude, this essay has examined the work of two Muslim-identified
writers for film, Hanif Kureishi and Ayub Khan-Din. After the watershed of
the Rushdie affair, both authors are concerned to probe the ethics of Muslim
religious "tradition," leveling particularly pointed criticisms at the Muslim

29. Khan-Din 1996/1997, 57.
30. Khan-Din 1999, 125.
31. Procter 2006, 77.

community in relation to sexuality. If Kureishi's pre-1989 film, *My Beautiful Laundrette*, has little to say about Islam, his later screenplay, *My Son the Fanatic*, as well as Khan-Din's *East Is East*, explore specifically Muslim rather than South Asian concerns. Both 1990s films delineate Muslim-associated subjects such as prayer, halal dietary requirements, and *maulvis*. They also shift the focus onto working-class Muslims living in the north of England (rather than Kureishi's earlier interest in more cosmopolitan communities in London) and to attacks on them through racist microaggressions in the form of jokes. Several years before 9/11, these British films were making a troubling and stereotypical link between Muslims, patriarchy, and domestic abuse.

Works Cited

Agard, J. 2004/2013. "Half-Caste." *Half-Caste and Other Poems.* London, 11–13.

Ahmed, S. 2010. *The Promise of Happiness.* Durham.

Anwar, M. 1979. *The Myth of Return: Pakistanis in Britain.* London.

Bhanot, K. 2011. *Too Asian, Not Asian Enough: An Anthology of New British Asian Fiction.* Birmingham.

Buonanno, G., V. Sams, and C. Schlote. 2011. "Between Tradaption and Adaptation: Glocal Imaginaries in British Asian Drama." *Postcolonial Text* 6.2:1–18. http://journals.sfu.ca/pocol/index.php/pct/article/view/1259/1161

Butler, J. 2004. *Precarious Life: The Powers of Mourning and Violence.* London.

Caute, D. 1998. *Fatima's Scarf.* London.

Charsley, K. and A. Liversage. 2013. "Transforming Polygamy: Migration, Transnationalism and Multiple Marriages Among Muslim minorities." *Global Networks* 13.1: 60–78.

Dahya, B. 1974. "The Notion of Pakistani Ethnicity." In *Urban Ethnicity*, edited by A. Cohen, 77–118. London.

Hingorani, D. 2010. *British Asian Theatre: Dramaturgy, Process, Performance.* Basingstoke.

Hubbard, P. 2006. *City: Key Ideas in Geography.* Abingdon.

Hussein, A. 1987. "The Journey Back." In *Downfall by Degrees: And Other Stories*, edited and translated by M. Umar Memon, 128–96. Toronto.

Khan-Din, A. 1996/1997. *East Is East.* London.

———. 1999. *East Is East: Screenplay.* London.

Kipling, R. 1889/2001. "The Ballad of East and West." In *The Collected Poems of Rudyard Kipling.* Ware.

Kureishi, H. 1986. *My Beautiful Laundrette and The Rainbow Sign.* London.

———. 1990. *The Buddha of Suburbia.* London.

——, dir. 1991. *London Kills Me*. Written by H. Kureishi. Actors: J. Chadwick, F. Shaw, B. Dourif, N. Andrews, S. Rimkus. London.

——. 1995. *The Black Album*. London.

——. 1997a. "My Son the Fanatic." In *Love in a Blue Time*. London. 119–31.

——. 1997b. *My Son the Fanatic*. London.

——. 2011. *Collected Essays*. London.

Michell, R., dir. 1993. *The Buddha of Suburbia*. Written by H. Kureishi. London.

Nobil, A. 2009. "Is East … East?" *Third Text* 13.49:105–7.

O'Donnell, D, dir. 1999/2007. *East Is East*. Written by A. Khan-Din. London.

Procter, J. 2006. "The Postcolonial Everyday." *New Formations* 58 (Summer): 62–80.

Ramesh, R. 1998. "Mid-Life Kureishi." *Independent* 2 May. http://www.independent.co.uk/life-style/interview-hanif-kureishi-mid-life-kureishi-1161701.html

Runnymede Trust. 1997. *Islamophobia: A Challenge for Us All*. London.

Rushdie, S. 1988. *The Satanic Verses*. London.

——. 2012. *Joseph Anton: A Memoir*. London.

Ruthven, M. 1990. *A Satanic Affair: Salman Rushdie and the Wrath of Islam*. London.

Said, E. W. 1997/1981. *Covering Islam: How the Media and the Experts Determine How We See the Rest of the World*. London.

Sharma, S. 2009. "Teaching British South Asian Cinema: Towards a 'Materialist' Reading Practice." *South Asian Popular Cinema* 7.1:21–35.

Weldon, F. 1989. *Sacred Cows*. London.

Negotiating Queerness in the Ismaili Diaspora in the Films of Ian Iqbal Rashid[1]

Alberto Fernández Carbajal
University of Roehampton, UK.

INTRODUCTION: WHO ARE THE ISMAILIS?

The work of Canadian poet, screenwriter, and film director Ian Iqbal Rashid (b. 1964) follows the trail of Hanif Kureishi's seminal queer diasporic film, *My Beautiful Laundrette* (Stephen Frears), released in 1985. Like Kureishi, Rashid utilizes the medium of film as a site of conjoined ethnic and sexual resistance. As Jigna Desai, professor of Gender, Women, and Sexuality Studies, observes reflecting on the experience of seeing Kureishi's film: "As brown bodies trespassed the spaces of colonial anthropology and history to spaces marked as the present, I experienced a return and a rupture simultaneously."[2] Rashid's film-work undertakes such "return and rupture," extending the debates started by Kureishi, with the exploration of interethnic and diasporic queerness, the legacies of colonial modernity, and intergenerational ideological disparity of the Muslim diaspora. Yet, whereas *Laundrette* made accessible to a global audience its art-house and counter-cultural visual aesthetic, Rashid's first full-length film, *Touch of Pink* (2004), works differently: it *queers* the generally heteronormative mainstream genre of the Hollywood romantic comedy, appropriating, and playing with, its techniques, while focusing on an under-represented ethnic community, namely the East African Ismaili diaspora in Canada and its offshoots in Britain, which mirrors Rashid's own personal trajectory. As he himself confesses during an interview, "the themes that run through much of my work are concerned with the effects of migration on immigrant families."[3]

For Rashid, being Muslim is inseparable from having been born into the Ismaili community. In an early study published before their collective exile from Tanzania, Robert J. Bocock states the uniqueness of the Ismailis and

---

1. This chapter is a modified version of Chapter 2 from my book, *Queer Muslim Diasporas in Contemporary Literature and Film* (Manchester University Press, 2019), used with permission from Manchester University Press.
2. Sternberg 2004, vii.
3. Anonymous 2007, n.p.

their subscription to Shia Islam, the branch of the faith which believes in the hereditary nature of religious leadership.[4] There is an inherent paradox in the Ismailis' ability to "integrate" while clinging to a sense of cultural and religious distinctiveness. As Rashid himself has remarked, "[w]e do work well in the west. We do kind of assimilate better than a lot of other South Asian and Muslim communities who have migrated and yet we are very community minded. Family is so important and the community is so insular as well."[5] Peter B. Clarke observes that "[t]here is a 'givenness' about community in Ismailism. It stems from being born into this particular religious community," adding that "East African Ismailis tend to form together a group, and loyalty to and kinship among East African Ismailis accounts for some of the strength of the associational and communal bonds."[6]

This combination of integration, modernity, and tradition often entails a fraught relationship with issues of sexual liberation that are shared with other Muslims in the diaspora. Amir Hussain remarks how, for Canadian Muslims, "[t]raditional Islam recognizes the validity of only the heterosexual relationship," remarking on "the tremendous religious isolation that comes with being a gay Muslim in Toronto."[7] Membership in a religious community such as the Ismailis, who embrace modernity and social betterment, yet who steadfastly hold on to conservative religious morality, creates a rupture in the sense of identification of queer Ismailis, who are forced to attune their sensibilities to the various wavelengths of alleged Western sexual exceptionalism, resilient colonial forms of racism – both external and internalized – and Islamic heteronormativity.

As Karim H. Karim suggests, the Ismailis' "search for balance between tradition and modernity extends into interaction with the postmodern," arguing that "experience unfolds unendingly in the intervening spaces –

---

4. Bocock observes that "Shias believe that spiritual authority continues to be with man in the Imam, but today the Ismailis are the only group left who still think that the Imam is known and identifiable." See Bocock 1971, 366. According to Bocock, the Imam, like the Catholic Pope, is infallible; he is also free of sin, and although mainly a religious authority, he can advise on the material aspects of life. In Farhad Daftary's view (see Daftary 1998), and by contrast with Sunni Muslims, Ismailis do not participate in the compiling of *ahadith* or in the exegetical tradition of the *tafsir*, since the living Imam and his associates provide all necessary spiritual guidance derived from the esoteric interpretation of the Qur'an. Moreover, the Imam encourages loyalty to any of the countries where Ismailis have settled. This allegiance must be honoured regardless of whether these nations have a Muslim majority or a Muslim minority, and whether the largest Islamic group is Sunni or Shia.

5. Meherali 2004, n.p.

6. Clarke 1976, 490, 492.

7. Hussain 2004, 372.

the interstices – between tradition, modernity and postmodernity."[8] In this chapter, I examine Rashid's work as being placed in such interstices, constantly attempting to strike a balance between the demands of Ismaili and Muslim tradition, colonial modernity, and diasporic postmodernity. For the world's citizens, colonial modernity entails an encounter with the global hegemony of Western cultures. Postmodernity, in turn, involves a cultural relativism which de-essentializes knowledge and challenges the distinct contours of identity categories, but with similarly problematic consequences. I argue in this essay that outgrowing colonial modernity and diasporic postmodernity, especially the social hierarchies of British colonialism and the cultural hegemony of Hollywood cinema, is central to Rashid's characters.

SURVIVING SABU AND STAG: EMPIRE, DIASPORA, QUEERNESS

Rashid's first two short films as screenwriter and director, *Surviving Sabu* and *Stag*, released in 1998 and 2002, respectively, enact some of the diasporic themes and political issues that are fledged out in Rashid's 2004 feature film, *Touch of Pink*. *Stag*, a film around nine minutes long, depicts queerness and interethnic relationships. This short BBC piece features two characters, British Asian and bridegroom Sammi (Nitni Ganatra) and his best man, white British Luke (Stuart Laing). The film opens with photographic evidence of Sammi's bachelor party. We are witness here to a homosocial space of partly naked men with their arms around their shoulders. These Polaroid photographs are intercalated with images of Sammi and Luke sharing the same bed. A new scene offers us Luke spooning Sammi, while lying naked on Sammi's bed. When Sammi's arm reaches out to turn off the alarm clock, he gets out of bed in a panic. It takes both men a little while to recollect the significance of the previous night's sexual encounter, which allegedly leaves Luke "speechless."

The rest of the film examines the different ways in which both men attempt to reconcile their perspectives on their homoerotic encounter and on its implications for Sammi's imminent wedding. The relationship between Sammi and Luke is imbricated in existing structures of sexual and political domination historically linked not only to British imperialism, but also to classical Islamic and Greek civilizations. Luke never lets Sammi forget, either explicitly or through indirect allusion, that it was he who penetrated Sammi. Sammi's distaste for Luke's boasting angers him to the point of cultural disavowal, as he exclaims: "My culture didn't descend from

---

8. Karim 2010, 267.

the fucking Greeks like your lot." This is historically inaccurate. The work of Khaled El Rouayheb[9] links Islamic and Greek homoeroticism, revealing that the Muslim obsession with active and passive roles is drawn from classical Greek civilization. Sammi refuses to be placed in the subservient position connected to disease and effeminacy, demonstrating that his sensibility is more indebted to his Greek-inspired Islamic cultural legacy than he would be tempted to believe.

However, the political reverberations of Luke and Sammi's sexual encounter have more recent echoes. When Sammi asks Luke how it came to happen that Luke became the dominant one, Luke nonchalantly responds that "it's just how these things happen, I suppose," to which Sammi meaningfully retorts: "Yeah, for 300 years." Gayatri Gopinath argues in her analysis of *My Beautiful Laundrette* that "the barely submerged histories of colonialism and racism erupt into the present at the very moment when queer sexuality is being articulated."[10] The interpersonal relations in *Stag* also constitute an indictment of colonial racial hierarchies that become manifest simultaneously with queerness. Sammi finally denounces Luke's continued desire to be dominant, which is connected to the long history of British colonialism. As the men are about to leave Sammi's house, Luke descends the stairs and kisses Sammi's mouth, subsequently stating: "I don't wanna lose you, Sammi," to which Sammi responds: "You just don't wanna lose. [...] You've always hated losing." Instead of submitting to Luke's persistent hints that Sammi should postpone the wedding, Sammi honors his commitment to his fiancée, Yasmin. Rashid's film articulates a model of queerness whereby characters are not forced into a westernized and essentialized homosexual vs. heterosexual paradigm. Neither character identifies as "gay." Strikingly, the film's main act of representational defiance is refusing to collude with Western expectations of Muslims' need to "come out" and thus join modernity. In *Stag*, the act of fulfilling so-called "tradition" (i.e. honoring heterosexual matrimony) becomes an unusual act of political resistance, posited against the emotional demands of a white British citizen who is unable to come to terms with his loss of preponderance.

Rashid's first short film, *Surviving Sabu*, contributed its own critique of British imperialism and racism. *Surviving Sabu* explores the troubled relationship between a Pakistani father, Sadru (Suresh Oberoi), and his British son, Amin (Navin Chowdhry), during the shooting of Amin's first film, a short documentary about the Indian film star popularly known as "Sabu" (1924–1963), the star of a series of British and American Orientalist

9. El Rouayheb 2005.
10. Gopinath 2005, 2.

films who met an untimely death. Priya Jaikumar observes that Sabu's framing belies deeper meanings for a variety of audiences: "[Sabu's] body is effeminised, made sexually ambiguous with its attributes of over- or under-dress, yielding his figure to a range of desires outside those ruled by the conventions of heterosexuality, patriarchy and empire."[11] For Sadru, Sabu is an example of a successful Indian in the West and an embodiment of ideal South Asian masculinity. As Sternberg suggests, "Sabu's presence on the screen marks a certain moment in film history that provided migrant and diasporic audiences of earlier generations with the pleasure of recognition, seeing black or brown bodies at the heart of popular (if problematic) cinematic narratives."[12] To Sadru's migrant "pleasure of recognition," Rashid adds Amin's viewpoint.

As a second-generation migrant born and brought up in Britain, Sadru's son has become much more aware of the exoticizing gaze behind the camera lens. Amin's aim is to critique American and British racism, which exploited Sabu from the 1930s till his untimely death, and which also crushed his father's ambitions to become a policeman in 1970s London. Yet, for all his anti-colonial impetus, Amin is sensually drawn to Sabu, and the film seems to imply that Sadru's fascination with Sabu's physicality may have influenced his son's homosexuality. Upset by Amin's negative portrayal of Sabu's fate and by his fatalist perspective on his own fortunes in Britain, Sadru expels the film crew. Rashid then offers us two intercalated soliloquies illustrating what father and son have learnt from each other. Amin tells the camera: "he left Uganda with no money; started from scratch; he rebuilt his life. That's courage." Amin's perception of his father's disapproval of his homosexuality contrasts with Sadru's reflection. As Sadru states: "On the night he told us, he stayed over. That took courage. He knew we were upset. He wanted us to be alright." Both father and son need to appreciate each other's "courage" in order to trigger their reconciliation: Sadru's daring in starting afresh in the racially volatile Britain of the 1970s; and Amin's bravery in considering his parents' culturally and generationally conditioned outlook on his homosexuality.

TOUCH OF PINK: QUEER MUSLIMS IN THE INTERSTICES

Rashid's first short film is critiqued by Gopinath for avoiding depicting the figure of Amin's mother. Rashid's feature film début, *Touch of Pink*, redresses this gender imbalance by focusing on an Ismaili diasporic mother-and-son relationship. *Touch of Pink* illustrates queer diasporic Muslims' arduous

11. Jaikumar 2012, 64.
12. Sternberg 2010, 269.

existence at the interstices between tradition, modernity, and postmodernity. If Rashid's short films were more intent on exploring issues of Muslim diasporic masculinities, *Touch of Pink* is also concerned with the dilemmas of migrant women, who are not immune to the competing values of tradition and modernity. The film is a romantic comedy with explicit references to the Hollywood of the "Golden Age", and Rashid uses his penchant for films featuring Cary Grant and Doris Day in order to comment on the pitfalls of postmodernity. However, by self-consciously deploying the techniques of classic romantic comedies in a narrative zoomed in on a diasporic Ismaili community, I argue that Rashid is queering and diversifying the cinematic mainstream.

To offer a short summary of the film, its protagonist is Alim (Jimi Mistry), a Canadian young man of Ismaili Kenyan heritage living in London with his partner Giles (Kris Holden-Ried), a white British man, without the knowledge of his Ismaili community in Canada. As we gradually find out, Alim's childhood trauma surrounding his homosexuality, his father's untimely death, and his mother's subsequent move to London, all drove him to the creation of an imaginary friend, the so-called spirit of Cary Grant (Kyle MacLachlan), who constantly offers him relationship advice and who feeds his escapist obsession with old Hollywood films. The film's premise is the visit of Alim's mother Nuru (Suleka Mathew) to London to convince Alim to attend his cousin Khaled's (Raoul Bhaneja) traditional Ismaili wedding, which she uses as an attempt to lure him back to Canada and to a heteronormative lifestyle with a potential Ismaili wife. The film explores Alim's difficulty in "coming out" to his mother, as well as his mother's dilemmas once she learns about his homosexuality. Alim's relationships with Giles and with Nuru are tested by two emotional stumbling blocks, which are the result of his assumptions about Nuru's Ismaili traditionalism and his related inability to reconcile ethno-religious tradition with modernity, and with his own postmodern diasporic worldview. Nuru, whose growing intimacy with Giles is cut short by Alim's coming out, leaves London in anger about her son and Giles' deception of her. Giles then leaves Alim, alienated as much by Alim's "closetedness" as by his heavy-handedness with his mother. Alim eventually follows Nuru to Toronto, where he attends Khaled's wedding preparations, thus rekindling his connection with his Ismaili family. He is then joined by Giles, whose presence prompts their joint "coming out" to Alim's Ismaili community, including Nuru's public sanctioning of their same-sex and interracial relationship, which leads to their final reconciliation.

Such a predictable narrative arc and happy ending do not do full justice to Rashid's complex formal and thematic endeavours. Thomas Waugh hails the film as an "excellent queer subversion of the oppressively heterocentric diasporic wedding cycle of the 1990s and 2000s. *Pink* is an intercontinental, intercultural couple comedy-romance and family melodrama."[13] As such, it garnered polarized responses from the international Ismaili community. Some viewers felt "thoroughly humiliated, very insulted, ashamed of ourselves as to how our Ismailis are being portrayed," including being depicted as "racist as well, not building bridges with *dhorias* [white people]"[14] and focused on material gain and social climbing through education. Despite the fact that Nuru builds a bridge with Giles, it would seem her sanction of his relationship with her son is not deemed representative of Ismaili sentiments about homosexuality. Film critic Zahra Meherali observes that "[t]he film was criticized for its 'deliberate exposing' of aberration"[15] in the community. These responses to Rashid's film need to be framed within the context of the global Ismaili community. On the one hand, Clarke argues that criticism within the Ismaili community "is always made in private," due to "the social stigma attached to being branded a critic."[16] On the other hand, Momin Rahman and Amir Hussain affirm that "[d]iasporic communities in the large urban centres of the West have openings for those raising critical questions about traditional religious and cultural ideas."[17]

Dissenting Muslim voices either remove themselves from their ethno-religious communities, which matches Alim's initial predicament in *Touch of Pink*, or attempt to change attitudes from within, as becomes the case later on in the film. Rahman and Hussain explain that "social traditionalism may well be strengthened by the relatively recent migration of the great majority of Muslims to both Canada and the United States as well as by the starkly conservative norms relating to gender and sexuality that prevail in the countries from which they migrated."[18] Nonetheless, values are constantly on the move, and Rashid's film is testament to the ways in which diasporic Ismaili citizens have to negotiate the conflicting demands of their community's traditions and of global modernity. The downside of Alim's position is that he is unable to fathom his mother as anything but a strict traditionalist bound to East African colonial values. Brainwashed by Cary Grant's spirit into believing that Nuru is a "Muslim from the Third World," he forces himself to adapt his lifestyle to her alleged expectations, evicting Giles to the spare room and thus pretending they are mere "roommates."

13. Waugh 2006, 495.
14. Al-Solaylee 2004, n.p.
15. Meherali 2004, n.p.
16. Clarke 1976, 487.
17. Rahman and Hussain 2014, 262.
18. Rahman and Hussain 2014, 263.

Lastly, Alim avoids coming out to his mother by pretending to be engaged to
Giles's sister Delia (Liisa Repo-Martell).

The scene of Alim's announcement to his mother of his imaginary
engagement to Delia posits an ethnic understanding of being "in the closet"
articulated through techniques inherited from classical Hollywood romantic
comedies. When Nuru taunts Alim about how he expects to "attract a nice
professional girl when [he is] living with a lodger," Alim caves in and tells her
he is in a relationship. Giles and Delia barge in mid-conversation, and Giles
gleefully assumes that Alim has told Nuru about their same-sex relationship.
In this moment of confusion, which already resembles classical comedies'
typical misunderstandings, Giles hugs stunned Alim and tells Nuru they
were "concerned about how [she] would handle it," to which Nuru retorts:
"Who could this frightening creature be I can't handle"? Cary Grant's spirit,
who is thoroughly enjoying the scene, motions towards Delia to Ali, who
calls her name and kisses her on the cheek, announcing their engagement,
to everyone's astonishment, and Cary Grant's ghost's delight. Here, Rashid
self-consciously references the identity swapping plot device of one of his
main intertexts, the 1940 romantic comedy *The Philadelphia Story*, directed
by George Cukor and starring Katharine Hepburn, Cary Grant, and James
Stewart, in which the identities of Hepburn's character's father and uncle are
swapped in order to avoid social scandal about her father's infidelity-related
absence at her wedding. In *Touch of Pink*, this technique is deployed in order
to signal the unresolved tensions between Alim's ethno-religious identity
and his sexual orientation. While avoiding "coming out" to his mother, he
rebels against her qualms about Delia not being a Muslim by stating that
he is no longer a Muslim, ironically adding that he is not going to pretend.
Nuru is dismayed by this revelation, which Alim attempts to downplay by
stating: "I just mean I don't believe in God." Rashid utilizes religion here as a
substitute for a debate about sexual orientation that Alim is not prepared to
have: it reveals that he needs to come out to himself as both a Muslim and a
homosexual in order to reconcile himself with his various identities.

Shamira Meghani proposes that queer Muslim narratives construct the
closet as an ethnic space:

> [T]he coming-out narrative is one of religion and ethnicity that
> needs to be overcome, in order for the closet to reopen. It is not
> sexual identity that needs to be discovered, but rather religion and
> ethnicity that stand in the way of what is already known. [...] *Touch
> of Pink* presents religion and ethnicity as ideas that have become
> overdetermined and that can be undone.[19]

19. Meghani 2014, 183.

Meghani suggests that, while Alim's homosexuality has already been internally accepted and externally acknowledged in select social situations, his conflict about his faith and ethnicity is stopping the "closet" from reopening. This situation is exacerbated by a diminished sense of self-worth and by internalized racism, which Rashid calls an "inferiority complex,"[20] which constitute the lingering legacies of colonial relations.

Following her disagreement with Alim over his faith, Nuru becomes more intimate with Giles, who takes her out sightseeing in London and who persuades her to buy a two-piece suit that reminds her of her favorite film in her youth, *That Touch of Mink*, starring Doris Day and Cary Grant. This episode of interethnic bonding begins unravelling Nuru's life story and her own experience of metropolitan racism and modernity. In a manner similar to the father figure in *Surviving Sabu*, Nuru experienced the insidious workings of British racism as a young woman in 1970s London. Later in the film, in the wake of a heart-to-heart with Alim about his relationship with Giles, Nuru shares her own life story. She dwells on how she "went to London to be Doris Day." After Alim's father unexpectedly died, Nuru confesses: "For weeks I just felt nothing. Then, one afternoon, I went to a film. Suddenly there was a way out. Suddenly, I could be Doris Day, flying off to a new life in London. Trouble is, London wasn't interested in any Indian Doris Days. Then or now."

The love of Hollywood films Alim has inherited from his mother do not offer either of them a suitable model for their lives as South Asian Muslims in the diaspora. Nonetheless, Nuru's encounter with Western modernity entails both negative and positive lessons, involving a gradual detachment from socio-cultural Islamic traditionalism. As she candidly tells Alim, "I'm not completely backwards. I know about men with men. I subscribe to *Reader's Digest* [...]. I didn't know about you and Giles. I didn't know that you had such feelings for him." Nuru's lack of a word for same-sex desire demonstrates, as Rashid tells Al-Solaylee, that "there's no word for homosexual in Kutchi,"[21] or at least an affirmative and non-derogatory one, which indexes the taboo of homosexuality within the Ismaili community. Nonetheless, Nuru's gradual acceptance of Alim and Giles' same-sex relationship is symptomatic of her own experience as woman at the interstices between tradition and modernity, between the heteronormativity of her Ismaili community and the variegated knowledges attained in the diaspora.

The emotional conversation between Nuru and Alim is prompted by her exposure to the duplicity of her nephew, Khaled. When he is about to

20. Meherali 2004, n.p.
21. Al-Solaylee 2004, n.p.

go home for the night, Alim asks Khaled whether he is happy; the latter responds: "Sure. [...] I'm doing what's expected of me; what I expect of myself." Khaled is a respected member of his community because he has qualified as a dentist and he has bought his parents an opulent house where they all live together. *Touch of Pink*'s characters' stress on education and on financial betterment is in keeping with ongoing developments in the Ismaili community. As Farhad Daftary observes,[22] the present spiritual leader of the Ismaili, the fourth Aga Khan, who was educated at Harvard University, has extended his father's modernization plans, founding learning programs and institutions which generally benefit all Muslims in so-called Third World countries and elsewhere.

However, this educational and economic embrace of global modernity still needs to wrestle with religious and moral traditionalism, and *Touch of Pink*'s characters demonstrate their struggle with their ideological inheritance. After Khaled's stag party, as he drunkenly rummages through cupboards looking for more alcohol, he makes a sexual pass on Alim, who rejects his advances, alleging he is in love with someone else, not the imaginary female brain surgeon Nuru has been bragging about, but Giles. Khaled charges: "You're in love with a guy? You don't love men, Alim. Fuck 'em, by all means. Hey, he's just in it for the squirt. I bet he doesn't love you. [...] It's just not normal," to which Alim retorts: "Hey, if you're normal, count me out. Look at you: a closet drunk, closet queer. Name a closet. You're hanging there." Khaled is incensed by Alim's "accusation," telling him not to play "high and mighty with me. [...] You ever think of your mother"? Ironically, eavesdropping Nuru has been privy to their heated encounter. When she makes her presence known, Khaled backtracks in a panic: "Auntie, it's not what you were imagining," to which she responds: "I'm not imagining. I'm seeing."

Nuru's eyes have become open to the doubleness of some queer Muslims' lives: to their internalized homophobia and their attempt to conform to familial ideas of social propriety, which only mask their queer desires. Khaled's closeted queerness is disguised not only by himself, but also by his family. When Nuru's sister Dolly (Veena Sood) notices that Nuru looks troubled, she tells her:

> It's all right, Nuru. I know. [...] About Alim. Our room used to be next to Khaled's and your boy's got quite a set of lungs. [...] I've always given Khaled his freedom. He's given me all this. [...] Look, I want grandchildren and ice sculptures and place cards. And so do you,

22. Daftary 1998.

Nuru, don't pretend. But if Khaled can do his duty, there's no reason why Alim can't.

Dolly's confession demonstrates that, despite her knowledge of Khaled and Alim's queerness, discovered early on in their lives, her material aspirations require her son to kowtow to the heteronormativity of their Ismaili community. This sexual normativity is constructed as Khaled's "duty" to his family, which Alim is also expected to fulfil. As John Esposito suggests, "Muslim minority communities have faced many hurdles in making the transition [between countries]; other hurdles continue to exist. Muslims and non-Muslim citizens and communities alike face the challenges of living in a pluralistic society."[23] The acceptance of homosexuality is one such hurdle that still needs to be overcome, as is the acknowledgement of different ideological hurdles for queer citizens of different ethnicities. Indeed, while Alim's Ismaili community needs to become attuned to his queerness, his partner Giles also needs to tune himself to the different sociocultural demands placed on Alim as a member of an ethno-religious minority which clings on to Islam as a way of reaffirming their diasporic group identity.

CONCLUSION: POSTMODERNITY AND THE SHEDDING OF COLONIAL TUTELAGE

In addition to the tensions between tradition and modernity, Alim's diasporic predicament also requires his self-effacing negotiation of postmodernity. The ready availability of Western cultural artefacts, such as old Hollywood films, does not provide models that can fruitfully encompass the complexity of his position as a queer Muslim in the diaspora. Karim suggests that

> The eclectic consumption of the products of many cultures in a way that negates the distinctiveness of each and all is [...] viewed as a feature of postmodernism. Muslims participate along with other people in a global consumerism that has served to rearrange relationships that were constructed by both tradition and modernity.[24]

The postmodern culture embodied by Hollywood film does not offer a suitable model for Alim. Instead, it only triggers a negation of his identity as a Muslim and a gay man. Hence, aside from his "coming out" to his Ismaili community in Canada, Alim's other main liberation in the film is outgrowing the influence of Cary Grant's ghost, a figure who is simultaneously condescending, racially and culturally biased, and also closeted. Lured by

23. Esposito 2002, viii.
24. Karim 2010, 275.

his Hollywood glamour, Alim initially hangs on to Cary Grant's every word, until, as Rashid points out, he learns to "stop living by Hollywood's values the way that the movies tell you."[25] Meghani observes that "[t]he coming-out story is subtended by the imaginary friendship Alim has with the film star Cary Grant, whose sexuality has been the subject of contentious debate since his death," adding that "Cary Grant functions as his closet-gay closet-coach."[26] As a white male surrogate father figure, Cary Grant's spirit provides both camp comic relief and the perpetuation of racist ideologies.

Meghani further argues that Alim's relationship with the spirit of Cary Grant constitutes an externalization of what Frantz Fanon calls "third person consciousness," and which is "productive of non-belonging."[27] Apart from the fuelling of a sense of non-belonging and the occasional fostering of ethnic inferiority, Cary Grant's spirit encourages superficial social heteronormativity and private transgression, as he favors pretence over truthfulness. The last straw is the ghost's comical donning of a Gunga Din outfit for Khaled's wedding, which signifies the persistence of Hollywood's Orientalist imageries. When it eventually dawns on the ghost that Alim is trying to get rid of him, he finally relents and confesses: "I envy you. Live every moment of it. Live it for me.... Be happy, my little samosa." Cary Grant's spirit is envious of Alim because he is now out of the closet, unlike the real Cary Grant, and because he has a chance to live his own life in the open, as a queer diasporic Muslim of South Asian and East African Ismaili ethnic heritage. Finally accepting all facets of his complex personality, Alim learns to reject the relativism of postmodern consumer culture.

In the end, Alim's shedding of Hollywood film's glamorous signifier as the ultimate "message," together with Giles' reconciliation with the personal and cultural distinctiveness of Alim's experience, allows for their relationship to be rekindled, not before one last moment of Hollywood-style misunderstanding. When Alim tells Giles "there's been another man," meaning Cary Grant, Giles assumes he is referring to Alisdair Keith (Dean McDermott), whom he had an affair with while Alim was busy reconnecting with his family in Toronto. "Oh, him. Yeah," retorts embarrassed Alim. Giles then looks into Alim's eyes and asks: "Alim, are we on the same wavelength?" to which Alim smiles back and responds: "We are now," after which they embrace in a balcony overlooking misty Toronto, fading to pink. Alim and Giles are finally on the same wavelength because of their interethnic negotiation of the competing and intersecting demands of Ismaili Muslim

25. Meherali 2004, n.p.
26. Meghani 2014, 180.
27. Meghani 2014, 182.

traditionalism, colonial and postcolonial modernity, and diasporic postmodernity. Rashid's short and long films provide distinctive articulations of Muslim identities which must wrestle with the complexities of diaspora and globalization. Rashid's queer work challenges the interwoven exigencies of British colonial racism, monolithic Western sexual exceptionalism, and Islamic homophobia, in a manner that shows queer Muslims in the movies to be constantly, both physically and figuratively, on the move.

Works Cited

Al-Solaylee, K. 2004. "A Touch Too Pink?" *Saturday's Globe and Mail*, July 24. http://www.theglobeandmail.com/arts/a-touch-too-pink/article18268745/.

Anonymous. 2007. "Ian Iqbal Rashid: 'My main influences were the dance films I grew up with.'" *Indiwire*. January 17. http://www.indiewire.com/2007/01/park-city-07-interview-ian-iqbal-rashid-my-main-influences-were-the-dance-films-i-grew-up-with-75383/.

Clarke, P. B. 1976. "The Ismailis: A Study of Community." *British Journal of Sociology* 27:484–94.

Daftary, F. 1998. *A Short History of the Ismailis: Traditions of a Muslim Community*. Edinburgh.

El Rouayheb, K. 2005. *Before Homosexuality in the Arab-Islamic World, 1500–1800*. Chicago and London.

Esposito, J. L. 2002. "Preface." In *Muslims in the West: From Sojourners to Citizens*, edited by Y. Y. Haddad, vii–viii. New York.

Hussain, A. 2004. "Muslims in Canada: Opportunities and Challenges." *Studies in Religion/Sciences Religieuses*, 33.3/4:359–79.

Jaikumar. P. 2012. "Sabu's Skins." *Wasafiri* 27.2:60–67.

Karim, K. H. 2010. "At the Interstices of Tradition, Modernity and Postmodernity: Ismaili Engagements with Contemporary Canadian Society." In *Modern History of the Ismailis: A Continuity and Change in a Muslim Community*, edited by F. Daftary, 265–94. London and New York.

Meghani, S. A. 2014. "Queer South Asian Muslims: The Ethnic Closet and its Secular Limits." In *Imagining Muslims in South Asia and the Diaspora: Secularism, Religion, Representations*, edited by C. Chambers and C. Herbert, 172–84. London and New York.

Meherali, Z. 2004. "Pride and Prejudice." *Samar Magazine*. March 11. http://www.samarmagazine.org/archive/articles/174.

The Philadelphia Story. 1940. Directed by George Cukor. MGM.

Rahman, M., and A. Hussain. 2014. "Muslims and Sexual Diversity in North America." In *Faith, Politics, and Sexual Diversity in Canada and the United*

States, edited by D. Rayside and C. Wilcox, 255–74. Vancouver and Toronto.

Sternberg, C. 2010. "Migration, Diaspora and Metacinematic Reflection." In *European Cinema in Motion: Migrant and Diasporic Film in Contemporary Europe*, edited by D. Berghnd and C. Sternberg, 256–74. Basingstoke and New York.

Stag. 2002. Directed by I. I. Rashid. BBC.

Surviving Sabu. 1998. Directed by I. I. Rashid. Hindi Pictures.

That Touch of Mink. 1962. Directed by D. Mann. Universal.

Touch of Pink. 2003. Directed by I. I. Rashid. Sienna Films.

Waugh, T. 2006. *Romance of Transgression in Canada: Queering Sexualities, Nations, Cinemas*. Montreal and Kingston, London, Ithaca.

Integration Through Conversion: Discourses of Islam and the *musulman laïc* in Contemporary French Cinema

Nancy Demerdash-Fatemi

INTRODUCTION: INTEGRATION AND THE DOUBLE BIND OF THE *MUSULMAN LAÏC*

I planted jasmine this morning in my HLM neighborhood
And I wondered what I had to do for France to love me
for France to love me.[1]

This essay focuses on the processes and filmic representations of Islam and religious conversion in relation to matters of integration and identity construction in contemporary France, in two recent films: *Qu'Allah bénisse la France* (*May Allah Bless France*, Abd al Malik, 2014) and *L'Apôtre* (*The Apostate*, Cheyenne Carron, 2014). These films have grappled not only with the politics of marginalization, ethnicity, and class in the *banlieues* (or ghettoized/stigmatized suburbs) of French cities, but have touched on a controversial subject that has been heretofore insufficiently addressed in the critical literature in cinema: Islam, conversion, and their relationships to secularism. *May Allah Bless France*, based on the autobiography of the rapper and writer Abd al-Malik (né Régis Fayette-Mikano), portrays the life of Abd Al Malik, who rose to prominence from his life in the HLM (Habitation à Loyer Modéré, i.e. low-income, rent-controlled housing), converted to Islam, and effectively spread his message of tolerance and integration through his compositions. By contrast, *The Apostate* narrates the path of Akim, a young Maghrebi Muslim in France who is destined to become an imam, but in a fraught turn of events, converts to Christianity against the wishes of his family and community.

Locating these films amidst the rise of Islamophobia in France, this essay positions these works dialogically with respect to debates on *laïcité*, anxieties about immigration and terrorism, and the postcolonial critiques of acculturation and transculturation. *Laïcité* – the widely contested notion derived from the 1946 and 1958 French Constitutions, that France is an "indivisible, secular, democratic, and social Republic" – is predicated on

1. Al Malik 2012, 48.

the republican idea that to live collectively in a society, that society must subscribe to the same set of values.[2] The questions in this analysis fall within two primary prongs: What does it mean to embrace or reject Islam in a culture that denigrates, ostracizes, and racializes Islam? How is the subject of conversion, piety, and religiosity treated cinematically in a country of *laïcité* and how are these on-screen representations connected to off-screen political discourses and debates on race, faith, ethnicity and belonging in France? What are the external and internal motivations undergirding such conversions to and denunciations of Islam? How do these films propagate the idea of a *musulman laïc*, or secular Muslim? How can we understand the complexities of identity, faith, and collective belonging against this troubled cultural ethos? This essay builds on the abundant scholarship on *beur* cinema[3] by putting these discourses in conversation with the cacophony of xenophobic and integrationist rhetoric that has permeated the public sphere. Another goal of this essay is to foreground the underlying issues of identification and social integration inherent to processes of religious conversion, and to examine the cinematic representations and French media's reception of these introspective and identitarian transformations.

The release of these films in 2014 was undoubtedly timely, in the very midst of the escalation of the civil war in Syria, the graphically broadcasted violence of ISIS/Daesh on Muslims and Christians alike in Syria and Iraq, and the so-called "refugee crisis" in Europe. With the horrific terror attacks on *Charlie Hebdo* and the kosher supermarket, and Bataclan massacre in Paris, of January and November 2015, respectively, these films' reception has, without question, been filtered through the lens of these atrocities. But their production as well is also indicative of a political drive and governmental necessity to "do something"[4] about this extremist violence and speak directly to those perpetrators, and more broadly, to the subjectivities and values of young Muslim males in France.[5]

Integration is a highly polemical and politicized issue in contemporary French discourses. The term itself superseded phrases that uncomfortably echoed the civilizing mission and ideology of the French colonial system of the Third Republic (1870–1940), such as "assimilation" or "insertion," which

---

2. Bowen 2007, 29; 33. "...there is no historical actor called "laïcité": only a series of debates, laws, and multiple efforts to assert claims over public space."

3. Bosséno 1992, 49. Beur films are defined as those "made by a young person of North African origin who was born or who has spent his or her youth in France, and which features beur characters."

4. Bowen 2007, 7.

5. Tarr 2005, 44. Tarr notes that much of beur-focused cinema centers on issues of masculinity and identity.

remained in usage even to the tail end of the *Trente Glorieuses*, (or "Thirty Glorious [Years]," referring to the roughly thirty years of postwar growth in France up to the mid-1970s).[6] In a deliberate shift away from this colonial rhetoric, more recent governments have preferred the term "integration" in an acknowledgement of cultural diversity and the right to cultural difference within the universalism of the Republic. However, as Abdelmalek Sayad has suggested, this placed the responsibility of adaptation solely on the migrants and their children, who are expected to not only jettison their perceptibly foreign values and traditions but repeatedly prove themselves and their desire to integrate through language acquisition, socio-cultural blending, and so on, in spite of their continued spatial/residential alienation and general ostracism from the mainstream public.[7] As of a law passed in July 2006, those immigrants seeking long-term residency are mandated to sign a *Contrat d'accueil et d'intégration* (Contract of Settlement and Integration), underscoring their obligations to accept and conform to principles of *laïcité* and gender equality (in male-female unions).[8] With these pressures in mind, Sylvie Durmelat and Vinay Swamy aptly define the act of integrating as "a screening process that can either exclude or include, and through which differences are created, maintained, and/or displaced."[9]

Being at once French and Maghrébin, is often treated as a contradictory ethno-national identity. But in spite of French Maghrébins' religiosity, piety or beliefs, they are automatically cast as Muslim due to Islam's predominance in the Maghreb itself. As Jean Beaman illustrates in her ethnographic study of second-generation Maghrébins in France, the manner in which these individuals outwardly display their affinities for Islam or their degree of Muslim religiosity is directly related to their attempt to challenge their marginalized position in French society.[10] Beaman asserts that respondents "frame their religiosity in ways that allow them to agentically respond to their marginalization and legitimate their inclusion within mainstream French society," and that they tend to express their faith identities in ways that accommodate and complement, rather than obstruct, French republicanism.[11]

As these films make clear, within France the position of French Muslims and their perceived failure to fully integrate in society continue to be

---

6. Hargreaves 1995,195–196. Cited in Durmelat and Swamy 2011, 9.
7. Sayad 1999. Cited in Durmelat and Swamy 2011, 9.
8. Durmelat and Swamy 2011, 10.
9. Durmelat and Swamy 2011, 11.
10. Beaman 2017.
11. Beaman 2016, 43.

issues of scholarly and public debate.[12] Islamophobia in France cannot be understood though, without inquiries into widely accepted conceptions of French republican identity and its relation to, and negotiations with, French Muslim identities. Much discussed in this literature are the popular concerns about the display of "conspicuous religious symbols," the impact of the resulting 2004 ban of the headscarf (*hijab*) and head-to-toe, black *niqab* in public schools and its socio-cultural impact.[13] A *musulman laïc*, or roughly, a secular Muslim, would have to respect the neutrality of the public space which allows for the coexistence of people from multiple faiths.[14] For Jennifer Fredette, Muslims who integrate in this fashion are perceived of as "deserving citizens," but these individuals are understood to be outliers, and in most instances, French media coverage associates Muslims with "violence, extreme religiosity, and disrespect for France's secularism."[15] Across these two films' representations of Muslims and Muslim life in France, the producers and writers secularize Muslim subjects so as to make them more palatable to a dominantly white, French viewing audience.

Rrepresenting Islam between *Beur* and *Banlieue*

Although *May Allah Bless France* and *The Apostate* were directed by individuals who do not self-identify as *beur* – the Franco-Congolese rapper, writer, and Muslim convert, Abd Al Malik (né Regis Fayette-Mikano), and Cheyenne Carron, a prominent French director of Kabyle (indigenous Algerian) descent, though adopted by French, practicing Catholic parents[16] – these two films in particular share and grapple with an array of issues so prevalent to the cinematic canon of "*beur*" cinema, the term stemming from the *verlan* back-slang reversal of the syllables in the word "*arabe*." Novels, literature or cinema made by or about descendants of Maghrebi immigrants carry the label of *beur*. More than a cinema based on ethnicity, at the time of their emergence *beur* films in the 1980s and 1990s sought to explore the vast and complex socio-cultural imaginaries of Maghrebi populations in France, as testimonials of their fraught lived experiences in urban centers and suburban peripheries. Soon enough, by virtue of their common thematic and formal attentiveness to minorities' political disenfranchisement, everyday

12. Beaman 2016, 41–42. See also Bleich 2006, 3–7; Bleich 2009, 379–400; Fernando 2005, 12–17; Kastoryano 2002; Kastoryano 2004, 66–88; Voas and Fleischmann 2012, 525–45.

13. Beaman 2016, 41–42. See also Bleich 2006, 3–7; Bleich, 2009, 379–400; Fernando 2005, 12–17; Kastoryano 2002; Kastoryano 2004, 66–88; Voas and Fleischmann 2012 525–45.

14. Bowen 2007, 29.

15. Fredette 2014, 39.

16. Millot 2013.

indignities, social alienation, and environment of urban decay within the *banlieues* (suburbs) of major French cities like Paris, Lille, Lyon, Grenoble, Strasbourg, *beur* films became conflated with yet another subgenre of "*banlieue* film," a term coined by the critic Thierry Jousse in reference to narratives of disenchanted, disenfranchised, and frequently misrepresented and misunderstood youth in the French *banlieues*.[17] Stories of this subgenre shed light on the realities and hardships of life in the *banlieue*, with all of its social ills and political injustices: the discriminatory deprivation of opportunity to French youth of multiethnic backgrounds (leading to high unemployment rates), intergenerational cultural clashes between foreign-born elders and their second- and third-generation offspring (often relating to integrational challenges), as well as drug trafficking, petty crime, high rates of incarceration, overdose, and so forth. Like much of this cinematic canon, *May Allah Bless France* and *The Apostate* address similar questions of social integration, acceptance and identity.

   Yet Al Malik's and Carron's works confront head-on three variables in this complicated socio-political and cultural matrix that are otherwise left untouched in *beur* or *banlieue* cinema: Islam, its extremist iterations, and religious conversions. What muddles these already charged interrelationships further is the reading of these phenomena against the backdrop of violence in France, both real and discursive. According to Franco-Maghrebi and émigré film specialist Will Higbee, this relative absence of Islam in French cinema is palpable; filmmakers of *beur* or *banlieue*-oriented productions tend to avoid tackling Islam altogether for a number of reasons, though many times out of a desire to sidestep the potential minefield of controversy and enter the mainstream.[18] There are exceptional precedents of course. It is the risk of testing audiences' values that many Franco-Maghrebi or émigré filmmakers opt not to take, for fear of releasing a film that monetarily flops. Moreover, there is ambient pressure in the film industry to facilitate off-screen integration through on-screen assimilations. So, apart from Islam constituting untouchable content for market reasons, its treatment is dodged for political ends.

   Given this evasion of Islamic subject matter and plot content more generally, it is striking that in this ethos, both Abd Al Malik's and Carron's films were widely lauded in the French media – why? Even before deciding to produce the film based on his eponymous autobiography, Abd Al Malik's celebrated rap albums *Le Face à face des cœurs* (2004), *Gibraltar* (2006) (for which he won the "Victoire de la musique," or French version of a Grammy

17. Durmelat and Swamy 1995: 37–39.
18. Higbee 2013. Cadé 2011, 43–44.

Award), and *Dante* (2008) catapulted him to stardom, but his literary writings and appearances on French radio and television talk shows brought his art and political presence to a much wider audience, and the aim of his film, so he says, was to further disseminate his story.[19] Unsurprisingly, *The Apostate* received, in the same year, the Special Prize of the Capax Dei Foundation at the Mirabile Dictu Catholic International Film Festival, and was an official selection of numerous film festivals throughout the world, marketed by Carron and the press as a film of "peace" and "tolerance."[20] Though, problematically, Carron knew that her movie project was a hazardous endeavor[21], as she initially could find no financial sponsors. In the analysis that follows, I argue that what has rendered these films so popular to French audiences are their secularized accounts of Islam and religious conversion. Before delving into this critique, outlining these films' narratives and their discursive operations is essential.

MAY ALLAH BLESS FRANCE (2014): ABD AL MALIK AS A SECULAR MUSLIM RAPPER

The film *May Allah Bless France* is based on the eponymous autobiographical memoir (2004) of French hip-hop artist Abd Al Malik (né Régis Fayette-Mikano) and his life story, beginning with his troubled upbringing in the *banlieue* of Neuhof (in the outskirts of Strasbourg) and solace in poetry and music, to his inner reformation and conversion to Islam and eventual rise to multi-platinum success as a rapper in the French music industry. Born to Congolese (ethnically Vili and Teke), Catholic parents and a family of brothers (Fayette and Arnaud), the Dickensian plot traces the formative experiences of teenaged Régis (played by Marc Zinga), in his schizophrenic upbringing as both skilled pickpocket and drug dealer, on the one hand, and academic wunderkind in private schools, on the other. Narratively and thematically speaking, the film parallels the kind of introspective transformations of Curtis Hanson becoming Eminem, and indeed, this has been repeatedly compared in the French press to the American movie *8 Mile* (Curtis Hanson, 2002) based on the life of Detroit rapper, with its emphases on socioeconomic struggles, racial politics, and urban blight.[22] Both the memoir and film (shot entirely in gray-scale) capture the spectrum of the young Régis's Neuhof posse, who are evocatively portrayed in the film as well, but as they either

19. Duhamel 2015, 40.
20. Lachasse 2015. The film was censored from showings in Nantes and Neuilly due to intelligence from the Direction générale de la sécurité intérieure (DGSI).
21. Carron. Cheyenne Carron comments in an interview on her own website that she solicited sponsors by reaching out to some of the wealthiest individuals in France.
22. Sotinel 2014.

fall prey to drug addiction and overdose, get killed in violent gang standoffs, or arrested and sent to jail, the realization sets in that his fate could be sealed with one misstep (both the memoir and movie commemorate these perished peers). Along Régis' correctional journey to the straight-and-narrow path, his brother Arnaud had a vision one night, in which he was summoned by a black man dressed in white to embrace Islam.[23] Arnaud's subsequent conversion (notably adopting "Bilal" as his new Muslim name, after the black African *muezzin* and companion to the Prophet Muhammad) and upright lifestyle affected Régis deeply, as he worked towards his own purification of mind and spirit. This, coinciding with his own cultural awakening to the writings of African-American intellectuals, the Négritude and Civil Rights movements, and anti-colonial theory,[24] led him in turn to heroize Malcolm X. It is easy to comprehend the allure of Malcolm X for impressionable youth of the *banlieues*, given his own battles against a system of racist discrimination, his criminal background and incarceration, and redemption and resilience through Islam. But it was the verse of rap and hip-hop, in his 1988-founded group, New African Poets (N.A.P), that gave voice to the injustices of social exclusion and criminalization of multiethnic youth of the *banlieue* of Neuhof.[25]

Abd Al Malik has been described as a "man of conversion [homme de conversion]."[26] The conversion process that Abd Al Malik undergoes, and the Islamic revivalism that his Maghrébin peers experience alongside him, share qualities with other religious converts and revivalists who rely on foundational texts (e.g. the Qur'an, Sunnah, and *hadīth*), aspire towards "purification" and seek seemingly authentic notions of Islam.[27] Initially, he subscribed to what he later deemed a fundamentalist interpretation of Islam, for instance, in his dressing in traditional garb of the *sunna*.[28] His memoir recounts his frustrations with Muslim immigrants' tendency to associate by nationality rather than religious affiliation,[29] but in the memoir

---

23. Al Malik 2014, 46–47. "He told me one night he was awakened by a strange gleam above his bed. He swore he was perfectly awake when he saw this black man dressed in white who was floating barefoot over his bed and asked him to embrace Islam."

24. Al Malik 2012, 56.

25. Al Malik 2012, 69. From N.A.P.'s song, "Au sommet de Paris [At the Top of Paris]": "The animal spirit 'gun blah' possessed us/ Thousands of desperados like me living in these concrete towers knew/ The life we had was dark, gray and just plain rotten/ Project dwellers, immigrants, the poor all have dreamed of a better life/ This is how we took rap, to escape life's prison."

26. Pingeot 2012, 11.

27. Deeb 2006, 20. See also Grewal 2013.

28. Al Malik 2012, 89–90.

29. Al Malik 2012, 114–15.

and movie we can see the active processes of acculturation and deculturation that Abd Al Malik undergoes.[30] In the movie, he and his friends all reinforce their sense of communal adhesion and identity through these exteriorizing modes of dress and immerse themselves in debates about appropriate codes of Muslim behavior.[31]

Over time, Abd Al Malik gravitated toward Sufi interpretations of Islam, in part pushed to it by the intransigent orthodoxy of the "Islam de *banlieue*" but also because of the spiritual mentorship of Sidi Hamza al-Qadiri al-Butchichi, a member of the Qadiriyya Butchichiyya *confrérie* (brotherhood) in Madah, Morocco. In his dedication to al-Butchichi at the beginning of his memoir, Abd Al Malik credits al-Butchichi with teaching him, "in the intimacy of our hearts, how to be a universal man filled with love for all humanity."[32] In a powerful, expansive shot in the film, showing Abd Al Malik on the ferry passing through the Strait of Gibraltar, from Algeciras, Spain, to Tangier, Morocco, one can apperceive the vastness of these Sufi ideals in this literal and spiritual passage.

Through his espousal of Sufi Islam – a path that marries universalism and the idea of a loving, benevolent God[33] – Abd Al Malik has morphed into something of a darling of the French state, and by extension, the media as well. Accolades and awards lavished on him include the highly prestigious and exclusive Chevalier des Arts et des Lettres issued by the state, the Prix Constantin, and the Edgar Faure Prize for political literature for his *La guerre des banlieues n'aura pas lieu* (2010). As a product of the *banlieue* who also honors and is indebted to his own French education, some argue that Abd Al Malik has become appropriated as a kind of poster child or voice-box for the state, to show that kids from the projects can and should have a sense of gratitude to the government, patriotism, and pride in their Frenchness.[34] Olivier Bourderionnet suggests that Abd Al Malik is "being played" by the media, given, for instance, his sponsorships and partnerships with *Télérama* and *Le Monde* on his 2006 album *Gibraltar*. Consequently, he has been widely perceived as the kind of voice-box or poster child for a pacifist, placatory, or "conciliatory rap discourse" – that is, a brand of rap that renders him *le rappeur idéal* (ideal rapper) for his invocation of traditional French *chanson poétique* (French popular songs), and for his non-threatening and

---

30. Özyürek 2015, 3, 7.
31. Al Malik 2012, 93.
32. Al Malik 2012, 93, dedication to the book to Sidi Hamza al-Qadiri al-Butchichi.
33. This idea is perhaps more palatable to a general French public due to its compatibility with French Catholic notions of God/Christ as being the embodiment of love.
34. Poteau-Tralie and Cook 2017, 165.

non-violent content.[35] Ironically enough, it is precisely this state and media-sanctioned legitimacy that has diminished his reputational authenticity and "street cred" among his primary, intended demographic: the disillusioned *beur* and/or Muslim youth of the French *banlieues*.[36]

And yet, the film, mirroring Abd Al Malik's rap lyrics, carries a didacticism in the dramatizations and unique authorial subjectivity that is hard to dismiss as simply "cooptation" by the state. In spite of the fact that the sentiments of his memoir and film do not internalize the symbolic, revolutionary violence that is espoused by many French rap artists,[37] the poetics of the film and his music nevertheless discursively employ the political, ethical project of "engagement" (*littérature de l'engagement*) in its intentions to challenge existing social structures and cultural norms.[38] The historiographic, and indeed, revisionist dimensions of Abd Al Malik's cross-referencing, palimpsestic art forms[39] add new currency to the productive dialogues he seeks to initiate. Though he has been charged with cherry-picking, name-dropping and mere citation of the literary canon by some in the French media,[40] the arsenal of cultural capital that he deploys bears a keen and undeniable critical historical consciousness, as with much of French rap and hip-hop.[41] Even if Abd Al Malik's message of *citoyenneté transnationale* (transnational citizenship) inherent to his Sufi understanding of the world is, in turn, appropriated and promoted by the state as a kind of "favorable" brand of Islam, his nuanced perspectives and rich life experiences speak compellingly to the growing plurality of Islams practiced today in France.[42]

THE APOSTATE (2014): CONVERTING THE PUBLIC OPINION OF "GOOD VS. "BAD" MUSLIM

Cheyenne Carron's film *The Apostate* charts the transformational arc of a young, Franco-Algerian man's religious inquiries, inspirations, and subsequent conversion from Islam to Catholicism. Though the main plot follows a fictitious storyline, elements are rooted in true events. The intense opening scene is one such portrayal, in which a woman (we later find out, the sister of a priest) is strangled to death in a domestic setting by a man of

35. Bourderionnet 2011, 154–55.
36. Poteau-Tralie and Cook 2017, 165.
37. Etoke 2009, 167.
38. Martinez 2011.
39. Poteau-Tralie and Cook 2017.
40. Bourderionnet 2011, 157.
41. Martinez 2011.
42. Muedini 2015. Chapter 6 offers a discussion of how Sufism is deployed in British and US foreign policy.

color; this is based on the real-life strangulation of a woman who was the sister of a priest in Carron's hometown of Valence, in the region of Drôme.[43] The next scene closes in on two brothers, Akim (played by Fayçal Safi), the protagonist, and Youssef (Brahim Tekfa), praying side by side outdoors in the backyard of their parents' home. Their juxtaposition in this moment of solidarity and intimacy illustrates not only their physical differences, but gestures to the rifts in the brothers' temperaments, spiritual values, and worldviews, that only widen as the film progresses. While this contrast between the two characters certainly propels the plotline forward, the brothers merely serve as reductive typological foils for one another – Akim represents the open-minded, the curious and inquisitive, beauty-seeking pacifist, while Youssef depicts the dogmatic, rigid, bellicose, irrational traditionalist – flattening any iota of nuance to the brothers' disparate roles, ultimately doing a disservice to the actors' dynamic performances. This one-dimensionality to the character development is a shortcoming, playing into pre-existing, clash-of-civilizations dichotomies, colonial hangovers, and racist clichés of North African aggression; it is not out of line with the kinds of "reel bad Arab" representations that Jack Shaheen speaks of.[44] Given Carron's outspoken friction with her biological, Kabyle mother (who, as it turned out, violently sought to re-adopt Cheyenne as a teenage ward), it is difficult to resist a biographical reading of the director's personal crusade and biases as projected onto diasporic Maghrebi culture.[45]

Regardless, unlike most *beur* and *banlieue* cinema, the storyline does not fit neatly into any subgenre or capture concrete blights of the *quartiers*, social dysfunction, or intergenerational culture wars. We instead encounter a unified, wholesome, close-knit, middle class, practicing Muslim family, too picture perfect to be anything but surreal. Akim and Youssef's uncle Rachid serves as the local congregation's imam and is presented as a mild-mannered and upright, but orthodox leader. Akim, we learn, is being collectively groomed by his nuclear family, uncle Rachid, and the local *ummah* to fill the shoes of his uncle as imam. Gifted by uncle Rachid with a paid trip to go on the mandatory *hajj*, viewers can sense Akim's resignation through his facial expression, and the mixed, transactional nature of this blessing – simultaneously a promise, a privilege, and a burden.

These moments of subtle reluctance are amplified by the fault lines in his faith, as a sequence of incidents provoke bouts of self-doubt, revelation, and consternation. Walking past the crime scene of the priest's sister's murder, Akim becomes awestruck by the fact that the priest is helping the

43. Carron. Carron recounts the trauma of the incident on her website.
44. Shaheen 2015.
45. Millot 2013.

Muslim family of the man who killed his sister live through their tribulation. Shortly thereafter Akim finds himself entangled in a wreck after getting hit by a car while riding his bike, and the white male driver is quick to blame Akim for negligence, seeking to press charges at the nearby police station. Fabien, a street bystander and good Samaritan, advocates for Akim to the police, vouching that the driver is at fault. Without Fabien coming to his defense, as his literal savior – a white, ethnically French, non-foreign male – Akim admits that the law enforcement would have sided with the driver; he finds himself once again inspired by Christian kindness. By happenstance, days later, Fabien and Akim encounter one another again, and Fabien extends an invitation to Akim for his daughter Rose's baptism at a local cathedral. Touched by the intimacy of the gesture, Akim decides to attend, but this plan is met with rancor by the unrelentingly hot-tempered brother Youssef, who shuns the ritual as a celebration by infidels. In spite of his brother's admonishing disapproval, Akim sets out for the church, where he experiences his first revelatory epiphany, clearly affected by the service and words of the prayers and hymns. Holding onto the paper program from the baptism underneath his pillow, he later recites to himself the prayers in the privacy of his bedroom. As if the holy water had poured onto Akim as well, this symbolic baptismal rebirth ultimately transforms his relationship with himself, his family members, Uncle Rachid, and the Muslim community, who all begin to suspect that something is amiss. At this point he begins to regularly visit and question the priest who conducted the baptism. To broaden his perspectives on Christianity, he even seeks guidance from the Catholic priest and another Franco-Maghrebi Christian convert, who is labeled by his former Maghrebi Muslim brethren as an apostate (hence the name of the film), and, as evidenced by his bloody and bruised lip, supposedly beaten by this brotherhood too; he connects Akim to a small support group of ostensibly *beur* youth who have converted to Christianity, as they meet in relative secrecy (conjuring images of Christ's clandestine meetings with early disciples and converts).

The climax of the film coincides with Akim's eventual conversion to Catholicism, the upheaval and discord this wreaks on his family (in particular, Youssef), and his moving out of the parental nest. In one moving scene, Akim attempts to tell his mother that he is becoming a Christian, and in a state of disbelief, she replies: "You, your mother, your grandmother, and your great-grandmother are Muslim. You are Muslim." By distinguishing Youssef and Akim's religious zeal with the relatively calm demeanor of their parents, Carron points to the increasingly sharper intergenerational distinctions of piety and religiosity.[46] Only when members of the mosque congregation break into Akim's apartment and vengefully beat him nearly fatally for his apostasy, does his family forgive and accept him. A few years pass and we come upon a subdued Youssef ceremonially taking his oath to become an imam; the brothers pray side by side once more, but this time, we hear Youssef's āthān against Akim's Lord's Prayer. The film ends with passages honoring the victims of apostasy-related killings.

Admittedly, there is simply no "clean" way of depicting violence invoked in the name of religion. Even given the indelicate nature of representing religious defection, it can be nuanced and responsible. In light of the tragedies of Charlie Hebdo, it should not come as a shock that Christian audiences were more apprehensive about the film's release than Muslim ones, for "fear of polemics, disturbance, fear of being labeled Islamophobic."[47] What this film fails to produce are the fine grains, the overdetermined psycho-social and political motivations underlying religious conversion. Many converts, consciously or unconsciously, search for countless benefits of community, social acceptance, credibility, psychological peace, identification, a sense of selfhood, and so forth. In other instances, conversion may be prophylactically motivated – that is, to stave off discrimination or hate crimes. As viewers, we are meant to empathize with and dwell within the perspective of our protagonist, Akim. Youssef's character plays into a frankly colonial conception of an irrational, even tribalistic sketch of young Muslims in France as inherently belligerent and troubled. But in the end, Youssef becomes the idealized *musulman laïc*, accepting of his brother's transformation. Yet, contrary to the aim of conceiving of a film of "inter-religious tolerance," the film bluntly recapitulates the sensationalist right-wing discourse of secular (and Catholic) France being under attack by extremist Muslims.

CONCLUSION: POSITIONING CONVERSION WITHIN "POSITIVE PORTRAYALS" – SANITIZING ISLAM FOR THE PUBLIC PALATE

Because Islam is itself stigmatized in France, the ways in which religious and national identity, and their representations, are negotiated among French youth are all the more complex. In the pre- and post-9/11 United States, the conflation of Muslims with Islamic extremists as well as the racialization of Arabs and Muslims abound in Hollywood and mainstream media representations of Middle Eastern peoples. While 9/11 is typically

---

46. Carron.
47. Carron.

discussed as a transformational point in the negative stereotyping of Arabs and Muslims, many scholars have questioned the ways in which this privileging of the event has left us with a skewed historical perspective, obscuring the detrimental effects of a longstanding history of American interference in the region.[48] Evelyn Alsultany has wrestled not only with these derogatory portrayals in the media, but she has also examined the counter-surge of what she calls "positive" representations as well – instances in which compassionate images of Arabs and Muslims circulate with the intent of bolstering the United States' (purported) reputation of tolerance and its anti-racist stance: "the production and circulation of 'positive' representations of the (Arab and Muslim) 'enemy' has become so essential to projecting the United States as benevolent, especially in its declaration of war and official support of racist policies."[49] Alsultany dubs these sorts of depictions (e.g. as in the Fox series *24*, 2001–2010) as oxymoronic "simplified complex representations,"[50] as they superficially defy stereotypes and thus forward a multicultural, post-racial message, while employing those very same representational modes that instantiate and normalize disciplinary practices like incarceration and torture. While these American dramas appear to bend over backwards in humanizing Arab and Muslim characters, the frameworks of these programs nevertheless overload the viewer with explorations of terrorism.

We can see echoes of these representational tendencies in both *May Allah Bless France* and *The Apostate* to render Islam in a "positive" light. For the former memoir and film, the overarching objective is clear: to marry a celebration of Frenchness with a peaceful and love-based notion of Islam. Abd Al Malik has risen to stardom in France and received numerous awards because he is the embodiment of the ideal, multicultural *musulman laïc* so sought after by the government. With Carron's film, her stated goal was to present the "beauty of Catholicism without denigrating Islam."[51] While the topic of apostasy and hate crimes most definitely warrants public dialogue, Carron plays into and only reinforces simplistic popular binaries of the "good" and "bad" Muslims.

Ultimately, these transformations and transgressions tell us that religious conversion – whether intentionally so or not – is most often a political act in which status quo socio-cultural boundaries are challenged. The act of conversion entails so much more than simply practicing new rituals

48. Elseewi 2015.
49. Alsultany 2012, 6.
50. Alsultany 2012, 21.
51. Carron.

or adopting a new lifestyle, but it involves overdetermined motivations and a search for values otherwise missing in one's everyday life. Only time will tell how the future French media and culture industry will truly accept and accommodate all forms of difference, more than just the *musulman laïc*.

WORKS CITED

Al Malik, A. 2012. *Le dernier Français*. Paris.

———. 2014. *Qu'Allah bénisse la France!* Paris.

Alsultany, E. 2012. *Arabs and Muslims in the Media: Race and Representation After 9/11*. New York.

Beaman, J. 2016. "As French as Anyone Else: Islam and the North African Second Generation in France." *International Migration Review* 50 (1) (Spring 2016): 41–69.

———. 2017. *Citizen Outsider: Children of North African Immigrants in France*. Oakland.

Bleich, E. 2006. "Constructing Muslims as Ethno-Racial Outsiders in Western Europe." *Council for European Studies Newsletter* 36 (1) (2006): 3–7.

———. 2009. "Where do Muslims Stand on Ethno-Racial Hierarchies in Britain and France? Evidence From Public Opinion Surveys, 1988–2008." *Patterns of Prejudice* 43:379–400.

Bosséno, C. 1992. "Immigrant Cinema: National Cinema – The Case of Beur Film." In *Popular European Cinema*, edited by Richard Dyer and Ginette Vincendeau, 47–57. London.

Bourderionnet, O. 2011. "A 'Picture-Perfect' Banlieue Artist: Abd Al Malik or the Perils of a Conciliatory Rap Discourse." *French Cultural Studies* 22 (2): 151–61.

Bowen, J. 2007. *Why the French Don't Like Headscarves: Islam, the State, and Public Space*. Princeton.

Cadé, M. 2011. "Hidden Islam: The Role of the Religious in Beur and Banlieue Cinema." In *Screening Integration: Recasting Maghrebi Immigration in Contemporary France*, edited by S. Durmelat and V. Swamy, 41–57. Lincoln.

Carron. C. "Interview: L'Apôtre." http://www.cheyennecarron.com/itv7.php

Deeb, L. 2006. *An Enchanted Modern: Gender and Public Piety in Shi'i Lebanon*. Princeton.

Duhamel, B. 2015. "Qu'Allah bénisse la France: Entretien avec Abd Al Malik." *France-Amérique* April: 38–51.

Durmelat, S.and Swamy, V. 2011. "Introduction." In *Screening Integration: Recasting Maghrebi Immigration in Contemporary France*, edited by S. Durmelat, and V. Swamy, 1–24. Lincoln.

Elseewi, T. 2015. "Arabs and Muslims in the Media: Race and Representation after 9/11." *Cinema Journal* 54 (4) (Summer): 165–68.

Etoke, N. 2009. "Black Blanc Beur: Ma France à moi," *Nouvelles Études Francophones* 24 (1): 157–71.

Fernando, M. 2005. "The Republic's 'Second Religion': Recognizing Islam in France." *Middle East Report* 235:12–17.

Fredette, J. 2014. *Constructing Muslims in France: Discourse, Public Identity and the Politics of Citizenship*. Philadelphia.

Grewal. Z. 2013. *Islam Is a Foreign Country: American Muslims and the Global Crisis of Authority*. New York.

Hargreaves, A. 1995. *Immigration, "Race," and Ethnicity in Contemporary France*. London.

Higbee, W. 2013. *Post-Beur Cinema: North African Émigré and Maghrebi-French Filmmaking in France Since 2000*. Edinburgh.

Jousse, T. 1995. "Le banlieue-film existe-t-il?" *Cahiers du cinéma* 492:37–39.

Kastoryano, R. 2002. *Negotiating Identities: States and Immigrants in France and Germany*. Princeton.

———. 2004. "Race and Ethnicity in France." In *Social Inequalities in Comparative Perspective*, edited by F. Devine and M. C. Waters, 66–88. Malden.

Lachasse, J. 2015. "Cheyenne Carron: 'L'Apôtre est un film de paix.'" *Le Figaro*, 16 January. http://www.lefigaro.fr/cinema/2015/01/16/03002–20150116ARTFIG00294-cheyenne-carron-l-apotre-est-un-film-de-paix.php_

Martinez, I. M. 2011. "Intermediality, Rewriting Histories, and Identities in French Rap." *CLCWeb: Comparative Literature and Culture* 13 (3): 1–9.

Millot, O. 2013. "Cheyenne Carron. Mademoiselle sans gene." *Libération*, June 9. http://www.liberation.fr/societe/2013/06/09/cheyenne-carron-mademoiselle-sans-gene_909455

Muedini, F. 2015. *Sponsoring Sufism: How Governments Promote "Mystical Islam" in their Domestic and Foreign Politics*. New York.

Özyürek, E. 2015 *Being German, Becoming Muslim: Race, Religion and Conversion in the New Europe*. Princeton.

Pingeot, M. 2012. "Preface," In *Le dernier français*, Abd Al Malik, 7–10. Paris.

Poteau-Tralie, M. and C. Cook. 2017. "Palimpsest in the Rap Lyrics of Abd Al Malik: Rejuvenating the Study of Poetry." *The French Review* 90 (4): 159–70.

Sayad, A. 1999. *La double absence: Des illusions de l'émigré aux souffrances de l'immigré*. Paris.

Shaheen, J. 2015. *Reel Bad Arabs: How Hollywood Vilifies a People*. Northampton.

Sotinel, T. 2014. "'Qu'Allah bénisse la France': Abd Al Malik filme son passage d'un côté à l'autre de la rue." *Le Monde*, September 12. http://www.lemonde.fr/cinema/article/2014/12/09/qu-allah-benisse-la-france-abd-al-malik-filme-son-passage-d-un-cote-a-l-autre-de-la-rue_4536995_3476.html

Tarr, C. 2005. *Reframing Difference: Beur and Banlieue Filmmaking in France*. Manchester.

Voas, D. and F. Fleischmann. 2012. "Islam Moves West: Religious Change in the First and Second Generations." *Annual Review of Sociology* 38:525–545.

Laughing at the Other:
Muslims in Italian Comedies

Michela Ardizzoni
University of Colorado Boulder

IN FEBRUARY 2017, the *Washington Post* published an article titled "In Italy, Islam Doesn't Officially Exist." What the catchy headline refers to is the lack of official recognition for Italy's second major religion, embraced by more than two million people, according to the latest census.[1] Unlike Catholicism and Judaism, Islam is not officially recognized by the government, with consequences that vary from the unavailability of public funds to build mosques to the illegality of Islamic weddings.[2] In 2017, though, a narrow aperture seemed to be on the horizon as leaders of the nine major Islamic organizations in Italy met with the country's interior minister to discuss the possibility of charting a pathway for Islam's official recognition. As is often the case, the promise to consider the possibility of an official recognition came with some heavy trade-offs. Indeed, Italian Muslim leaders agreed to create a registry of the imams in the country, who are also obligated to give sermons only in Italian.[3] The conspicuous double-standard at the heart of this agreement, known as the "National Pact for an Italian Islam," invokes an articulation of Islam as a threatening and perilous religion, whose Otherness is lessened by the adoption of standard linguistic codes. Indeed, while numerous Catholic churches in Italy offer masses in a variety of languages to cater to increasingly diversified congregations, mosques are asked to reverse this process by adopting solely Italian as the language that mediates between the imam (and the institution he represents) and the believers. Despite being clearly singled out with this agreement, most Muslim leaders agree that this is small price to pay in a country that still has overwhelming reservations towards Muslims: indeed, according to a recent Pew survey, 69% of Italians hold unfavorable views of Muslims and Islam, the second highest percentage in Europe, after Hungary.[4]

In many European countries, the uncertainty and cultural fluidity

1. Centro Studi sulle Nuove Religioni 2014.
2. Momigliano 2017.
3. Momigliano 2017.
4. Wike, Stokes, and Simmons 2016.

accelerated by migratory flows and anglophile attitudes have resulted in increased quotidian encounters with the Other and the weakening of the ideological and metaphorical margins of the nation-state.[5] What Appadurai calls a civilization of clashes (in opposition to the infamous clash of civilizations proposed by Huntington) thrives on principles of exclusivity and inevitable superiority resulting in local and/or regional confrontations, where the Muslim Other figures as an unwanted imposer unable (and unwilling) to assimilate. As Ottavia Schmidt di Friedberg noted in the Italian context,

> After September 11, graffiti against Islam and Muslims in Italian cities have replaced those on politics or soccer. In bookshops the translation of Huntington's work on the clash of civilisations is sold out, while studies on the Arab world are selling well. Classics on Islam are dug out and transferred from the highest bookshelves to the window displays, while studies quickly thrown together are popping out everywhere. In bars and on TV exotic words like "jihad" and "mullah" have become common language.[6]

The antagonistic approach to Islam in the Italian public discourse has, for years, fostered a Manichean approach privileging inflexibility and Orientalism and emphasizing cultural differences. In the first decade of the new century, two emblematic events in Italian cultural life shaped the discourse on Islam in mainstream media. The first was the publication of Oriana Fallaci's *La rabbia e l'orgoglio* (*The Rage and the Pride*, 2002), a book written as a response to the 9/11 events by one of Italy's most influential writers and journalists.[7] In her controversial writing, Fallaci relied on her experience as Middle East correspondent to proclaim Islam as a fossilized enemy of the West, "an ahistorical, indifferentiated monad, without distinctions or internal tensions worthy of analysis."[8] Cautioning readers against the spread of Islam, Fallaci rails vociferously against this imminent threat to democracy:

> You don't understand or you don't want to understand that, if we don't oppose it, if we don't defend ourselves, if we don't fight, Jihad will win. It will destroy the world that, in one way or another, we've been able to build, to change, to improve, to render more intelligent,

5. Appadurai 2006; Ardizzoni 2013.

6. Schmidt di Friedberg, n.d.

7. Oriana Fallaci was an Italian journalist and author, who became famous worldwide for her important interviews with many political leaders, from Indira Ghandi, Golda Meir, and Yasser Arafat to Henry Kissinger and Iran's Shah.

8. Cousin and Vitale 2016, 48.

that is less sanctimonious or not sanctimonious at all. And it will destroy our culture, our art, our science, our morals, our values, our pleasures.... Don't you realize that the many Osama bin Ladens feel they have a right to kill you and your children because you drink wine or beer, because you don't wear a chador or sport a beard, because you go to the theater or the movies, because you listen to music and sing folk songs, because you dance in clubs or in your own house, because you watch television, because you wear mini-skirts or shorts, because you are naked or semi-naked when you go to the beach or the swimming pool?[9]

Despite the forceful criticisms directed at Fallaci's offensive generalizations, her position was widely publicized in mainstream media as Fallaci became the legitimate expert on Islamic culture in the post-9/11 culture of fear.[10]

The second mediatic event that marked public discourse on Islam in Italy in the new millennium was the conversion to Catholicism of one of Italy's best-known Muslim intellectuals and journalists, Magdi (Cristiano) Allam. Born in Egypt in a Muslim family, Allam was baptized by Pope Benedict XVI on Easter day 2008 as he denounced Islam for its violence, intolerance, and close-mindedness. Allam's conversion was the subject of many headlines in Italy and across the world because of his extremist position and his former role as Middle East correspondent for several national newspapers. In 2013 Allam left the Catholic Church because of its recognition of Islam as a religion that must be respected. As Allam stated, his conversion to Catholicism ceased because of "its legitimation of Islam as a true religion, of Allah as true God, of Mohammed as true prophet, of the Quran as a sacred text, of mosques as places of worship. Instead," he continues, "I believe that Islam is an intrinsically violent ideology ... and that Europe will end up being subjugated to Islam."[11] Allam's words are particularly resonant in the Italian context precisely because of his background and his presumed expertise on the Muslim world.[12]

More recent headlines insist on highlighting Islam's otherness and its innate propensity for violence, as exemplified by the following 2017 titles: "Islam in Italia: la paura della convivenza" (Islam in Italy: fear to coexist), "Islam in Veneto: sposa-bambina di 9 anni violentata dal marito" (Islam in the region of Veneto: 9-year-old child-bride raped by her husband), "Islam, orrore nel Pavese: l'ex-marito perseguita la moglie" (Islam,

9. Fallaci 2001; my translation.
10. Allievi 2004.
11. Anonymous 2013.
12. For more on the practice of neo-orientalism in today's US culture, see Bayoumi 2015.

horror in the Pavia area: ex-husband stalks his wife), "Migranti e Islam, l'apocalisse dell'Italia" (Migrants and Islam, the Italian apocalypse). The tone remains somber when covering Islam, and the emphasis on crime and utter incompatibility bespeaks Appadurai's anxiety of incompleteness, the core of the relationships between the majority (Catholic, white) and the Muslim minority.[13] Here, the social uncertainty and identitarian ideology precipitated by increased mobility and globalization reveal a latent angst about multiculturalism and diversity, particularly when these are embodied by physical and religious traits.

CONTEMPORARY MAINSTREAM COMEDIES

Elsewhere I have analyzed the representation of the Muslim Other in Italian drama, by focusing on productions that attempted to complicate the relationship between Italians and Muslim migrants.[14] These dramatic films, while not flawless, constitute a felicitous attempt to offer a somewhat nuanced depiction of diversity and thereby to mainstream Otherness as an increasingly acceptable form of Italianness. Yet, these films could also be considered part of a niche market that eschews the large appeal of blockbusters and does not reach a large number of viewers. Hence, despite their artistic and intellectual value, one could argue that the complex representation of Islam in these recent dramas is tailored to cultured audiences and rarely challenges the common public discourse on Islam. It is therefore important to address also those cinematic productions (mostly comedies) aimed at mainstream audiences and screened throughout the country in multiplex theaters and later television broadcasts. Indeed, the five comedies I analyze in this chapter were distributed in all the major cities, earning a total of over 20 million euros (approximately $25 million) in their opening weekends. Regardless of their debatable artistic value, these films cannot be easily dismissed in studies on contemporary Italian cinema because they contribute to a myopic discourse on Islam that is reflected also in the news media. A brief summary of the plots is necessary before delving into the analysis of the tropes embraced in the films.

The protagonists of *Lezioni di cioccolato* (*Chocolate Lessons*, Claudio Cupellini, 2007) are Mattia, a young Italian contractor, and his older, Egyptian illegal worker, Kamal. When Kamal is injured at work and ends up in a cast, to cover up the incident and help him fulfill his dream, Mattia takes his place in an advanced chocolate-making competition. Mattia tries hard to pass as Kamal in the chocolate-making class by accentuating Egyptian features,

13. Appadurai 2006.
14. Ardizzoni 2013.

such as clothing, accent, and behavior. The sequel to the film was released four years later with *Lezioni di cioccolato 2* (*Chocolate Lessons 2*, Alessio Maria Federici, 2011), where Mattia and Kamal become once again partners to escape the pervasive economic recession. A twist is added to the plot as Mattia falls in love with Kamal's beautiful daughter, Nawal.

Che bella giornata (*What a Beautiful Day*, 2011), directed by Gennaro Nunziante, is the second highest-grossing film in the history of Italian cinema with over 43 million euros earned at the box office.[15] The narrative centers on Checco, an ignorant, incompetent security guard who lands a job at Milan's Duomo cathedral only thanks to his uncle's recommendation. Checco falls in love with Farah, a young Maghrebi woman, who pretends to be an architecture student to gain access to the cathedral and uses their relationship to plant a bomb atop the Duomo to avenge her parents' death in the Gulf War. Farah is torn between her plan to destroy the cathedral and the kindness shown to her by Checco and his family. At the end, the latter will prevail.

2015's *Pitza e datteri* (*Pizza and Dates*, Fariborz Kamkari) tells the story of a small Muslim community in Venice as they navigate their integration into mainstream Italian society. The group figures a handful of different characters (the newly arrived Afghani imam Saladino, the Italian convert Bepi, the rebellious women Zara and Fatima) and displays an eclectic range of reactions to Italian traditional customs – from complete assimilation to total rejection. The plot revolves around the group as they look for a new location for their weekly prayer service and debate their position as Muslims in Italian society. As the only film among the ones analyzed here with a non-Italian director,[16] *Pizza and Dates* is slightly less simplistic in its depiction of Islam.

The most recent film, *Non c'è più religione* (*There's No More Religion*, Luca Miniero, 2016), is set in a small southern island, where two communities – the Catholics and the Muslims – come together to organize the traditional Christmas nativity scene. The forced cooperation between the two groups originates in the Italians' low birth rate and the need to replace a Christian child with a Muslim baby Jesus. Cecco, the local mayor, asks his longtime friend Marietto, who converted to Islam, if he can lend them his soon-to-be born son for the island's nativity performance.

RELENTLESS MUSLIM MASCULINITY

In these recent comedies, Muslim characters follow a trite pattern of gender differentiation that, in most cases, juxtaposes the exoticized Muslim woman

15. The highest-grossing film is James Cameron's *Avatar* (2009) with 65 million euros. *What a Beautiful Day* overtook one of Italy's most successful films in the national and international markets, Roberto Benigni's *La vita è bella* (*Life Is Beautiful*, 1997).

16. *Pizza and Dates* was directed by Kurdish-Iranian Fariborz Kamkari

to her unintegrated male counterpart. This characterization becomes particularly ossified in national blockbusters such as *What a Beautiful Day*, whose crude and politically incorrect humor provides the apt framework to sustain the stereotyped representation. In Nunziante's film, the Muslim male characters feature typically Mediterranean looks, an ominous gaze, and seemingly suspicious behaviors. The three Muslim men, all played by second-generation Italian actors (Mehdi Mehdloo, Matteo Reza Azchirvani, Hossein Taheri), speak with a vague, French-North-African accent and address Italians with short, truncated sentences, displaying an inability and unwillingness to interact beyond the necessary pleasantries. Among themselves Sufien and his two sidekicks speak in a whisper, thereby highlighting the secretive (and inherently dangerous) nature of their conversations. Yet, their determination to avenge the death of Sufien's and Farah's parents at the hands of the West is easily tested when the protagonist's father invites them to dinner. Eating mussels and other Italian delicacies proves to be a successful strategy to divert their initial plans. Here, their religiosity becomes fickle and gives in to the ostensibly superior joie de vivre of the locals. In these narratives, Islam entails a lifestyle of constrictions and deprivations, which can be conveniently neglected when one is faced with the titillating choices of *la dolce vita*. Hence, Islam is perceived more as an ideology than one of the monotheistic religions, its very existence made fun of by the film's main Italian character. Checco Zalone, the character impersonated by the homonymous actor, is a maladroit forty-something, whose humor derives from his blatant ignorance and callowness. Hence, upon meeting the wannabe terrorists and unaware of their origins, he asks them, "Do you live in Islam?" and quickly adds, "I live in Cattolica." Here Zalone plays on the double meaning of "Cattolica" as both "Catholic" and a town in Northern Italy. *What a Beautiful Day* brims with jokes of this nature, highly localized and boldly neglectful of cultural differences. The nauseating repetition of these gags reiterates the Us vs. Them logic the Italian public is exposed to on a daily basis in headlines and talk shows. The visual representation of Islam as inherently Other is reiterated in *There's No More Religion*, whose Muslim community partakes in a lifestyle demanding traditional clothing, regardless of one's ideological position. Hence, both Ali (played by Italian Mehdi Meskar), an open-minded youth who develops a relationship with the Buddhist daughter of the town's mayor, and the Italian convert Bilal (played by Italian star actor Alessandro Gassman) wear a small cap (*taqiyah*) and a kaftan, as do all the other male members of the community. Indeed, in many interactions with the Catholic coterie dress becomes the only sign of difference and the only clue for viewers to identify membership in one side or the other. When the emphasis on alterity cannot be underlined by evident physical traits, recent Italian comedies recur to well-known accoutrements as unmistakable identifiers. Indeed, with the exception of few Italian converts – loose cannons experimenting with religion – Islam is never portrayed as a legitimate thread of the contemporary Italian fabric. Rather, it has been imported by immigrants, who embrace it either to destroy Western symbols (as in the case of the plotted attack on Milan's cathedral in *What a Beautiful Day*) or to follow family traditions with superficial obsequiousness. For instance, Kamal, the cunning and resolute Egyptian chocolatier in *Chocolate Lessons*, displays a certain degree of flexibility towards his religion and defies orthodoxy when circumstances drive him to: he hides a bottle of wine under his favorite chair and, when he is caught eating pork, he says nonchalantly, "Oh, I was convinced that was beef." What seems problematic in such characterization is not the depiction of Muslims as unwilling to follow the pillars of Islam or questioning blind spirituality. Indeed, these characters are not endowed with such nuances. Rather, the flatness of these characters and their scarcity in Italian cinema reflect the stereotypical view of Islam as incompatible with Italian mores and, ultimately, inferior. Italy and Italian practices shine a brighter light in these narratives and cannot be resisted. The only route to integration is assimilation and the consequent disavowal of previously held beliefs.

This is the situation facing Saladino, the young imam in *Pizza and Dates*. Played by Meskar, the same actor in *There's No More Religion*, at the beginning of the film Saladino has just arrived from Afghanistan, where he grew up as an orphan in an Italian hospital. His first encounters with the Venetian society bare his orthodox views and are thus laughing cues for the audience: he covers his eyes when a waitress serves him pizza or a scantily dressed woman walks by, he tries to convince the other Muslims that women's stoning is the only way to secure the space now occupied by the hair salon, and defies local customs by chanting the call to prayer from atop a crane. Despite the film's otherwise more layered portrayal of Muslim identities, the young imam comes through as extremist and inexperienced, an inept leader for the multi-ethnic Muslim community, who soon realize his limitations.

As mentioned above, *Pizza and Dates* is the only film among the ones analyzed here that attempts to address the possible coexistence between Muslims and non-Muslims in Italy. Director Kamkari accentuates this attention to multiculturalism by setting the story in Venice, a cosmopolitan city with a rich cultural history, and entrusting the Orchestra di Piazza Vittorio,[17] a well-known multi-ethnic ensemble, with the original soundtrack. As Kamkari

17. The Orchestra di Piazza Vittorio, created in Rome in 2002, fuses various musical traditions and thrives on its own composite nature. Indeed, the group includes members from Argentina, Brazil, Cuba, Ecuador, Hungary, India, Italy, Senegal, Tunisia, and the US.

asserts, "with its music the Orchestra di Piazza Vittorio perfectly embodies the union between East and West and it is evidence of how frontiers can be when they are crossed by human talent" ("Pitza e Datteri, esce la colonna sonora," n.d.).

MUSLIM WOMEN'S EXOTIC APPEAL

In these comedies the Arab Muslim woman is cast as the ploy for the development of the Italian protagonist and their inevitable, ensuing relationship. With the exception of *Pizza and Dates*, the films center on a sensual, attractive young woman of North-African origins whose physical difference is visible enough to be exoticized, yet not too conspicuous to inhibit romance. In the three largest-grossing films I discuss here (*There's No More Religion, What a Beautiful Day,* and *Chocolate Lessons 2*), the Muslim woman is portrayed by the same Franco-Tunisian actress, Nabiha Akkari. Dark hair, brown eyes, and olive skin, Akkari's looks are traditionally Mediterranean and easily translatable into a variety of national origins. Yet, her looks fall outside the stereotypical standards of Italian beauty and, for this reason, have attracted Italian casting directors looking for a "Muslim-looking" actress. In *What a Beautiful Day* Akkari was selected after many days of casting, during which many (first- or second-generation) Italian women auditioned for the part and were immediately dismissed for being too Italian. Akkari, on the other hand, got the role thanks to her foreign accent, which positioned her outside the realm of Italianness, and thus more plausible as a Muslim character.

As seen in the case of the Muslim men, in Nunziante's film humor is used frequently to underscore Farah's Otherness. For instance, when Farah brings her couscous dish to a picnic, Checco mistakes this for animal food and ignorantly uses it to feed the ducks, much to the audience's and Farah's hilarity.[18] Similarly, Checco's family caution him against her in several scenes. His father, for instance, reiterates, "The problem is that they are Arabs. They are different from us. They are weird." When Farah falls sick with a high fever and subconsciously speaks Arabic, Checco's mother appears alarmed by a language she inherently associates with peril and enigma. "She [Farah] sounded crazy," she confides to her son. These utterances, interspersed throughout the narrative, are problematic on different fronts. On the one hand, they incessantly characterize Arab and Muslim culture as so utterly

18. This scene clearly bypasses the popularity of couscous in some parts of Italy, such as Sicily, where a history of Arab colonialism has resulted in typical North African food staples being assimilated into the local cuisine (as in the case of the traditional Sicilian couscous dish).

different that one cannot but joke about it. Its sounds are puzzling to Italian ears, and its flavors cannot compare to Italian cuisine. On the other hand, at the level of the narrative, Farah's relationship with Checco relies purely on physical attraction. Given their clashing cultural backgrounds, Checco's interest is sustained exclusively by Farah's voluptuousness: it is thus the Muslim female body, object of many Orientalist tales, that entices the naïve protagonist. The objectifying sexism behind this story line is inscribed in Checco's overall treatment of women, whom he judges based on their breast size, with unapologetic nonchalance and a certain sense of entitlement.

In *Chocolate Lessons 2*, Akkari plays Nawal, the chocolatier's daughter, who has recently returned to Italy after studying abroad in France. Nawal, a new character who did not exist in the prequel, is introduced in the opening credits: the atmosphere is jolly and upbeat as Nawal says goodbye to a friend and walks confidently down a busy urban street on her way to the bus station. She wears make-up and a stretchy, colorful mini-dress, which falls on the side, baring her shoulder. Her curly, thick hair bounces along the vivacious soundtrack. As she makes her way to the bus and later arrives in her family's hometown, Nawal is transformed into a more modest woman: the dress is pulled down to cover her knees, her shoulders are covered by a pastel-colored cardigan, the lipstick has been wiped off, and her hair is tightly pulled into a bun and covered with a foulard. From the very beginning, Nawal is shown straddling two cultures and adapting adroitly to her role in each. When the Italian protagonist Mattia falls in love with Nawal (who uses a fake name with him), he is unaware of her family ties and asks Kamal advice on how to conquer a Muslim woman. Once again, albeit in much softer tones than *What a Beautiful Day*, the Muslim woman is different from her Italian counterparts and must be dealt with as such: no longer an individual, she belongs to a cultural cluster aggregated by common characteristics, to which Mattia, as an outsider, is not privy. In this narrative, it is the father, unbeknownst to him and against his parenting goals, who fans the fire of their relationship by subjecting his daughter to the stereotyped expectations of the Italian man.

In *There's No More Religion* Akkari is, one more time, a Muslim woman in a relationship with the Italian protagonist. Here, she portrays Aida, the beautiful Tunisian woman for whom Marietto (now Bilal) converts to Islam. Like all the Muslim women of the island, she wears a traditional loose outer robe (*djellaba*) in every scene, changing only the color and the amount of jewelry to go with it. Aida is visibly younger and more attractive than her Italian husband, as the camera emphasizes with frequent close-up shots.

Her inherently mysterious nature is actualized when she blows up the star atop the nativity's manger by simply looking at it. In this scene, her aesthetic rejection of the star is sufficient to send it into flames and alert the nearby Catholics of her powers. More than a simple comedic twist, this story line reinforces widespread notions of Islamic culture as inscrutable and inexplicably tied to some form of violence, whether this will indeed come into being or not.

A slightly subtler portrayal of Muslim womanhood is presented in Kamkari's film *Pizza and Dates*, which foregrounds more speaking roles for Muslim women. The main female character is Zara, a Maghrebi hairdresser, who is fiercely occupying the space that used to accommodate the local mosque. The movie opens with the camera zooming in on Zara as she gets dolled up to sing alone in her empty salon: on the notes of an original tango, close-up shots of her cigarette, her brightly red lipstick, her shiny earrings, and her alluring outfit signal Zara's subversive nature in her otherwise traditional community. True to Italian and Mediterranean cultures in general, her parlor becomes the meeting point for a handful of local Muslim women, who converge at Zara's to share their secrets, discuss their position in the Muslim community, and gossip about their partners or spouses. The small, effervescent space holds a microcosm of Muslim identities and offers the viewer a peephole into the heterogeneity of this community. Cesarina, the blond Venetian woman married to a Senegalese, entertains the group with her brash jokes on sex. Mina is a rebellious teenager born in Italy from an Egyptian family; she dons revealing outfits, which enrage her father, and is equally fluent in standard Italian and the Venetian dialect. Miriam, Mina's mother, is fairly conservative, but well integrated into Italian society, and has mastered the local cuisine. Lastly, native speaker Fatima is veiled and a staunch supporter of equal rights for men and women in Islam. When Saladino, the inexperienced imam, attempts to spread his extremist views on Islamic orthodoxy, it is well-educated Fatima who stands up to him, inveighing, "Stop preaching violence.... I know God's orders very well, I follow and practice them every day. What you preach are your tribe's rules! Men take advantage of your own rules to subjugate their wives and daughters even more ... and with your benediction!" This interaction takes place in the hair salon, this symbolic feminine space where Saladino is an outcast and is soon chased off by all the other women. In this sense, the independent comedy *Pizza and Dates* succeeds in part in rectifying the monochromatic representation of Muslim womanhood illustrated in the other films. Unfortunately, but unsurprisingly, *Pizza and Dates* is also the lowest-grossing film among the five I analyze here.

THE ITALIAN CONVERTS AS (OPPORTUNISTIC) COMMUNITY LEADERS

The last trope used to depict Islam in Italy centers on the Italian convert. Two films (*There's No More Religion* and *Pizza and Dates*), otherwise quite different in their approach to Muslim communities, focus on the bromidic convert as the main narrative ploy. As mentioned above, Marietto-turned-Bilal converted to Islam in his attempt to attract and later marry Tunisian Aida. Since his conversion, he has become the leader of the Muslim community in the small southern island, despite his superficial understanding of Islam. Indeed, his conversion highlights mostly external symbols of religiosity, such as dress code and food limitations, the latter being a constant, comedic point of contention with his Italian, traditional mother. In Kamkari's film, instead, Bepi converted to Islam as a personal way to express his hatred towards the "infidel capitalists": indeed, Bepi finds refuge in an extremist form of Islam as he tries to evade the confiscation of his inherited building. Bepi's interpretation of Islam is conservative and inflexible and, as such, welcomes the initially uncompromising nature of the new imam. In fact, when the imam's position softens, warming up to Italian customs and the possibility of finding a new space for the mosque, Bepi locks himself in the hair salon and attempts to blow himself up. In these comedies, the Italian converts are played by well-established Italian actors (Alessandro Gassman and Giuseppe Battiston), thereby asserting their central role in the narratives. The characters are consistently framed as fickle and opportunistic, and Islam becomes for them an experimental route to achieve personal goals. The superficial elements of their faith take center stage over Islamic spiritual principles and position these characters in a chronic battle between cultures. Indeed, in the case of Bepi in *Pizza and Dates*, his faithfulness to Islam (and his consequent rejection of capitalism) correlate with his radicalism. In both instances, the Italian converts display a degree of religious expertise far superior to their non-Italian counterparts'. Despite their relative ignorance, the Italian converts become the leaders of their respective communities and, as such, uphold the pillars of Islam for their fellow Muslims.[19]

Recent Italian comedies derive their comedic edge from an emphasis on Muslims' utter Otherness and their mostly ineluctable alienation from Italian society. Their speech is accented even when the actors are native Italian speakers. Their exotic clothing – veils, *djellabas*, kaftans – sets them apart from the Western, Christian lifestyle. Their food options are seen as

---

19. For more on the trope of conversion see: Demerdash-Fatemi's chapter in this volume.

prohibitive and a little bizarre. In general, the outward accoutrements of the kind of Islam highlighted in these productions exacerbate difference instead of similarity: the shared Mediterranean basin becomes, in these fictions, a site of divisions, an insurmountable rhetorical and ideological chasm that mainstream storytelling refuses to bridge. The joined destinies of northern and southern Mediterranean cultures are beclouded by Islam's dark shadow, which makes honest, selfless relationships unattainable. As seen in this analysis, the very existence of a Muslim community, with its quirky characters, is doomed to create problems, arouse suspicion, and engender controversies. The reality of a sizeable community of second-generation Italians of Muslim origins is completely silenced here in favor of a more palatable depiction of Muslims as immigrants and foreigners.[20] Hence, their cluelessness about Italian customs and their naïveté on Western social norms give audiences a reason to laugh at them and their incessant alterity. The purely entertaining goal of these comedies does not preclude their problematicity, because they are re-inscribed in a socio-cultural, mediatic context that embraces Muslims as Others. In its contemporary form, mainstream Italian comedy misses an urgent opportunity to reverse the blatant reductionism of news headlines and the blaring consignment of Muslims as eternal, unbridgeable outcasts.

WORKS CITED

Allievi, S. 2002. "Muslims in Italy." In *New European Identity and Citizenship*, edited by R. Leveau, K. Mohsen-Finan, C. Wihtol de Wenden, 37–49. Aldershot.

———. 2004. *Ragioni senza forza, forze senza ragione* (Reasons without Force. Force without Reason). Bologna.

Anonymous. "Pitza e Datteri, esce la colonna sonora." (Pizza and Dates: The Soundtrack is Out). *Movieplayer*. https://movieplayer.it/news/pitza-e-datteri-esce-la-colonna-sonora_35297/

Anonymous. 2013. "Magdi Allam: 'La mia conversione al cattolicesimo è conclusa' (Magdi Allam: My Conversion to Catholicism Is Over)." *Huffington Post*, March 25. https://www.huffingtonpost.it/2013/03/25/magdi-allam--la-mia-conversione-cattolicesimo-conclusa_n_2947196.html

Appadurai, A. 2006. *Fear of Small Numbers: An Essay on the Geography of Anger*. Durham.

20. For more on Muslims in Italy see Roggero 2002; Spena 2010; Allievi 2002; Coppi and Spreafico 2008; Mezran, 2013; Toronto 2008.

Ardizzoni, M. 2013. "Nuove narrative sull'Altro: Arabi e musulmani nel cinema italiano contemporaneo (New Narratives on the Other: Arabs and Muslims in Contemporary Italian Cinema)." In *Un nuovo cinema politico italiano?*, edited by W. Hope, L. D'Arcangeli, and S. Serra, 152–62. Leicester.

Bayoumi, M. 2015. *This Muslim American Life: Dispatches from the War on Terror*. New York.

Centro Studi sulle Nuove Religioni (Center for Studies on New Religions) (CESNUR). 2014. "L'Islam e i movimenti di matrice islamica in Italia (Islam and Muslim Movements in Italy). https://cesnur.com/lislam-e-i-movimenti-di-matrice-islamica-in-italia/

Coppi, A. and A. Spreafico. 2008. "The Long Path from Recognition to Representation of Muslims in Italy." *The International Spectator*, 43 (3): 101–115.

Cousin, B. and T. Vitale. 2016. "Italian Intellectuals and the Promotion of Islamophobia after 9/11." In *Global Islamophobia: Muslims and Moral Panic in the West*, edited by G. Morgan, 47–65. New York.

Cupellini, C. 2007. *Lezioni di cioccolato* (Chocolate Lessons).

Fallaci, O. 2001. *La rabbia e l'orgoglio* (Rage and Pride).

Federici, A. M. 2011. *Lezioni di cioccolato 2* (Chocolate Lessons 2).

Kamkari, F. 2015. *Pitza e datteri* (Pizza and Dates).

Mezran, K. 2013. "Muslims in Italy: The Need for an 'Intesa' with the Italian State." *The International Spectator*, 48.1:58–71.

Miniero, L. 2016. *Non c'è più religione* (There's No More Religion). Cattleya.

Momigliano, A. 2017. "In Italy, Islam Doesn't Officially Exist. Here's What Muslims Must Accept to Change That." *Washington Post*, February 8. https://www.washingtonpost.com/news/worldviews/wp/2017/02/08/in-italy-islam-doesnt-officially-exist-heres-what-muslims-must-accept-to-change-that/

Nunziante, G. 2011. *Che bella giornata* (What a Beautiful Day). Medusa Distribuzione.

Roggero, M. A. 2002. "Muslims in Italy." In *Muslims in the West. From Sojourners to Citizens*, edited by Y. Yazbeck Haddad, 131–43. Oxford.

Schmidt di Friedberg, O. "Building the Enemy: Islamophobia in Italy." http://inhouse.lau.edu.lb/bima/papers/Ottavia.pdf

Spena, M. R. U. 2010. "Muslims in Italy: Models of Integration and New Citizenship." In *Muslims in 21st Century Europe: Structural and Cultural Perspectives*, edited by Anna Triandafyllidou, 170–90. New York.

Toronto, J. A. 2008. "Islam Italiano: Prospects for Integration of Muslims in Italy's Religious Landscape." *Journal of Muslim Minority Affairs*, 28.1:61–82.

Wike, R., B. Stokes, and K. Simmons. 2016. "Negative Views of Minorities, Refugees Common in EU." *Pew Research Center*, July 11. http://www.pewglobal.org/2016/07/11/negative-views-of-minorities-refugees-common-in-eu/

Strong Girls and Lost Boys?
Growing up Muslim in Nordic Films

Sofia Sjö

INTRODUCTION

In spring 2017, the fourth season of the Norwegian online-series *Skam* (*Shame*, Julie Andem) premiered. The series, produced by the Norwegian public broadcasting company, NRK, is about a group of high school students in Oslo. *Shame* has been immensely popular in Norway and abroad. Each season of *Shame* follows one character. In season four, the focus was finally on a character many fans had long wanted to get to know better, Sana – a devout young Muslim woman. From the very beginning of the series, Sana is represented as strong, loyal and creative, but also as a character who has to face prejudice and who struggles with how to be a devout Muslim and have secular Norwegian friends. Sana inspired a great deal of both public[1] and academic[2] discussion concerning Muslims in popular culture, and religion and ethnicity in popular culture more broadly.

Though I would argue that Sana is in many ways a noteworthy character, she is also only one in a line of fictional representations of young Muslims in Nordic popular culture. Particularly in film, and particularly since the turn of the millennium, Muslim characters have become more common, especially in Danish, Norwegian, and Swedish productions.[3] Predominantly the films focus on characters with a migrant background, a theme highlighted as key to many films of late, not just in the Nordic countries.[4] These films can be seen as a natural outcome of the fact that the Nordic countries are becoming more ethnically and religiously diverse. As Mette Hjort has argued regarding Danish film, the process has been slow and it took quite some time before a cultural interest for these stories came about. However, Hjort describes a noticeable ethnic turn, which started with ethnic Danish filmmakers making films about immigrants and has now led to filmmakers with a migrant background taking executive control and making films relating to their own

1. Andulkarim 2017.
2. Moffat and Kääpä 2018.
3. Sjö and Daníelsson 2013, 53–56.
4. Berghahn and Sternberg 2010.

experiences.[5] Similar turns have been identified in both Norwegian[6] and Swedish[7] film and in Finnish film, too, some changes are noticeable.[8]

A number of concepts have been presented to capture the identified new focus on multiple belongings and complex identities in Nordic and other cinemas that is connected to the ethnic turn and aspects of migration. Hamid Naficy talks about an accented cinema, a cinema he connects to exilic, diasporic, and postcolonial ethnic and identity filmmakers. Naficy argues that these filmmakers, through their experiences and perspectives, provide different stories and different ways of making films – in other words, accented films.[9] Naficy's work is discussed in studies of Nordic films about migrants, but it is often argued that filmmakers in the Nordic countries have stuck closer to traditional genre motifs than the filmmakers Naficy explores.[10] Still, their films do provide new perspectives, as will be highlighted in this chapter.

A lot of the research on migrants in film focuses on filmmakers with some form of immigrant background. Berghahn and Sternberg make a distinction between migrant filmmakers, who have themselves experienced migration, and diasporic filmmakers who are second or third generation immigrants, for whom migration still plays a central role. They underline that a filmmaker is not a migrant or diasporic filmmaker just because of his or her background; they also need to deal with issues relating to migration in their films.[11] The focus on migrant and diasporic filmmakers highlights that it matters who is allowed to tell whose stories. However, migrant and Muslims characters are of course not only to be found in films by migrant or diasporic directors.

The ethnic turn in Nordic films is clearly not only about Muslims, but the topic of growing up Muslim and the challenges this entails – and the focus is generally on the challenges – is a recurring topic in many films. In this chapter, I discuss one film directed by what Berghahn and Sternberg would define as a migrant filmmaker, Reza Bagher's *Vingar av glas* (*Wings of Glass*), made in Sweden in 2001, one film by a diasporic filmmaker, Ulrik Imtiaz Rolfsen's *Izzat*, made in Norway in 2005, and one film by a filmmaker with a Danish background, Natasha Arthy's *Fighter* made in 2007. I have wanted to be sure to capture varied views on the topic by including films by directors

5. Hjort 2005, 243.
6. Bakøy 2010.
7. Wright 2005.
8. Hiltunen 2016.
9. Naficy 2001.
10. Bakøy 2010, 149.
11. Berghahn and Sternberg 2010.

with different backgrounds. The films are primarily chosen because they capture many recurring themes in Nordic films about Muslims, but still the films also all present unique features.

In my analysis of *Wings of Glass, Izzat,* and *Fighter* I specifically focus on how Islam is brought into the films, how the characters relate to their religious background, and how their background not just as Muslims, but as migrants, or children of migrants, is presented. I particularly highlight aspects of the coming-of-age-theme, emphasizing both well-known features and less usual topics that the films present. In the final section of this chapter, I reflect on what understandings and possible misunderstandings the films provide, and what one can learn and what one might miss with stories of this kind.

FINDING ONE'S WAY – *WINGS OF GLASS*

Coming-of-age stories are quite common in films and tend to include certain themes. Though some have argued that there is a difference between Nordic coming-of-age films and the internationally more known American versions, similarities have also been highlighted.[12] Nordic filmmakers have often taken inspiration from American genre films, but added their own twists. Generally, coming-of-age films are about finding oneself and breaking free, or at least declaring a form of independence in relation to parents and other caregivers. As Moseng has highlighted in his study of Norwegian youth films, other recurring themes are marginalization, questions of sexuality and romance, and related issues of the body and gender.[13] Reza Bagher's *Wings of Glass* focuses on marginalization and coming to grips with who you are, but romance also plays a part.

The main character in *Wings of Glass* is Nazli, a young woman of Iranian decent, who grew up in Sweden and, in the beginning of the film, tries very hard to behave like her Swedish friends, even calling herself Sara instead of Nazli. From the first scene on though, Nazli's complicated situation becomes obvious. When she arrives at a job interview, the employers are expecting the very Swedish sounding Sara Lindström and Nazli admits to using a Swedish name to get the interview, since she does not believe that she would be interviewed if she used her real name. Nazli does not get the job and throughout the film, she struggles to find employment and thereby independence from her family.

The family is a second area of struggle for Nazli. She lives with her sister Mahin and their father Abbas, who is a widower. Abbas promised his late wife

12. Moseng 2011.
13. Moseng 2011.

to make sure that their daughters would marry well and he chooses partners for them. While Mahin happily obliges – Abbas chose for her a young man he knows she is in love with – Nazli refuses and shows no interest in Hamid, her cousin, who Abbas picked as her future husband. Nazli, however, willingly accepts a job in Hamid's store. Hamid tries to make Nazli see how good a husband he would be, mostly by bragging about his financial success, but their relationship comes to an abrupt end when Hamid tries to rape Nazli.

Nazli attempts to convince her father to cut the contact with Hamid, but since her father is financially dependent on him he takes Hamid's side. In protest, Nazli moves in with her Swedish boyfriend Johan, a boyfriend she has kept secret from her family. Nazli and Abbas are both very stubborn and unwilling to take the first step towards reconciliation. Though Abbas does come across as a dominant patriarch by trying to decide whom his daughters should marry, the picture becomes more complicated when one takes into consideration that Abbas does in fact fulfill both traditional male and female roles in the film. He is the one who is always cooking and taking care of the home and he genuinely seems to want his daughters to be happy, but without breaking with his views of what is correct behavior.

What is the role of Islam in this film? At the job interview in the beginning of the film, Nazli explains that she did not give her real name because people would then start thinking that she wears a veil. Already in this scene Islam or being a Muslim is indicated as a part of Nazli's identity, but a part she is not comfortable with. When Nazli tells her Swedish friend that Abbas wants Nazli to marry a cousin, the friend is shocked, calling the proposal incestuous. Nazli explains that it is not considered incest among Muslims, which again shocks her friend, who asks if Nazli is a Muslim, to which Nazli responds that she does not know what she is. Generally, Nazli's family does not come across as particularly religious. In a somewhat comic scene, Abbas takes out a religious wall decoration and dusts it off in preparation for the visit of Mahin's soon to be in-laws, who are devout Muslims. For the most part in the film, Islam is thus connected to a traditional life with marriage and children for young women and the family as central focus. Nazli is not comfortable with these ideals.

Though religion and traditional values connected to the family's roots in Iran are parts of Nazli's challenges and things she seems to want to break with, the final resolution of the film offers a more complex picture. When Johan declares Nazli's family to be strange, Nazli gets very upset. Soon after, she is shown watching a young girl in a chador rollerblading in the street. In the beginning of the film, she watched the same girl and, as Andrew

Nestingen has highlighted, this scene seems to entail a symbolic turn for Nazli.[14] In the next scene, she enters a driving school, introduces herself as Nazli and declares that she is Muslim, but also Swedish. The owner of the driving school, whose accent indicates that he is an immigrant from Finland, is not particularly interested in who Nazli is, but is willing to work out a deal with her, which means she will work in the office and get cheap driving lessons. This means she can fulfill her dream of getting a motorcycle driving license. In this scene then, Nazli seems to have decided to accept her Muslim background, but also a Swedish identity.

In *Wings of Glass*, Islam also becomes more than just rules and traditions that need to be followed through Abbas. When Abbas finally comes to visit Nazli in Johan's apartment, after having been encouraged by Johan, Abbas mentions that he has not been to the mosque since he came to Sweden. However, now he tells Nazli he has visited the mosque and prayed on his knees for the strength to come see Nazli. In this scene, Nazli and Abbas take time to listen to each other and try to understand each other. Johan's role in their reconciliation cannot be ignored, but this is not a case of the more balanced Swede helping the lost immigrants. Johan is in many ways just as lost as Nazli. He is an orphan who lives with the constant threat of being evicted since he cannot pay his rent. When Abbas finally accepts Johan as Nazli's boyfriend, he is provided with a family he seems to be in need of.

Though Nazli's story is to some extent unique, it does at the same time include several recurring features that can also be found in films such as Susan Taslimi's *Hus i helvete* (*All Hell Let Loose*), made in Sweden in 2002, Khalid Hussain's *Import-eksport* (*Import Export*), made in Norway in 2005, and Natasha Arthy's *Fighter*, which I will return to later. As Tigervall discusses in her thesis on migrants in Swedish films, the characters are often represented as "Other" and different, but many films at the same time present the migrant characters very sympathetically. The resolution in these films is often not a case of choosing one identity and leaving another, instead a compromise is reached. In addition, natives Swedes are often shown to have a great deal to learn from the migrant families and the independence ethnic Swedish characters represent is generally not shown to be an altogether positive thing, as it often leaves them lost and lonely, as is the case with Johan.[15] Recurrently though, male Muslim characters are represented rather unsympathetically and as a hindrance for the young Muslim women wanting to find themselves and their place in Scandinavian societies. While films focusing on young

14. Nestingen 2008, 139.
15. Tigervall 2005.

Muslim women include a hopeful view, suggesting a better future ahead, the same is generally not the case in films focusing on young Muslim men.

A VIOLENT WAY – *IZZAT*

Nordic noir, or crime fiction, is currently very popular both in the Nordic countries and internationally. We come across Muslim characters in these stories too. For the most part, Muslim characters play the roles of criminals or victims of crime. These characters are seldom given much of a background. However, in a number of gangster films and thrillers an emphasis is put on Muslim characters as part of criminal gangs. The main characters in these cases are often young Muslim men.[16] On the surface, one could argue that Nordic films offer the same stereotypes found in Hollywood films, where violence, masculinity, and Islam are often interconnected.[17] However, there are films that try to go beyond the clichés. I have previously discussed the violent crime drama *Gå med fred Jamil - Ma Salama Jamil* (*Go with Peace Jamil*), made in Denmark in 2008 by Omar Shargawi, and argued for the complex characters that hide behind the violent central narrative.[18] Here I focus on Ulrik Imtiaz Rolfsen's *Izzat*, a film that even more obviously focuses on the question of growing up Muslim and growing into violence.

Rolfsen has indicated that the story of *Izzat* is based on his experiences growing up in a migrant community in Oslo.[19] The main character in *Izzat* is Wasim, a second-generation immigrant whose parents moved to Norway from Pakistan. The story, told in voice-over by the grown-up Wasim, starts in 1982. Wasim and his brother are walking down the street together with their father, who Wasim tells the viewer knew every Pakistani in town, which meant walking down the street took forever. As with Nazli, Wasim's marginalized status is indicated from the beginning. This is not only done by underlining Wasim's migrant background, but also by early on show-ing how ethnic Norwegians bully Wasim. The school system does little to support Wasim. He is required to learn about Christianity and considered insolent when he asks the teacher how he is expected to know the sayings of Jesus.

From the very start Wasim is presented as an outsider; however, this does not mean that he is alone or unable to find a place for himself. Wasim has two good friends who are also of immigrant decent, Riaz and Munawar. The boys soon befriend the toughest Pakistani gang in town and quickly develop into to hardened criminals. As young men, they are three of the

16. Sjö 2015.
17. Ramji 2010.
18. Sjö 2013.
19. Larsen 2015, 173.

closest allies of the gang leader, Saddiq, and successful drug dealers. According to Wasim, they considered themselves kings, with money and power at their fingertips. This is, however, when it all changes.

Munawar has become tired of following Saddiq's orders. When he finds out that Saddiq's relative, Khalid, is courting his girlfriend, Munawar gets Khalid arrested. Khalid, who is not a legal resident in Norway, is deported and Saddiq decides to get his revenge. When they find Munawar, he is first severely beaten and Wasim is then forced to kill his friend. When Riaz decides to leave the country shortly after, Wasim is left on his own with problems that just seem to expand. Wasim tries to break with Saddiq and another drug dealer, Kula, by blackmailing them and thereby forcing them to leave him and his family alone. His plan backfires and Wasim's younger sister is kidnapped and raped. In the end, while trying to save his sister, Wasim shoots Kula and Saddiq and ends up in jail. In the final scene, the viewer finds out that he is telling his story to a representative of a review board that will discuss his parole.

Wasim does not come across as a devout Muslim, and in general his behavior upsets his religious parents. However, the viewer is told that Wasim drives his parents and sister to the mosque every week, though he does not seem to go there himself. Wasim is thus not represented as particularly interested in religion, yet he does seem to be a devoted son and brother, or at least he tries to be. In one of the few scenes where Islam is clearly connected to Wasim's life, it is presented as a form of punishment. When Wasim's father finds out that Wasim has not been to school for several weeks he sends Wasim to a Qurʾān school in Pakistan. Here Wasim is shown being beaten by his teacher when he cannot repeat lines from the Qurʾān. According to Wasim, he was sent to Pakistan to become more respectful, but all he felt was lonely and nagged at, just as in Norway. Back in Norway, Wasim quickly returns to his life of crime.

Islam and religion thus play a marginal role in *Izzat*, but from the very beginning the characters are identified not only as people with migrant backgrounds but also as Muslims. The story as a whole does not give a particularly cheerful image of what it is like growing up as a Muslim boy in Norway. Still, the film does, similarly to *Wings of Glass*, highlight the hybrid identity of the main characters, but also their delight in being Norwegian and something else. For Wasim being a Norwegian citizen has a very practical consequence. It means that he, if he is arrested, is not deported but gets to spend time in a Norwegian jail, which is according to him preferable to having to spend the rest of his life in Pakistan. Consequently, the scenes in the jail are filmed in a clean room with a soft yellow light and with Wasim looking well and ready to be a free man.

The Kung Fu Way – *Fighter*

The last film I want to discuss, *Fighter*, has similarities with both *Wings of Glass* and *Izzat*, blending narratives of violent young Muslim men, as seen in *Izzat*, with issues of navigating identity, as in *Wings of Glass*. The film has a somewhat un-original plotline, but explores issues of Muslims in a very un-common Nordic genre: a martial arts film. In *Fighter*, the struggle with growing up Muslim and having to deal with family expectations, strict gender norms, and threats of violence from men in your community is combined with the story of a young person falling in love with martial arts and developing into a talented kung fu fighter. What the film also underlines even more than *Wings of Glass* is the challenge of living as a Muslim woman among secular youth.

The main character in this film is Aicha, whose parents are from Turkey. As in the other films, her parents have very strict ideas about how their children should behave. Aicha's parents, similar to Nazli's and Wasim's parents, have sacrificed a great deal for their children and worked hard to provide for them, something they all let their children know. Aicha's parents expect her to study hard, and become a doctor, just like her brother Ali – who very clearly breaks with the recurring image of young Muslim men being violent criminals. They also expect her to marry a Muslim and emphasize that she cannot get involved with someone who is not a Muslim. Aicha is also expected to behave well so as not to risk anything going wrong with her brother's engagement to Yasemin, a woman he is secretly dating. What Aicha wants is of little interest to anyone, but it is her dreams that the film is about.

When the film starts, Aicha trains in a martial arts group for women, but does not get along with the other girls. Her trainer encourages her to find a different team because she thinks Aicha has potential to become a talented kung fu fighter. The problem is that the new team is a mixed group with women and men training together, something Aicha's father does not accept. Aicha starts training with the team in secret and is befriended by the top fighter Emil. Emil is clearly infatuated with Aicha, but Aicha is reluctant to get involved with him, knowing her family would never accept their relationship.

Training kung fu and hanging out with a native Danish man are not the only secrets Aicha keeps from her family. She also hides the fact that she is failing school. Things get more difficult when Omar, a friend of Yasemin's brother Mehmet, joins Aicha's training group. Omar refuses to fight women and is consequently thrown out of the team. He tells on Aicha at her brother's engagement party, which results in a fight between Aicha and Omar and Aicha's brother's engagement being broken off. Aicha's brother is distraught, and things get worse when it transpires that his ex-bride-to-be is pregnant. Yasemin's brother and his friends, except Omar, go looking for Ali. Aicha is warned by Yasemin and saves Ali, thanks to her kung fu skills. No one is grateful though, but Ali does take Aicha's advice, to go apologize to Yasemin's parents. Apologizing is something Aicha has done throughout the film.

Fighter does not have as clear a resolution as *Wings of Glass*, but here too a way forward is suggested. The film ends with Aicha taking part in a tournament, where she wins over Emil and loses to Omar, a result everyone seems happy with. After the competition, she suggests to Emil that they should take it slow, which he accepts. Aicha then speaks to her father and hopes that he someday will be able to forgive her and be proud of her. She will not become a doctor, but she is determined to become something, though she does not yet know what. Aicha's father does not reply, but takes her hand, indicating that he cares for his daughter.

Similar to Nazli, identifying as a Muslim or being identified as a Muslim is an issue for Aicha. Early in the film when Emil asks, "So you're a Muslim from a Muslim country?" Aicha sarcastically answers, "Yes. So I'm a Muslim from a Muslim country. And you're a Christian from a Christian country, or what?", suggesting she does not like the generalization Emil is making. Emil apologizes and tries to explain that he does not know many Muslims and therefore does not know how to talk to her, to which Aicha replies that he should talk to her as if she was not a Muslim. However, that Aicha is not like other girls becomes clear in scene after scene. She is uncomfortable with getting physically close to Emil, either in training or in other situations. When it becomes clear that Emil is interested in being more than friends Aicha tells him that they can never date and never marry, to which Emil responds with a surprised laugh since marriage is nothing he, as a young Danish man, is thinking about. When Aicha's friends ask Aicha if she is sleeping with Emil, Aicha responds that they are not dating. They reply, "What does that have to do with anything?" For her friends having sex, drinking, and partying is a natural part of being young, but not for Aicha.

Fighter and *Wings of Glass* both show that there are many expectations of Muslim women, especially around sexuality, because of familial relationships and attitudes. Aicha is very hesitant to get in a situation where sexual desires might be encouraged and coy with her friends about sex. Similarly, Nazli tries very much to behave like her ethnic Swedish friends but is reluctant to sleep with her boyfriend, and is not shown doing so in the film. The severe reaction to Yasemin's pregnancy also underlines this theme. Sex before marriage, or at least women having sex before marriage, is highlighted as being a particularly sensitive issue among Muslim migrants. The issue is not exclusively tied to religion, but since the characters are clearly presented as Muslims this is something that in the films comes across as being central in Islam.

THE NORDIC WAY?

The themes woven across these Nordic films are not unique to the Nordic contexts. Issues relating to finding one's place in between cultures are common in films by migrant and diasporic filmmakers in other contexts too[20] and in many films focusing on Muslim characters.[21] While in countries such as Britain some researchers have suggested that the migrant and Muslim background of characters is today less of an issue,[22] Nordic films are not there yet. Still in Nordic countries recent films about characters with migrant backgrounds would seem to put less of a focus on Islam and play more with preconceptions. For example, in the humorous 2010 Norwegian horror-film *Trolljegeren* (*Troll Hunter*) by André Øvredal it is clear that trolls can smell Christian blood and Christians should therefore stay away from trolls, but the troll expert is confounded when asked if it is a problem that one person in the team is a Muslim. However, as the reactions to Sana in *Shame* indicate, there is a need for strong and complex Muslim characters in the Nordic countries, but there is also a need to think through the narratives about Muslims in Nordic popular culture.

Taken together the films discussed in this chapter demonstrate common themes across Nordic films. The films highlight that growing up Muslim in the Nordic countries today is challenging. One has to deal with prejudice from many quarters and young people have to negotiate their own path. What is somewhat problematic though is that the characters' marginalized position is largely portrayed as a personal choice or related to their families. This has been argued to be a problem with coming-of-age stories more generally as well.[23] This setup ignores the social and structural aspects that might be behind the marginalization, such as discrimination in the job market and an un-supporting school system. The films can at times be read as a critique of society, but this is often a minor theme. The opening scene in *Wings of Glass* indicates the lack of understanding that Nazli and

20. Berghahn 2010.
21. Ramji 2010.
22. Malik 2010.
23. Moseng 2011.

similar characters have to deal with. While one of Nazli's interviewers is somewhat supportive, the other is confused about the fact that she is not the ethnic Swede they expected and the fact that she chose to lie about her name ends up being her downfall. In a similar vein, the school system does not seem able to provide an option for Wasim and his friends, who end up looking for other contexts in which to strive. However, the film, by focusing on them and their views, presents the criminal path as their choice, not as the outcome of a lacking system.

The problem is thus that the focus on the internal and personal struggles of characters coming of age means that the social structures behind the character's marginalization are largely made invisible. One of the few exceptional examples of a Nordic film in which a Muslim character disrupts these patterns is Gabriela Pitcher's *Äta, sova, dö* (*Eat, Sleep, Die*), made in Sweden in 2012.[24] In this film, the viewers are introduced in several scenes to governing agents that underline a systematic lack of concern through their actions and put the blame on those who are marginalized. The main character is the young Muslim woman Rasa, who is represented as strong-willed and imaginative, but unable to break free from a faulty system.

What the films that I have analyzed here likewise hide is the relatively long history of Muslims in some Nordic countries. The films do highlight the fact that most Muslims in the Nordic countries today have a migrant background. However, with the story of migrant Muslims being so dominant other histories and Muslim identities are easily ignored. In Finland, for example, there has been a Muslim minority since the nineteenth century, when Tatar merchants settled in the country.[25] The focus on young Muslims with a migrant background coming of age also ignores the fact that ethnic Scandinavians sometimes convert to Islam.[26] The films also do not generally focus on characters with a mixed background, that is to say with one parent with a migrant background and one who is an ethnic Scandinavian. One exception is the Finnish film *Leijonasydän* (*Heart of a Lion*) from 2013, directed by Dome Karukoski, about a neo-Nazi who falls in love with a woman who has a child who is a Muslim.[27] In general though, the story is somewhat generic.

Despite their limitations, the films discussed in this chapter also have many noteworthy features. Films about growing up often receive less schol-

---

24. Lindvall 2013.
25. Daher 1999.
26. Roald 2004.
27. Hiltunen 2016.

arly attention than other genres, but they do obviously fill a purpose.[28] The stories might seem somewhat similar, differing mostly in their details and whom they give center stage. However, they do also provide important voices to both individuals and groups while bringing additional topics to traditional themes in coming-of-age stories. Particularly the films that focus on young Muslim women underscore issues concerning the body, love, and sexuality and being different and in-between. The stories are thus not just about the struggles of falling in love, exploring your sexuality and finding yourself, but doing this while juggling expectations of your secular friends and your often more traditionally oriented family. The films about the young Muslim man's road to crime in turn illustrate the many layers of marginalization, another recurring theme in stories about growing up.[29]

Growing up is tough – particularly in film, where the story requires some conflicts to be worth telling – but often in real life too. However, having parents of not just a different generation but also from a different cultural context, having to make your way between varied ideas about how and who you should be, and, independent of what you choose, still risking to be categorized by others according to their preconceived notions, is no doubt even more challenging. In this situation, to see someone on the silver screen – or some other screen – dealing with issues that you too struggle with can without a doubt be important. In addition, it can help those around you better comprehend your struggles. The reactions to Sana in *Shame* clearly illustrate this, but the stories of Nazlis, Wasim, and Aicha can certainly work in the same way. Films and other popular cultural narratives can of course also create prejudice, but at their best they can be a sounding board for understanding and accepting difference, an understanding greatly needed today.

Works Cited

Abdulkarim, M. 2017. Maryan Abdulkarim: Det var befriande att se Sana och Skam bryta normerna. Svenska Yle. https://svenska.yle.fi/artikel/2017/07/09/maryan-abdulkarim-det-var-befriande-att-se-sana-och-skam-bryta-normerna

Bakøy, E. 2010. "From Lonely Guest Workers to Conflict-Ridden Diasporas: A Historical Survey of Norwegian Migrant Cinema." In *Media in Motion: Cultural Complexity and Migration in the Nordic Region*, edited by E. Eide and K. Nikunen, 145–62. London.

Berghahn, D. 2010. "Coming of Age in 'the Hood': The Diasporic Youth Film and Questions of Genre." In *European Cinema in Motion: Migrant*

28. Shary 2014.
29. Moseng 2011.

and *Diasporic Film in Contemporary Europe,* edited by D. Berghahn and C. Sternberg, 235–55. New York.

Berghahn, D. and C. Sternberg. 2010. "Introduction." In *European Cinema in Motion: Migrant and Diasporic Film in Contemporary Europe,* edited by D. Berghahn and C. Sternberg, 1–11. New York.

Daher, O. 1999. "Orthographical Traditions among the Tatar Minority in Finland." *Studia Orientalia* 87:41–48.

Hiltunen, K. 2016. "Encounters with Immigrants in Recent Finnish Feature Films." *Journal of Scandinavian Cinema* 6 (3): 235–52.

Hjort, M. 2005. *Small Nation, Global Cinema: The New Danish Cinema.* Minneapolis.

Larsen, L. O. 2015. "New Voices, New Stories: Migrant Cinema and Television in Norway." In *European Cinema and Television: Cultural Policy and Everyday Life,* edited by I. Bondebjerg, E. N. Redvall and A. Higson, 169–91. New York.

Lindvall, D. 2013. "Class, Ethnicity, and Immigration in Sweden: Two Films, Two Strategies." *The Journal of Labor & Society* 16 (4): 457–70.

Malik, S. 2010. "The Dark Side of Hybridity: Contemporary Black and Asian British Cinema." In *European Cinema in Motion: Migrant and Diasporic Film in Contemporary Europe,* edited by D. Berghahn and C. Sternberg, 132–51. New York.

Moseng, J. S. 2011. *Himmel og helvete: Ungdom i norsk film 1969–2010.* Trondheim.

Naficy, H. 2001. *An Accented Cinema: Exilic and Diasporic Filmmaking.* Princeton.

Nestingen, A. K. 2008. *Crime and Fantasy in Scandinavia: Fiction, Film, and Social Change.* Seattle.

Moffat, K and P. Kääpä. 2018. "Unthinking Ethnocentrism: Ecocritical Approaches to Ethnic Diversity in Nordic Screen Meida." *Journal of Scandinavian Cinema* 8 (2): 149–65.

Ramji, R. 2009. "Muslim in the Movies." In *The Continuum Companion to Religion and Film,* edited by W. L. Blizek, 177–78. New York.

Roald, A. S. 2004. *New Muslims in the European Context: The Experience of Scandinavian Converts.* Leiden.

Shary, T. 2014. *Generation Multiplex: The Image of Youth in American Cinema since 1980.* Austin.

Sjö, S. 2013. "Go with Peace Jamil: Affirmation and Challenge of the Image of the Muslim Man. *Journal of Religion & Film* 17 (2). http://digitalcommons.unomaha.edu/cgi/viewcontent.cgi?article=1136&context=jrf

———. 2015. "Madness, Otherness and Transformation: Exploring
     Religion in Nordic Crime Films." *Journal of Religion & Film* 20
     (1). http://digitalcommons.unomaha.edu/cgi/viewcontent.
     cgi?article=1370&context=jrf
Sjö, S., and Á. S. Daníelsson. 2013. "Detraditionalization, Diversity, and
     Mediatization: Explorations of Religion in Nordic films." *Nordic Journal
     of Religion and Society* 26 (1): 47–64.
Tigervall, C. 2005. *Folkhemsk film: Med "invandraren" i rollen som den
     sympatiske andre*. Umeå.
Wright, R. 2005. "'Immigrant film' in Sweden at the Millennium." In
     Transnational Cinema in a Global North: Nordic Cinema in Transition, edited
     by A. Nestingen and T. G. Elkington, 55–72. Detroit.

Muslims in Australian Cinema:
The Future of Listening Across Difference

Mehal Krayem

DIVERSITY IN AUSTRALIAN CINEMA

Cinema can normalize diversity and acknowledge a history of social inequality. By allowing cultural and religious minorities, in this case Muslim-Australians, the opportunity to tell their own stories on the big screen, histories and experiences are written into a broader national narrative. This chapter explores the place of two recent romantic comedies, *Alex and Eve* (Peter Andrikidis, 2015) and *Ali's Wedding* (Jeffrey Walker, 2017) in the broader national landscape. It considers how these films displace a long-standing whiteness in Australian cinema and calls on Australian audiences and the media industry to engage in a form of "listening across difference."[1] This concept is informed by feminist and political theories of listening. It is understood as a political listening that undoes the oppression that occurs "through not hearing certain kinds of expression from certain kinds of people."[2] "Listening across difference suggests a subtle shift, from seeking better understanding of an "other" to listening for better understanding of relationships and complicities, issues, and the workings of privilege."[3] I argue that this listening creates further opportunities for dialogue between mainstream communities and cultural minorities by removing the burden from minority communities and decentering a "free speech" approach to communication, and instead asking mainstream communities to actively consider their own position and conditions of privilege.[4] Such a shift centers an understanding of how institutions and individuals are complicit in histories of misrepresentation and allows industries to actively begin changing into the future. In a media context this asks mainstream media institutions to consider the conditions that centralize "whiteness" in Australian storytelling.

Scholars of film, practitioners, and community members from cultur-

1. Dreher 2009.
2. Dreher 2009, 449.
3. Dreher 2009, 451.
4. Dreher 2009, 447.

ally diverse backgrounds have been commenting on the overall whiteness of the industry and also the problematic portrayal of community groups who have been underrepresented, for decades.[5] It wasn't until the release of the Galbally report (a government report written by lawyer, Frank Galbally, which was instrumental in highlighting the increased need for services catering to recently arrived migrants) in 1978 that Australians began to consider the importance of diversity in the media they were consuming.[6] While Australia prides itself on being "the most successful multicultural nation in the world," a line oft repeated by politicians to placate minorities and ignore grave forms of discrimination, Australia's representational media culture is rarely reflective of this diversity. The dominance of whiteness in the Australian film industry has meant that stories of Others have existed mostly on the margins.[7] While there have been a number of films from cultural minorities that have found a home as part of Australian cinema, such as *The Wog Boy* (Aleksi Vellis, 2000) and *Fat Pizza* (Paul Fenech, 2003), these films have been largely built on stereotypes of the Greek and Lebanese communities respectively. *The Wog Boy* tells the story of a second-generation Greek migrant who battles for belonging. It reinforces stereotypes of Greek-Australians as welfare bludgers and lazy migrants for the entertainment of the audience. *Fat Pizza* produced and written by Paul Fenech, is based off the award winning comedy show, *Pizza* (2003–2007) which screened on the Special Broadcasting Service (SBS), Australia's designated multicultural television station. The film focused on a pizza shop run by Bobo Giglioti, who is threatened by the competition of a new pizzeria opening up on the same street. The film is over the top and makes no claim to politically correct language or attitudes.

Collins (2009) and Speed (2005) argue that both *The Wog Boy* and *Fat Pizza* reinvent the "national type" in Australian comedy by challenging images of quintessential Australian masculinity.[8] However, these films do not encourage a "listening across difference" because their reliance on stereotypes continues to allow white Australia to set the agenda.[9] They employ stereotypes of ethnic men as vile, rough, gaudy and dishonest. They may disrupt the national space but they do nothing to further a public conversation about racial inequality and the role of whiteness in maintaining these hierarchies.[10] These films rely heavily on the notion of "unbelonging"

5. Mitchell 1992; Goodall et al. 1994; Stratton 2005; Elder 2007; Klocker 2014; Krayem 2015; Krayem 2016; Krayem 2017a; Krayem 2017b.
6. Jakubowicz 1987.
7. Elder 2007.
8. Collins 2009, 73.
9. Dreher 2009, 451.
10. Collins 2009.

as a backdrop for understanding the plight of the protagonist. We see the relationship of the men in the above films as defined by their relationship to whiteness and their being situated outside it. As a breakaway from this, *Ali's Wedding* and *Alex and Eve* focus on internal community conflicts by circumventing the white center, giving writers a space within which to demand a politics of listening that is not led by concerns of the white mainstream.

MUSLIMS IN AUSTRALIAN CINEMA

There has been an increase in Islamophobia post 9/11,[11] a general distrust of and resistance to accepting refugees from Muslim majority countries,[12] a broad demonization of the Arabic language, and a strong reproduction of Orientalist understandings of Muslims as Other.[13] These circumstances draw attention to the importance of nuanced representations of Muslims in cinema. Prior to the early 2000s there were few cinematic representations of which to speak. Tom Zubrycki's documentary *Bilal* (1996) tells the story of a 16-year old, Sydney-based, Lebanese Muslim man who has been left with brain damage after "a racially motivated hit-and-run accident."[14] The story becomes as much about Bilal's readjustment to the world as it is about his family's broader sense of belonging. The 1997 production *Heaven's Burning*, directed by Craig Lahiff, features a violent Afghan family involved in a bank robbery, with Russell Crowe. Outside of these representations, however, Muslim stories were mostly absent from the big screen.

The early 2000s mark a mainstream curiosity in the lives of Muslim-Australians as they become increasingly visible in public discourse, and a small number of documentary and drama films are made about the community as is outlined below. Often, however, these depictions have Muslims as the subjects but are written, produced and directed by people outside of the community. Muslim-Australian self-representation, therefore, has had a delayed actualization in Australian cinema.

Films featuring Muslims as refugees became a common trope during this period.[15] These are often stories of belonging, pain, and suffering. This can be seen in *Letters to Ali* (Clara Law, 2004) a documentary about a 15-year-old Afghan refugee who, through letter writing, bonds with an Australian family. Directed by Asian-Australian filmmaker, Clara Law, the film makes salient commentary on broader race relations in light of national

11. Itaoui 2016, 264; Dunn et al. 2004.
12. Dunn et al. 2007, 565.
13. Dandy and Pe-Pua 2010, 38.
14. Khamis 2009, 150.
15. Tascon 2009.

belonging.[16] Almost all films made about Muslim-Australians by non-Muslim Australians reference the political climate and begin by framing Muslims as social deviants. For example, the 2016 film *Down Under*, directed by Abe Forsythe, intended to satirize the historic events of the Cronulla Riots in Sydney's south, but failed spectacularly as it attempted to poke fun at the racial tensions between Middle Eastern youth (a term that has become a kind of code for Muslim) and white Australians on Cronulla beach.[17] An issue that was reported to be brewing for years came to a head in December of 2005, when residents from the areas around Cronulla declared a "Leb and Wog bashing day," resulting in the injury of a number of people of "Middle-Eastern appearance." The issues did not stop there; young Middle Eastern men then took to the streets of Maroubra for "revenge attacks."

Forsythe's film *Down Under* drew on stereotypes of Muslim youth as incompetent and unintelligent thugs who perform an inferior, ethnicized masculinity. Such Oriental stereotyping has also been seen in films like Mojgan Khadem's *Serenades* (2001). *Serenades* tells the story of a woman named Jila – the daughter of an Aboriginal mother and an Afghan father. The film is reminiscent of 1962's *Lawrence of Arabia* (David Lean), with Arab men in traditional clothing. Radio National presenter Rachel Kohn describes the film as being "about religious conflict, a search for identity, and the triumph of love."[18] Jila's father serves as the dominant patriarch, controlling of Jila's life and leaving her unable to make her own choices. Khadem, who was born in Iran but now lives in Adelaide says she drew on her experiences of the oppression of women in the Middle East to inform the conflicted story of Jila. While Khadem's experiences are not to be dismissed, the portrayal of Jila in the Australian outback reinforces images of the oppressed Muslim woman.

Tom Zubrycki's documentary *Molly and Mobarak* (2004) is what Sonia Tascon describes as a cross-cultural romance film.[19] *Molly and Mobarak* tells the story of a Hazara refugee, Mobarak, as he navigates his refugee status, distance from his family, and new relationships. Mobarak falls in love with Molly, a young woman from the country town of Young, after she and her mother, Lyn, welcome Mobarak into the folds of their family. Molly does not reciprocate this love and Mobarak is left devastated.[20] The expression

---

16. Johnston 2008.
17. Grewal 2007, 117; Lattas 2007, 301; Evers 2009, 187.
18. Kohn 2001.
19. Tascon 2009, 51.
20. Tascon 2009, 55.

of cross-cultural love on screen has been investigated by Natasha Klocker.[21] Klocker argues, "The presence and acceptability of such 'mixing' in our society, and on our screens, is instructive about the nature of prejudice and the limits of tolerance" and that "media representations of minority groups have material implications for social cohesion, interpersonal relationships and the formation of identities and social norms."[22] These intercultural intimacies, even if they fail, tell us something about the extent of social cohesion and belonging, indeed the frequency of these representations also normalizes common experiences of intercultural relationships.[23]

Unlike the previous examples, *Alex and Eve* and *Ali's Wedding* do not use a white character to mediate the cultural realities of being an ethnic or religious minority in Australia. These films ask the audience to engage in a new kind of listening.

WHITENESS IN AUSTRALIA AND THE IMPORTANCE OF "LISTENING ACROSS DIFFERENCE"

It has been acknowledged time and again that the longevity of the colonial legacy in Australia contributes to the ordering of the nation around the invisibility of whiteness. Hage considers "Whiteness" to be itself a fantasy position of cultural dominance born out of the history of European expansion."[24] For Ruth Frankenburg,

> Whiteness is a location of structural advantage, of race privilege. Second, it is a "standpoint", a place from which White people look at [themselves], at others, and at society. Third, "Whiteness" refers to a set of cultural practices that are usually unmarked and unnamed.[25]

Whiteness in an Australian context makes invisible the racial markers and identifiers of the dominant culture. It gives the illusion of a "benign mainstream" with which legitimate control lies.[26] This definition applies to what Hage terms "White multiculturalists" and "White-racists" alike.[27] Both groups of people conceive of the "nation as a space structured around a White culture, where Aboriginal people and non-White 'ethnics' are mere-

21. Klocker 2014.
22. Klocker 2014, 35–36.
23. Klocker 2014.
24. Hage 1998, 20.
25. Frankenburg 1993, 1.
26. Elder et al. 2004, 210.
27. Hage 1998, 18.

ly national objects to be moved or removed according to a White national will."[28] In *Heroes, Villains and the Muslim Exception: Muslim and Arab Men in Australian Crime Drama*, I established the way whiteness operates in both the film and television industries in Australia.[29] Here it is important that despite craving stories of difference within the industry, the Australian film industry is only comfortable retelling stories that respond directly to the public discourse around Muslim populations in Australia. For example, one budding filmmaker, who upon presenting a script for what he calls a "love story" to a production company was asked to include a scene where Lebanese men rape a white woman to "spice it up."[30] These kinds of occurrences make the concept of listening across difference particularly important for Australian audiences as it asks us to consider to whom would such a scene seem "spicy" and why?

A shift, even if only slight, away from whiteness is important for giving voice to non-Anglo and non-white experiences. By demonstrating that, even in the absence of white characters, films about cultural minorities are worthy of being told, because they ask the audience to engage in "listening across difference." Listening across difference takes into account "political listening, listening and privilege, and the politics of recognition."[31] A recognition of privilege in the concept of listening makes it possible to ask the dominant group, in this case white Australia, to "work" in the listening process. Listening no longer becomes passive but rather asks the party or parties who possess cultural privilege to move away from colonial experiences of trying to "understand" the other and instead to equally "listen for one's own complicities and privileges," and "instead gravitate towards understanding networks of privilege and power and one's own location within them ... [and] enable a politics of listening to avoid the pitfalls of identity in favour of a politics of interaction."[32] The goal of "listening across difference" in a cinematic context is to make cinema where white characters are sometimes peripheral and industry gatekeepers and audiences question their assumptions. Primarily that experiences of the other do not require the accommodation of white characters in order to be adequately heard. This is a powerful and deeply political act that potentially begins to create space for new kinds of stories because assumptions about the privilege attributed to the white mainstream when thinking about "audience," i.e. that they are the dominant audience, are questioned.

28. Hage 1998, 18.
29. Krayem 2017b.
30. Krayem 2017b, 79.
31. Dreher 2009, 446.
32. Dreher 2009, 451.

Beyond Whiteness: Romance and Muslim-Australians

Ali's Wedding and *Alex and Eve* reveal the potential of Australian cinema as a place where whiteness can be decentered, at least narratively. Both films pivot around the stories of Muslims who fall in love while white characters play a very marginal role. These depictions normalize the reality of intercultural relationships and show that ethnic relationships do not need to be mediated by white Australia.

Alex and Eve

Alex and Eve is a romantic comedy set in Sydney. Alex, a Greek-Australian high school mathematics teacher (played by Richard Bracatisano), and Eve (played by Andrea Demetriades), a high-powered lawyer from a Lebanese-Muslim-Australian family, fall in love despite the racist objections of their families. The couple meet in the iconic Opera-bar in Circular Quay. The bar boasts stunning views of both the Sydney Harbor Bridge and the Sydney Opera House. The location is recognizable and makes symbolic the meeting of two second-generation Australians. From the perspective of a second-generation audience their relationship makes sense as they share similar struggles of belonging, having both experienced the reality of growing up with migrant parents. However, intergenerational conflict arises when their families discover the relationship and begin to place pressure on them to stop seeing one another.

Humor as used by non-Anglo or non-white communities can either exacerbate and reinforce the general power dynamic or bring them to light and challenge them. Mitchell worries that the use of caricatures when associated with people from non-English speaking backgrounds mocks migrant groups rather than integrates them.[33] Often the features that are exaggerated for comedic purposes are things like physical attributes and an accented English.

> The comic stereotype looks good-natured, even affectionate; yet ... it "infantilises" the ethnic group, portraying its members as abnormal and ridiculous, and thereby undermines their chances of being taken seriously.[34]

Alex and Eve relies in part on comedy produced through continued mispronunciation. Eve's mother for example continues to refer to Skype, the online communication application, as "skippy." This is presumably funny

---

33. Mitchell 1992.
34. White 1989, as cited in Mitchell 1992, 123.

because the Australian slang word for a white person is a "skip" or "Skippy." Again, as Alex's father George (played by Tony Nikolakopoulos) comes with his wife Chloe (played by Zoe Carides) to meet Eve's parents, Salwa (played by Helen Chebatte) and Bassam (played by Simon Elrahi) for the first time, Salwa greets George by asking "*kefak?*" meaning "how are you?" in Arabic. George responds with, "no, you get fucked." The misunderstanding is less "infantilizing" than noted above because it comes from a community that itself has been marginalized and has suffered the effects of racism; however, it still makes language fodder for comedy.

Alex and Eve has been adapted from a trilogy of theater performances written by Alex Lyoks "based loosely on his own experience."[35] Though not itself unproblematic, what makes *Alex and Eve* an exciting glimpse into the future is the decentering of whiteness in Australian cinema. This makes for a refreshing change as race politics are contested implicitly. Australian race politics are built on the idea that white Australia is the legitimate center of the nation and that white Australians are responsible for managing non-English speaking and Indigenous communities in both an official policy sense and in everyday interactions.[36] In Australian cinema the existence of a white center often manifests in the way stories are mediated by a white actor or actress in a lead role. This character becomes the protagonist with which the wider audience associates and therefore the film is deemed marginally fit for mainstream audiences.

Alex and Eve is not a particularly strong film in dealing with the cultural or nuanced struggles of second-generation migrants. All the conflict in the film comes to a loggerhead too suddenly and is awkwardly resolved. Eve and Alex know that their parents hold bigoted views about the culture of the other partner from the very beginning. Alex's father in particular feels that his son's relationship with a Muslim woman would be a direct affront to the history of struggle. Below is an excerpt of an argument between Alex and his father mediated by Alex's older brother, Stavros (played by Alex Lykos).

> George: Why can't you be like the other boys in the church?
>
> Alex: They don't go there to pray, they go there to pick up.
>
> George: Yeah, if only you did we wouldn't be in this mess.
>
> Alex: We're not in a mess.
>
> George: Do know the history between the Greeks and the Muslimanis?

35. Rolfe 2015, 53; Byrnes 2015, 30.
36. Elder et al. 2004.

Stavros: Dad, we live in Australia, that stuff has nothing to do with us.

George: You want him to marry the Lebanese eh? [moving toward Alex] For 400 years the Muslimanis occupied the Greeks. They let the women live but they killed the men to get rid of the Greek Orthodox. But we fought for our independence. If you marry this Muslimana you undermine 400 years of suffering. The Greeks, what they did for their people, their religion and for the cause of the people alive. Ok she's a nice girl, but this is bigger than love. If you don't leave her, you lose your home, your family, everything!

While Eve's brother, Shadi (played by Rahel Romahn), is portrayed affectionately as playful and ditzy, he is still made to be a bit of a thug. He speaks aggressively regardless of the content. He threatens to kill Alex after the relationship between Alex and Eve is first discovered, and later threatens Alex in order to get him to reveal the depth of his feelings toward his sister. In advance of the final scene, Alex and Shadi meet in an alley behind the school as Alex is, in the style of a true romcom, rushing to tell Eve he loves her before she marries someone else. Shadi confronts Alex to an audience of Alex's students.

Shadi: Been seeing my sister, aye?

Alex: What? Nah.

Shadi: Don't fool with me, man.

...

Shadi: Do you love my sister?

Alex: Look man, I didn't

Shadi: Hey! Answer my questions man!

Alex: [nods]

Shadi: Then go and tell her before she gets married, you dumb klutz. If you break her heart, I'll kill ya.

Alex: [nods]

Alex drives away, to a unanimous thumbs-up from his students. Shadi here acts out of love; in fact both Eve's father and her brother subvert the image of the Muslim patriarch as oppressive and controlling. Both Bassam and Shadi are the ones who facilitate Eve's happiness. Eve's father is the one who suggests that Eve invite Alex and his parents over to meet him and his wife Salwa. The meeting goes tail up thanks to the brutal fighting between

Salwa and George, who are unable to put aside their prejudice. Salwa insists repeatedly that the best thing for Eve to do is to "forget about Alex" but her father and brother actively encourage her to pursue Alex.

Thus while *Alex and Eve* makes attempts to challenge the stereotype of men as upholders of patriarchy and tradition, it struggles to move away from depicting young Muslim men as thugs and criminals. It is increasingly important to rethink the ways in which we conceive of Muslim men in public discourse. If indeed film is to assist in presenting more progressive representations of any minority group, then it is important that we look beyond the use of the "thug" as a form of comedic fodder, a trope which appears to be a direct result of modern Orientalist caricatures of Muslim and Arab men, and instead imagine new possibilities for Muslim masculinities on screen.

Despite the religiosity of Eve's family, this film does not posit religion as a problem per se. As we see both Bassam and Shadi accepting the marriage we realize the issue is with the prejudice held by her mother, who is more concerned with what the community will think than any religious mandate that forbids Eve from being with Alex. Similarly, Alex's father is concerned with this marriage being viewed as a betrayal of his history and community. In this way while culture is still problematized, it is presented as an issue on both sides. The fact that both Lebanese-Australians and Greek-Australians have been victims of broader policies of discrimination in relation to Australia's longstanding White Australia policy means that there is no power differential. By eliminating the White standard against which most Muslim characters or Greek characters are compared, *Alex and Eve* can tell a story about love and conflict without inherently blaming either culture.

Alex and Eve provides the opportunity to speak for both Greek and Lebanese Australian communities. However, the constraints of the genre of romantic comedy mean that themes are somewhat superficial. The progress made, though minor, is important for "listening." It demonstrates that slowly the industry is creating space for others. The absence of a white character "decentres and denaturalises" whiteness and challenges mainstream viewers to listen without mediation.[37]

Ali's Wedding

Ali's Wedding is another romantic comedy, told from the perspective of a young Iraqi-Muslim man. Upon completing school, the not so academically gifted Ali (played by Osamah Sami) is expected to go to medical school. Set in Melbourne, the film portrays Ali's life as a series of comedic negotiations

37. Dreher 2009, 451.

with serious consequences. Ali lies about receiving a high score on his medical school entrance exam so as to upstage the son of one of his father's rivals and not embarrass his father, a popular Muslim cleric. The stakes for Ali are already high. They are again heightened when Ali is betrothed to a beautiful young woman from the Iraqi community, named Yomna (played by Maha Wilson). Yomna seems open to accepting Ali no matter how ridiculous his post-marital goals are. When he declares that he will get "fat and lazy" after marriage in order to turn Yomna off, Yomna simply assures him that if this makes him happy, she too will be happy.

While Ali really does not want to marry Yomna he feels he cannot tell her so. This does not stop him from pursuing an intelligent young Lebanese-Muslim girl, Dianne (played by Helena Sawires). Unlike Ali, Dianne did get into medical school. Dianne's father, however, does not think a good Muslim girl goes to medical school. Ali, pretending to be a customer at Dianne's father's fish and chips shop, takes it upon himself to assure him that if Dianne goes to medical school she'll be able to cure his ailments. Upon realizing this to be true, he allows Dianne to go to medical school. Ali begins attending medical school regardless of the fact that he has not been admitted and Dianne quickly discovers his secret, but agrees to tutor him and help him get admitted next year. Of course, the romance escalates and Ali suggests that he and Dianne engage in a temporary marriage arrangement. Dianne agrees and just as the stakes are the highest Ali's life comes undone. Dianne had no idea he was engaged and now has to face the wrath of her community and is being sent to Lebanon to live with her aunty. Ali marries Yomna before realizing he truly cannot commit and runs away. Yomna, despite being publicly humiliated twice, is graceful enough to let Ali go.

Dianne is portrayed as an intelligent and autonomous being. In addition to Dianne, Ali's younger sister, is also deemed to be the brains of the family though she is overlooked in favor of Ali. However, one can't help but notice that Yomna barely speaks. Aside from a few very brief conversations with Ali we never hear from her. In fact, despite being treated poorly by Ali, Yomna never responds. She just seems resigned to accept her fate at Ali's hands. In some ways this film runs contrary to *Alex and Eve*, emphasizing the patriarchal structures that are often reproduced in some Muslim circles, in particular those that relate to community politics. Though Dianne's father plays but a minor role in this film, we see Dianne navigate the strict rules her father sets in a resourceful and clever manner, but she is ultimately at his mercy. In this way *Ali's Wedding* makes clear the conditions within which patriarchy can flourish. However, the mere fact that this tension takes place solely within the Arab-Muslim community in Melbourne eliminates the concerns of fuelling Islamophobia that often accompany stories like this.

Ali's Wedding is by no means a perfect representation despite being made by an Australian-Iraqi-Muslim. However, in not concerning itself with the broader perceptions of Islam by mainstream Australia, it offers refreshing potential as simply a love story. Most films in the current climate feel the need to respond to the overarching discourses of political Islam, terrorism, and social marginalization, but *Ali's Wedding* proves this needn't always be the case.

CONCLUSION

Both *Ali's Wedding* and *Alex and Eve* ignore the broader conversations about Islam and Muslims and focus solely on telling stories about the challenges of love. Both films remind us that the stories of Muslim Australians are not dominated by the events seen on the nightly news. These refreshing takes on being a young Muslim living in Australia remind us of the humanity in the life of the day-to-day Muslim. In particular they are a form of escapism for Muslim Australians who, for a couple of hours in viewing these films are allowed to forget how exhausting it is to continuously be on the defensive. As the scrutiny of the lives of Muslims increases in Australia it becomes more important to hear the stories that respond purely to an internal dialogue and not an agenda imposed upon the community by white Australia. The more these stories are told the more mainstream Australia is forced to truly listen to struggles and challenges on Muslim terms. This begins to create spaces where power hierarchies are disrupted and challenged, creating the conditions for a new approach to "listening" whereby the "right to be understood" is prioritized over the right to "free speech."

WORKS CITED

Byrnes, P. 2017. "Pain Behind the Gag Gives Romance Heart." *Sydney Morning Herald*, 22 October, 30.

Collins, F. 2009. "Wogboy Comedies and the Australian National Type." In *Diasporas of Australian Cinema*, edited by Catherine Simpson, Renata Murawska, and Anthony Lambert, 73–82. Bristol.

Dandy, J. P. and R. Pe-Pua. 2010. "Attitudes to Multiculturalism, Immigration and Cultural Diversity: Comparison of Dominant and Non-dominant Groups in Three Australian States." *International Journal of Intercultural Relations* 34 (1): 34–46.

Dreher, T. 2009. "Listening across Difference: Media and Multiculturalism beyond the Politics of Voice." *Continuum* 23 (4): 445–58.

Dunn, K., J. Forrest, I. Burnley, and A. McDonald. 2004. "Constructing Racism in Australia." *Australian Journal of Social Issues* 39 (4): 409–30.

Dunn, K., N. Klocker, and T. Salabay. 2007. "Contemporary Racism and Islamophobia in Australia: Racialising Religion." *Ethnicities* 7:568–89.

Elder, C. 2007. *Being Australian: Narratives of National Identity*. Sydney.

Elder, C., C. Ellis, and A. Pratt. 2004. "Whiteness in Constructions of Australian Nationhood: Indigenes, Immigrants and Governmentality." In *Whitening Race: Essays in Social and Cultural Criticism*, edited by A. Moreton-Robinson, 2nd edition, 208–21. Canberra

Evers, C. 2009 "'The Local Boys': Violence, Care, Masculinity and the Riots." In *Lines in the Sand: The Cronulla Riots, Multiculturalism and National Belonging*, edited by G. Noble, 185–99. Sydney.

Frankenburg, R. 1993. *The Social Construction of Whiteness: White Women, Race Matters*. Minneapolis.

Goodall, H., A. Jakubowicz, J. Martin, T. Mitchell, L. Randall, and K. Seneviratne. 1994. *Racism, Ethnicity and the Media*. Sydney.

Grewal, K. 2007 "The 'Young Muslim Man in Australian Public Discourse',", *Transforming Cultures eJournal* 2 (1): 116–34.

Hage, G. 1998. *White Nation: Fantasies of White Supremacy in a Multicultural Society*. New York.

Itaoui, R. 2016. "The Geography of Islamophobia in Sydney: Mapping the Spatial Imaginaries of Young Muslims." *Australian Geographer* 47 (3): 261–79.

Jakubowicz, A. 1987. "Days of Our Lives: Multiculturalism, Mainstreaming and 'Special Broadcasting'." *Media Information Australia* 45 (1): 18–32.

Johnston, M. 2008 "Unsettling Whiteness: The Slippage of Race and Nation in Clara Law's 'Letters to Ali'." *Studies in Australasian Cinema* 2 (2): 103–19.

Khamis, S. 2009. "Lebanese Muslims Speak Back: Two Films by Tom Zubrycki." In *Diasporas of Australian Cinema*, edited by Catherine Simpson, Renata Murawska, and Anthony Lambert, 147–58. Bristol.

Klocker, N. 2014 "Ethnic Diversity Within Australian Homes: Has Television Caught up to Social Reality?" *Journal of Intercultural Studies* 35 (1): 34–52.

Kohn, R. 2001. "An Exotic Tale of Afghan Islam in Australia." *Radio National*, 3 June. Sydney.

Krayem, M. 2015. "Heroes, Villains and More Villains: Representations of Arab and Muslim Men in Australian Popular Culture." PhD Thesis, University of Technology Sydney.

———. 2016. "Striking it Lucky: Arab Representation, Whiteness and 'Here Come the Habibs'." *Metro Magazine: Media and Education* 189:58–62.

———. 2017a. "Down and Out for 'Down Under': Critiquing Race and Representation in Abe Forsythe's Satire." *Metro Magazine: Media and Education* 191:14–19.

———. 2017b. *Heroes, Villains and the Muslim Exception: Australian Representations of Arab and Muslim Men on Screen.* Melbourne.

Lattas, A. 2007. "'They Always Seem to be Angry': The Cronulla Riot and the Civilising Pleasures of the Sun." *Australian Journal of Anthropology* 18 (3): 300–19.

Mitchell, T. 1992. "Wogs Still out of Work: Australian Television Comedy as Colonial Discourse." *Australasian Drama Studies* 20:119–33.

Rolfe, D. 2015. "Straddling Two Worlds." *Professional Development* 2 (10): 52–53.

Simpson, C. 2009. "Tinkering at the Borders: 'Lucky Miles' and the Disaporic (no) Road Movie." In *Diasporas of Australian Cinema*, edited by Catherine Simpson, Renata Murawska, and Anthony Lambert, 29–40. Bristol.

Speed, L. 2005. "Life as a Pizza: The Comic Traditions of Wogsploitation Films." *Metro Magazine: Media and Education* 146:136–44.

Stratton, J. 2005. "Lost in Music: Popular Music, Film and Multiculturalism." In *Reel Tracks: Australian Feature Film Music and Cultural Identities*, edited by Rebecca Coyle, 74–93. Oxon.

Tascon, S. M. 2009. "'I'm Falling in Your Love': Cross-cultural Romance and the Refugee Film." In *Diasporas of Australian Cinema*, edited by Catherine Simpson, Renata Murawska, and Anthony Lambert, 51–60. Bristol.

Wogs Out of Work. 1987. Theater production, written by Nick Giannopoulos, Simon Palomares, and Maria Portesi, Melbourne International Comedy Festival, Australia.

Truth, Lies, and Justice:
The Fragmented Picture in Asghar Farhadi's Films

Nacim Pak-Shiraz[*]
University of Edinburgh

RUTH AND JUSTICE ARE THEMES that appear in the Iranian cinema of both before and after the Islamic Revolution of 1979. As justice is bound up with notions of right and wrong, good and bad, its depiction in Iranian cinema provides an insight into the evolution of the idea of justice in Iranian society. The failure of the Islamic Republic's promise to uproot tyranny and social injustice through clerical rule has been the subject of numerous intellectual and artistic engagements. This chapter analyzes two films by Asghar Farhadi, one of the most acclaimed contemporary Iranian directors, whose success extends to both local and international audiences. Straddling art and commercial cinema, Farhadi's films depart from exotic images of rural landscapes and the struggles of the dispossessed that dominated much of the Iranian arthouse cinema in the 1990s and the noughties. Instead, his lens turned its focus on the angst of urban lower- and middle-class Iranians. By combining realism and melodrama, Farhadi "reintroduced mystery and suspense to the narrative of Iranian art films and depicted the complexity of the truths and lies of his characters."[1] Farhadi's films reflect upon Iranian society, including the Shi'i religious context. Here, I study *Shahr-e Ziba* (2004) and *Joda'yi Nader az Simin* (*A Separation*, 2011), in order to examine their critical engagement with the concepts of truth and justice in contemporary Iran.

TRUTH AND JUSTICE IN SHI'ISM

The concern with justice has been one of the clarion calls of Shi'ism, harking back to the early days of Islam immediately after the death of the Prophet Muhammad. Shi'as believe that the rightful successor to the Prophet was 'Ali, his cousin and son-in-law, and argue that the only just rulers of the Muslim community are the Shi'a imams. However, Abu Bakr and 'Umar, the first and second caliphs of Islam, respectively, usurped this right from 'Ali

---

* The author would like to thank Fayaz S. Alibhai for his comments on an earlier draft.
1. Pak-Shiraz 2019, 269–70.

and his successors. Thus, the idea of the just ruler was one of the arguments propounded historically by the Shi'a to support the legitimacy of the Shi'i imams over and above that of later Sunni rulers.

As Khadduri notes, the Umayyad rulers' persecution of heterodox groups led the Shi'a to "denounce Sunni rule as unjust," with them "continu[ing] to assert that their principle of the imamate was the only one which could insure justice."[2] Accordingly, from early on, many of the Shi'i sources on justice are preoccupied with the idea of political justice with a particular emphasis on the just ruler. In the *Nahj al-Balāghah* (*Peak of Eloquence*), a series of sermons and letters attributed to 'Ali, the first Shi'i imam, there is a frequent emphasis on the duty of justice that is incumbent upon rulers. This is evident from an excerpt of Ali's letter to Mālik al-Ashtar, the governor of Egypt:

> Be just with God and be just with people [giving them what is their
> due] from yourself, from your close relatives, and from those of your
> subjects towards whom you are most affectionate. If you fail to do
> this, you will be an oppressor. And he who oppresses the servants
> of God will find that God, as well as His servants, will oppose him....
> Nothing so surely induces the removal of God's grace and hastens His
> retribution as persistence in oppression.[3]

Justice was, therefore, not simply an imperative for the spiritual leader of the Muslim community, but an equal requirement for all those in positions of power over others.

In his battles against the Pahlavi regime, Ayatollah Khomeini invoked the Shi'i precepts of justice, criticizing the Shah as the *ṭāghūt* or tyrant who oppressed his people. Khomeini often invoked Yazid the Umayyad caliph, to refer to the Shah as the unjust and tyrant ruler. The army of Yazid had attacked Husayn, the grandson of the Prophet Muhammad and the third Shi'i imam, in 680 when he was on his way to Kufa after finally accepting the calls of the Kufans, who had long invited him to rise up against the Umayyad usurpers of the caliphate. Husayn and his small group of companions, including women and children, were brutally slain on 'Ashura, the tenth day of the month of Muharram, which became the central historical event in the lives and consciousness of the Shi'a.

With the occultation of the twelfth imam of the Ithnā 'Asharī Shi'as in 940, the issue of the leadership over the believers had to be reconsidered. During the physical absence of the imam, the spiritual guardianship of the

2. Khadduri 1984, 16–17.
3. Shah-Kazemi 2006, 220–21.

community was entrusted to the jurists, with worldly matters falling under the remit of the ruler. With the establishment of the Safavid dynasty in 1501 and the change of the official religion of Iran to Shi'ism, the Shi'i ulama began arrogating to themselves an elevatory role over the laity.[4] This power reached its zenith with the success of the Islamic Revolution in 1979. The introduction of the concept and institution of *velāyat-e faqīh* or "guardianship of the jurist" within the Islamic Republic's constitution finally gave the ulama not only spiritual but political authority over the people.

In a series of speeches leading up to the Revolution and delivered during exile in Najaf, Iraq, Ayatollah Khomeini had argued that the two essential qualifications for the ruler are "knowledge of the law and justice."[5] If the jurists who possess these qualities came together, Khomeini said, "they could establish a government of universal justice in the world."[6] However, a number of intellectuals from within the Islamic Republic, such as Abdolkarim Soroush, who began his career as a close ally of the Islamic Republic during the early years of the Revolution but has since become one of its staunch critics, have criticized the incompatibility of a theocratic state with the foundations of social justice.[7] Political justice and, particularly, the idea of the just ruler have remained central to Shi'i discourses on justice. The only exception is perhaps the discussions surrounding God's justice, which in any case lies within the limited domain of theology.

TRUTH AND JUSTICE IN IRANIAN CINEMA

Iranian commercial films of the pre-Revolutionary period, known as *filmfārsī*, largely depicted a black and white image of good and bad. These included hugely popular films such as the1950 movie *Sharmsar* (*Shamefaced*, Esmail Kushan), *Lat-e Javanmard* (*The Chivalrous Tough Guy*, Majid Mohseni, 1958), *The Champion of Champions* (*Qahraman-e Qahramanan*, Siyamak Yasemi, 1965), *Jahan Pahlavan* (*The World Hero*, Esmail Riyahi, 1966), Siamak Yasemi's hugely successful *Ganj-e Qarun* (*Qarun's Treasure*, 1965) that broke all previous box-office records in Iran,[8] Mohammad Ali Fardin's all-time favorite, *Soltan-e Qalbha* (*King of Hearts*, 1968), *Javanmard* (*The Chivalrous Man*, Faraydun Zhurak, 1974) and *Hamsafar* (*Companions*, Maʿssoud Asadollahi, 1975). However, *filmfārsī* was not simply "cheap entertainment," a label with which many

4. For a discussion of the growth of the Shi'i clergy's power in Iran see Keddie 1995, Algar 1980, and Mir-Hosseini and Tapper 2006.

5. Khomeini 1985, 59.

6. Khomeini 1985,   62.

7. For his discussion of social justice within clerical rule see Soroush 1999, 273–84.

8. Naficy 2011, 198.

critics and scholars dismissed the entire oeuvre.[9] Although notorious for their borrowing and adaptation from "western" images, such as the scantily clad women and erotic scenes, many of these films, in fact, ultimately endorsed a return to religion and traditional values, a point overlooked by the religious strata and other critics of the genre who condemned these films as immoral. Indeed, the films didactically depicted the consequences of sin and deviating from tradition, denouncing many of the supposedly "western" values especially when it came to women. By the mid twentieth century, Iranians had to navigate their lives by the triple standards within which they found themselves being governed: the religious law (Shari'a), societal customs ('urf), and rapid modernization.[10] Most of the *filmfārsī* films, however, drew their morals only from religious traditions and societal customs.

At the turn of the twentieth century, many Iranian intellectuals welcomed modernization as a cure for what they perceived as the backward state of their country. As Ervand Abrahamian states, many reformers of this period "shunned religion because of their own personal experiences during the Constitutional Revolution. When conservatives, headed by Shaykh Fazlallah Nouri, had opposed reforms, including representative government, civic codes, women's rights, equality before the law, and individual freedoms."[11] By the 1960s, however, they began articulating their disenchantment with the modernization process and what it had to offer. Instead, they proposed "nativism," a return to the Self against the westernization process, which found expression in literary and artistic works.[12] Jalal Al-e Ahmad (d. 1969) and Ali Shari'ati (d. 1977), two of the most influential intellectuals in the 1960s and 1970s respectively, couched their criticism of the Pahlavi regime by emphasizing the social injustices within Iran.[13] In the arena of cinema, nativism found expression in what came to be known as the Iranian New Wave Cinema, a new approach that sought to intelligently explore "the complexities of the social and political context"[14] and distance itself from the low-brow movies of the dominant *filmfārsī*. While the dominant theme of the commercial films of the pre-Revolutionary period, known as *filmfārsī*, was a return to religion and tradition, some pre-Revolutionary films, particularly a few of the New Wave cinema, were read as critical of

---

9. For a critical study of filmfārsī see Rekabtalaei 2019, Pak-Shiraz 2013, Moezezinia 1999.

10. For an analysis of these three competing forces see Amir-Ebrahimi 2008, 89–118.

11. Abrahamian 2004, 269.

12. See for instance, Ahmad 1997. For a case study in art, see Keshmershekan 2004.

13. For a study of Jalal Al-e Ahmad and Ali Shari'ati's anti-western rhetoric see Mirsepassi 2006, 416–33.

14. Sadr 2006, 152.

religion. For example, Bahman Famanara's *Sayeha-ye Boland-e Bad* (*Tall Shadows of the Wind*, 1978) criticized the irrational beliefs of a village fearful of a scarecrow that they had built themselves. Ironically, the film was banned both before and after the Revolution. It was first seen as a criticism of the Pahlavi regime, and later the Islamic Republic saw the scarecrow as a symbolic reference to the irrationality of religion and its destructive power over the masses.[15]

Justice is usually portrayed through the juxtaposition of good and evil. In Iranian cinema, the melodramatic *filmfārsī* narratives of the pre-Revolution commercial cinema revolved around the heroism of the protagonist and his courage in battling the villains. In my study of the constructions of heroes, I have demonstrated how *filmfārsī* "subverted masculine hierarchies by reversing the state's most desired and most disenfranchised masculine prototypes into villains and heroes respectively."[16] The injustices that the poor and the weak suffer are also motifs that appear in the two well-known early New Wave films made in 1969: Dariush Mehrjui's *Cow* (*Gav*) and Masud Kimiayi's *Qeysar*. In *Qeysar*, like many *filmfārsīs*, attaining justice is associated with violence as the protagonist, Qeysar, seeks to redeem his male honor. He single-handedly sets out to kill those responsible for the rape and subsequent suicide of his sister and the murder of his brother, who had tried to avenge this dishonor. Qeysar sees the only way to obtain justice by taking matters into his own hands, and one by one kills the malefactors. Like most of the *filmfārsīs*, the good and evil are clearly demarcated in this New Wave film. The good men of *filmfārsī* were strong, honorable men who acted chivalrously (as *javanmards*) against the villains who oppressed the weak and threatened the honor of good women. Good women were innocent, obedient daughters, wives and mothers who upheld the family honor and reputation, in contrast to the loose women who acted outside the accepted norms of society. The narrative of Mehrjui's *Cow* departs from that of *filmfārsī*. There are no heroic protagonists but the weak and oppressed are clearly seen through the destitute village dwellers, who live in fear of the enigmatic, shadowy figures of the three men lurking in the outskirts of the village. Similarly, the narratives of Ebrahim Golestan's *Khesht va 'Ayeneh* (*Brick and Mirror*, 1964) and Bahram Beyzaie's *Ragbar* (*Downpour*, 1972) are devoid of any heroes or villains.[17]

After the 1979 Revolution, the good and evil in the narrative of many

---

15. Farmanara speaks about this in Hassan Solhjoo's documentary about him, Sangi dar Ab Biyandaz (Throw a Stone in the Water, 2011).

16. Pak-Shiraz 2008, 316.

17. For an analysis of heroes and villains in these two films, see Pak-Shiraz 2008, 297–318.

of the early post-Revolutionary films continued to retain a stark black and white image with one-dimensional protagonists and antagonists. In propagating the ideology of the new Islamic Republic, many of these early popular films condemned the Pahlavis (r. 1925–1979) by depicting the regime and its lackeys as wealthy, westernized Iranians who oppressed the larger weak, poor and religious population. With the eruption of the Iran-Iraq war in 1980 soon after the Revolution, evil found expression on the silver screen in the invading Iraqi forces in contrast to the *basījis*, voluntary militia, who were depicted as selflessly giving up their lives in what was termed "the sacred defense." The focus, however, remained on the Iranian side and their bravery and sacrifices rather than the demonization of the Iraqi forces. The good characters in these films extended beyond the Iranian soldiers on the battlefield to include men and women who supported the fighters behind the front line and readily sacrificed not only their material wealth but also their loved ones in this unjust war. Mothers on screen resolutely sent son after son to the front lines and proudly bore the news of their martyrdom.

Gradually, however, this black and white image began to give way to a more complex depiction of post-revolutionary Iranian society. The earlier, uncompromising images now slowly shifted their focus from the imposed war to domestic injustices. A few filmmakers began subtly criticizing the inequities imposed not by a previous regime, the enemies of the Islamic Republic or an invading foreign force, but the very Islamic Republic which had found popular support in its commitment to uprooting oppression. For example, Mohsen Makhmalbaf, a fervent ally of the Islamic Republic in its early years, made a number of propagandist radio programs and films in the first decade after the Revolution. However, by the end of the eight-year Iran-Iraq war, the disillusionment with what the Islamic Republic had offered society could be traced in his films. His *Arousi-ye Khouban* (*Marriage of the Blessed,* 1989) is the first of such films, which specifically examines the war, its aftermath, and the state's failure in removing tyranny or installing the promised social justice. In a less pointed approach, Abbas Kiarostami's *Close Up* (1990) is a "a meditation on perplexities of justice, social inequity, and personal identity"[18] as it re-enacts the real-life story of a penniless man whose desire for social recognition and respect leads him to deceive a wealthy family into believing he is the famous director, Mohsen Makhmalbaf.

JUSTICE IN ASGHAR FARHADI'S FILMS

Asghar Farhadi was born in 1972 and graduated from the University of Tehran. He began his career in cinema by making shorts at the Young

18. Cheshire 2010.

Cinema Society in Isfahan, after which he worked for the Islamic Republic of Iran Broadcast Television as a screenwriter for several television series. He made his feature film debut, *Raqs Dar Ghobar* (*Dancing in the Dust*), in 2002 and within less than ten years had five feature films under his belt, most of which have won prestigious national and international awards. His *A Separation* garnered the 2012 Academy Award for Best Foreign Film, Iran's first ever Oscar prize followed by a second one for his *Forushandeh* (*The Salesman*, 2016). Both Farhadi's filmmaking style and his authorial role in the screenplays of his films have given his works a distinctive cinematic language.

Whereas all of Farhadi's films are preoccupied with truth, lies, and justice, here I will examine but two of them in detail: *A Separation* and *Shahr-e Ziba* (2004). *Shahr-e Ziba* is literally *Beautiful City*, but it is also the name of a neighborhood in Tehran housing the juvenile prison in which the film starts and to which the protagonist returns in the closing shot. In this regard, I prefer to use *Shahr-e Ziba* rather than *Beautiful City*, the title in international screenings, in an attempt to maintain the complexities evoked by the original title. The inspiration for the film began with the concepts of "retribution" and "compensation." Farhadi had visited the Ministry of Justice to film a sequence of a television series and had come across families of various murder victims and perpetrators with the former demanding retribution and the latter looking for ways to appease them to save their loved ones from capital punishment. This later on developed into the final screenplay of *Shahr-e Ziba*.[19]

In *Shahr-e Ziba*, Akbar, an eighteen-year-old boy having reached legal age awaits his execution for murdering a sixteen-year-old girl in an act of passion two years earlier. The narrative of the film builds upon the attempts of Ala, a young petty thief who had befriended Akbar in prison, to save his friend from execution. To do so, Ala requires the consent of the father of the murdered girl. According to the Iranian penal code, those convicted of murder can escape capital punishment if the victim's heirs forgive the killer. In this case, however, the father's grief and anger have failed to subside over time and he continues to insist on obtaining justice through *qesas* or retribution. An alternative to *qesas* is the payment of *diyeh* (compensation) also referred to as blood money in cases of compensation for murder. *Diyeh* "is a substitute for the law of private vengeance."[20] However, the full amount is assigned to a male victim as women's blood money is worth half that of men.

19. Farhadi 2013, 127.
20. Tyan 2012.

Farhadi raises the problem of justice by questioning not only the validity of capital punishment but also the purported justice demanded by laws in which one life is not equal to another. Since the victim was a woman, her life is worth half that of a man; ergo, the father of the murdered girl has to pay the difference of the blood money to Akbar's family before the death sentence can be carried out. Abol Qasem, the victim's father, is an impoverished and jobless man whose sole possession is a humble house in a poor neighborhood of Tehran. His only way of attaining "justice," therefore, is to put up his home for sale so as to pay this difference of the blood money owed to his daughter's murderer. Although a devout Muslim, Abol Qasem is unable to accept the justice in which, as he puts it, "the life of his innocent daughter is only worth half that of the rogue boy."

Farhadi challenges viewers to rethink their convictions about good and bad, right and wrong. Like Krzysztof Kieslowksi's *Krótki film o zabijaniu* (*A Short Film About Killing*, 1988), which raises complex ethical questions surrounding capital punishment, Farhadi, too, refrains from creating villains, heroes, and victims in his narrative. Thus, even though Akbar in *Shahr-e Ziba* has murdered an innocent girl, he is nevertheless not depicted as the villain either. In fact, he only appears in the opening sequence, even though it is the social and legal consequences of his action that drive the narrative. Instead, we follow the desperate attempts of Akbar's friend, Ala, and the former's sister to save him from death, allowing the audience to identify and empathize with their struggle. On the other hand, we also witness Abol Qasem's pain and his desperate efforts to obtain justice for his daughter's wrongful death. Although the murder is clearly depicted as morally reprehensible, the course of justice in responding to this evil act is questioned by the film. As a theocracy, Iran's administration of justice is based on religious sources. As Mir-Hosseini states, "[t]he most drastic changes in the Iranian legal system after the Revolution, took place in the area of criminal law, where Islamic legal concepts [had been] entirely put aside in the 1920s."[21] As Abrahamian also observes, "the regime codified the chief features of the sharia into the *Qanon-e Qesas* (Retribution Law) and the *Qanon-e Tazir* (Law of Discretionary Punishments)."[22]

Since the religious authorities are in charge of administering justice, how do they respond when purported justice is questioned? Farhadi approaches this hugely sensitive issue in a number of scenes where characters are unconvinced about the justice of the legal solutions they are offered. Indeed, both sides protest against being treated unjustly. I will

21. Mir-Hosseini 2010, 334.
22. Abrahamian 2004, 273.

examine three particular sequences in which a cleric is challenged about the justice of the legal rulings; the first two are raised by Abol Qasem and the third by Ala.

In the first sequence, Abol Qasem is dissatisfied with the court clerk's justification and complains to a court judge-cleric about having to pay blood money to the murderer. Interestingly, this scene has been deleted in later copies of the film, which includes the following dialogue:[23]

> Judge-Cleric: Tell me, are you a Muslim or not?
>
> Abol Qasem: Of course! I believe in the same God and Prophet as you do.
>
> JC: This is what the Shari'a says.
>
> AQ: Does the Shari'a say whoever's loved one is killed, take millions from them as well and then perform justice? Does Shari'a say this or do you?
>
> JC: It doesn't go into my pocket or that of the regime. It goes to the boy's family. I don't have time to explain its wisdom.
>
> AQ: Does exaction have any wisdom in it?
>
> JC: That very religion in which you believe, loathes that one life is taken for another. It places obstructions in your way so that you may spare the killing of another life.
>
> AQ: I will not forgive!
>
> JC: God willing you will! There is more spiritual recompense in that!
>
> AQ: What we destitutes have a lot of in this world is spiritual recompense!
>
> JC: Then find a way to arrange for the blood money.

This conversation ultimately fails to rationalize the administration of this kind of justice in society. At first, the judge attempts to silence Abol Qasem by implying that a true Muslim would never doubt the Shari'a, or religious law. Interestingly, Abol Qasem is depicted as a devout Muslim, but he is not convinced by the religious ruling; the injustices he so plainly argues against in this law of retribution are far too great for him to believe it to be the will of God. He thus directly challenges not only the religious authorities but also

---

23. I only realized that the section was omitted when I was attempting to cut this particular scene from a subtitled copy for a presentation. The BBC screenings did not include this section either.

the sanctity attributed to the laws when he questions if it is the Shari'a or the cleric that has come up with such a law.

The judge's second attempt at explaining away the injustice as a way of saving another life is a flawed argument.[24] It does not address the inequality between the genders which Abol Qasem is indirectly questioning. The wisdom of placing the so-called "obstruction" to spare another life only works in sparing male and not female lives. Had the sexes of the killer and the victim been reversed, that is, had a woman killed a man, the obstruction would no longer apply to spare the female murderer's life. Indeed, she would be killed without her victim's family having to pay anything to her family for obtaining justice. The cleric's final attempt is a recourse to spiritual recompense, ostensibly in the next world. Abol Qasem refutes this argument as well: instead of attaining social justice in this world, the impoverished like him have been accumulating abundant spiritual recompense redeemable only in the next world. Abol Qasem's response clearly points to the state's failure in providing the social justice it had promised the disenfranchised when it first came to power.

The second sequence in which Abol Qasem challenges religious authority is when the *pish namaz* (prayer leader) of the neighborhood mosque invokes the Qur'an's emphasis on forgiveness to convince him to forgive Akbar. However, the cleric is unable to reconcile the contradictions that Abol Qasem juxtaposes between justice through retribution and the emphasis on forgiveness. Instead, like the court judge, the cleric here also tries to silence Abol Qasem by reminding him of the dangerous religious consequences of such doubts. He exhorts Abol Qasem not to waste a lifetime of observing religious rituals by asking such questions and not to blaspheme by challenging the justice of God. In both these sequences, the religious authorities fail to respond convincingly when challenged. Instead, they resort to threats of the ramifications of blasphemy or the rewards in the afterlife. The inability of both clerics to satisfactorily address Abol Qasem's interrogations represents a failure on their part to justify their very authority, and by extension, their privileged position over laity, predicated

---

24. This may be seen as a reference to Qur'an 17:33, "Nor take life – which Allah has made sacred – except for just cause. And if anyone is slain wrongfully, we have given his heir authority (to demand qesas or to forgive): but let him not exceed bounds in the matter of taking life; for he is helped (by the Law)"; as well as to 5:32, "On that account: We ordained for the Children of Israel that if any one slew a person – unless it be for murder or for spreading mischief in the land – it would be as if he slew the whole people: and if any one saved a life, it would be as if he saved the life of the whole people. Then although there came to them Our messengers with clear signs, yet, even after that, many of them continued to commit excesses in the land." Ali 1983.

as it is on the clergy being the best placed of all people to administer justice in society.

The third sequence is Ala's conversation with the same prayer leader. Having found out that Abol Qasem is about to sell his home so that he can raise the blood money for Akbar's execution to go ahead, he wants the cleric to intervene and convince him against it. He argues that Abol Qasem's acquiescence would benefit all parties involved; there would be no need to lose the family home and Abol Qasem could use his daughter's blood money to pay for the treatment of his disabled step-daughter. This would result, Ala argues, in more spiritual recompense than the retribution. The cleric dismisses Ala's logic not because it does not make sense but because any discussion on the matter is the prerogative of only those within the circle of *ijtihād*, the jurist's privilege to endeavor in deriving law from the religious sources. He sarcastically asks Ala: "When did you achieve the degree of *ijtihād*?" Ala does not appear to know the meaning of *ijtihād* but he is not one to be silenced easily and remains unfazed by the cleric's assumed superiority in the matter. For him, reasoning and understanding cannot be the monopoly of a certain class of people who arrogate to themselves the exclusive capacity of divining the will of God. He debunks the claim by responding that, "This is something that even a five-year-old can realize is a better option." Unlike Abol Qasem, Ala is neither a religious person nor is he well-versed in religious knowledge. Yet, he is able to cleverly (even if ultimately unsuccessfully) argue for the cleric to intervene in the progression of a contract – the sale of Abol Qasem's house – that could result in even more evil.

In fact, it is Ala's "theological" reasoning with Abol Qasem in a later scene that appears to be the most effective as he convincingly argues against retribution and the taking of life being the best way of attaining divine justice. Ala visits the local mosque where Abol Qasem prays as the latter has refused to receive him at home. He forces Abol Qasem to listen to him by talking when Abol Qasem is praying. He pleads:

> Do you believe in the God in front of whom you are standing and praying?... Isn't it that you think he [Akbar] deserves to die, then leave him to God. He knows justice and injustice better than you and I ... do you think it's going to be difficult for Him? God will take care of the retribution. If you don't believe in what I'm saying, then it means that you doubt God!

Ala, the petty thief, is not a scholar of religious law but an ordinary man who uses slang to articulate the problems of a retributive system of justice.

The power of Ala's arguments on the hitherto unresponsive Abol Qasem is evident in the way he finally acknowledges Ala and turns to face him.

In all of this Farhadi does not, however, suggest that religion, or indeed the Qur'an and other religious sources from which these laws are derived, are irrelevant. Instead, he invites us to reconsider the de facto wisdom of sanctifying the law through religion and in so doing reflect upon the human and, therefore, fallible dimensions of administrating justice. Farhadi questions a literal approach to the word of God that overlooks the complexity of human life and the circumstances surrounding it, highlighting the absurdity of laws that remain rigid, are impervious to reason and the exigencies of context, but which are nevertheless claimed to be perfect. This in turn, as mentioned earlier, challenges the legitimacy of the jurists' claims to being the most appropriate rulers vis-à-vis their essential qualifications, namely "knowledge of the law and justice" as argued by the proponents of the concept of *velāyat-e faqīh*, guardianship of the jurists.

Farhadi returns to the issue of blood money once again in *A Separation*. Nader and Simin are middle-class Tehranis whose marital discord appears to stem from their disagreements about staying in Iran. Simin wishes to leave the country before their immigration visa, acquired with great difficulty, expires but Nader is reluctant to leave behind his ailing father, who is suffering from Alzheimer's disease. The main dispute taken to court, however, is over their adolescent daughter Termeh. According to Iranian law, children cannot acquire a passport or leave the country without their father's permission. Nader has consented to the divorce but not to Termeh's departure, prolonging and complicating the proceedings as Simin refuses to leave without her daughter.

With Simin having moved out of the marital home, Nader hires Raziyeh, a devout Muslim woman, from a deprived part of the city, to look after his senile father and undertake some domestic chores during the day. Within just three days this leads to events that drag Nader and Raziyeh to court in a complicated case. Nader accuses Raziyeh of stealing the missing cash from his house. The indignant Raziyeh refuses to leave before she has defended her honor and demands to be paid for her services for the day. Nader is infuriated and pushes her out of the door leading her to fall down a flight of stairs. If the court is convinced that Nader knew about Raziyeh's pregnancy before he pushed her out of his flat, he would be charged with manslaughter and the payment of the full amount of blood money for the death of the male fetus.

While the clerics in *Shahr-e Ziba* invoked the sanctity of the law to stave off any questioning of it, the judge in *A Separation*, who is not a cleric, is seen to engage rather more meaningfully with the aggrieved parties in an attempt at legal parity. Ultimately, however, he too is circumscribed by the law and has little, if any, leeway in its interpretation. While secular law can be revisited to examine its continued applicability, religious law is invariably premised on the permanence of its sources beyond time and place. As we saw earlier for *Shahr-e Ziba* in the cleric's response to Ala, the derivation and subsequent interpretation of the law is limited to a small group of people who are allowed to practice *ijtihād*. It is not the preserve of others, such as the judge in *A Separation* who says his hands are tied. Even though the judge in *A Separation* is not a cleric, he is bound in his rulings to the Shi'i state's theological framework. This rigidity of the law in addressing the needs of a modern society ignores that messy and intricate web of all-too-human conditions and contingencies. The issue of the blood money itself further complicates the situation, becoming a negotiating tool that commodifies human life. When the taking away of another life, as in *Shahr-e Ziba*, is rationally institutionalized as the religious right of a victim and the outcome of a true course of justice, any other solution can only be perceived as a compromise and an expedient sop over the life of one's loved ones.

The possibility of attaining justice recedes even further in *A Separation*. Unlike the New Wave film *Qeysar*, discussed earlier, there are no villains or innocents in *A Separation*, making a sharp identification of justice being seen to be served all the more difficult. Indeed, none of the characters are either good or evil; they are ordinary people with their own foibles, suffering human imperfection in dealing with their daily challenges and the banality of life. In all of this, religion, which can otherwise provide solace and hope and comfort to bear the vicissitudes of life, becomes merely a scale that coldly measures the punishment of each person. In this case, religion as embodied by the state has failed to address the underlying causes of injustice, to ask why families have to suffer such poverty that blood money becomes a temporary relief from the pressures of creditors. It also fails to respond to the challenges of a modern society where traditional structures of care for the weak, the ailing, the needy and the elderly, also enshrined within sacred texts[25] are increasingly difficult to sustain: Nader should be

---

25. See Qur'an 2:83: "And remember We took a covenant from the Children of Israel (to this effect): Worship none but Allah; treat with kindness your parents and kindred, and orphans and those in need; speak fair to the people; be steadfast in prayer; and practice regular charity. Then did ye turn back, except a few among you, and ye backslide (even now)," and 4:36: "Serve Allah, and join not any partners with Him; and do good to parents, kinsfolk, orphans, those in need, neighbours who are near, neighbours who are strangers, the companion by your side, the wayfarer (ye meet), and what your right hands possess: For Allah loveth not the arrogant, the vainglorious." Ali 1983.

imprisoned if he is unable to come up with bail, even if this results in his ailing father's life being put in grave danger. In a blind following of the letter rather than the spirit of the law, the prayer leader in *Shahr-e Ziba* has to attend to his prayers rather than exert himself for a greater good. It is easier to follow the prescriptive aspect of religion than to critically engage with its ethical imperatives in speaking to the human condition as it relates to good and evil and justice.

TRUTH IN ASGHAR FARHADI'S FILMS

Whereas in *Shahr-e Ziba* it was clear that Akbar had murdered the girl, the cause of Raziyeh's miscarriage remains uncertain. While *Shahr-e Ziba* questions the adeptness of a theological framework in responding justly to a particular kind of crime, in *A Separation*, attaining the very truth of the events themselves becomes impossible. Not everything is as it appears in the films of Farhadi. Just as we think we know what has happened, our certainty is proven wrong. In Shi'i and Sufi thought, truth is multi-layered. It has a *ẓāhir*, outward or exoteric, and *bāṭin*, internal or esoteric, meaning. The manifest truth is, therefore, only part of the Truth, which includes the hidden truth. Thus, every unveiling of the esoteric meaning results in yet further layers and complexities in the process of arriving at a complete picture. The impossibility of ever attaining the whole truth has a striking implication in Farhadi's films: it underlines the fallibility and, ultimately, arbitrary nature of human justice. Since man cannot truly and fully be just, religious laws, which are derived by an exclusive group of men, cannot set out to maintain truth and justice in society and be its sole arbiter. Farhadi, therefore, challenges the convictions of religious law. While Truth is not denied, human shortcomings in arriving at it are thrown into sharp relief.

This subtle reference to the general impossibility of attaining truth finds particular significance in the context of Iran. The impossibility of any one character, or even us as viewers who are privy to far more than the characters themselves, attaining the whole picture (that is, truth) may be read as questioning the legitimacy of a theocracy that claims to behold, protect and enforce the "Truth" upon its citizens even as it disregards the fallibility and, therefore, plurality of human religious understanding and interpretation. The film itself, as Farhadi mentions in an interview, is open to diverse interpretations.[26] His fragmented images of characters and events resonate deeply with our fragmented understanding of ourselves, each other, and ultimately life. Even ostensibly "objective" reality is understood and articulated differently by people. This is exemplified from very early on

---

26. See the interview with Asghar Farhadi in the Special Features of the film's DVD.

in the film in a seemingly inconsequential scene when movers are carrying out the piano from Nader and Simin's apartment. The argument between Simin and the movers is about whether or not her flat is on the second or third floor – the main disagreement centering on each party perceiving and, therefore, naming the starting point for the floor differently as being either "ground" or "first."

But the truth is not all that Farhadi is concerned with. He also records the little white and great lies his characters tell. *Shahr-e Ziba* starts off with a lie. Ala pretends to have cut his wrist in the juvenile prison only to drag Akbar to the surprise birthday party they have arranged for him. This celebration, however, becomes a bitter rather than a joyous event for Akbar for this, his eighteenth birthday, is a harbinger of his impeding execution. Whilst Ala's first pretense in the film is an innocent, boyish playfulness for a birthday surprise, his later pretenses are far more serious. In his efforts to secure Abol Qasem's clemency for Akbar he begins "good behavior" to qualify for early release from prison. Despite being the rowdiest of the lot, he ingratiates himself to the prison wardens by turning over the contraband belonging to his cellmates, and pretends that he is a changed man who even performs his daily prayers. Once he finds out that Abol Qasem is a religious man, he buttons up his shirt before seeing him to ask for his forgiveness and intersperses his vocabulary with religious terms. This pretense of piety and religiosity also extends to Akbar's sister, who puts on a chador whenever she goes to see Abol Qasem to beg for her brother's life.

Akbar's sister lives with an even greater lie, pretending to still be married to her now ex-husband. As she tells Ala, she continues to wear the wedding ring from a drug-addict in order to survive in her neighborhood, for "here if you don't have a man," she says, "a hundred others will come to you every night." In Shi'i belief, truth can be veiled to protect oneself. Indeed, the historical principle of *taqiyya* or precautionary dissimulation was used by the Shi'a to protect themselves from Sunni persecution.[27] Similarly, each of the characters in the films lies to protect themselves from the evil that might befall them. Although the Shi'a in Iran no longer face the threat of religious persecution, the culture of a separate public and private life still dominates much of Iranian society. In this regard, Akbar's sister's remark is telling, for even though it is acceptable for a woman to be divorced according to the religious law or the Shari'a, '*urf* or the traditional customs within certain social strata frown upon a woman's single status.

A Separation demonstrates how the concealment of truth is imbibed from an early age. When Raziyeh is conflicted between attending to Nader's

27. Daftary 2007, 82.

father, an ailing old man who has soiled his clothes, and adherence to the religious prohibitions regulating men's and women's interactions, she calls a religious hotline to seek advice. Even though she is granted permission to change the old man's clothes, the weight of *'urf* that presses on Raziyeh is evident in the way her four-year-old daughter, Somayeh, reacts to her mother's fear. She looks solemnly at her mother and says: "I won't tell daddy!"

People not only lie to each other but they also collaborate with each other in these lies. Raziyeh's sister-in-law has not told her own brother about finding a job for his wife. Raziyeh herself later pretends to her husband that she has found the phone number of a potential employer in the newspaper and Nader collaborates in this lie with her. Initially, Nader and Simin pretend to each other that they want to separate. Their daughter Termeh, however, fails in collaborating with her mother's pretense, and by the end, the separation eventually becomes a reality.

People also lie to themselves. We believe Nader did not know Raziyeh was pregnant, not only because he appears to believe it himself, but also because he seems so principled in upholding the importance of truth that we cannot believe he himself would act otherwise. When going over the Persian equivalent of "foreign" terms that Termeh has to learn as part of her schoolwork, Nader takes issue with the substitution of an Arabic term for the European word "guarantee":

> Nader: That's Arabic, not Persian
>
> Termeh: That's what our teacher has said.
>
> Nader: Don't ever say that sentence to me again! What's wrong is wrong, no matter who says it or where it's been written.

In having Nader dismiss the teacher's authority and her sources ("or where it's been written" was omitted in the subtitles), Farhadi challenges the blind following of the absolute rule of religious authorities and their sources, which continues to dictate people's lives. When we find out that Nader did know of Raziyeh's pregnancy, it is almost as though we have just discovered this truth alongside him. But if an ordinary person like Nader can fool himself, what of those who wield power and authority? In this way, Farhadi turns the lens on us, just as much as he has on the state and its functionaries. We are as culpable in the deception.

Similarly, Raziyeh is convinced her miscarriage is Nader's fault. Her doubts about this are revealed to us almost as gradually as they are revealed to her. This ever-changing perception of reality is what makes what is on the surface a simple story a gripping study of a gamut of human emotions, from hope and hopelessness to risk-taking, pride, honor, and if-only regrets. Termeh is perhaps the only voice in the film who is keen on prevailing the truth but even she is forced to lie when put in the difficult position of choosing in front of the judge to either protect her father or speak the truth.

Farhadi himself has to lie in his film. In an interview, he states that he was not allowed to shoot on location in the courthouse.[28] The crew, therefore, transformed two school buildings into a courthouse. This itself points to an intensification in state censorship of cinema. In 1998, Ziba Mir-Hosseini was not only able to shoot *Divorce Iranian Style* on location and in the judge's court, she was also granted permission to document the real proceedings of the cases submitted to the judge.[29] To go even further back, in 1990, Abbas Kiarostami was not only permitted to the real court proceedings on location, but also allowed to reconstruct the proceedings for a further eight hours with all parties involved, without the presence of a judge, which he later edited into his film *Close Up*. Not only have the red lines of censorship been clearly tightened up over the years, but the transparency of justice itself being literally seen to be done in situ also seems to have increasingly become opaque.

CONCLUSION

Nothing is as it appears in the films of Asghar Farhadi. They depict the challenges that contemporary Iranians face by living in a modern theocratic society that is governed by a range of contradictory demands. These often result not only in internal conflicts of the characters themselves, but also in conflicts and disparities between the public and private, men and women, and between the social classes. In navigating their way through these contradictions, Farhadi's characters often do not reveal the complete "truth" about themselves; indeed they choose to selectively disclose it, conceive and present themselves in a particular way, or feel obliged to lie. Aside from the characters, the filmmaker himself does not provide the complete picture by not telling his audiences the full story.

The social justice promised by Ayatollah Khomeini at the beginning of the revolution in 1979 has yet to materialize despite the just rule of the *velāyat-e faqīh*. Many of the urban middle class are disillusioned with the convictions proffered by the religious discourse in administrating social justice and apprehending the Truth. Even those within the religious strata themselves appear to question their religious convictions.[30] Coupled with

28. Farhadi 2011.
29. See Mir-Hosseini 2002, 167–99.
30. See Mir-Hosseini and Tapper 2006, and Pak-Shiraz 2011, 67–92.

the authorities' dismissal of any approach to ethics and truth that falls outside the religious discourse, the films depict the disorientation and isolation of the individual. It is as though society has lost its moral compass and is desperately trying to find a way to save itself. It is ironic, therefore, that the "immoral" pre-Revolutionary *filmfārsī* cinema reflected a society that questioned the values of modernity and in so doing proposed a return to religious and traditional values to define justice, truth, and lies. In the contemporary Islamic Republic, however, the conviction of religious truth is no longer the ultimate answer to the challenges of human life, as Farhadi observes. Indeed, in his films Farhadi invites us to once again reconsider the place of truth, justice and lies in society, reminding us that it is humanly impossible to ever behold them completely.

WORKS CITED

Abrahamian, E. 2004. "The Islamic Left: From Radicalism to Liberalism." In *Reformers and Revolutionaries in Modern Iran: New Perspectives on the Iranian Left*, edited by S. Cronin, 268–79. London and New York.

Ahmad, Jalal Al-e. 1997 [1962]. *Gharbzadegi (Westoxication)*. Translated by J. Green and A. Alizadeh. Costa Mesa, CA.

Ali, A.Y. 1983. *The Holy Qur'an: Text, Translation and Commentary*. Beltsville, MD.

Algar, H. 1980. *Religion and State in Iran, 1785–1906: The Role of the Ulama in the Qajar Period*. Berkeley, CA.

Amir-Ebrahimi, M. 2008. "Transgression in Narration: The Lives of Iranian Women in Cyberspace." *Journal of Middle East Women's Studies* 4 (3): 89–118.

Cheshire, G. 2010. "Close-up: Prison and Escape." *Criterion*, June 22. http://www.criterion.com/current/posts/1492-close-up-prison-and-escape.

Daftary, F. 2007. *The Ismailis: Their History and Doctrines*. 2nd edition. Cambridge, UK.

Farhadi, A. 2011. "A Separation: Sony Pictures Classics Press Kit." http://www.sonyclassics.com/aseparation/aseparation_presskit.pdf.

———. 2013. "Kojay-e Shahr Zibast? (What is Beautiful about the City?)" In *Shahr-e Ziba (Beautiful City)*. London.

Keddie, N. 1995. *Iran and the Muslim World: Resistance and Revolution*. New York and London.

Keshmershekan, A. 2004. *Contemporary Iranian Painting: Neotraditionalism during the 1960s to 1990s*. School of Oriental and African Studies, University of London, Ph.D. dissertation.

Khadduri, M. 1984. *The Islamic Conception of Justice*. Baltimore, MD.

Khomeini, Ruhollah. 1985. "Islamic Government (*Hokumat-e Islami*)." In *Islam and Revolution: Writings and Declarations of Imam Khomeini*, translated by H. Algar. London.

Mir-Hosseini, Z. 2002. "Negotiating the Politics of Gender in Iran: An Ethnography of a Documentary" In *The New Iranian Cinema: Politics, Representation and Identity*, edited by R. Tapper, 167–99. London and New York.

———. 2010. "Sharia and National Law in Iran." In *Sharia Incorporated: A Comparative Overview of the Legal Systems of Twelve Muslim Countries in Past and Present*, edited by J. M. Otto, 318–71. Leiden.

Mir-Hosseini, Z. and R. Tapper. 2006. *Islam and Democracy: Eshkevari and the Quest for Reform*. London and New York.

Mirsepassi, A. 2006. "Religious Intellectuals and Western Critiques of Secular Modernity." *Comparative Studies of South Asia, Africa and the Middle East* 26 (3): 416–33.

Mu'azzizī'niyā. H. 1999. *Fīlmfārsī Chist?* (What is *Fīlmfārsī?*). Tehran.

Naficy, H. 2011. *A Social History of Iranian Cinema, Volume 2: The Industrializing Years, 1941-1978*. Durham, NC.

Pak-Shiraz, N. 2008. "Constructing Masculinities through Javanmards in Pre-Revolutionary Iranian Cinema." In *Javanmardi: The Ethics and Practice of Persianate Perfection*, edited by Lloyd Ridgeon, 297–318. London.

———. 2011. *Shi'i Islam in Iranian Cinema: Religion and Spirituality in Film*. London and New York.

———. 2013. "Imagining the Diaspora in the New Millennium Comedies of Iranian Cinema." *Iranian Studies* 46 (2): 165–84.

———. 2019. "Iranian Cinema Today: An Ode to the Past and New Directions in the Future?" In *Islamic Art: Past, Present, Future*, edited by J. Bloom and S. Blair, 260–77. New Haven and London.

Rekabtalaei, G. 2019. *Iranian Cosmopolitanism: A Cinematic History*. Cambridge.

Sadr, H. R. 2006. *Iranian Cinema: A Political History*. London and New York.

Shah-Kazemi, R. 2006. *Justice and Remembrance: Introducing the Spirituality of Imam Ali*. London.

Soroush, A. 1999. "Hukumat-e Dimukratik-e Dini' (The Democratic Religious Government)." In *Farbeh-tar az Idiuluzhi* (*More Obese than Ideology*), edited by A. Soroush. 273–84. Tehran.

Tyan, E. 2012. "Diya." In *Encyclopaedia of Islam*, Second Edition, edited by P. Bearman, Th. Bianquis, C. E. Bosworth, E. van Donzel, W. P. Heinrichs. Leiden.

Subverting Stereotypes through a Saudi Film: *Wadjda*, Gender, and Islam[1]

Elliott Bazzano

Le Moyne College

ALTHOUGH THERE IS A RICH HISTORY OF ARAB CINEMA and well-established national Arab film industries, one country has avoided developing film production until only recently. The Kingdom of Saudi Arabia's conservative stance on film exhibition has shaped a "non-public film culture," where film-going is prohibited and filmmaking unsupported.[2] *Keif al Hal* (*How's It Going?*, Izidore Musallam, 2006) – produced by Saudis but filmed in the United Arab Emirates with a Jordanian lead actress – was released for in-home viewing only in 2006.[3] More recently, *Wadjda*, directed by Haifaa Al Mansour, debuted in 2012 to much international acclaim. It tells the tale of a young, spirited girl named Wadjda who longs to own a bicycle.

But why is this film with a simple narrative about a girl and her bike such a big deal? Saudi Arabian cultural norms have traditionally allowed only boys to ride bicycles; and until the summer of 2018 women were not even allowed to drive cars in the country. Wadjda's story takes place before a backdrop of a Muslim-majority society, institutional corruption at her all-girls school, the crumbling marriage of her parents, and in a world of multi-faceted gender dynamics that on the whole disadvantage women. In this essay, I argue that the complementary themes of gender, family life, and religion – often infused with tropes of paradox – position *Wadjda* well as a film for Western audiences that productively challenges harmful stereotypes towards Muslims and Arabs.

The broader political context of the film also offers much for reflection, for although it is not the first film made by Saudis, it is the first feature film shot entirely in-country, and which stars all Saudi actors. It also stands out because of its Saudi female director.[4] With few exceptions, moreover, Saudi

1. This chapter draws on an essay I contributed to the Wabash Center's blog series, "Teaching Islam." Bazzano 2017a.

2. Ciecko 2010.

3. Sakr 2011.

4. Al Mansour's previous films include three short films and a documentary about women in the Gulf, *Women Without Shadows* (2005). She was an associate producer for the first Saudi-produced film, *Keif al Hal* (*How's It Going?* 2006).

Arabia boasts no movie theaters, but this cultural norm is now changing with Saudi's "Vision 2030" plan aiming to build hundreds of theaters.[5] Given these social circumstances within Saudi Arabia we must understand the film as aimed at multiple audiences, both local and international. Given the country's strictures surrounding gender and the arts, therefore, many cultural critics see *Wadjda* – both as a symbol but also through its themes – as reflecting a systemic, even progressive, change in Saudi Arabian society.[6]

WADJDA'S INTERNATIONAL RECEPTION

Al Mansour's debut feature film has received acclaim across many venues, including the *New York Times*, which refers to the film as "sweetly subversive."[7] Saudi authorities also submitted it for the foreign language film category in the 2014 Academy Awards – even if it didn't make the final short list. Its screening at the Tribeca Film Festival "was attended by Queen Noor of Jordan and followed by a discussion led by Gloria Steinem."[8] The film was also later adapted into an English-language novel, *The Green Bicycle*.[9]

Despite *Wadjda*'s international success, scholarly publications on the film remain scarce, but there are lots of published reviews, interviews with Al Mansour, and quick snapshots of the film. Milja Radovic's chapter on the film, from her monograph *Film, Religion and Activist Citizens* provides one of the richer analyses of *Wadjda*, as it combines scholarly literature and personal interviews with Al Mansour.[10] Amrita Deb also published a thoughtful article that explores the film from a psychological perspective with attention to the positive growth of the film's characters. As Deb observes, "despite the misfortunes, the characters in the film are not merely living a satisfactory life but making every effort to make the most of whatever opportunities come their way."[11] In this way, the film not only speaks to audiences interested in Islam or the Arab world, but indeed relates even more broadly to the human condition and processes of internal development – all marks of a tactful and compelling narrative. I agree with Deb's assessment in this regard and think it is one of the reasons, on the whole, that *Wadjda*'s international reception continues to be overwhelmingly positive.[12]

5. Ellyatt 2018.
6. Wazir 2013, 48.
7. Bloom 2013.
8. Bloom 2013.
9. Al Mansour 2015.
10. Radovic 2017.
11. Deb 2016, 531.
12. In terms of its reception in the Arab world, this is a topic that deserves its own consideration but one that I will not spend much time exploring in this chapter. Time will tell what

Given Al Mansour's international travels, it is not surprising that she made the film with a global audience in mind. Al Mansour earned a master's degree in Australia, the film was co-produced by a German company, and she currently lives in California. Precisely because filming in Saudi Arabia has remained so unusual, *Wadjda* also acts as one of the first occasions for many people to see life inside "a world on screen that, until now, has been largely hidden from the filmgoing world at large."[13] Notably, many films about the annual Muslim pilgrimage (*hajj*) to Mecca have been shot in Saudi Arabia, but these films don't focus on the inner lives of Saudis; instead they turn to international travelers' experience in Mecca, and Medina – cities not even mentioned in *Wadjda*.

To the extent the film gives people in Saudi Arabia a chance to see a depiction of life there through a feature film, it also targets a Saudi audience, but its reach is much larger. Despite explicit attention to the political context of the film, in this essay and through interviews with Al Mansour, few assumptions about Saudi political life or its relationship to the Western world feature anywhere in the film. Additionally, unless the viewer knows how to interpret some small clues (e.g. a shirt with "KSA" on it), or previously learned the context for the film, it is not even completely clear where the film takes place.

Because much of *Wadjda*'s global audience is situated in non-Muslim majority European and North American societies where international film festivals are based and film distribution rights were purchased, we can consider a certain line of questioning: In what ways does *Wadjda* challenge popular stereotypes about Islam? Or confirm stereotypes about Islam? These questions push the viewer to reflect on the complex choices and characters in the film as well as on the viewer's own complexity as agent in the world with inevitable – often sensational – preconceptions about Islam, Muslims, and Arabs.[14] *Wadjda* is so effective in deconstructing the idea of Islam as a homogenous entity because there is not merely *one* central question that

---

kinds of change the evolving political scene in the Kingdom of Saudi Arabia will produce, but I will note here that shortly after *Wadjda* was completed, "the Saudi Arabian government decided to lift the ban from girls and women riding bicycles," and because "the decision was made 'right after the film,' al-Mansour felt that there was a correlation between her film and the reaction of the Saudi government." Radovic 2017, 132.

13. Hornaday 2013.

14. A particularly scathing critique of Western stereotypes towards Arabs and Muslims, which explores intersections of racism and media bias comes in the form of a segment from comedy news show, *The Colbert Report*, in which its host Stephen Colbert demonstrates how journalists were quick to assume Muslims were responsible for a mass-murder carried out by an anti-Muslim man, simply because it was a mass murder that targeted non-Muslims (*The Colbert Report* 2011).

animates the film. Rather, it touches effectively on so many themes, and one of Al Mansour's key strengths is that she can tackle these issues with subtlety, emotion, and authority.[15]

STORY OF A GIRL

Wadjda explores many humanistic themes, including gender, friendship, marriage, religion, justice, and freedom. The characters are relatable, especially the protagonist, Wadjda; her adolescent rebellious search for truth and meaning mirrors a transcultural experience of many children around the world. There are several scenes expressing tenderness between Wadjda and her mother that have a moving power over the emotions. Islamic studies scholar Kathleen Foody argues that paying attention to affect in media can help combat Islamophobia as well, because not only, or even mostly, intellectual facts push people to change their minds.[16] So when we feel emotionally connected to characters, it is more difficult to retain harmful stereotypes associated with a character's various layers of identity.

According to Al Mansour, seeing the story through the eyes of Wadjda is significant not only for relatability but also because "children ask very simple questions that make us rethink the basics of right and wrong."[17] This framework is one of many ways that the film offers subtle social and political critiques. As scholar and film critic Omer Mozaffer puts it, Wadjda:

is a walking package of pre-teen sarcasm and snide comments. Most Disney Princesses clash with authority through song and secret skills; Wadjda is no Disney Princess. Her song is noisy rock music blaring from her cassette player. Her secret skill is her wit and intelligence.[18]

Wadjda is an adorable, clever, and perseverant young girl and it is easy to become engrossed in her story and form an emotional connection with her, which complicates prevailing stereotypes about strict and burdensome religiosity in productive ways. On the other hand, there are filmic components that confirm stereotypes if one wishes; for example, women wear face veils in public and Wadjda's religious school is very strict. A viewer could easily interpret these signifiers in ways that perpetuate stereotypes about the lack of Muslim women's rights and Islam as an unfair religion, rather than understanding these behaviors as socially conditioned by any number of factors, including religion, but also Saudi state and society. On the other hand, and I think this comes through most clearly, the mundane nature of

15. Bloom 2013.
16. Foody 2018.
17. Al Mansour and Powell 2012, 50.
18. Mozaffer 2014.

Wadjda's story keeps notions of religious transcendence in the background and allows viewers to focus on the story rather than sensational ideas about Wadjda's religious or cultural context. In a brief scene, for example, we see Wadjda somberly perform the Islamic ritual prayer with her mother. But her conversations in the film almost never revolve around God, afterlife, or the Qur'an.

Al Mansour seems to have crafted the film with demonstrating the diversity of Islam in mind because she gives due attention to culturally pervasive dynamics, even if they are unsavory at times, to say the least. There are positive and negative implications for religion that take place in the larger story that force the viewer to reconsider monolithic ideas about Islam and religious practice. About Saudi Arabia, Al Mansour notes, "yeah, it's conservative, and there are radical ideologies and very religious people, but beneath that, there are really nice people.... Beneath all the politics and conservative cover, you'll find lots of humor. It's a great place to tell a story."[19]

FAMILY LIFE: MEN AND WOMEN, BOYS AND GIRLS

Throughout the film, Wadjda's aloof father explores the possibility of a second marriage in order to sire a son, while Wadjda's mother struggles to provide and create a good life for her only child. Wadjda, meanwhile, confronts her own challenges, including navigating the strict environment at her school and developing her relationship with the Qur'an as a means to win money to purchase her prized bicycle by way of a recitation competition at her school.

Wadjda communicates her wit and free spirit throughout the film by arguing with authority figures, sometimes with sarcasm, and listening to Western music, but she also lives innocently in her own challenging world of early adolescence. In fact, this delicate balance of drawing on symbols from the "West" and the "East" has drawn critique from Waleed Mahdi:

> Al-Mansour's empowerment narrative certainly subscribes to East-West binaries. Capturing Wadjda's rebellion through her consumption of Western commodities, i.e., insistence on wearing Converse All Star boots and selling rock music mixtapes, adds insult to injury. The film seriously lacks the vision to foreground the possibility of producing a feminist narrative that reconciles religion, tradition, and locality. Its message could be easily dismissed as another example of works produced to satisfy a curious Western gaze.[20]

19. Eggers et al. 2013, 85.
20. Mahdi 2016, 103.

Mahdi goes on, however, to assert that "regardless of its flaws, the work should still be applauded for many reasons."[21] Although I appreciate this author's concern about simplistic binaries "produced to satisfy a curious Western gaze," some of these alleged binaries probably arose inevitably given the globalized cultural, political, and economic interests that combined to fuel the film in the first place.

Wadjda may succumb to some other Orientalism-inspired tropes as well, such as "evoking sympathy for the Muslim woman" and "regulating sympathy for the Muslim man."[22] Wadjda and her mother are portrayed as complex agents, for example, who develop as the film unfolds, but Wadjda's father is less complex. He is out of touch with his family, and set on taking a second wife. Thus he embodies quite well a particular stereotype of the lecherous, authoritarian Arab/Muslim man; hence the viewer's regulated sympathy for him. In fact, men don't make lengthy appearances in the film. Wadjda's best friend is a boy, which is significant, but he's still a secondary character compared to the many lead female roles.

One of the many ways that subversion reveals itself in the film, in fact, is the way women behave, because, in the words of Al Mansour, "outside, they are invisible, but when they go home, they inhabit the space, they sing, and they dance. That in-between is so interesting."[23] Speaking to this theme of "in-between" and paradox, Omer Mozaffer puts it this way: "Girls are not allowed to ride bikes, yet the store owner sells girls' bikes. And, the market is stiff enough that Wadjda worries her prized green bike will sell. So, if there is a prohibition on girls riding bikes, it exists in the imaginations of some people."[24]

Beyond imagination, however, Wadjda's mother, for example, opposes the bicycle at first. So even if there is overarching social pressure banning bikes for females, in the case of Wadjda the ban comes directly through her mother. In fact, one of the provocative themes in the film is that in the patriarchal world where the characters live, it is women who regulate one another. This could be a natural consequence of making a film about women (who else would impose regulations besides the main characters?) but more likely, I think, Al Mansour wants to demonstrate the multi-faceted dynamics of gender norms, including how and why they are adopted by people who are not presumably served well by them. Roy Armes notes that the "regime is reinforced by other women, such as Wadjda's teacher, who schools the girls

21. Mahdi 2016, 103.
22. Alsultany 2012, 71–131.
23. Bloom 2013.
24. Mozaffer 2014.

in submission and denies them any sort of freedom or self-expression."[25] But with almost every example from the film of women regulating one another according to supposed gender norms, there is also paradox or contradiction; Wadjda's best friend in the film is a boy, for example, and no one in the film says a critical word about it.

Additionally, because *Wadjda* features primarily female characters, it pushes Western viewers all the more, given the naïve ideas many viewers have not only about Muslims in general but about Muslim women in particular. Historically, there have been state-sponsored projects and public imperialist-inspired American sentiments to help Muslim women abroad, in the name of freedom and democracy. Lila Abu-Lughod points out that these sentiments are often misguided by assumptions that Muslim women across the globe experience oppression qua Muslim women, lack agency, and require the assistance of (white) foreigners to set them free.[26] Beyond simplistic assumptions about gender, for many viewers understanding Islam and Muslims in the today's socio-political climate requires a process of unlearning or, in the words of Sahar Ullah "de-programming."[27] *Wadjda* works well in this regard precisely because of its storytelling, and so viewers get a chance to reprogram their ideas of what Muslims might be like, beyond superficial media headlines.

In this respect *Wadjda* adds to the complex portrait of Muslim women and religious practice presented in several documentary films. For example, *The Light in Her Eyes* (Julia Meltzer and Laura Nix, 2011) follows a female preacher in Damascus (pre-civil war), with attention to a girls' Qur'an school. *Me and the Mosque* (Zarqa Nawaz, 2005) interrogates the challenges of female participation in mosques throughout the United States and Canada. Again, themes of gender and social justice are central to the film. Finally, *Koran by Heart* (Greg Barker, 2011) follows several kids from around the world as they participate in an international Qur'an recitation competition in Cairo. Additionally, feature films, such as those of Iranian director Majid Majidi, for example, *Bacha-hā-ye Asmān* (*Children of Heaven*, 1997) *Baran* (*Rain*, 2001), *Rang-e Khodā* (*Color of Paradise*, 1999), also narrativize Muslim children's experiences that are shaped by religion as their stories unfold, much like in *Wadjda*. Thinking about *Wadjda* with this filmic backdrop in mind is helpful, moreover, because Al Mansour notes that Iranian cinema was a key inspira-

---

25. Armes 2015, 304.

26. Abu-Lughod 2002.

27. Ullah 2014. Green 2015 provides an excellent resource for understanding the contours of Islamophobia and could successfully complement films about Islam and Muslims.

tion for her to navigate sensitive political themes in a cultural environment marked by censorship.[28]

WADJDA'S ENCOUNTERS WITH THE QUR'AN

Toward the aim of acquiring the bicycle, Wadjda learns to negotiate a few clandestine deals with members from her community (for example, charging a fee for delivering secret messages between sweethearts), but her primary strategy to earn money involves entering herself in a Qur'an recitation competition. Her mother helps her, but mostly Wadjda practices on her own with dedication. This component of the film's plot does well to illustrate the performative and aesthetic life of the Qur'an, which non-Muslims often find difficult to understand. Films like *Wadjda* (cf. *Koran by Heart*), therefore, illustrate well that Muslims engage with the Qur'an not only or even primarily through reading comprehension but also through sound, memorization, and emotional connection.

Several of the Qur'an recitation scenes in the film are somber, melodic, even meditative, and invite the viewer to focus on words that are likely foreign, but nonetheless resound with meaning. The Qur'an recitation scenes in *Wadjda* not only serve the plot of the film, but also give the viewer a chance to interact with the most oft-recited book in the world.[29] Muslims of course value the linguistic meaning of the Qur'an as well, and the verses we hear in *Wadjda* speak to many of the themes in the film. Thus these scenes invite reflection not only on the narrative of the film itself but also on why Al Mansour chose particular verses from the Qur'an to be recited.[30]

From the lens of a casual viewer, the function of the Qur'an in *Wadjda* serves at least a few ends. Wadjda's recitation practice and eventual victory in her school's competition provide the context in which she pursues her dream of owning a bicycle. The avenue through which she trains for the competition is a video game, which pushes against popular Orientalist stereotypes that all Muslims live in what Jack Shaheen calls "Arabland," a

28. O'Falt 2013; Ciecko 2013, 254.

29. Also, importantly, the Qur'an has consistently contributed toward Islamic art, ranging from calligraphy to poetry, and film is perhaps part of a natural progression of the Qur'an's place in Islamic art.

30. I explore related themes of Qur'anic commentary outside the genre of traditional exegesis in Bazzano 2016. Stemming from arguments I make in the article, *Wadjda* also functions as a form of meaningful Qur'anic exegesis (*tafsīr*). Another even more recent work that also explores the Qur'an in context is El-Badawi and Sanders 2019, which further helps to contextualize why Al Mansour makes certain choices when it comes to including scriptural references in *Wadjda*.

fantastical world that authors and film makers often imagine as "a violent, backward place complete with goats, daggers, giant gongs, souks, ornate palaces, dungeons and dark alleys."[31] And as Sophia Arjana adroitly notes, in Hollywood cinema, "Muslims are surrounded with fictions that would be considered obscene if applied to other social groups, but through Orientalism [including portrayals in film], they are validated."[32] In *Wadjda*, there are no goats or dungeons, but there are Qur'an video games. And Wadjda practices with the game while happily wearing a bicycle helmet.

A closer examination of the Qur'an in *Wadjda* also reveals some subtle and significant themes, which I would like to explore by considering each of four recitation scenes from the film. The first two take place with Wadjda's teacher, followed by a scene with her mother, and finally the scene toward the end whose performance earns her first place in the recitation competition. Because the Qur'an runs about four hundred pages, it was no accident that Al Mansour selected particular passages to convey particular meanings, even if those meanings might remain a bit cryptic to some viewers.

In the first extended recitation, Wadjda struggles to read in front of her classmates and her teacher, indicating that she is a novice. On the instruction of her teacher, Wadjda recites the following verse: "You who believe, obey God and the Messenger, and those in authority among you. If you are in dispute over any matter refer it to God and the Messenger" (Q 4:59).[33] One could surmise what Al Mansour intended, but I do not think the interpretation is obvious; the polyvalence works well in this regard, as it signals another way in which Al Mansour invites the viewer to experience and interpret the film: Who are "those in authority," and according to whom?

A bit later in the story, a more practiced Wadjda gives the recitation in front of her teacher another go: "If anyone opposes the Messenger after guidance has been made clear to him, and follows a path other than that of the believers, We shall leave him on his chosen path – We shall burn him in Hell, an evil destination" (4:115). Her classmate continues: "God does not forgive the worship of others beside Him – though He does forgive whoever He will for lesser sins – for whoever does this has gone far, far astray" (4:116).

Appropriately, Wadjda's recitation at school explores themes of obedience and punishment, as the school's principal conveys a punitive and petty attitude toward the students. Later, however, when Wadjda's mother helps her with recitation in their home, the words from the Islamic holy book convey a much different tone: "Another of His signs is that He created spouses from among yourselves for you to live with in tranquility:

31. Shaheen 2009, 542.
32. Arjana 2015, 11.
33. Qur'an citations in this chapter draw on the translation of Abdel Haleem 2005.

He ordained love and kindness between you. There truly are signs in this for those who reflect" (30:21). This scene takes place in the context of Wadjda's father pursuing a second wife (legal in Saudi Arabia but not in many Muslim-majority countries), which breaks her mother's heart.

Although Wadjda's mother is decidedly not experiencing "love and kindness" with her husband, the bond that she shares with Wadjda is unmistakable. The plain meaning of this Qur'an verse appears to relate to marriage. The term for "spouse" (*zawj*) in the verse stems etymologically from a verb meaning "to pair," so one could also understand that the verse functions not only to lament the relationship between Wadjda's mother and father but also to demonstrate gratitude for what Wadjda and her mother share.

In the final Qur'an recitation scene, where Wadjda's performance merits victory in the competition, the verses she recites frame one of the most powerful scenes in the film. The principal, who also directs the competition, had earlier suggested impropriety between two girls because they were sitting together alone, and she implicated Wadjda, even as a passive observer. It then came to light that the principal herself may be involved in her own affair, so the theme of hypocrisy hits home when Wadjda recites in front of the principal and her classmates while the camera pans across the faces of those present:

> God has sealed their hearts and their ears, and their eyes are covered. They will have a great torment. Some people say, "We believe in God and the Last Day," when really they do not believe. They seek to deceive God and the believers but they only deceive themselves, though they do not realize it. There is a disease in their hearts, which God has added to. Agonizing torment awaits them for their persistent lying. When it is said to them, "Do not cause corruption in the land," they say, "We are only putting things right." (Q 2:7–2:11)

In my reading, the verse in the context of the film is about superficiality, hypocrisy, and justice. The principal sees herself in the young protagonist but has already chosen a life of conformity and must continue down the path, so she at once resents and admires Wadjda. Insofar as the principal uses the Qur'an like a carrot on a stick – to encourage conformity among the school's students – it is perhaps divine secondarily to her material goals, which also underscores hypocrisy. In the end, Wadjda wins the competition, thanks to her own dedication, supportive mother, and the motivation of owning her very own bike. But the principal forces Wadjda to donate the money upon hearing her true intentions. Wadjda eventually acquires the bike, though, no thanks to her school principal.

Conclusions

Because Saudi Arabia is often assumed to be representative of Muslims around the world – it is the birthplace of Islam and hosts an annual pilgrimage for Muslims across the globe – this film will confuse many Western viewers. In the context of Muslim-majority countries, it is very small, having only about thirty-five million citizens. So the film is hardly representative of any kind of global Muslim experience, but the film never claims to be that. Film scholar Rubina Ramji elaborates on this idea, though, and explains that even if the film does not make this claim, viewers may nonetheless assume that it does:

> The discourse of the Muslim identity has been formulated in a global context. Cinema itself is part of the message, in that it participates in the discourse of the society and culture in which it is situated. There is a multiplicity of publics, and thus the identity of Islam is manifold as well. Depending on which brand of Islam one 'consumes', one will expect that brand to behave in a universal way.[34]

Thus tales of human complexity not only offer relatable personalities for diverse viewers to consider but also challenge Muslims and non-Muslims alike to think beyond comfortable assumptions that they have, which suggest any religion or society ever acts in a "universal way."

What the film does represent is the affective nature of storytelling as a means of (personal and political) transformation. In Al Mansour's own words, considering the sensitive political landscape of her home country, "I don't want to offend people or fight.... It's more like: Tell them a story and have them feel it." Al Mansour harnesses the power of the emotional connection that can be generated through narrative film. When dealing with sensitive material, I think it can be a mistake to give too much attention to direct critiques, and as Jannis Hagman notes, "the critique is cleverly subtle."[35] Direct critiques are important and necessary, but so is subtlety and building narratives.[36] Similarly, according to film critic Hanna Brown, that *Wadjda* "is subtly rather than openly critical of the [Saudi] government ... makes it both more entertaining and more subversive."[37] As a cultural trailblazer, Al Mansour elaborates on the delicate political implications of her work: "I'm not in a position to defend or educate as much as tell human stories, like opening a window and letting people discover for themselves.

34. Ramji 2009, 187.
35. Hagman 2013.
36. I elaborate on the importance of building narratives in Bazzano 2017b.
37. Brown 2013.

It's safer for me as an artist to step away."[38] In this way, *Wadjda* functions and ends on an optimistic note. As the film concludes, the sweet relationship between mother and daughter is reinforced, the aloof father remains withdrawn, Wadjda encounters freedom on her new bike, and leaves the audience rooting for her as she heads toward an unknown but presumably hopeful future, racing her best friend, Abdullah, on her new bicycle.

WORKS CITED

Abdel Haleem, M. A. S., translator and editor. 2005. *The Qur'an.* Oxford.

Abu Lughod, L. 2002. "Do Muslim Women Really Need Saving? Anthropological Reflections on Cultural Relativism and its Others." *American Anthropologist* 104 (3): 783–90.

Al Mansour, H. 2016. *The Green Bicycle.* New York.

Al Mansour, H. and L. Powell. 2012. "10 Minutes with Haifaa Al Mansour." *The World Today*, 68 (6): 50.

Alsultany, E. 2012. *Arabs and Muslims in the Media: Race and Representation after 9/11.* New York.

Armes, R. 2015. *New Voices in Arab Cinema.* Bloomington.

Arjana, S. 2015. *Muslims in the Western Imagination.* New York.

Bazzano, E. 2016. "Normative Readings of the Qur'an: From the Premodern Middle East to the Modern West." *Journal of the American Academy of Religion* 84 (1), 74–97.

———. 2017a. "Introducing Islam through a Subversive Saudi Drama." *Wabash Center*, April 5. https://www.wabashcenter.wabash.edu/2017/04/introducing-islam-through-a-subversive-saudi-drama/

———. 2017b. "A Post-Trump Islamic Studies Pedagogy?." *Religious Studies News*, May 26. http://rsn.aarweb.org/spotlight-on/teaching/after-the-2016-election/post-trump-islamic-studies-pedagogy

Bloom, J. 2013. "Where a Bicycle is Sweetly Subversive." *New York Times*, September 15. http://www.nytimes.com/2013/09/15/movies/wadjda-by-haifaa-al-mansour-made-in-saudi-arabia.html

Brown, H. 2013. "The One to Watch." *Jerusalem Post*, December 5. http://www.jpost.com/Arts-and-Culture/Entertainment/The-one-to-watch-334050

Ciecko, A. 2016. "Bicycle Borrowers after Neoliberalism: Global Nou-velo Cinema." In *Culture on Two Wheels: The Bicycle in Literature and Film,* edited by J. Withers and D. P. Shea, 44–262. Lincoln, NE.

———. 2011. "Cinema 'Of' Yemen And Saudi Arabia: Narrative Strategies, Cultural Challenges, Contemporary Features." *Wide Screen* 3 (1): 1–16.

38. Eggers et al. 2013, 83.

The Colbert Report. 2011. "Norwegian Muslish Gunman's Islam-esque
    Atrocity." July 25. http://www.cc.com/video-clips/fbd6kf/the-colbert-
    report-norwegian-muslish-gunman-s-islam-esque-atrocity
Deb, A. 2016. "A Qualitative Exploration of Positive Psychology Concepts
    in the Film *Wadjda* and Implications for Future Research." *Journal of
    Human Behavior in the Social Environment* 26 (6): 521–32.
El-Badawi, E. and P. Sanders. 2019. *Communities of the Qur'an*. London.
Eggers, D., M. Al-Harthy, H. Hatrash, and H. Al-Mansour. 2013. "Arabia
    Yesterday, Today, and Tomorrow." *World Policy Journal*, 30 (1): 78–85.
Ellyatt, H. 2018. "Saudi Arabia brings back movie theaters – and
    'staggering' demand is expected." *CNBC*. April 18. https://www.cnbc.
    com/2018/04/18/saudi-arabia-reopens-movie-theaters-with-black-
    panther.html
Foody, K. 2018. "Muslims in the American Media: From Texts to Affects."
    Journal of Islamic Studies 27 (2): 230–51.
Garcia, M. 2013. "Review of *Wadjda*." *Cinéaste* 38 (4): 51–53.
Garcia, M and H. Al Mansour. 2013. "A Woman's Voice Is Her Nakedness: An
    Interview with Haifaa Al Mansour." *Cinéaste* 38 (2): 34–37.
Green, T. 2015. *The Fear of Islam: An Introduction to Islamophobia in the West*.
    Minneapolis.
Hagmann, J. 2013. "A Children's Story in a Grown-Up World." *Qantara*,
    October 4. http://en.qantara.de/content/the-saudi-arabian-film-
    wadjda-a-childrens-story-in-a-grown-up-world
Hornaday, A. 2013. "*Wadjda* Movie review." *Washington Post*, September 18.
    https://www.washingtonpost.com/goingoutguide/wadjda-movie-
    review/2013/09/18/73e63734–1fae-11e3–94a2–6c66b668ea55_story.
    html
Mahdi, W. 2016. "Review of *Wadjda*." *Journal of Islamic and Muslim Studies* 1
    (1): 100–102.
Muzaffer, O. 2014. "Western Wrestling with *Wadjda*." *Roger Ebert*, February
    27. https://www.rogerebert.com/far-flung-correspondents/western-
    wrestling-with-wadjda
O'Falt, C. 2013. "Influences: The Movies that Inspired *Wadjda* Director
    Haiffa [sic] Al-Mansour to Make History." *Hollywood Reporter*, December
    18. https://www.hollywoodreporter.com/news/influences-movies-
    inspired-wadjda-director-665035
Radovic, M. 2017. "Creating a Rupture: *Wadjda*." In *Film, Religion and Activist
    Citizens: An Ontology of Transformative Acts*, 117–35. New York.
Ramji, R. 2009. "Muslims in the Movies." In *The Continuum Companion to
    Religion and Film*, edited by W. Blizek, 177–87. New York.

Sakr, N. 2011. "Placing Political Economy in Relation to Cultural Studies: Reflections on the Case of Cinema in Saudi Arabia." In *Arab Cultural Studies: Mapping the Field*, edited by T. Sabry. London.

Shaheen, J. 2009. *Reel Bad Arabs: How Hollywood Vilifies a People.* Northampton, MA.

Ullah, S. 2014. "Teaching Notes III: Islamic Studies and 'De-programming.'" *Baraza: Critical Collaboration on the Middle East, South Asia, and Africa,* September 14. https://baraza.cdrs.columbia.edu/teaching-notes-iii/

Wazir, B. 2013. "Saudi Arabia Lifts the Veil." *The World Today* 69 (4): 48.

Harems and *Ḥudūd*:
Gendered Space in Farida Benlyazid's *Bab al-Sama Maftuh*

Rebecca Moody

IN A SIMPLE YET TELLING SHOT early in her 1988 *Bab al-Sama Maftuh* (*Door to the Sky*), Farida Benlyazid's camera captures the simultaneous enormity and enclosure of Nadia's *riad* (house): its long, flat stucco walls, its ornate woodwork and *zallīj* (traditional Moroccan tile), its roof opening onto the bright sky above. Filmed from the courtyard below, the shot is split – brown walls; blue sky – but not neatly halved. Instead, at the top of the screen, the sky is encased on three sides by a brown roof and on the fourth by the film frame. Viewers seemingly glimpse but do not experience tran-

scendence. Instead, our gaze moves from the sky down to the frame's center: a *mūsharabī* (covered window).[1] After a brief pause, the camera cuts to a shot-reverse shot of the courtyard as three women crisscross it, then, in a

1. With its ornate arabesque patterns, a *mūsharabī* allows those inside – presumably women – to see out without allowing others to see in. Today, they are being replaced by frosted glass or heavy curtains that compromise the view that those within the house have of the spaces outside.

medium shot, back to the window. Noticeably absent now is the sky. Slightly out of focus, slightly off center, in what at first appeared an empty window stands Nadia, leaning against the *mūsharabī* that dwarfs her, her dark hair and dark shirt blending into the dark frame so that we see only her face. Benlyazid's mise-en-scène fixes her within the multiple frames of reference that she will aesthetically explicate over the course of the film: France and Fes, secular and Muslim, Sunni and Sufi.

Farida Benlyazid is among Morocco's most recognizable directors, part of a generation of post-independence filmmakers who strove to transition its film industry beyond state propaganda and into a site of rich cinematic production that is increasingly recognized locally and globally.[2] While much has been written about her role at the forefront of Moroccan cinema and her focus on women, I want to sit with her vibrant cinematography, her focus on Moroccan Muslim women as they articulate their own iterations of Islam, and her subtle negotiation with recent cultural moments, including secular and Islamic feminisms.[3] To narrow my perspective, I will focus on her use of lived space to press against dominant notions of Muslim women.

2. Benlyazid was respected within Morocco's film community before *Bab al-Sama Maftuh*, working as screenwriter with Jilali Ferhati (*Reed Dolls*, 1981) and M. A. Tazi (*Searching for My Wife's Husband*, 1994), among others. Throughout her corpus, she remains focused on Moroccan women's quotidian realities.

3. See Carter 2000, Gauch 2016, Martin 2011, Shohat 2003, and Van de Peer 2015. For more on Benlyazid in the context of Moroccan cinema, see Carter 2009 and Dwyer 2004.

Through the lens of Fatima Mernissi's *Dreams of Trespass: Tales of a Harem Girl-hood*, Kathleen Stewart's *Ordinary Affects,* and Ranjana Khanna's *Algeria Cuts: Women & Representation, 1830 to the Present*, I will focus on *Bab al-Sama Maftuh*, touted as Morocco's first feature-length fiction film by a woman.[4]

Morocco's most prominent feminist, Mernissi's reflections on women's (often heterodox) Islam offer a useful way to approach what I see as distinctive about Benlyazid's cinematography: her representation of Islam outside of normative, often masculine, spaces. Rather than in mosques, Mernissi and Benlyazid locate women's Islam in women's lived spaces. These careful divisions are mirrored in Benlyazid's cinematography, with much of *Bab al-Sama Maftuh* tightly framed within the *riad*, occasionally giving way to transcendent pans up to open skies. Yet rather than confirming certain stereotypical assumptions, I argue that Benlyazid's framing does not convert to a Western sense of oppression or segregation but to an endemically Moroccan gendered spatial logic that speaks directly to a different kind of gendered possibility, one centered around Islam. Through this possibility, perhaps even hope, Benlyazid channels Mernissi to resist static iterations of "Western feminism" (that is, secular, liberal, colonial or poststructuralist searches for freedom, choice, and agency) and perhaps equally static interpretations of orthodox or conservative Islam as routes through which to recognize women's and men's equality.[5]

HAREMS AND ḤUDŪD

The Nadia that we see framed by the window is in a state of flux. Having returned to Fes from Paris to be with her dying father, she disembarks the plane wearing a black leather jacket, her black hair tipped in fire-engine red, a black bag slung over her shoulder. She cannot stay long, she tells her sister Leyla. In fact, she never leaves. Instead, by the film's close, we see a decidedly different Nadia wandering Morocco's countryside with her new

---

4. Mernissi 1994, Stewart 2007, Khanna 2008.

5. See Mernissi 1987, Mernissi 1991, and Mernissi 2001 for more on her approach to the concepts of feminism and equality within Islam. I'm also drawing on Saba Mahmood and Jeanette Jouili: Mahmood (2005) questions post-Enlightenment liberal (and arguably neolibЕ eral) subjectivity and associated implied freedoms read through the lens of poststructural feminisms. Urging readers to uncouple agency from resistance, she insists that these liberal constructs often do not map onto local structures. Jouili (2015) draws on while also resisting aspects of Mahmood's argument, illustrating an important reminder about the multiple and varied forms that feminisms and resistance can and do take. Finally, I'm drawing on Leila Ahmed's and Asma Barlas' meticulously researched reminders that current understandings of Islam, including women's historical and current public and private roles and the relationship between the Qur'an, Hadith and Sunnah, emerge through their use by people in power (both social and governmental), most often men. See Ahmed 1992 and Barlas 2002.

husband in shots suggesting a pilgrimage. Nadia's multiple transitions – from French to Fassi, secular to Sufi – take place within the *riad*, where she learns to pray, reads Al Ghazali and Ibn 'Arabi, becomes a renowned Sufi healer, and ultimately makes the decision to leave the *riad* but not Morocco. Here, in the window, in what Kathleen Stewart might call a still life – "a static state filled with vibratory motion or resonance" – we see the start of her journey.[6]

Her father has passed away, yet Nadia refuses to don traditional mourning dress - white *djellaba* (long, loose robe), white *balgha* (slippers), white *hijab* (scarf) – favoring her t-shirt, whiskey, and cigarettes. Rather than join the mourners below, she remains in a salon above the courtyard surrounded by memories of her French mother.[7] Reluctantly, at Leyla's urging, Nadia moves to the window to hear Kirana's recitation praising the Prophet Mohammed, a marker of mourning. Framing the *mūsharabī*, the camera locates the France of her mother's salon behind her and Fes' Islam below to form a still life: "A quivering in the stability of a category or a trajectory, it gives the ordinary the charge of an unfolding."[8] The camera cuts to that same shot of the courtyard, now filmed from eye level, as Nadia enters dressed in white, quietly crossing it to pause at another *mūsharabī*. Hereafter, rather than t-shirts, we see her dressed in *sarwāl qandrīsī* (loose pants), *djellaba* or *pajamas* (house dresses that Moroccan women often wear indoors and, when out, under their *djellaba*), her hair often covered in *hijab*. Gone is her whiskey. She will go on to save the *riad* from Driss, her brother, who is adamant about selling it and who, by Islamic law, inherits half while she and Leyla each inherit one-quarter.[9]

Nadia's entrance into the courtyard marks her visual and affective unfolding into Fes and a non-normative Islam evidenced by Moroccan women. Here, Benlyazid also locates the *riad*'s role in her transition, situating it as one of the film's main characters.[10] She offers few establishing

6. Stewart 2007, 19. Stewart says of still lifes: a painting is "charged with the textures of paint and desire;" it represents "a state of calm, a lull in the action" (18).

7. While not addressed in the narrative, Nadia's mother, a French woman who did not speak Darija (Moroccan colloquial Arabic), died when she was young. She was an artist; many of her canvases still populate the salon. She was also a follower of Ba Sassi, a Sufi with whom Nadia became close following her death.

8. Stewart 2007, 19.

9. See Qurʾān 4:11–12.

10. "According to the character sketch provided by Benlyazid, the house is another character: 'It is in a certain manner the principal character. It is a vestige of a civilization in the process of disappearing. It represents the cradle of the Arabo-Andalusian (Moroccan) culture of which the city of Fez has long been proud'" (Carter 2009, 293, fn 179, quoting a "Document in Benlyazid's file in CCM [Centre Cinématographique Marocain, Morocco's government-affiliated film board]," my translation).

shots of the Medina, instead tightly framing the narrative within the *riad*'s walls.[11] While perhaps proving claustrophobic to some Western viewers accustomed to more open shots, for Nadia these walls form a cocoon. In her memoir *Dreams of Trespass*, Fatima Mernissi offers a lens through which to approach the significance of private spaces in Moroccan women's lives, starting with her opening passage:

> I was born in a harem in 1940 in Fez, a ninth-century Moroccan city some five thousand kilometers west of Mecca, and one thousand kilometers south of Madrid, one of the dangerous capitals of the Christians. The problems with the Christians start, said Father, as with women, when the *hudud* – a sacred frontier or boundary – is not respected.[12]

Formed by the *riad*'s walls and the cultural and familial norms that surround Mernissi, *ḥudūd* prove an ever-present specter in the lives of the women who populate her memoir, regulating their movement without and within and forming an affective frame that marks their daily routines.[13] From her paternal grandmother and aunt who deeply respect the dual institutions to her mother and cousin who consistently resist them, Mernissi's childhood is structured around the harem and *ḥudūd*. "[S]ince then, looking for the frontier has become my life's occupation," she continues. "Anxiety eats at me whenever I cannot situate the geometric line organizing my powerlessness."[14]

For Mernissi, harem life is ordinary, its physical layout reiterating the import of private space in Morocco.[15] Houses are set up so that they re-

11. Fes is divided into three distinct neighborhoods. Founded in the eighth century, its densely-populated, labyrinthine Medina (old city) is home to myriad shrines, *madāris* (singular: *madrasah*), *ṭuruq* (singular: *ṭarīqah*; Sufi orders), and mosques, including Qarawiyyin University and Mosque, the world's oldest university, founded in 859 CE by Fatima al Fihri. Adjacent to it in one direction is Fes J'dīd (new Fes), dating to the eleventh century, known for its Mellah (Jewish quarter) and the King's palace. During the Protectorate era (1912–1956), the French built the Ville Nouvelle adjacent the Medina and Fes J'dīd. Nadia's *riad* is in the Medina; Leyla lives in the Ville Nouvelle, where wide, tree-lined streets contrast the Medina's narrow alleys.

12. Mernissi 1994, 1.

13. *Ḥudūd* (حدود) is the plural form, *ḥad* (حد) the singular. It would be more colloquially appropriate to refer to *ḥudūd* as a concept (rather than a specific instance) using the singular, definite construction: *al-ḥad* (الحد). With *ḥudūd*, I am drawing on and deferring to Mernissi's repeated use of the word.

14. Mernissi 1994, 3. Affect theory, such as Stewart 2007, helps me convey this sense of the quotidian indexed in women's private spaces.

15. Ḥ-r-m, the triliteral root for harem, carries meanings ranging from forbidden (*ḥaram*) to that which is sacred, taboo or private (*ḥurma*). Many Moroccans suggest that one should not enter a home uninvited because it is *ḥurma*. This is especially true of adolescent or adult men, who might encounter a woman without her *hijab*.

main invisible from the outside; still today, many include rooms near the entrance where men who are not family members are welcomed but beyond which they do not wander. For many Westerners, these configurations can translate into a sense of gender segregation, yielding staid Orientalist and Islamophobic tropes about oppression. Mernissi and Benlyazid resist this characterization, situating the private space of the *riad* as one in which women nourish each other, learn from each other, and directly contradict and confront each other. Rather than a space of silence, it is one of engaged activity with, to be sure, complex gendered and spatial hierarchies. This, for Mernissi, is a harem: its purpose is to safeguard the women within. Moreover, she distinguishes what she calls a domestic harem from the lascivious creations of Ottoman history: they are "rather dull" with "hardly any erotic dimension to speak of.... What defines it as a harem is not polygamy, but the men's desire to seclude their wives, and their wish to maintain an extended household rather than break into nuclear units."[16] For her father and uncle, the harem offers security to women who have nowhere else to go. Yet alongside this sense of security, Mernissi situates persistent resistance as "women dreamed of trespassing [the *ḥudūd*] all the time. The world beyond the gate was their obsession."[17] Benlyazid pushes beyond this representation, perhaps evidencing a generational divide: in *Bab al-Sama Maftuh*, women freely come and go within the *riad* with Nadia and Kirana traveling across Morocco and into Europe to religious festivals and on pilgrimages.

(RE)FRAMING HAREMS AND ḤUDŪD

Mernissi's *ḥudūd* frame her childhood. She spends sleepless nights on her maternal grandmother's farm where "the frontiers were not clear enough"; in Fes, she traces them by braving the *riad*'s highest terraces.[18] They form a normative structure on which she leans and against which she presses. Collectively, they serve as conduits for what Kathleen Stewart calls ordinary affects: pulses or pricks, surges or shocks that mark dominant norms and daily routines. Building on what she terms the ordinary – "a shifting assemblage of practices and practical knowledges" – ordinary affects are "the varied, surging capacities to affect and to be affected that give everyday life the quality of a continual motion of relations, scenes, contingencies, and emergences."[19] Mernissi's ordinary includes learning to navigate her *ḥudūd* by watching her mother's, cousin's, and aunt's differently structured resis-

16. Mernissi 1994, 35.
17. Mernissi 1994, 1–2.
18. Mernissi 1994, 25.
19. Stewart 2007, 1–2.

tance, marking Mernissi even if she does not (re)cognize it. Their ordinary affects circulate around gender politics: women confronting spatial and familial hierarchies expressed by where in the *riad* one's salon is located; Mernissi's evolving relationship with her best friend – her male cousin – as, with age, they confront an emergent *ḥudūd* separating them.

Ordinary affects are simultaneously collective and individual. They mark Moroccans who remain saturated by persistent gender norms about women occupying public and private spaces that constitute their ordinary. They differently mark Western audiences pressing against sedimented ideas about Orientalist iterations of the harem. While the vibrant colors and rich textures of Ingres' *La Grande Odalisque* – blues and yellows, silks and velvets – may ring true in Mernissi's and Benlyazid's narratives, the lasciviousness does not.[20] For many viewers, these contradictions form a pulse or prick in the form of a disconnect, impacting how they interact with Nadia and the *riad*. Finally, ordinary affects form flows in our routines that do not stop us in our tracks but function as "an empty pause or a dragging undertow."[21] We are not traumatized by Benlyazid's closed shots but may, after a while, register a subtle discomfort; while our eyes may gravitate to the patch of blue sky, the limitations imposed by the *riad*'s roof remain part of our peripheral vision, subtly framing the shot and, by extension, what we visually and affectively take away from it.

In my approach to *riad*s as framing devices – in my insistence that Benlyazid's filmic representation of it as a main character contributes to our affective engagement with it – I am merging physical space with its powerful affect. Different viewers – Moroccan and foreign; women and men – will draw on their ordinary affects as their own differently configured framing devices: their sense of the *riad* as a claustrophobic space or supportive cocoon is informed by their gender, class, and geographic backgrounds that come together to form their *ḥudūd*. To help enflesh my approach to the private space of the *riad* as a framing device for the film and our affective engagement with it, I turn to Ranjanna Khanna's theorization of a frame as a device that "both determines and supplements meaning" by functioning as a "protective enclosure," regulating the information flowing into it.[22] Khanna's frames are filmic and photographic: the shiny white paper, for example, that surrounds an image on four sides and that, by extension, determines what we can and cannot see. I would like to add others: spatially,

---

20. For a fascinating visual resistance to lascivious representations of harem life, see Moroccan artist Lalla Essaydi (2005).

21. Stewart 2007, 2.

22. Khanna 2008, 33, 36.

the frame of the *riad* and its walls; culturally, the frame of the harem and its *ḥudūd*. Stewart's ordinary affects, when felt as circulating through Khanna's frames, productively amplify the cinematic affect that Benlyazid conveys through the *riad*'s simultaneous openness and enclosure.

Benlyaid's still lifes underscore her emphasis on affect over narrative specificity in marking Nadia's transitions. They are only briefly still and often without context. Rather than relying on explication, Benlyazid conveys information affectively: the prick of a bright but abbreviated sky. Finally, Benlyazid structures these still lifes around the *riad*. Or, differently stated: women's private space structures Nadia's transitions; Benlyazid frames them in the vibratory potential of her still lifes. Following a confrontation with Leyla – when they learn that a young, unmarried maid who works in the *riad* is pregnant, Leyla wants to fire her while Nadia insists she can stay – Nadia declares to Kirana her frustration with religion: those with power use it to oppress those without. Dressed in the white *pajama* torn along the shoulder and bottom hem that she has worn since her father's funeral, her hair noticeably disheveled, she stands slightly left of center screen, her back to the camera, facing large windows that dwarf her, as did the *mūsharabī*. Framed in blue, she faces the *riad*'s sun-drenched courtyard. Surrounding her is *zallīj*: intricate, multi-colored tile, a marker of Fassi architecture that, to the uninitiated, can also appear chaotic; the windows are populated by multiple panes so that, rather than an unbroken view of the courtyard, it is fractured. Behind them, off-screen, are her mother's paintings. In front of them is the courtyard, toward which she will turn her attention. The vibratory potential of an unfolding felt in the affect circulating through the frame: Kirana encourages Nadia to rethink the normative Islam that yields her fear of oppression, therein orienting her toward another transition.

Given its multiple colors and textures, this still life's aesthetics and affect take precedence over the scene's narrative content. It is almost easy to gloss Kirana's advice without internalizing its role in the Islam that Nadia embraces. Yet rather than encouraging her to visit a mosque, to seek guidance from an imam (inevitably a man) – rather than encouraging her to embrace an orthodox Islam – Kirana directs her toward the margins of Fes's normative. She therein prioritizes the private sphere – the space of women's Islam over men's; of a more heterodox iteration of Islam such as Sufism – rather than the orthodox space of the mosque.[23] In fact, Benlyazid

---

23. In *Dreams of Trespass* (1994), Mernissi touches on women's Islam within the private sphere, as does Leila Ahmed (2000). For more on the interplay of Sufism, Sunni, and sharifi Islam in Morocco, see Cornell 1988 and Spadola 2014. For a critique of Benlyazid's representation of Sufism, see Gauch 2009.

never takes viewers inside a mosque and only once focuses her lens on one.[24] Kirana's suggestion that Nadia read Al Ghazali, a central figure for Sufi and Sunni practitioners, further substantiates her and, by extension, Nadia's path. Finally, the cumulative impact of her overt emphasis on Sufism opens up the space for the role that the *riad* will take on as it begins to function more as a Sufi order.

Faced with its imminent sale, Nadia announces to a lawyer her intention to use it as a *zāwiyah*. While the word is subtitled in the film as shelter, this translation elides its relationship to Sufism: *al-zawāyā* (plural of *zāwiyah*) have long functioned as shelters; the word also refers to a Sufi *ṭarīqah*'s (order) physical space. Her lawyer – a woman in Western dress contrasting Nadia's *djellaba* – warns her that the law is on Driss's side but encourages her to press forward. As with many others, the scene is brief. It is also remarkable for its overt reference to feminism. The lawyer dryly asks, "so, then, you want to create women's lib in Fes?" Taking a drag on her cigarette, reminding us that, beneath the *djellaba*, this is the same Nadia we first met, she counters: "No, it always existed in our country. The problem is that we're losing the best aspects of our culture, and only keeping the skeleton of the traditional, devoid of its meaning." Nadia's insistence that "in Islam, women have always used their wealth freely and financed shelters for deprived and unhappy women" lends this scene an overtly feminist narrative. Still, I find the sequence that follows more telling in terms of Benlyazid's aesthetics and her use of the *riad* as a framing device focused toward secular and Islamic feminisms.

Following a still life of Nadia praying in a salon, bathed in its ubiquitous blue, the camera cuts to her sitting on the *riad*'s brown roof in the bright Fassi sun with the expansive Medina behind her: a decidedly different color palette. Kirana enters and, over a long, slow pan of the Medina, they discuss Moulay Abssesalam, a twelfth-century Sufi mystic from northern Morocco. As the two slowly circle the roof arm in arm, the courtyard below edges into the frame, reversing Benlyazid's previous shot of the sky, while viewers finally take in the Medina's dense, crowded expansiveness. As Nadia recounts her intent to use the *riad* as a *zāwiyah*, into the back of the frame creeps a visibly disheveled girl who has been badly beaten. Nadia immediately takes this as a sign. The camera cuts to her in the courtyard watering verdant green plants. In her shot-reverse shots of the roof and courtyard, Benlyazid sutures

24. Benlyazid opens *Bab al-Sama Maftuh* on the phallic minaret of a Medina mosque shot from a low angle and set against the open blue sky, clearly juxtaposing the sky over the *riad*'s courtyard. A pre-credit flashback sequence, here Nadia's father, dressed in a Western-style suit and hat, meanders the narrow streets of the Medina, passing the mosque en route to the *riad*.

many spatial and affective aspects of Nadia's transitions. The circumscribed transcendence of the enframed sky shot from the courtyard below seems fractured – opened – first in the shot of Nadia over the expansive Medina and here in the enclosed courtyard. This is the first time we have seen her dwell in this space rather than cross it; it is the first time since the pre-credit sequence that we have seen the courtyard teeming with plant life. Since she emerged dressed in her white *djellaba*, it is the first time we have seen her in different colors: here, bright yellow *sarwāl qandrīsī*, a black shirt layered over a red shirt. Another transition, another unfolding, another "static state filled with vibratory motion" that is based around the *riad*'s physical frame.[25] Here, we see the emergence of Nadia's own domestic harem. By the film's close, multiple women live within its walls, including those who have weathered unplanned pregnancies, child abuse, and domestic violence, as well as free spirits who simply do not conform to Fes's gender norms.

(Re)Framing a Cultural Moment

Mernissi's father wondered where, without the domestic harem, all the "troubled women" would go.[26] He welcomed divorced women, widows, and former slaves into its routines and rituals. In contrast, Nadia's harem – the *zāwiyah* – does not lean on men's traditional roles in harem hierarchies: men had no say in its founding; they do not monitor its *ḥudūd*. Nadia establishes it, directly contradicting her brother and the patriarchy he represents. Moreover, she does so recognizing that, once a *zāwiyah*, the *riad* cannot be repurposed. Yet, while she therein deviates from the dominant, do her actions contradict the norm? According to her, "women's lib" has "always existed in Morocco." As does Mernissi across her corpus, through Nadia, Benlyazid reiterates Muslim women's roles in the history of Islam: Nadia does not need Driss. She takes her own active steps. In so doing, she implicitly contradicts common misperceptions about Muslim women's oppression. In her representation of the *zāwiyah*, Benlyazid is not rejecting or radically exploding existing cultural and religious *ḥudūd*, nor is she interjecting an anachronistic iteration of women's rights in Islam. Instead, she is reminding Moroccan viewers and reeducating Western viewers about them.

Benlyazid released *Bab al-Sama Maftuh* during what proved a significant historical moment. As the UN Decade for Women (1976–85) heightened rhetoric about women's rights, transnational feminists pressed against Western feminisms' colonial legacies; Gayatri Chakravorty Spivak's "Can the Subaltern Speak?" emerged as a foundational postcolonial feminist text the

25. Stewart 2007, 19.
26. Mernissi 1994, 16.

same year that Benlyazid released *Bab al-Sama Maftuh*.[27] In the early 1980s, the World Bank and International Monetary Fund mandated structural readjustment programs that wreaked havoc on Morocco's economy; by the decade's close, King Hassan II began slowly easing the extreme censorship and torture that marked his tenure, although artists, activists, and citizens alike continued to police themselves in fear of his security apparatus.[28] *Al-Mujāhadīn* returning from the war in Afghanistan brought fundamentalist Wahhabi- and Salafi-infused iterations of Islam while Marxist and socialist groups gained visibility on university campuses. Finally, secular and Islamist women's groups grew in number and visibility, manifesting in multiple organizations such as the Association Démocratique des Femmes du Maroc and the Women's Section of Al-Adl wal-Ihsan. Both in part turned their attention to Morocco's *mudawwanah* (family code) as a marker of women's quotidian realities: secular feminists argued for significant changes; Islamist women resisted change by pointing to its status as *sharia* (and thus divine) law.[29] In many ways, *Bab al-Sama Maftuh* reflects this moment. Rather than mapping onto secular feminists or Islamist women, Benlyazid translates the opposition into still lifes – frames – that can be shot through with opposing affective dynamics. By showing women's relationship with Islam, including its place in the private sphere, Nadia's *zāwiyah* evidences an endemically Moroccan gendered spatial logic that indexes a different kind of gendered possibility. To be sure, she was critiqued for her positive representation of veiled women and Islam. Sandra Carter says "[s]ome considered it a beautifully crafted inquiry into a personal dilemma of development and change" while others saw a "folkloric depiction of backward Morocco," perhaps a marker of secular feminists' orientation away from Islam.[30]

With its focus on women's spaces and their unique sense of gendered possibility, Nadia's harem represents what Stewart refers to as a "weirdly floating 'we' snap[ping] into a blurry focus."[31] Men are rarely seen on

27. Spivak 1988. Originally published in the journal *Wedge* in 1985, "Can the Subaltern Speak?" is much more widely cited in the Cary Nelson and Lawrence Grossberg 1988 edited volume *Marxism and the Interpretation of Culture*.

28. For more on the Lead Years, see Slyomovics 2005. For filmmakers' response to censorship during Hassan II's reign, see Dwyer 2012.

29. Morocco's only legal code based in *sharia* rather than French law, the *mudawwanah* governs family life, including marriage, divorce, and custody. First codified in 1958 by Mohammed V, it denied women legal subjectivity, granting fathers, brothers, and husbands guardianship; Mohammed VI changed this with his 2004 revisions. For more, see Elliott 2015 and Salime 2011.

30. Carter 2009, 250.

31. Stewart 2007, 27. Similarly, Mernissi's harem is visibly populated by women. Her father and uncle are central characters in their role as men, but they occupy different spaces in the *riad* than do the women and thus remain on the memoir's margins.

screen alone. The film's two male-only sequences are filmed outside of the *riad* and function as flashbacks, falling outside of its narrative structure.[32] Instead, women dictate and enforce the harem's *ḥudūd* with close attention to their own iterations of Islam. Nadia's harem thus illustrates a feminist resistance that, to draw on Saba Mahmood, did not involve rupturing the surrounding structures.[33] Instead, by drawing on her own interpretations of mystics and philosophers such as Al Ghazali, Ibn 'Arabi, and Moulay Abdessalam, Nadia gently reframes them and, in so doing, shifts them into configurations through which she can feel and comport herself differently. Mernissi undertook a similar trajectory, another important context for Benlyazd's frames: one of the earliest academics to engage in an overtly feminist rereading of Islam, rather than rejecting it, Mernissi leaned on her own interpretation that insisted on its compatibility with women's rights.

The Nadia we first glimpse within the *mūsharabī*'s frame overtly rejects the *ḥudūd*, insisting that what she does is no one's business. Crossing into the bright courtyard, she also crosses into their frame. Out of the norms of propriety, Leyla presses her to move from the open courtyard into the crowded salon where Kirana and a group of women are gathered: from a space of expansiveness to one of enclosure. This constellation is central to my reading of *Bab al-Sama Maftuh* as a generative gendered space that defies a Western sense of oppression. It is telling that a woman leads women in the mourning recitation. Gone are the men who have been hovering on the film's margins in her father's final days: Nadia's brother, her brother-in-law, her nephew; they will not hereafter return to the *riad*. To a certain extent, their absence here in this mourning sequence is expected. One guesses they are at the cemetery, where women are often not permitted during burial ceremonies. Yet rather than waiting for them to return to lead them in the recitation, rather than hiring a *talbah* or *firqat al-madīḥ* (both men) to perform it, as is common practice, the women do it themselves: with Kirana as *al-madīḥah*, reciting praise of the Prophet, the women participate in a typical call-and-response pattern.[34] Benlyazid does not show them rupturing the harem's *ḥudūd* by going to the cemetery. At the same time, they shift them by projecting their voices in open defiance of patriarchal interpretations that silence Muslim women's voices in public spaces of worship. Theirs is a

32. In the pre-credit sequence, Nadia's father meanders the Medina's alleys; later, as a child, he and his father encounter a Daria-speaking Westerner in the Medina.

33. Mahmood 2005.

34. A *talbah* is a group hired to recite the Qurʾān and perform *duʿaaʾ*: supplications to Allah. A *madīḥ* (man) and *madīḥah* (woman) orally praise the Prophet; those around her respond with a refrain that varies regionally and across religious orders. While women can fill these roles, in a city as conservative as Fes, they rarely do.

decidedly non-normative gender performance that proves so productive for Nadia and the *riad*.

Benlyazid's cinematography in this sequence is striking. In a medium shot, Nadia emerges into the courtyard in a white *djellaba* and white *hijab* against the visual chaos of the courtyard's *zallīj* and *mūsharabī*. Following a cut – a brief shot from the opposite side of the courtyard looking into the

salon, again dwarfing Nadia – she reverses the shot: within the salon looking out into the courtyard. Between Nadia and the camera lies the *mūsharabī*, fracturing the frame with its intricate arabesque pattern and tacitly implying the trope of the oppressed Muslim woman. While Nadia's movements are slow and deliberate, Benlyazid's mise-en-scène is set in the vibrant motion of colors, patterns, and textures. From here, Nadia allows Leyla to guide her into the salon; as they cross its threshold, Benlyazid's frame shrinks, yielding to the salon's walls and shadows: another visual reference to the claustrophobia of the enclosed private sphere. Yet here she fractures this frame of reference, from the recitation through the film's narrative arc. Allowing another woman to take her elbow and guide her to a seat, Nadia is differently framed than she has been. Rather than alone in her mother's salon, she is saturated by the women's fluid, rhythmic recitation and surrounded by the women themselves: they line each wall of the salon, one after another. Throughout the sequence, Benlyazid's frames defy a parallel between enclosure and oppression. Instead, she visually demonstrates Moroccan women's quotidian lives, framing them in contrast to representations by increasingly verbal strains of secular feminisms and conservative Islam. Benlyazid pushes against both: she resists the stereotypical spatial connotations of public and private spaces by productively engaging Moroccan women's roles in the private sphere.

WORKS CITED

Ahmed, L. 1992. *Women and Gender in Islam: Historical Roots of a Modern Debate.* New Haven, CT.

———. 2000. *A Border Passage: From Cairo to America – A Woman's Journey.* New York.

Barlas, A. 2002. *Believing Women in Islam: Understanding Patriarchal Interpretations of the Qur'an.* Austin, TX.

Carter, S. G. 2000. "Farida Benlyazid's Moroccan Women," *Quarterly Review of Film & Video* 17 (4): 343–69.

———. 2009. *What Moroccan Cinema?: A Historical and Critical Study, 1956-2006.* Lanham, MD.

Cornell, V. 1988. *Realm of the Saint: Power and Authority in Moroccan Sufism.* Austin, TX.

Dwyer, K. 2004. *Beyond Casablanca: M. A. Tazi and the Adventure of Moroccan Cinema.* Bloomington, IN.

Elliott, K. Z. 2015. *Modernizing Patriarchy: The Politics of Women's Rights in Morocco.* Austin, TX.

Essaydi, L. 2005. *Converging Territories.* New York.

Gauch, S. 2016. *Maghrebs in Motion: North African Cinema in Nine Movements.* New York.

———. 2009. "Now You See It, Now You Don't: Transnational Feminist Spectatorship and Farida Benlyazid's *A Door to the Sky.*" *Camera Obscure* 24 (2): 107–37.

Jouili, J. 2015. *Pious Practice and Secular Constraint: Women in the Islamic Revival in Europe.* Stanford, CA.

Khanna, R. 2008. *Algeria Cuts: Women & Representation, 1830 to the Present.* Stanford, CA.

Mahmood, S. 2005. *Politics of Piety: The Islamic Revival and the Feminist Subject.* Princeton, NJ.

Martin, F. 2011. *Screens and Veils: Maghrebi Women's Cinema.* Bloomington, IN.

Mernissi, F. 1987. *Beyond the Veil: Male-Female Dynamics in Modern Muslim Society.* Bloomington, IN.

———. 1991. *The Veil and the Male Elite: A Feminist Interpretation of Women's Rights in Islam.* Translated by Mary Jo Lakeland. New York.

———. 1993. *The Forgotten Queens of Islam.* Translated by Mary Jo Lakeland. Minneapolis, MN.

———. 1994. *Dreams of Trespass: Tales of a Harem Girlhood.* Cambridge, MA.

———. 1996. *Women's Rebellion & Islamic Memory.* New York.

———. 2001. *Scheherazade Goes West: Different Cultures, Different Harems.* New York.

Salime, Z. 2011. *Between Feminism and Islam: Human Rights and Sharia Law in Morocco.* Minneapolis, MN.

Shohat, E. 2003. "Post-Third-Worldist Culture: Gender, Nation, and the Cinema." In *Rethinking Third Cinema,* edited by Anthony Guneratne and Wimal Dissanayke, 51–78. New York.

Slyomovics, S. 2005. *The Performance of Human Rights in Morocco.* Philadelphia.

Spadola, E. 2014. *The Calls of Islam: Sufis, Islamists, and Mass Mediation in Urban Morocco.* Bloomington, IN.

Spivak, G. C. 1988. "Can the Subaltern Speak?" In *Marxism and the Interpretation of Culture,* edited by Cary Nelson and Lawrence Grossberg, 271–316. Champaign, IL.

Stewart, K. 2007. *Ordinary Affects.* Durham, NC.

Van de Peer, S. 2015. "Morocco." In *Women Screenwriters: An International Guide,* edited by Jill Nelmes and Julie Selbo, 23–28. New York.

School of Satan:
al-Azhar's Censure of Egyptian Cinema Coincides with the Vogue of Islamic History Films

Mohannad Ghawanmeh

THE RELATIONSHIP BETWEEN THE EGYPTIAN STATE and the venerated, millennium-old institution of (Sunni) Islam named al-Azhar has influenced Egyptian cinema over the decades, especially films whose content is deemed "Islamic" in subject or theme. In *Majallat Al-Azhar*, the namesake publication of the institution, authors commented on cinema repeatedly. Muslim scholars generally did not care for cinema or its social effects and the magazine's content illustrates al-Azhar's censure of Egyptian films over much of the last century. For example, a 1957 essay claims cinema corrupts moviegoers because it is a school of Satan.[1] This chapter examines al-Azhar's role in approving the roughly fifteen or so films dealing with Islamic history, which belong to a production trend in Egypt that began in earnest with *Dhuhour al-Islam* (*The Emergence of Islam*, Ibrahim ʿIz al-Din, 1951) and ending with *al-Sheimaʿ* (Husam al-Din Mustafa, 1972).[2] Overall, al-Azhar's disavowal of Islam-centered films served as an extra-legal instrument of government censorship and as a public critique of the cinema. However, al-Azhar's position on the depiction of Muhammad's contemporaries permitted visual storytelling that would have been impossible had al-Azhar taken a more strident line, such as that of its contemporary, Muslim Brotherhood.

An extensive conceptual or cultural analysis of Egyptian mid-twentieth-century Islamic history films is not a task I can perform in a single chapter.[3]

---

1. Al-Shirbasi, A. 1957.
2. *Al-Sheimaʿ* was the Prophet Muhammad's "milk sibling," who embraced Islam after long supporting the Prophet clandestinely, according to the film's account.
3. See Salahʾl-Din 1998, Qasim 2017, and Ahmad 2018. Such studies of Egyptian cinema's links to Islam do not exist in English to my knowledge, though Shafik 1998, 47–49, touches on Arab cinema's interaction with Islam, in terms of strictures, and Egyptian Islamic history films (170–73). Shafik 2007, 201–5, assesses the sexism of increasingly vociferous censures of the cinema on the grounds of immorality, by public figures and institutions, and offers a couple of Egyptian works of resistance. Khouri 2010, 167–83, focuses on the renowned director, Youssef Chahine's confrontation with fundamentalist and political Islam. Most valuable in this chap-

Instead this essay references Egyptian religious and cultural journals, variety magazines, and industry papers of the era, to discuss the relationship between the Egyptian government's cinema censorship apparatus and al-Azhar's participation in assessing film projects' propriety for production. It begins with a review of al-Azhar's censorship function and tradition of censure in relation to the cinema and to the Egpytian government. Then it focuses on the allowance that al-Azhar made for portraying most of Muhammad's companions (*Sahaba*) in theater and cinema, arguing for how such allowance emboldened producers to embark on film projects Islamic in theme or subject. It concludes with an assessment of how Islamic history films negotiated industry trends, audience expectations, al-Azhar's strictures, and the censor's eye in vying for success at the box office and beyond.

AL-AZHAR'S FUNCTION IN CENSORING THE EGYPTIAN CINEMA

Censorship history in Egypt is a relatively well traversed subject.[4] Two film projects are documented to have been censored on the grounds of religious insensitivity before the emergence of the Islamic history films, both of which proposed to have an actor portray the Prophet Muhammad. Both Egyptian projects were aborted, having been assailed in the press. Both were proposed as foreign productions, but the first, and far better remembered project involved one of Egypt's celebrities, theater director and actor Yousef Wahby, in the role of Muhammad.[5] These projects predate a definite trend of Islamic films that begins two decades thereafter but establishes al-Azhar's position on depiction of hallowed persons, which is most significant to this study's analysis. Al-Azhar declared its stance in response to published news that Yousef Wahby's signed, in the German embassy, a contract for the exorbitant amount of ten thousand Egyptian pounds to perform the role of Muhammad.[6] Al-Azhar's director, Abu'l-Fadl al-Jizawi,[7] argued to the effect that Islam utterly forbade imagery of the prophets, messengers, and their companions.[8] This position would be attenuated so as to allow for depiction of most companions of Muhammad, an allowance a few of the Islamic history films in question would certainly take advantage of.

---

ter is the analysis of Chahine's choice to use colloquial Egyptian Arabic in his film *Destiny* (*al-Masir*, 1997), rather than standard/classical Arabic as is customary in historical films, including all of the Islamic history films examined herein.

4. See Bayoumi 2002, Farid 2002, Ali 2004, and Ali 2008.
5. El-Hadary 1987, 199–204 and a whole chapter on the scandalous affair in Farid 2002, 26–52.
6. Farid 2002, 27.
7. Al-Namnam 2012, 126
8. Farid 2002, 27.

Egyptian state censorship of the cinema, first affected its exhibitors in 1909.[9] Thereafter, various ministries and supervisory bodies would take on the charge of overseeing exhibition houses and the films that they screened. Significant for this essay's purpose is that the censorship function was bifurcated by the Egyptian government in 1946, only a few years before the onset of the Islamic history films. This bifurcation was administrative – the Ministry of Social Affairs oversaw issues of sensitivity toward common decency, family, and tradition while the Ministry of the Interior minded public safety and national interests.[10] This segmentation is confirmed by Muhammad ʿAli Nasif and his successor, Mustafa Darwish,[11] both having served as director of censorship within the Ministry of Social Guidance, established in 1952 in the wake of the Free Officers Revolution,[12] during this study's period of interest.[13] Nasif cites religion as the subject of films that pose the greatest threat to Egyptian society, following sex.[14] Indeed, restrictions and requirements on representing religion, especially Islam, its practices, and sanctities appears in the censorship table produced by the Egyptian government in 1947.[15]

Darwish does correctly identify depiction of prophets as among the prohibitions, for it appears in the censorship table.[16] The table does not, however, mention Muhammad's companions; as such depicting them was not illegal according to the censor's letter, including the venerated Rightly Guided Caliphs Abu Bakr, ʿUmar, ʿUthman, and ʿAli. Although it had been written, the 1947 code had not been made public at the time of Darwish's first appointment as director of censorship in 1962, so as to shroud the censorship process in secrecy, he gathered.[17] Notable, is that the code's points of prohibition are particularly abstract in the "religion" segment. Of the five points delineated two begin with "To be taken into consideration":

> ... 2. To take into consideration presentation of ceremonies and rituals especially those Islamic in a dignified, respectable fashion ... and 5. To be considered is respect of religions and not opposing doctrines while

9. ʿAli 2008, 17.

10. ʿAli 2008, 74–75.

11. Nasif 1963, 78; Darwish 1995, 93.

12. ʿAli 2008, 77.

13. Nasif served for three years, 1960–1962 and Darwish served twice for a total of two years during 1962, 1966–1967. Nasif 1963, 75; Darwish 1995, 91.

14. Nasif 1963, 81.

15. ʿAli 2008, 97–107.

16. "Showing the images of the prophets" is stated in the first point under "religion." ʿAli 2008, 99.

17. Darwish 1995, 92. The code has been since published, as my examination of it would indicate.

avoiding subjects and dialogues that propagate religious or national discord. [18]

Since a practice of taking a thing into consideration hardly directs the considerer to act in any way definitive, such points as above only furthered the censorship code's vagueness. Yet, such ambiguity seemed well suited to al-Azhar's being unofficially assigned the task of approving film projects with Islamic themes.

Al-Azhar sanctioned films in a single stage of oversight, whereas the censorship office did so in at least three, signifying al-Azhar's authority relative to that of the censorship department. The Egyptian censor required three submissions before issuing approval for domestic exhibition. Two of these occurred in pre-production: first the producer would present a treatment of the screenplay to the censor to be accepted or rejected, in which case amendments were suggested. Having received a pass for the treatment, a producer would then submit a completed screenplay for a similar assessment. Once approval of the screenplay was secured, the completed film would be reviewed before granting a permit for domestic exhibition. The object of such a system is that a tiered approval process prevented unnecessary investments of time, energy, and funds into a commercial product that would not be sellable. In the years leading up to the study the Egyptian censor had on multiple occasions denied an exhibition permit after reviewing the film, even though it had been made to the letter of an already approved screenplay![19]

Indeed, al-Azhar's approval of a film's idea or treatment at minimum was necessary for the censor's allowance to proceed with shooting an approved script of Islamic theme or subject. Al-Azhar reviewed screenplays as a matter of course, not merely treatments of the story.[20] On at least two occasions film project principles sought approval from al-Azhar directly for their projects. One is attorney 'Adli al-Moulad's biography of Muhammad, which he took to al-Azhar repeatedly until it agreed to his depicting 'Umar in the dark and wrapped in a robe, turning away from the camera. Al-Moulad reportedly also got approval for depicting Muhammad as a beam of light.[21] The other instance relates to a project to film the Qur'anic story of *Ahl al-Kahf* (*People of the Cave*), which never materialized. [22] Typically, productions hired historians and theologians not affiliated with al-Azhar to advise

18. The entire 1947 film censorship code is published in ʿAli 2008, 97–107.
19. Tawfiq 1971, 40.
20. Salah al-Din 1998, 121.
21. Rajab 1962.
22. Anonymous 1962, 67.

on the religious content of films, including Muhammad al-Banna, son of the founder of the Muslim Brotherhood Hasan al-Banna, and regular contributor to a journal with which the organization was affiliated – *Liwaʿ al-Islam* (*Banner of Islam*). Muhammad al-Banna participated in the two panel discussions on performing hallowed figures referenced in this essay and consulted on the film *al-Sayid al-Badawi* (Baha² al-Din Sharaf, 1954).[23]

Twice there was coordination between the censor and al-Azhar. The first was a reference to al-Azhar's involvement in censorship made by the aforementioned director of the censorship department, Muhammad ʿAli Naesif. He was asked if al-Azhar's opinion would compel two foreign producers that had each announced their intention of making a film about Muhammad to abandon "all of the elements that could play a role in commercial gain," presumably meaning the depiction of Muhammad, the principle character, and of his companions. Nasif responded that "etiquette compels that al-Azhar's opinion be binding from the literary aspect." Notable is Nasif's use of "literary aspect," to indicate that al-Azhar has no provenance over the photographic aspect, the filmic form of the text.[24] What is also notable about Nasif's response is his including the companions in the prohibition against depiction.[25] This is despite several Egyptian Islamic history films depicting the companions having been made prior to Nasif's tenure as censor. Nasif's ignorance of this recent production history consequential to his own function lends credence to his successor Mustafa Darwish's remark that the practice of the censor had been shrouded in secrecy.

Another example of the functional relationship between the government censor of cinema and al-Azhar is in the latter's eponymous *al-Azhar Magazine*. In it, director of al-Azhar Muhammad Shaltout writes an open letter to Vice-President Kamal al-Din Hussein in which he rails against two scenes in *Wa Islamah* (*Oh Islam*, Enrico Bomba and Andrew Marton, 1961; a film co-directed by American Marton), especially one involving incorrect prayer movements that Shaltout describes as "a farcical image known only to children and crazies." Shaltout goes on to announce that he is taking the opportunity of censuring *Oh Islam* to request that "films be screened to al-Azhar before screening them to the people, or at least to hire among the censor's members of al-Azhar ..." The vice-president's response committed next to nothing, other than to convey that he had "taken expeditious procedures to examine the matter of these observations ..."[26]

23. Salah al-Din 1998, 51.
24. Rajab 1962, February 9.
25. Rajab 1962, February 9.
26. Shaltout and Hussein 1961, 770–71.

Al-Azhar's oversight of cinema would not become official until 1985 for an exhibition of arts dealing with religion (Islam).[27] Until then al-Azhar's oversight differed from picture to picture. During this operative era, al-Azhar clearly functioned in a society not governed according to its interests or preferences, not least in the allowance for vice that Egyptians experienced. The cinema was one such vice. If a pocket of virtue in the prurient morass that is the cinema could be parsed by earnest Islamic-themed projects, then al-Azhar was increasingly willing to proffer its approval and offer its council. They even sent representatives upon request to the production site for a meet and greet of the cast and crew of *Fajr al-Islam* (*Dawn of Islam*, Salah Abouseif, 1971) and an on-set production consultant, in the case of the multinational production that would follow the vogue of films herein examined, namely *The Message* (initially titled *Muhammad, God's Messenger*, Moustapha Akkad, 1977). These two productions were among the most exorbitant among all Islamic history films, with *Dawn of Islam* costing 130,000 Egyptian pounds[28] and *The Message*'s budget amounting to a whopping $12 million,[29] so securing al-Azhar's sanction for their resulting film – not only for their source screenplay – was likely a precautionary measure, not least since both films' stories are set in the Mecca of the Prophet.

Emergence of Islam (1951) the film that launched the vogue of Islamic history films, even if it was not the very first,[30] was also set in Muhammad's Mecca. Like *The Message* and several other Islamic history films *Emergence of Islam* depicted a prominent member of the Sahaba named Bilal bin Rabah, who would become the central figure in the 1953 release *Bilal mu'adhin al-rasoul* (*Bilal, the Prophet's Muezzin*, Ahmed El Touki, 1953). Bilal bin Rabah was one of several Sahaba who would be personified on screen in these Islamic history films. Nasif's observation that materializing the Sahaba was out of bounds, though not consistent with Egypt's own recent production experience, was consistent with al-Azhar's proclaimed position regarding dating to the 1920s. Moreover, Nasif's relatively strict admonishment was shared by the Muslim Brotherhood contemporaneously, as discussed in the next segment.

27. Salah al-Din 1998, 116.

28. Al-Sa'dani 1971, 17.

29. Anonymous 1975, 77.

30. According to Mahmoud Qasim, the first film in this vogue is the film *Ibn 'Antar* (*Son of 'Antar*, Ahmed Salem, 1947). Qasim 2017, 53. However, the astonishing commercial and critical success of *Emergence of Islam* seems to have been responsible for the robust production of Islamic history films.

DEPICTING THE SAHABA SELECTIVELY,
AL-AZHAR'S ATTENUATED POSITION

It is perhaps convenient to consider al-Azhar a reactionary institution. They had for centuries acted as legitimators of regimes under which it had served and from which it had acquired funding.[31] Yet, al-Azhar arguably took a risk in permitting the depiction of most of the Sahaba, a position that waxes relatively progressive.[32] This position was expressed plainly in response to a query published in a regular feature of *Al-Azhar Magazine* dedicated to issuing edicts (*fatwa*) in response to reader queries, in this case one sent in from a member of the General Television Administration. The edict declares that personifying Sahaba in acting is permissible as long the performer is of a character that would not sully the reputation of the companion depicted. The edict excludes from this allowance depicting the "Sahaba's greats," such as the Rightly Guided Caliphs, as well as ʿAli's sons Hassan and Hussein, and Muʾawiya, founder of the Omayyad Empire, who were involved in the hostilities that engendered Islamic sects. This exclusion has held in all of the film and TV Islamic history productions that I have viewed.[33] According to Western film practices, it would seem regressive to discuss the propriety of depicting Muhammad, let alone his companions. We ought not ignore, however, that one of the two prohibitions applied by the British Board of Film Censorship at its creation in 1912 was the materialization of Christ (the other being nudity.)[34]

The film *Emergence of Islam* served to signal the marketability of historical and Islamic-themed films. The film compelled al-Azhar to attenuate its strident position on the depiction of the Sahaba because the film's director and screenwriter were particularly influential in the Egyptian government at the time of the film's release, although neither had worked in the cinema prior, nor would they again. Producer-director Ibrahim ʿIz al-Din had bought the rights to Taha Hussein's novel *The Divine Promise* (*al-Waʾd al-Haq*, 1949), upon which *Emergence of Islam* was based, under the condition that Hussein participate in writing the film's screenplay.[35] With the forming of

31. Al-Namnam 2012, 2–4

32. Al-Asil 1962, 120.

33. A notable exception to the established practice of not depicting the Rightly Guided Caliphs was the Ramadan series *Omar* (Hatem Ali, 2012), about the life of the second Rightly Guided Caliph, but this series was a Qatari, not Egyptian, production.

34. The British Board of Film Censorship would develop a longer catalogue of prohibitions over time, but according to Neville Hunnings these two were the original (Hunnings 1967, 55).

35. It is notable that *The Emergence of Islam* is the only film in the examined collection to

a new parliamentary government in 1950, a year before the film's release, Ibrahim ʿIz al-Din's brother Muhammad Salah al-Din was appointed minist ter of foreign affairs, and Taha Hussein himself was appointed minister of education.[36] The censor approved the project despite protests by person- alities associated with al-Azhar in the press.[37] It seems that the solemnity of the story, the mannered earnestness of the film's performances and dia- logue, the eloquence of the continual narration (uncommon to this vogue of Islamic history films), the frequent use of still photography and highly deliberate pacing, along with the relative authority of the film's government affiliated principles, not only overcame al-Azhar's protests, but attenuated its stance on depicting the Sahaba permanently. Al-Azhar's edict, its official sanction of representing most of the Sahaba and all of the *Tabi'in* (followers) arguably allayed anxieties that producers and funders might have felt in taking on Islamic history films whose characters could not be depicted. As it was, only a dozen or so characters could not be depicted.

Depicting the Sahaba photographically, with limited exceptions, was rejected by other Islamic institutions and figures, most notably those as- sociated with the Muslim Brotherhood, as demonstrated by two seminars conducted by the journal *Banner of Islam* (*Liwaʿ al-Islam*).[38] Panelists disagreed on the propriety and value of telling stories about early Islam in films. They not only voiced concern about how stories about a sensitive era of Islamic history were contained textually, but also about how such accounts were depicted, particularly who performed the roles of the Prophet Muhammad's companions.

One of the two dozen or so panelists that participated in the two semi- nars was Islamic scholar and author Ahmed al-Shirbasi, who had worked for al-Azhar for nearly a decade.[39] He remarked that after watching a film about the life of Christ, he discovered that the Vatican in this case required that

---

be named as a positive example of the cinema by no less than the director of al-Azhar himself, despite highly publicized, accusatory feud between al-Azhar and Taha Hussein in the press, including in the pages of *Majallat al-Azhar*. Anonymous 1960, 889–90.

36. This Muhammad Salah al-Din is not the author of *al-Din wa al-ʿaqida ri al-sinima al-mis- riya*, a principle secondary source in this essay, including of this information about the two ministers! (Salah al-Din 1998, 18).

37. Salah al-Din 1998, 18.

38. *Banner of Islam* was established the year the first post-independence Egyptian govern- ment was founded, in 1923, and as such predates the Muslim Brotherhood. For more on the magazine's advocacy for the Muslim Brotherhood see Mellor 2018, 148–71.

39. Panelist Ahmed al-Shirbasi, following this panel discussion, would consult the govern- ment censor of printed materials, including religious texts. Also notable is that al-Shirbasi was among the first to author Islamic history plays, including some dramatizing events contempo- raneous to the Prophet Muhammad (Tamam 2007).

the actor portraying Jesus not act again, and issued him a salary after the release of the film.[40] Although I doubt the account, care in casting for the role of Christ is long established in the tradition of the most renowned passion play of all, that of Oberammergau, named after the German village in which it has been performed decennially since 1634.[41] Until the most recent rendition of 2010, all actors selected to perform, including the role of Jesus, have been amateur actors who must reside in the village of 5,000 and who "must have high moral and ethical principles."[42] Those selected to perform receive a wage intended to make up for wages lost by committing to a run of five months, but no more. Nor do the actors wear makeup while acting.[43] Such practices suggest an interest in audience-perceived "purity" of the performers worthy of the pure people represented.

Similarities in the strictures of representation and performance in two monotheistic traditions should not surprise us, not least in matters of purity and pollution. Like the standard applied by overseers of Oberammergau, I have noticed two trends in the collection of Egyptian Islamic history films related to casting. The first of these recalls Oberammergau in casting relative unknowns to perform hallowed female figures, so as to insure public acceptance of female characters as performed; virtue being associated with a certain occupational virginity, or at least a novelty of sorts. This is true of Nabila Obeid, whose titular role in *Rabiʿa al-ʿAdawiya* (Niazi Mostafa, 1963) was her first lead, having performed a small part in a single film prior. She was such an unknown that an advert for the film presents her as "the new face: Nabila Nour,"[44] whereas the opening credits introduce her as "the new face: Nabila."

Najwa Ibrahim was also a relative newcomer, whose top female billing in *Dawn of Islam* (1971) was her second acting performance. She had come into the cinema from broadcast television[45] and had replaced contracted star Suʾad Husni, who withdrew from the project after the press attacked her casting in the role of a virtuous odalisque at the dawn of Islam. The incommensurateness of performing characters on opposite ends of a normative virtue continuum would turn up relating to other Islamic history films. Samira Ahmed, who performed the titular role of Muhammad's sister in the last of these films *al-Sheimaʿ* (1972) did not come into the project with a métier for what the Egyptian press dubbed *adwar al-ighraʾ* – seduc-

---

40. As stated by Ahmed al-Shirbasi (Anonymous 1959, 324.
41. For more on the passion play of Oberammergau see Shapiro 2001 and Wetmore 2017.
42. Anonymous 2009.
43. Wetmore 2017, 21.
44. Anonymous 1962, 1945.
45. Saʾd 1970, 2374.

tion roles. Rather, Ahmed signed on to play the part of a sexually expressive woman and to dance in a film for the first time in a role to follow her part in *al-Sheima*ᶜ. Ahmed disclaimed reports that she had agreed not to perform in any *aflam six* (sex films) for two years after *al-Sheima*ᶜ to protect its reputation.[46] According to Muhammad Salah al-Din, the ensuing controversy in the press about actor suitability to play hallowed personalities, considering the licentiousness of Egyptian films of the time, contributed to the demise of the Islamic history film.[47]

Beside the strategy of casting relative newcomers, ingénues, in the roles of hallowed figures was a practice of repeat casting in these films, a particular typecasting whereby audiences would be persuaded to accept an actors' worthiness in personifying historical figures by having seen them in such roles previously. Star actor Magda (nicknamed Virgin of the Screen!) appeared in three lead roles, as did Ahmad Mazhar, a military officer whose role in *Emergence of Islam* was his first stint as actor. Secondary actors also appeared repeatedly in Islamic history films, possibly because of their dependability to perform in classical Arabic, actors such as Emad Hamdy (three films), Tawfiq al-Daqn (five films), Abbas Fares (five films), Mahmoud El Meleigy (three films), Hussein Riad (six films), Farid Shawqi (three films), Omar El-Hariri (three films), and Fouad El Tokhy (whose performances in four Islamic history films were his only in the cinema) among others. This repeated engagement in Islamic history films was not restricted to actors, but extended to directors, producers, and writers.*Banner of Islam* seminar panelist Ahmed al-Shirbasi, who had worked in three capacities for al-Azhar in nearly a decade of service, surprisingly disproved of the portrayal of Muhammad's companions.[48] However, he approved of portrayal of the Prophet's *tabiʾin* (followers) in cases of performers being actors pure enough and the environs of the arts clean enough to deserve such portrayal. Curiously, al-Shirbasi admits in the latter seminar that a year prior to this panel he had consulted on the Islamic history film *Khalid bin al-Walid* (Husain Sidqi, 1958), but to his reported dissatisfaction in having realized a "very dangerous" aspect of cinema, namely the exaggeration for effect integral to cinematic representation and deemed necessary for audience appeal.[49] Presumably, al-Shirbasi had made sure that such infractions upon Islamic history would not take place in the next Islamic history film for which he

46. The film had been initially titled *Chanteuse of Islam* (*Shadiyat al-Islam*), as indicated by the title herewith cited – "Samira Ahmed's Difficulties because of Shadiyat al-Islam." Anonymous 1971, 42:791.

47. Salah al-Din 1998, 134.

48. Anonymous 1959, 326.

49. Anonymous 1959, 325.

consulted, *Hijrat al-Rasoul* (*The Messenger's Hijra*, Ibrahim ʾImara, 1964),[50] in that he had confirmed that not a single documented historical character of the Sahaba was included in its plot, a plot whose only nonfictional characters are followers (among whom is the daughter of the Caliph Abu Bakr named Asmaʿ, who the camera avoids anyway) and infidels who had defied Muhammad. Al-Shirbasi's affiliation with the cinema recalls al-Azhar's own, and with Islamic history films specifically – an ambivalent and fluid affiliation, modifying and mollifying to appease powerful personalities and influence the masses. The next segment examines this as it links al-Azhar's proclamations and edicts to the content and production of the noted fifteen or so Islamic history films.

AL-AZHAR'S STRICTURES, INDUSTRIAL CURRENTS AND THE RUN THAT WOULD END

Al-Shirbasi may have believed that his involvement in filmmaking could produce works of culture to stand against the corrupted preponderance of the art industry's output, to demonstrate that the cinema could aspire to virtue with good faith and determination. Yet, he equivocated so that a more conflicted relationship with the cinema manifested. Al-Shirbasi likely did not think the cinema could be rectified, or he would not have penned an essay in *Al-Azhar Magazine* condemning it and dubbing it a "school of Satan." Contradictorily, al-Shirbasi published his essay the year of the release of *Khalid bin al-Walid*, the first film for which he had consulted. In the piece, al-Shirbasi lambastes the cinema for the prurient, immoral content and for its venues, which prey upon the youth, literally luring them away from their schools by day to attend their screenings.[51] Nor was al-Shirbasi's piece the only published in *Al-Azhar Magazine* to criticize exhibitors.[52] That said, the publication more commonly railed against the content of Egyptian films, including Islamic history films,[53] its depravity exemplified in three ubiquitous matters of content in films of the day: dancing, cabarets, and kissing.[54] Such publicized scorn may seem incommensurate with al-Azhar's charge of approving screenplays for filming, only that al-Azhar would certainly not have missed that most of the Islamic history films in question contain one or more dance, kiss, or cabaret. Indeed, all but three films – *Emergence*

50. Salah al-Din 1998, 118–27.
51. Al-Shirbasi 1957, 506–12.
52. See Fayid 1955.
53. These sentiments were expressed in such pieces as Al-Khatib 1955, 609–14; "Libertinism and Crime Films," 1954, 538; Al-Sunousi 1957, 834–37.
54. These depicted prohibitions were delineated in a two-part article, titled "Manifestations of Ruin in Egyptian films" (Al-Sunousi 1954, 517–21 and 442–45).

of Islam, Khalid bin al-Walid, and *al-Nasir Salah al-Din* (*Saladin the Victorious,* Youssef Chahine, 1963) – included one more dance, usually sexually suggestive and at times performed by scantily clad dancers. These dances are often performed in cabaret-like environs – dens, tents, and royal courts in which voracious men consume alcohol with female hostesses at their sides. When performed outdoors, attending men delimit the performance space by lining its periphery.

Nor would al-Azhar have failed to notice the convenience of having non-believers perform such acts or attend such spaces, usually in one of two ways. 1) Characters begin the film as nonbelievers or impious, thereafter converting to or embracing Islam. In such films the dancing and cabarets are performed or attended by unbelieving or unfaithful characters before embracing Islam definitively. Such films include *Instisar al-Islam* (*Victory of Islam,* Ahmed El Touki, 1952), in which the dancer herself utters the *shahada,* thereby embracing Islam, as she takes her final breaths; *al-Sayid al-Badawi* (1954); *Shahidat al-hub al-ilahi* (*Martyr of the Godly Love,* Abbas Kamel, 1962); and *Rabiʿa al-ʿAdawiya.*[55] 2) Nonbelievers defy Muslims throughout the film until defeated at the end of the picture. They are the ones who perform or attend dances, in such films as *Bilal, the Messenger's Muezzin* (1953), *Bait Allah al-haram* (*The Sacred House of God,* Ahmed El Touki, 1957), *Allah Akbar* (*God Is Great,* Ibrahim El Sayed, 1959), *The Messenger's Hijra* (1964), *Oh Islam* (1961), *Dawn of Islam* (1971), and *al-Sheimaʿ* (1972).

Islamic history films smacked of prestige, which was a point of appeal for funders, producers, filmmakers, and stars who sought to work on them. Yet, none seemed to replicate the success of their progenitor *Emergence of Islam.*[56] And even though such films had "legs" longer than most, especially in terms of revenues recouped from foreign sales to governments and distributors in majority Muslim countries, such proceeds took long to realize.[57] Further, the generic link between such films and spectacle epics increasingly compelled producers to have them shot in color, which though costly proved vital for enhanced appeal as evidenced by the relative success of the color *Rabiʿa al-ʿAdawiya* to the black and white *Martyr of the Godly Love* as both films centered on the same historical personality and told her tale in highly similar narratives.[58] Indeed, it is unlikely that *Saladin the Victorious* (1963), the most expensive Egyptian film to date, would have been made as a lavish epic in color had it not been co-produced by the state owned Egyptian

---

55. Even kissing turns up in *Rabiʾa al-ʿAdawiya*!
56. Saʾd 1970.
57. Salah al-Din 1998, 48, 115–16, 128, and 161.
58. Salah al-Din 1998, 111.

Cinema Organization.[59] The operative vogue may well have ended the following year with the making of *The Messenger's Hijra* (1964), were it not for two films coproduced by the General Egyptian Cinema Organization in the early 1970s. *Dawn of Islam* was not only co-produced by the "Organization" as it was commonly dubbed, but was also made from an original screenplay written by the director of the Organization, Abd El Hamid El Sahar.[60] Moreover, it was released in the year when news of the Organization's corruption and incompetence began to appear in the press.[61] *Al-Sheimaʿ* was among the last crop of films that the Organization produced, as it was liquidated in 1972, a year after *Al-Azhar Magazine* had published a piece condemning performing the Sahaba,[62] as if to signal a hardening of the religious institution's positions soon to come, now that Anwar al-Sadat had succeeded Nasser as Egypt's president.

The *Message*, a multinational production of an Islamic history spectacular, would follow in 1976, but Egyptian Islamic history production had firmly and successfully moved to television, at this point, state owned and run, a medium whose inherent strictures because of its broadcast service suited Islamic subjects and themes,[63] a shift that has maintained to this day.

Works Cited

Abu Sharba, M. 1971. "Presenting Qurʾanic Storytelling by Way of Cinema and Theater, ("ʾArd al-qisas al-qurʿani ʿan tariq al sinima wa al-masrah"). *Al-Azhar Magazine* (*Majallat al-Azhar*) 42:785–91.

Ahmad, N. A. 2018. *Religious Cinema and Qurʾanic and Historical Referencing: A Comparative Narrative Study* (*al-Sinima al-diniyah wa al-iqtibas al-Qurʾani wa-al-tarikhi: dirasah sardiyah muqarana*). Beirut.

Ali, M. 2004. *Cinema and Censorship in Egypt, 1896–1952* [*al-sinima wa al-raqaba fi Misr (1896–1952)*]. Cairo.

———. 2008. *A Hundred Years of Censorship of Egyptian Cinema* (*Maʾat ʾam min al-raqabah ʾala al-sinima al-misriyah*). Cairo.

Anonymous. 1954. "Films about Crimes and Dissoluteness" ("Aflam al-jaraʿim wa al-fujour"). *Al-Azhar Magazine* 26:538.

Anonymous. 1955. "*Banner of Islam* Seminar" ("Nadwat Liwaʾ al-Islam"). *Banner of Islam* 9:579–87.

---

59. Anonymous 1963.
60. This conflict of interest was not missed on the Egyptian press. Al-Saʾdani 1971, 17.
61. Cinema reporter Raʾouf Tafiq broke and pursued this story beginning in 1971 with a report titled "Six Million: The Cinema's Debts," *Sabah al-Khaeir* 1972, 14–17.
62. Abu Shahba 1971, 789.
63. ʿUmar 1972.

Anonymous. 1959. *"Banner of Islam* Seminar: Performing Prophets" ("Nadwat Liwaᵓ al-Islam: tamthil al-anbiyaᵓ" 13: 318–29.

Anonymous. 1960. "Opinions and Discussions: The Cinema from the Point of View of Religion" ("Araᵓ wa ahadith: al-sinima min wijhata nadhar al-din"). *Al-Azhar Magazine* 31:888–90.

Anonymous. 1963. "A New era for the Egyptian Cinema" ("ʿAhd jadid li al-sinima al-misriya"). *Al-Musawar.* June 26.

Anonymous. 1971. "Samira Ahmed's Difficulties because of Shadiyat al-Islam" ("Masaʿib Samira Ahmed bisabab Shadiyat al-Islam"). *Sabah al-Khaeir* 42:791.

Anonymous. 1975. "Iranians, Too, Rap Prophet Pic." *Variety.* Jan 8: 77.

Anonymous. 2009. "Passion Play Director Selects Actors for Roles of Jesus, Mary, Judas." *Deutsche Welle,* April 19. http://www.dw.com/en/passion-play-director-selects-actors-for-roles-of-jesus-mary-judas/a-4189575.

Asil, M. 1962. "Of the Edict Committee's Conclusions" ("Min adabir lajnat al-fatwa"). *Al-Azhar Magazine* 34:119–21.

Bayoumi, H. 2002. *Censorship of Cinema: restrictions and limitations (Al-Raqaba ʿala al-sinima: al-quyoud wa al-hudoud).* Cairo.

Darwish, M. 1995. "Censorship and the Other Cinema: A Censor's Testimony" ("al-Raqaba wa al-sinima al-ukhra: shahadat raqib"). *Alif* 15:91–98.

El-Hadary, A. 1987. *History of Cinema in Egypt, Part I (1896-1930) (Tarikh al-sinima fi misr, al-juzᵓ al-awwal min bidayat 1896 ila akhir 1930).* Cairo.

Farid, S. 2002. *History of Censorship on Cinema in Egypt (Tarikh al-raqaba ʿala al-sinima fi Misr).* Cairo.

Fayid, M. 1955. "Our Problem in the View of Islam: Houses of Amusement and Cinemas" ("*Mushkilatuna fi nadhar al-Islam: dour al-lahw wa al-sinima*"). *Al-Azhar Magazine* 26:579–81.

Hunnings, N. 1967. *Film Censors and the Law.* New York.

Al-Khatib, M. 1955. "The Impact of the Press and Cinema in Directing Society" ("Taʿthir al-sahafa wa al-sinima fi tawjih al-mujtama"). *Al-Azhar Magazine* 26:609–14.

Khouri, M. 2010. *The Arab National Project in Youssef Chahine's Cinema.* Cairo.

Mellor, N. 2018. *Voice of the Muslim Brotherhood: Daᵓwa, Discourse, and Political Communication.* New York.

Al-Namnam, H. 2012. *The Azhar ... The Sheikh and the Sheikhdom (Al-Azhar... al-sheikh wa al-mashyakha).* Cairo.

Nasif, M. 1963. "Censorship and Art" ("al-Raqib wa al-fan"). *Dialogue (Hiwar),* April 1.

Qasim, M. 2017. *The Historic Film in Egyptian Cinema (al-Film al-tarikhi fi al-sinima al-misriya).* Cairo.

Rajab, A. 1962. "Will the Prophet [Muhammad] Appear on Cinema Screens? All of Our Actors Refuse to Perform Part of the Prophet!" ("Hal yadhhar al-nabei ʿala shashat al-sinima? Kul al-mumathilin ʿindana yarfudoun tamthil dawr al-nabei!"). *Al-Musawar*, February 9.

Saʿd, K. 1970, "Among the Idols Prior to Islam and the Kaaba" ("Bain al-asnam ma qabl al-Islam wa al-Kaʾba"). *Al-Musawar*, April 10.

Al-Saʾdani, M. 1971. "This Man's Film" ("Film hadha al-rajul") *Sabah al-Khaeir*, February 25.

Salahʾl-Din, M. 1998. *Religion and Doctrine in Egyptian Cinema (Al-din wa al-ʿaqida fi al-sinima al-misriya)*. Cairo.

Shafik, V. 1998. *Arab Cinema: History and Cultural Identity.*

———. 2007. *Popular Egyptian Cinema: Gender, Class, and Nation*. Cairo.

Shaltout, M. and Hussein K. 1961. "The Magazine's Mail: Religious Infractions in 'Barid al-majalla: Mukhalafat diniya fi film.'" *Al-Azhar Magazine* 33:770–71.

Shapiro, J. 2001. *Oberammergau: The Troubling Story of the World's Most Famous Passion Play*. New York.

Al-Shirbasi, A. 1957. "About the Cinema's Problem: A School that has Become Satan's" ("Hawl mushkilat al-sinima: Madrasa sarat lil-sheitan"). *Al-Azhar Magazine* 29:506–12.

Al-Sunousi, A. 1954. "Symptoms of Destruction in Egyptian Films, I" ("Madhahir al-hadm fi al-aflam al-misriya, 1"). *Al-Azhar Magazine* 26:442–45.

———. 1954. "Symptoms of Destruction in Egyptian Films, II" ("Madhahir al-hadm fi al-aflam al-misriya, 2"). *Al-Azhar Magazine* 26:517–21.

———. 1957. "Cinema and Its Influence on Teenagers and Youth" ("Al-sinima wa taʾthiruha ʿala al-murahiqin wa al-ahdath"). *Al-Azhar Magazine* 29:834–37.

Tamam, A. 2007. "Character of Dr. Ahmed al-Shirbasi" ("Shakhsiyat al-ductour Ahmed al-Shirbasi"). "Fora of the Story of Islam" ("Muntadayat qissat al-Islam"), November 16. http://forum.islamstory.com/2020-%D4%CE%D5%ED%C9-%C7%E1%CF%DF%CA%E6%D1-%C3%CD%E3%CF-%C7%E1%D4%D1%C8%C7%D5%ED.html.

Tawfiq, R. 1971. "Cinema's Censorship Wounds Itself with a Scissors" ("Raqabat al-sinima tajrah nafsaha bilmaqass"). *Sabah al-Khaeir*, March 4.

ʿUmar, H. 1972. "Caravan of Light Travels with God's Blessings" ("Qafilat al-nour tasir ʿala barakat Allah!"). *Al-Musawar*. October 13.

Wetmore, Kevin J 2017. *The Oberammergau Passion Play: Essays on the 2010 Performance and the Centuries-Long Tradition*. Jefferson, NC.

"There Goes the Neighborhood":
Film Soundstages and the Islamicate
Public in Northern Nigeria

Abdalla Uba Adamu

INTRODUCTION

THE HAUSA VIDEO FILM INDUSTRY, known as "Kanywood" was established in March 1990 with the release of a video film, *Turmin Danya* (*The Draw*, Salisu Galadanci). From 1990 to 1999 the Hausa video film releases were basically extended television dramas featured boy-meets-girl situations that centered on parental opposition. By 2000, and under the influence of transnational flow of media through electronic media, which provided alternative ways of looking at consumption patterns,[1] leading to many instances of what Gopal and Moorti call "translated modernities,"[2] the Hausa video film had become an African commodity communicating an African translation of modernity. Hausa filmmakers started experimenting with various configurations of figurative representation of the female body. This focused on the creative characteristics of Hausa films, which follow Indian film narrative structure. These are forced marriage, love triangles, and song and dance. All these focus on the female space and female body form, and drew the ire of the Muslim clerical class, who consider such focus on the female body form immoral and an Islamic transgression. For instance, the singing and dancing sequences tended to show women in tight-fitting Western clothes and act as erotic soft sell to essentially young male urban audiences.

When the Shari'a law was fully enforced in 2000 in most of northern Nigeria, many individual states established "moral police" to monitor the public culture, such as the Kano State Hisbah Corps (*hisbah* literally means "accountability"). One of the first points of clash with the new laws was in the film industry because of its mixed-gender settings. Subsequently, a battle line was drawn between enforcement of Islamic law and public entertainment culture, which was increasingly transnationally oriented – what is seen in local terms as "global" – in terms of audience, and which deviated

1. Appadurai 1996.
2. Gopal and Moorti 2008, 40.

from Islamic tenets of decent behavior according to local clerics. This was further reflected in the way two Hausa actresses, Maryam "Hiyana" Usman in 2007 and Rahama Sadau in 2016, became objects of derision because of their violation of the Islamic code of conduct in visual public space.

In cautioning against the use of theoretical frameworks in contemporary analysis of gender spaces particularly in the Muslim world, Hanita Brand argued that the very dichotomy between the public and the private spheres needs some modification.[3] This is because in between the public and the private are several layers of society that are more private than public but contain elements of both. These layers are especially pertinent with regard to women, as they may turn out to be the only extra-private, or semi-public, spheres that women occupy.

This situation is explained in a study of women and spaces in Sudan, in which Salma Nageeb explores the concept of "neo-harem," which explains the gender-specific ways in which women experience the process of Islamization.[4] Nageeb developed this theoretical concept in studying how two quite contrasting groups of women restructure the use of female space in Sudan. While Salma Nageeb's study is rooted in re-mapping the use of physical gender space, my focus in this chapter is on the virtual/visual space segregation of the genders, which indeed in Muslim societies translates into physical space delineations, and its consequences for the critical public sphere.

THE FEMALE BODY AND THE PUBLIC SPHERE IN ISLAM

A contentious issue between Islamic law and the public sphere is that of the *'awrah* (genitals, or shameful nakedness). Both men and women have parts that are *'awrah* and must be covered, both in private and especially in public. However, "in some Muslim texts and social contexts, the female body is uniquely associated with sex and shame."[5] In this context, the greatest degree of covering is required when a woman is in the presence of non-*mahram* men other than her husband. As stated in the Qu'rān (24:31):

> And tell the believing women to reduce [some] of their vision and
> guard their private parts and not expose their adornment except that
> which [necessarily] appears thereof and to wrap [a portion of] their
> headcovers over their chests and not expose their adornment except
> to their husbands, their fathers, their husbands' fathers, their sons,

3. Hanita Brand 2003, 84–85.
4. Nageeb 2002; Nageeb 2004.
5. Leaman and Ali 2008, 12.

their husbands' sons, their brothers, their brothers' sons, their sisters' sons, their women, that which their right hands possess, or those male attendants having no physical desire, or children who are not yet aware of the private aspects of women. And let them not stamp their feet to make known what they conceal of their adornment.[6]

In July 2016, the Nigerian government revealed plans to establish a "film village," which was the local term for a soundstage, in Kano. A massive public protest erupted, led by local Islamic clerics who were joined in the public debate on social networks, which led to the generation of numerous memes and YouTube videos against the proposal. The protesters were against the idea of what they perceived as a residential "village," which they believed would further dilute the Islamic purity of the State and encourage immorality among young filmmakers.

This chapter traces these reactions to the film industry in an African Islamic society against the background of the development of what can be termed "alternative" cinema in an African economy.

THE ISLAMICATE NORTHERN NIGERIA

Shari'a, the Islamic legal code, was re-introduced (having been in the public culture for years, especially after the 1804 Islamic jihad, but subsumed under Nigeria's secular constitution) into the northern Nigerian political economy from 1999, when the country returned to democratic rule after years of military dictatorship, and the core northern Muslim states, freed from the shackles of military rule, embraced democracy by demonstrating their right to religious worship.[7] On 27 January 2000 Zamfara State enacted the first Shari'a Penal Code in Northern Nigeria. Shari'a courts had already been established earlier. The example of Zamfara was followed by Niger (May 2000), Sokoto (May 2000), Katsina (August 2000), Jigawa (August 2000), Yobe (October 2000), Kebbi (December 2000), Kano (November 2000), Bauchi (March 2001), Borno (June 2001), and Kaduna (November 2001).

The adoption of an Islamic legal framework within a secular constitution as declared by Nigeria poses an interesting issue of defining the public spaces of such spheres where Islam predominates. In this regard, Marshal Hodgson uses "Islamicate" to "refer not directly to the religion, Islam, itself, but to the social and cultural complex historically associated with Islam and the Muslims, both among Muslims themselves and even when found among

6. Sahih International 1997.
7. Ostien 2007.

non-Muslims."[8] Consequently, although the Nigerian state uses a secular constitution, individual Nigerian states that have adopted the Shari'a as a social fabric operate an Islamic public space within the overall secular constitution of the country that can be referred to as Islamicate. This Islamic public space came to dominate every aspect of life such that in 2000 the Kano State government established a Hisbah Board, which recruited over 9,000 "Shari'a police" (referred to as the "Hisbah") who are enjoined to promote what is good and prevent what is bad in Kano's social spaces. One of the earliest clashes between the Hisbah and creativity was with the Hausa video film industry, which due to its emphasis on gender-mixing and song and dances became part of Hisbah's mandate of "stopping what is bad."

While the current Hausa film industry is referred to as "Kanywood," before its appearance in 1990 Muslim Hausa audiences were entertained by cinemas screening European and Indian films and later local TV dramas. From the 1960s to the 1970s cinema houses throughout northern Nigeria screened films mainly from India, the United States and Hong Kong. Neither Arabic nor other African films were screened by the Lebanese owners of the cinemas. The 1980s saw a drastic drop in cinema audiences. Larking quotes one of his respondents in Kano as stating that cinemas "mainly played Indian films whose actresses were so beautiful they aroused audiences and corrupted their hearts. Moreover, the non-Islamic origins of many actresses ('they worship cows') could lead Muslim men astray."[9] An Islamic revival in northern Nigeria in 1979 focused more attention on the illicit nature of films screened in cinema houses, and reduced attendance, and raised the profile of TV dramas in Hausa. The dramas, mainly situation comedies and extended series were extremely popular among Hausa audiences due to the natural authenticity of their storylines. As Bourgault noted:

> Storylines were created out of the stream of urban gossip pervading the city of Kano. Producers transposed these stories to suit their creative means and didactic purposes and to satisfy the demands of the television medium. Storylines were submitted by other employees at the station, and sometimes by outsiders who were welcomed by the station when submitting ideas for productions.... Some producers were even known to frequent public viewing centres to "eavesdrop" on their audiences and to incorporate feedback into developing storylines or future episodes.[10]

8. Hodgson 1977, 59.
9. Larking 2008, 138.
10. Bourgault 1996, 66.

The cultural spontaneity of these productions established them as the "typical" Hausa cinema – shot in natural settings, with clear gender delineation, dealing with everyday issues, and appealing to family values. These TV dramas were always quoted by the Islamicate culture as being the proper and correct way a Hausa film should be produced.[11]

One way the Kano State government came up with for controlling the film, and indeed general entertainment industry was the institution of a Censorship Board on13th December 2000. An association, Motion Picture Practitioners Association of Nigeria (MOPPAN) was created in 2001 by the filmmakers themselves as a support to the Shari'a, and became the subsequent contact point between the industry and government in Kano, and later in other parts of northern Nigeria, in regulating the behaviors of filmmakers, although, curiously enough, not film production itself. The clashes between female spaces and figurative representations were encapsulated in two cases involving two popular Hausa female actresses within a nine-year period.

Crossing the Line - Sexuality, Female Film Stars, and Public Culture

In late July 2007 a short cell phone video clip surfaced among the Hausa film industry practitioners in Kano. It shows a very popular Hausa video film actress, Maryam Usman, engaged in explicit sex with her boyfriend. Usman was popularly referred to as *"Hiyana"* (fraud) named after her hit film of the same name. What made its appearance so electric was that it came at a time when the Hausa film industry was accused by the Islamicate public and critical space as getting increasingly Westernized and immoral, principally due to the suggestive song and dance sequences as well as overwhelming focus on romantic themes.[12] The *Hiyana* clip provided a perfect ground for backlash against not only Hausa filmmakers, but also the entire industry itself. What the public heard was that a Hausa actress has made a pornographic film, ignoring the fact that the "film" was not part of any organized film production and was a private recording of an encounter between two consenting adults. A series of reactions followed the appearance of this clip.

The first were threats, intimidations, and attacks on Hausa female video film stars, such that quite a few of them relocated to other states. Maryam Usman herself disappeared and went into hiding. The local newspapers and FM stations became awash with comments condemning not only the appearance of the porn clip, but also the entire film industry.

11. For an extensive study on this, based on fieldwork in Kano, see Bourgault 1996.
12. Adamu 2010.

The second reaction was from filmmakers themselves. MOPPAN, of which Maryam Usman was a member, expelled Maryam from the film industry. The Kano State Censorship Board also suspended all filmmaking activities in the state for six months beginning September 2007, in addition to denying a license to any film producer who featured Maryam Usman in their film for five years.

The third was public action of "film burning" by both the government and Islamic religious organizations, led by the Kano Government officials, when on 11th September 2007, hundreds of Hausa video films were burned as being immoral to Hausa Islamicate culture as a protest against what Maryam Usman did. This was followed by *Imam Malik* organization, an extremist Salafist-leaning association in Katsina, when in October 2007 it burned 2,013 Hausa video films.[13] In January 2008, *Manarul Al-huda Assanawiyya Al-Islamiyyah* (*TRANSLATION*), a coalition of religious schools for Muslim women in Kano held its own Hausa film burning event.[14] The reason given was that the films teach immorality, corrupt youth, and are against the teachings of Islam. About 1,000 films were burned at the event. All these were aimed at showing public support for moral cleansing of the Hausa video film industry of its urban-sexual image. None of these "film burnings" led to any significant impact in either the economy of the industry or the viewership of the films.

The *Hiyana* case became a pointed display of how Hausa women in the typically urban public theater – film, in this case – are seen as bait. Further, the youth fascinating with the "singing chambermaid" in prudish Victorian era Britain translates as the same youth fascination with the "singing Hausa video film actress" in Shari'a state of Kano in 2007. The moral prudence of both societies merely seems to escalate the desire for the illicit, such that the stage fantasy of the actresses became ultimately their fundamental reality.

Almost ten years after the Maryam Usman incidence in Hausa video films, and just when the industry seemed to have moved beyond ostracization and regaining its credibility, another incidence, again involving a popular Hausa actress, occurred.

Barnabas Buba Luka, aka ClassiQ, is a Christian Rapper from the northern Nigerian state of Bauchi, although based in Lagos, southern Nigeria. To attract more audiences to his music, he shot a music video featuring one of the most successful and glamorous Muslim Hausa actresses, Rahama Sadau, in September 2016. In the music video, "I Love You," Sadau plays the role of a

13. Yahuza 2007.
14. El-Hajeej 2008.

fruit and vegetable vendor who catches the singer's eye as he strolls through the market. In a series of fantasy scenes, the video moved from adoration to intimacy with the singer and the actress locking and holding hands, and hugging each other.

On 2nd October 2016 Rahma Sadau was expelled from the Hausa film industry by MOPPAN for appearing in the music video. Part of the reason for her expulsion was "as a result of her recent immoral appearance in a certain video song where she appeared in series of visuals (video and pictorial) hugging and cuddling the music artist ClassiQ in his newly released video."[15] A fan of hers, Maryam Umar, was quoted as stating: "Rahama has crossed the boundary line this time around. The video is all revealing and this is not proper for a Muslim girl to go this extreme in an open video."[16] Sadau promptly accepted the decision on her and apologized to her fans on her via Kannywoodscene Twitter handle on 4th October 2016. ClassiQ himself issued a letter of public apology to both Rahama Sadau and his fans about the way things turned out.

What brought about the religious perspective in her case was that despite the fact that the female actresses wear tight-fitting clothes during song and dance routines in Hausa films, there was hardly any direct physical contact, at least on the screen, between male and female actors. In the case of the ClassiQ music video, not only was she hugging and holding hands with a male in public who was not her *mahram* (a male whom a woman cannot marry at any time in her life whatsoever), but it happened to be a Christian male, while she is Muslim.

Sadau's case differed from Usman's in the sense that in the intervening nine years since the Usman incident in 2007, Hausa filmmakers had latched onto the Internet and Rahama quickly seized this medium to humble herself. Her apology was retweeted many times and picked up by international news media, including *The Washington Post*.[17] The entire episode suddenly propelled her into international limelight – far more than she could ever get into while remaining in a locally based indigenous film industry in Africa. Thus on 15th October 2016, through her Twitter handle, Rahama Sadau confirmed being invited to the United States by Akon, the American-Senegalese rapper and actor, and a Muslim. The invitation was to observe the shooting, in Los Angeles, of Akon and Jeta Amata's new film *The American King: As Told by An African Priestess* (2019).

It took Sadau almost a year to respond to the banning. On 7th July 2017,

15. Lere 2016.
16. Lere 2016.
17. Bearak 2016.

she participated in a panel discussion on "Art, Activism and the Northern Nigerian Narrative" during the Kaduna Book and Arts Festival. Responding to her banning by MOPPAN over her appearance in the music video, she stated:

> I believe things like this happen because I am a woman, I keep saying it, because there are a lot of my co-actors that did things that are worse than me, worse than what I did, but they passed with it.... To my thought, there was nothing in that video. It is just an artist trying to showcase the art and creativity that she has.... And I think that is the best thing I did, even done, I am so proud of myself till today.... I don't regret anything I did that has to do with my craft or my art, because it is a completely different person from who I am.... I don't let my religion come in the way of my profession actually. So I do what I have done as me, as the artist, and then besides that, I don't let anything cross in the way.[18]

These responses, the bravest ever made by a Muslim woman in contemporary northern Nigeria, seek to confer a creative independence on women regardless of Islamicate reaction. With her banning, she became more attractive to other entertainment industries. An urban legend rapidly developed around her insinuating that she had converted to Christianity, a claim which she debunked in press statements issued while she was with Akon in California.

FILM SOUNDSTAGES AND PUBLIC RESISTANCE

On Thursday 14th July 2016 the Nigerian Government announced plans to establish a film soundstage, which was locally referred to as a film village. This was announced by a member of the Nigerian House of Representatives, Abdulmumi Jibrin at an interactive session with Hausa filmmakers. He announced, "the film village has a cinematography center, 400-capacity auditorium for training, hostel, sound stage, eatery block, three-star hotel, shopping mall, stadium, clinic, among others."[19] The Nigerian Government planned to release one billion naira for the start of the 20-hectar village, modeled on similar sound stages in other parts of the world.

On Friday 15th July 2016, the reaction to the project swept Kano mosques. More than ten Imams took to the *minbar* (pulpit) to express their understanding of the project. The sermons were divided into two: condemnation and accommodation. Interestingly, it also revealed the cleavage that exists among the clerics that follow the Saudi Wahabbi ultraorthodox

18. This is AREWA 2016.
19. Izuzu 2016a.

interpretation of Islam, and the followers of the mystic orders of Sufi brotherhoods in Kano.

The loudest condemnation of the film village project was from Wahabbi Imams who belong to the Society of Removal of Innovation and Re-establishment of the Sunna (*Jama'atu Izalatul Bid'a Wa'ikamatus Sunnah*) (JIBWIS), commonly referred to as Izala. This was an Islamic movement originally established in Northern Nigeria in 1978 to fight what it sees as the *bid'a*, (heretical innovation), practiced by the Sufi brotherhoods.[20] Soon after the announcement of the film village, Imams in five mosques belonging to the Izala in Kano seized the opportunity of their Friday sermons to attack the project. This was led by Sheikh Dr. Abdallah Usman Umar at the Gadon Kaya mosque. In a fiery sermon in the Hausa language, Sheikh Umar announced,

> There is a calamity they are planning for this State of ours
> (Kano). This was the plan to establish a film village at Bebeji Local
> Government.... Is this the first contribution they will make to Muslims
> in Kano or even the country? To establish a national or international
> film village which will attract people from all over the world to
> shoot films ... to come and do shamelessness? ... I am calling on all
> those who can write to do so and inform them we don't want it.
> Southern Nigerians want it, but because they know that Kano is an
> Islamic State, they want to corrupt our religion and behavior (the
> Government decided to bring it here). And by Allah, we will pray and
> curse: whoever brings this to us may Allah deny him His favors. We
> don't want this, they can discard it, and take it to those who want it,
> we don't need it. Write on Facebook and WhatsApp, explain as much
> as you can, we don't want, we don't want it, we don't want.[21]

This was followed by other similar sermons and general preaching against the project at mosques located in Kano, most notably from areas in the city (called Quarters) such as Arzai, Kofar Nassarawa, Tudun Murtala, and 'Yan Kaba, most of which were uploaded on the YouTube channel of Manara TV, owned by JIBWIS. Virtually all the discussions on the issue in the various YouTube clips as well as audio of the actual sermons uploaded to MP3 depositories by eager followers of JIBWIS revolve around the central messages of Sheikh Abdallah Usman Umar of the Gadon Kaya mosque: the film village was a diabolical plot to dilute the Muslim purity of Kano State and corrupt the morals of Muslims. Its rejection by some of these Muslim clerics amounts to rejection of any newcomers into any neighborhood. This is because in all the sermons and public opinions on radio programs

20. Kane 2003.
21. Umar 2016a.

in Kano and other northern states, the impression given was that a residential village is about to be created in a deeply Muslim state and would invite filmmakers with their immoral baggage as residents. The on-going tension between the Islamicate social culture and film industry had now been brought to the fore.

Visual and video memes were created based on the billboard announcing the establishment of the project and circulated widely in social media. (See Fig. 1)

Fig. 1. Kano film village protest meme

Verbally abusive dialogues on Hausa film stars from various Hausa films were edited by Danbuzu and segued into a single clip – giving the impression that even the Hausa actors condemn themselves – ignoring that the actors were reading a script.[22]

A second group of Muslim clerics, mainly either from Sufi brotherhoods, or just liberal enough to see with a different lens, endorsed the film village project, but chose not to be vocal in their support. However, by and large, the Imams of the Sufi brotherhoods perceived the project as a good idea if carefully monitored by public authorities to ensure conformity with Islamicate social behavior. A strong supporter of the project was the emir of Kano, Alhaji Sanusi Lamido Sanusi, who became emir on 8th June 2014.

In the end, the pressure became so much and the possibilities of political fallout so glaring that the Federal Government capitulated to the demands and canceled the film village project on 24th July 2016.[23] On 28th July 2016,

22. Danbuzu 2016.
23. Bawa 2016.

Sheikh Dr. Abdallah Usman Umar of the Gadon Kaya mosque posted on his Facebook wall gratitude to the Nigerian government for scrapping the film village project.

> I am extending gratitude and appreciation on behalf of all loving innocent citizens to PMB President of Nigeria from the deep thoughts and acknowledgement that He showed to our Country elders, teachers and analyst that have far vision for stopping the FILM VILLAGE PROJECT He did in Kano, a state that is in need of more better projects of course.... We are forwarding our advice to change this project of 3 billion naira on Agriculture, establishment of University or higher institutions, hospitals, rehabilitation of industries, youth programmes, helping fire victims in their markets (Kano).[24]

Sheikh Muhammad bin Usman, another well-known and respected Muslim cleric and the imam of Sahaba Mosque in Kano, stated:

> Film village is stale news. We should not go back to it because scholars have already spoken and Allah has answered. The leaders have responded to the yearnings and concerns of the well-meaning Muslims of this part. Don't forget, we are typically a Muslim people, a characteristically Sunnatic [sic] people. We believe we have what you call civilizational values, norms and culture. The mere name Kannywood is an infringement and a slap on our traditional values.[25]

While by the end of July 2016 the film village incident was laid to rest, the Rahama Sadau incident came up barely two months later, in September 2016. It merely gave the Muslim clerics a gleeful justification for the stand they took with regard to their perception of Hausa filmmakers. More was to come, however. A year later, in July 2017, a film by Nollywood director, Tolu Lord Tanner, *Ajuwaya: The Haunted Village*, featured Rahama Sadau coyly deflecting an onscreen kiss from a male actor.

CONCLUSION

The reaction of the Islamicate social culture in Kano towards the Hausa film industry is predicated on the sexuality of gender relations in a Muslim society. And yet the reactions are more than a feminist critique of a female in the public sphere. Islamic authorities prescribe modes of engagement for the genders and the extent of the visibility of each. The overarching emphasis of

24. Umar 2006.
25. Williams 2016.

Hausa filmmakers on expressing the sexuality of the female is what created the feeling of "crossing the boundaries."

Paradoxically, for a visibly Muslim society, the success of the Hausa film industry was based not on the strength of the storylines, but on specifically projected female sexuality, particularly during the song and dance choreographies. Since the manifestation of such song and dance, the filmmakers have created a total link between the success of their films and the overt sexuality of the female dancers; films without erotic song and dance simply do not sell, even if the song and dance is deemed "traditional" within narratives of a historical film.

WORKS CITED

Adamu, A. U. 2010. "Islam, Shari'a and Censorship in Hausa Video Film." In *Viewing African Cinema in the Twenty-First Century: FESCAPO Art films and the Nollywood Video Revolution*, edited by M. Saul and R. A. Austen, 63–71. Cleveland.

———. 1999. *Confluences and Influences – The Emergence of Kano as a City-State.* Kano.

Appadurai, A. 1996. *Modernity at Large: Cultural Dimensions of Globalization.* Minneapolis.

Bawa, M. A. 2016. "Big Blow for Nigeria's Film Sector." BBC News, July 25. https://www.bbc.com/news/live/world-africa-36684140.

Bearak, M. 2016. "This 'Immoral' Hug Got a Nigerian Actress Banned from Acting." *Washington Post*, October 4. https://www.washingtonpost.com/news/worldviews/wp/2016/10/04/this-immoral-hug-got-a-nigerian-actress-banned-from-acting.

Bourgault, L. M. 1996. "Television Drama in Hausaland: The Search for a New Aesthetic and a New Ethic" *Critical Arts* 10, no. 1: 61–84.

Brand, H. 2003. "Loyalty, Belonging, and their Discontents: Women in the Public Sphere in Jewish and Palestinian Cultural Discourse." *Nashim: A Journal of Jewish Women's Studies & Gender Issues* 6:84–103.

Danbuzu. 2016. "An yarda a gina film village a Kano kuwa? (Can Building the Film Village be Allowed?)" Youtube, July 24. https://www.youtube.com/watch?v=wa8qsQbWZEA.

El-Hajeej, M. 2008. "Gangamin taron mata don kona Finanfinan Hausa (Large Crowd of Women at the Burning of Hausa Video Films)." *Leadership Hausa*, February 21: 14.

Gopal, S. and S. Moorti, eds. 2008. *Global Bollywood: Travels of Hindi Songs and Dance.* Minneapolis.

Hodgson, M. 1977. *The Venture of Islam, Volume 1: The Classical Age of Islam.* Chicago.

Hulmes, E. D. A. 2008. "Kanem Bornu." In *The Encyclopedia of Islamic Civilization and Religion*, edited by I. R. Netton, 342. New York.

Izuzu, C. 2016. "Federal Government to Establish Film Village in Kano." *Pulse NG*, July 15. http://www.pulse.ng/entertainment/movies/kanny-wood-federal-government-to-establish-film-village-in-kano-id5269249.html.

———. 2016. "ClassiQ Apologizes to Actress for Expulsion from Kannywood." *Pulse NG*, October 11. http://www.pulse.ng/entertainment/movies/rahama-sadau-classiq-apologizes-to-actress-for-expulsion-from-kannywood-id5590817.html.

Kane, O. 2013. *Muslim Modernity in Postcolonial Nigeria: A Study of the Society for the Removal of Innovation and Reinstatement of Tradition.* Leiden.

Larkin, B. 2008. *Signal and Noise: Media, Infrastructure, and Urban Culture in Nigeria.* Durham.

Leaman, O. and K. Ali. 2018. *Islam: The Key Concepts.* London.

Lere, M. 2016. "Why Popular Actress, Rahama Sadau, Was Expelled from Kannywood." *Premium Times*, October 3. https://www.premiumtimesng.com/entertainment/211837-popular-actress-rahama-sadau-expelled-kannywood.html.

Nageeb, Salma. 2004. *New Spaces and Old Frontiers. Women, Social Space and Islamization in Sudan.* Lanham.

———. 2002. "Stretching the Horizon: A Gender Perspective to Everyday Life and Islamic Practices of Women in an Islamist Subculture." In *Islam in Africa, Yearbook of the Sociology of Islam*, 3, edited by T. Bierschenk and G. Stauth, 17–42. Münster.

Palmer, H. R. 1980. "The Kano Chronicle." *The Journal of the Royal Anthropological Institute of Great Britain and Ireland* 38:58–98.

Sahih International. 1997. *The Qur'an: Arabic Text with Corresponding English Meanings.* Riyadh. https://quran.com/24/31.

This is AREWA. 2017. "Best Ever RAHAMA SADAU Interview (The Q&A at Kabafest July 2017)." Youtube. https://www.youtube.com/watch?v=a12Jow3znw4&t=1064s.

Umar, A. U. 2016. "Kano Film Village." Facebook, July 28. https://www.facebook.com/AbdallahUsmanUmarGadonKaya/posts/728361413969480.

Williams, D. 2017. "Kano Film Village and the Clerics." *The Politico.* http://thepolitico.com.ng/kano-film-village-and-the-clerics/.

Yahuza, B. M. 2007. "Bikin ƙona Finafinan Hausa na neman ta da rikici a Katsina" (Hausa Video Film Burning and its Potential to Public Disorder in Katsina). *Aminiya*, October19.

Sufi Aesthetics and the Making of Islam in Bollywood

Syed Haider

IT IS NOTEWORTHY that over its hundred-year history, Indian cinema has never produced a feature film based on Sufism or any of the major Sufi saints.[1] The Ministry of Information did commission a documentary on Sufism in 1990 titled, *The Lamp in the Niche* (Girish Karnad), with an aim to present Sufism as "a broadly tolerant movement, Islamic in its origin ... but more akin to the devotional Bhakti currents of Hinduism than anything else."[2] Ernst's assessment of the documentary reveals how Sufism is deployed as an embodiment of South Asian Islamicate culture. In this essay, I explore how "Sufism" serves as a floating signifier that is represented through a set of aesthetic techniques rather than understood as a purely Islamic mode of practice. This is demonstrated in two films, M. F. Husain's *Meenaxi: A Tale of Three Cities* (2004) and Milan Luthria's *Dirty Picture* (2011).

Although competing definitions of Sufism are available, "an absolute definition" as Nacim Pak-Shiraz acknowledges, is difficult to arrive at, even though she settles for using Sufism "to refer to a mystical dimension of Islam."[3] The problem that follows such a definition however, is the need to pin down what is meant by "mysticism", which she does by drawing on the work of Schimmel, Chittick, and Smith.[4] Schimmel for instance, defines mysticism as "love of the Absolute – for the power that separates true mysticism from mere asceticism is love. Divine love makes the seeker capable of bearing, even enjoying, all the pains and afflictions that God showers upon him in order to test him and purify his soul."[5] While the lexicon employed to describe Sufism differs from that used to describe more scripturalist forms of Islam,[6] the aspirations expressed often cross over the binary that places Sufism in opposition to a host of other Islams. Martin van Bruinessen argues this most persuasively and though he does not use

1. Deshpande 2009, 88.
2. Ernst 2005, 201.
3. Pak-Shiraz 2011, 99.
4. Schimmel 1975; Chittick 1983, 2000; and Smith 1995.
5. Pak-Shiraz 2011, 97.
6. I want to avoid using the term orthodox/orthodoxy, as certain literalist and scripturalist forms of Islam, like those associated with the Wahabist and Salafist traditions, self-identify as Orthodox in order to claim legitimacy and foreclose the historical diversity that has characterised Islamic practices and Islamicate cultures.

the word mysticism, he questions views that see mysticism as something that can be detached from Islam (more broadly conceived) and placed under the rubric of Sufism.[7] The opposition that Sufism is brought in to designate is something Bruinessen questions in his assessment of the work of Clifford Geertz and Ernest Gellner. Borrowing the terms "doctor" and "saint" from the latter, Bruinessen writes,

> The doctor and the saint ... do not necessarily represent competing styles of Islam but have been part of a single complex for most of the time. "High" and "Low" Islam, if those concepts have any value, cannot simply be identified with urban versus rural, and Salafi versus Sufi. Opposition to popular saint cults and the loud festivals at shrines has not only come from anti-Sufi scholars but has also been part of an ongoing debate within Sufism.[8]

What does this mean then? Is there no such thing as Sufism? Is Sufism merely "Islam" and Islam merely "Sufism"? The word "necessarily" in Bruinessen's quote above is helpful for my argument, regarding the way a softer Islam is imagined in Hindi cinema and how this is used for the expression of a distinct Muslim modernity. Certain strands of Sufism can be positioned in opposition to a more doctrinal, ulema-centric Islam – both Sunni and Shi'ah.[9] The "doctor" and "saint" distinction does not *necessarily* represent competing styles of Islam but they can come to do so, and this is how Hindi cinema has largely presented Indian Sufi Islam.

In Hindi cinema Sufism is a floating signifier; a shifting/malleable collection of motifs, symbols, and metaphors that together help give form to a particular imagination of Islam and Muslims. Hindi films that employ "Sufi" motifs and metaphors utilize particular aesthetic textures that are associated with an Islamicate culture historically rooted in India.[10] Articulated like this, it may not make much sense to ask too definitively what a "Sufi" film looks like given that a film deemed "Sufi" may simply be

---

7. van Bruinessen 2009.

8. van Bruinessen 2009, 140.

9. For a Shi'ah take on Sufism, see Nacim Pak-Shiraz 2011.

10. In his impressively erudite work, *The Venture of Islam*, Hodgson explains his use of the term Islamicate thus: "I plead that it has been all too common, in modern scholarship, to use the terms "Islam" and "Islamic" too casually both for what we may call religion and for the overall society and culture associated historically with the religion ... [hence] the society and culture [sometimes] called "Islamic" in the second sense are not necessarily "Islamic" in the first... I thus restrict the term "Islam" to the religion of the Muslims ... [and use the term] Islamicate ... [to] refer not directly to the religion, Islam, itself, but to the social and cultural complex historically associated with Islam and the Muslims, both among Muslims themselves and even when found among non-Muslims." Hodgson 1974, 57–59.

one that gives full scope to the interplay of these motifs and metaphors.[11]

Interpreted this way, a certain reading of Hindi films reveals the extent to which a Sufi face of Islam permeates Hindi cinema without the overt problems inherent in other forms of Muslim representation, and most notably so in the political representation of Muslims (in Muslim political thrillers or dramas for instance)[12]. The aesthetic emerges as an alternative modality through which an Indian imaginary engages with Islam and Muslims because it is in the aesthetics of Hindi films that Sufism finds its fullest expression.

ENTERING THE WORLD OF SUFISM

"Sufism," writes Adonis,[13] "is distinctive in that, in its search for the absolute, it resorts to poetry when it wishes to express its most profound feelings."[14] Nacim Pak-Shiraz acknowledges much the same when she suggests that the

> open-endedness of poetic language, in contrast to the argumentative language of science and logic, give it an elasticity that allows it to refer to multiple signifieds.... The mystical experience compels the mystic to share his unique perspective with others even though it is too ineffable or subtle to be precisely conveyed.[15]

Poetry (and the aesthetic more generally) is deployed as a more fitting vehicle to communicate nuances that are otherwise difficult to conceptualize. "Those readers," warns Adonis, "who enter this world [of Sufism] reliant on the ostensible external meanings of phrases will find it difficult. To put it another way, it is virtually impossible to enter the Sufi world by way of explanation, for allusion rather than explanation is the main portal."[16]

Such an interplay of meaning and ambiguity, allusion and evasion can be seen in M. F. Husain's[17] *Meenaxi: A Tale of Three Cities* (2004). *Meenaxi* has a disjointed narrative style, which underpins the film's arcane quality. Dealing with a Muslim novelist who is struggling to write a novel, the crux of the film centers around Nawab's meeting with the character of Meenaxi (played by Tabu), an encounter that begins the film's surreal foray into a

11. A good film to illustrate this is Ayesha Khan's 2008 Pakistani-US production, *Kashf: The Lifting of the Veil.*

12. See Haider 2013.

13. Adonis, or Adunis, is the pen name of Syrian poet and writer Ali Ahmad Said Esber.

14. Adonis 2005, 17.

15. Pak-Shiraz 2011, 100.

16. Adonis 2005, 18.

17. M. F. Hussain (1915–2011) was one of India's leading artists. For more on his art and politics, see Ramaswamy 2011 and 2016.

world of imagination and storytelling where the boundary between the real and the imagined blurs. Nawab is instantly drawn to Meenaxi, whom he imagines in different roles, from a perfume seller in Hyderabad to an orphan girl named Maria in Prague. Meenaxi meanwhile flits in and out of the narratives Nawab imagines for her, always sardonic and critical of his contrived tales. This flitting in and out, existing both in the diegetic world of the film and speaking from beyond it, *Meenaxi* displays the quintessential trait of liminality so central to the film both in terms of theme and style.

In a 2003 interview published on screenIndia.com, Husain spoke of how he enjoyed "playing with words," saying, "it's another kind of discipline altogether." *Meenaxi* is all about playing, mixing and blurring. Santosh Sivan's cinematography – for which he won a Screen Award – is perfuse with vivid colors and lighting that blend well with Ashley Rebello's and Raeesa Husain's costume designs.[18] Sivan spoke of working with Husain in an interview for *The Hindu* published in 2004:

> It was exciting to work for the first time with a painter. I realized from day one that [his] sensibility was something different. Husain has a deep understanding of color and tone, volume and dimension.... His visuals bore the imprint of a painter's feel for colors, arising from constant experimentation, and years of exploring their possibilities.

Blurring boundaries, mixing mediums and meaning, is a key motif in *Meenaxi*, a style that contributes to the film's avant garde aspirations and the creation of a cinematic (post)modern/mystical idiom.

Meenaxi sets up this paradigm of Sufism and postmodernism through a non-linear narrative structure, an overt use of Sufi imagery, and an ambiguity of character that complements postmodern and Sufi tropes. Patrick Hogan suggests that Husain "recruits the practices of postmodernism to Sufi ends" through a deliberate blurring of temporalities.[19] The frame story of Nawab weaves in and out of the subsequent stories of Meenaxi and Kameshwar (set in Jaisalmer) and Kameshwar and Maria (set in Prague) until the end, when the late Nawab stirs on his deathbed and we are returned to an earlier scene where Nawab first met Meenaxi. The frame story itself therefore appears as

18. Especially those of Tabu, who appears in bold colors throughout the film, as well as in costumes that are plain black or plain white. Being dressed in outfits that are entirely one color emphasises color over costume and contributes to the film's visual quality.

19. For example, common postmodern practices like fragmentation, a displacement of perspective, the utility of irony and contradiction, as well as the tropes of metafiction lend themselves well to convey Sufi beliefs in the ultimate illusion of the world and life, of the non-linearity of time; the conviction in esoteric knowledge, and the deliberate use of paradox as a pedagogical vehicle fitting for such knowledge. Hogan 2011, 111.

yet one more story amidst a medley of narratives thrown up on screen. This kaleidoscope of narratives where even the frame story offers an ultimately unstable frame does, superficially at least, lend the film a postmodern feel.

Similarly, Hogan interprets the rhythmic arrangement of shots in the opening (edited to have a mixture of short rapid succession scenes depicting everyday activity on the roads of Hyderabad) coupled with Nawab's voice over, as intimating Sufi themes that run parallel to what he sees as the film's postmodern inflections. The scene begins with a low angle tracking shot of a rickshaw before switching to a medium shot of Nawab riding the rickshaw and looking through his binoculars at the hustle and bustle of the city. The editing intercuts point-of-view shots with medium close-up shots of Nawab so that the viewer switches between observing Yadav's character as a distanciated observer (a little like Nawab himself, who is observing the city) and the visual position of Nawab, given that the camera reveals what he is seeing. This editing technique lends the scene an intimacy which is picked up in Nawab's stream of consciousness:

> What care has anyone here of reunions or separations;
> The world remains where it is; it is people that seek new stations.
> From the silences somewhere, a cry comes forth
> What seasons of spring have come from these forests of dreams;
> This dreamlike world is only for a while, as are its creations;
> The world remains where it is; it is people that seek new stations.

Hogan reads the juxtaposition in the poem of an appearance of flux in the world and the essential immutability of the world (or some broader reality) as Sufi, though he acknowledges that given there is little context at present of Sufism, the poem may seem "merely paradoxical."[20] But Sufi tropes, metaphors, and motifs are everywhere according to Hogan. In the next scene, when Nawab rushes to a press conference organized by his publisher, Nawab explains how his current project is "a story that may never be completed." Hogan comments:

> The point may seem postmodern. But here as elsewhere, it is also Sufi – as is made clear by Nawab's explanation that [the impediment to completing his story] is due to his "character." He uses the English word, thus suggesting his own character or ego (the standard impediment on the Sufi path) as well as the character or protagonist he is writing about. He explains that his mind is "cluttered with questions" a comment fitting for both a writer and a mystic.[21]

20. Hogan 2011, 112.
21. Hogan 2011, 112.

By dint of an accumulation of examples, Hogan makes a convincing case to see Sufism permeating the film as theme and providing its postmodern disunities an intensified "thematic or emotional unity."[22] Husain also uses Sufism as the context within which to interpret the vagaries of Meenaxi's character. The song *Noor un Ala Noor* (Light upon Light) employs several Sufi symbols and metaphors both at the level of picturization and in terms of its lyrical content. It also introduces Meenaxi, although she does not speak or lip-sync in the song and remains enigmatic throughout. This enigmatic aura, which is underscored by the other Sufi references in the song, persuades the audience to interpret Meenaxi as not only mysterious but signifying mysticism generally and Sufism specifically.

Beginning with an improvisatory melismatic vocal duet that is typical of *qawwalis* (a genre of music associated with Muslims and their devotional practices), A. R. Rahman inserts an atmospheric wind chime, which characterizes the emergent song as magical or mystical. When the initial *alap* (the improvized section of a *raga*, a combination of melody and scale) gives way to a convergence of harmonies and the introduction of percussion, the camera swoops down on Nawab's courtyard, transformed in the diegesis of the narrative for Nawab's sister's pre-wedding celebrations (*mehndi*), but also relating thematically to Sufism as the courtyard takes on the appearance of a quasi-shrine, the traditional setting for *qawwalis*. If the sounds of the song intimates Sufi tradition, the choreography does much the same. Drawing on the practice of the whirling dervishes from the Mevlevi order, the dancers are directed to perform movements that mix whirling with other similar gestures of hand and body, educing mental associations with the dervishes. This association is further emphasized by the costume that some of the dancers wear. The long gowns are weighted at the bottom to dramatize the whirling, so that the garment flares outward as the dancers spin round, and the iconic tall hats signify strongly a context of Sufism. Finally, the lyrical component of the song extends this context by borrowing heavily from the figurative language of Sufi literature: the play between imageries of light and dark, a declaration of the pervasiveness of divine light, and the ultimate mystery of life. Introduced at this point, the character of Meenaxi is deliberately made to function under the rubric of Sufism so that the esoteric/ethereal quality of the latter is presented as part of her characterization. She is elusive and flits between the real and the imagined in order to express an interstitial space that forms the horizon of Husain's intellectual and artistic vision.

The stylized Sufism of *Noor un Ala Noor*, however, ran into trouble with many Muslim organizations in India, including the All India Ulema Council,

22. Hogan 2011, 108.

Jamat-ul-Ulema-e-Hind, and the Raza Academy, amongst others.[23] While some of these organizations were scripturalists or (broadly) reformist, some like the Raza Academy were Barelvi, who have traditionally been more open to Sufism and Sufi practices.[24] In a statement to the press, Maulana Abdul Quddus Kashmiri, general secretary of the All India Ulema Council said, "For us, the term Noor-un-Ala-Noor is very sacred. It shouldn't be used to describe the physical beauty of a heroine." Ironically, the Maulana went on to say that he hadn't actually seen the film, but the controversy led to Husain withdrawing the film from cinemas nonetheless.

While this outcome may confirm for liberal minds the fundamental intolerance of organized religion[25], Husain's blending of postmodern practices with motifs, symbols, and metaphors that evoke Sufi beliefs, customs, and traditions may also be cast as an irreverent mimesis rather than a meaningful engagement with "authentic" forms. If read this way, Husain may be guilty of what Sardar sees as the proclivity of postmodernism to appropriate, package, and sell:

> Postmodernism ... posits that realities are something we can all acquire, or buy at a cut-price sale in the "bazaar of realities.".... The dupes of somnolent wishfulness who buy Karma Kola mysticism, quick-fix Hindu meditation schemes and perverted Sufism are getting just what they pay for: consumer products.[26]

While scathing, Sardar's point is borne out by Manuel's research into the popularity of Sufi music in "the North Indian music scene."[27] "A ... commonly voiced criticism," he writes, "is that the Sufi music vogue is a shallow urban bourgeois fad whose performers lack any serious or long standing engagement with or understanding of genuine Sufi traditions."[28] Quoting from an interview with artist Manjeet Bawa reported in *Newstime Weekend*, Manuel cites Bawa's reservations at the commercialization of Sufism: "[P]eople use Sufism ... to foster their own interests; that is why you see fashion shows and dance programs, and many other purely commercial ventures exploiting Sufism. It is just another way of making money."[29]

The allegation of exploitation, however, may not sit easily against

23. Kumar 2004.

24. Metcalf 1982, Werbner 2003, Bennett 2005.

25. Since the mid-1990s Husain had faced numerous protests from Hindu groups over a number of his paintings depicting Hindu deities.

26. Sardar 1998, 42.

27. Manuel 2008, 378.

28. Manuel 2008, 389.

29. Manuel 2008, 389. For more on popular critiques of Sufism in Bollywood see, Kortu 2017 and Goyal 2017. For an alternative view see, Anonymous 2010.

Husain, who withdrew *Meenaxi* after protests claiming, "I have not made the film to make money."[30] Nor can the allegation of a lack of understanding of the subject matter be levelled at him given his recurring professional interest in Sufism.[31] Sardar's scathing critique of postmodernism, therefore, cannot be extended easily to Husain or his film. But if the charge of exploitation, lack of understanding, or shallow engagement are too harsh and clumsy interpretations of the presence of Sufism in *Meenaxi*, a more nuanced reading reveals the presence of an impulse toward the aestheticization of Muslims and Islam in Bollywood, which the recent perfusion of Sufism on the Hindi screen represents.

THE AESTHETICIZATION OF MUSLIMS AND ISLAM IN BOLLYWOOD

Ian Almond's detailed analysis of Orhan Pamuk's *The Black Book* reveals interesting parallels with Husain's filmic use/s of Sufism. The same devices of narrative fragmentation, a play with meaning and liminality, and paradox as essential to characterization, operate in Pamuk's book as they do in Husain's film. Read as "an intensive examination of Turkish national identity," *The Black Book* has been enthusiastically termed postmodern (as has Pamuk himself) by Western critics "eager to find a writer who "delights in shredding preconceived dichotomies."[32] For Almond, Pamuk's protagonist, Jalal's fascination with "the fourteenth century Sufi Rumi ... not only invites us to see [him] as a modern-day Rumi but also implicitly proposes *The Black Book* itself as a kind of *Mesnevi*, a collection of Sufi stories."[33] Once again, Sufism and postmodernism are brought into a relationship and Almond proceeds to show the various ways in which "*The Black Book* reinvents and rewrites the various vocabularies of Islam." It is this play with "vocabularies" and signs which is most relevant for discussions of Sufism and Hindi cinema.

For Almond a thematic concern with identity runs through *The Black Book* and he partly foregrounds this through Pamuk's own words, demonstrating the dualism the novelist sees within himself: "At the centre of my life there is ... rationality. On the other hand...I open myself to other texts [those of the East and those of Sufism for example]. I don't see these texts as a necessity, I take pleasure in reading them, I feel joy... Perhaps my books find themselves without bickering or scuffling between these two centres." Almond interprets this as Pamuk admitting two selves: "a Western, secular,

30. Kumar 2004.

31. One of Husain's best-known early series was the "Calligraphy and Sufi Series" completed between 1970 and 1980s, and exhibited under the title "Sufi Paintings" in 1978 at the Pundole Art Gallery in Mumbai.

32. Almond 2007, 112.

33. Almond 2007, 113.

pro-Enlightenment rationalist, and an alternative self, implicitly Eastern, more closely linked with feelings and pleasure." The workings and illusions of identity feature as key thematic concerns in Pamuk's novels and also act as the plane on which Almond sees Pamuk's uses of Islam play out. In the first instance, Islam is used as a way of grounding a "true" and "original" Turkish identity through its utilization "as a politically useful storehouse of images to supply the citizen with a carefully constructed series of heritages, destinies and hopes." Yet "paradoxically ... Islam (in the form of Sufism) is also used to dismantle the notion of identity, in particular [the] notion of a self."[34] Almond shows how Pamuk's treatment of Rumi becomes a strategy to question and cultivate the possibility of different selves, so that Pamuk ends up using the figure of Rumi and his attendant histories as a way to:

> illustrate his own very secular beliefs concerning the illusion of the self. The key [tenet] in Sufism of *fanaa* ... [is] ultimately reappropriated by Pamuk with a much more secular aim in mind; re-narrated to us in a text like *The Black Book*, the story of Rumi as he wanders frantically around the streets of Damascus, looking for his dead lover loses its spiritual weight and becomes a deconstructive parable for the dissolution of selfhood into a confused "nothingness."[35]

This malleability of Sufism is what links Husain's film to Pamuk's novel. Both artists appropriate Sufism to a modern, secular, non-theistic end. In Husain's case, the Islam and Sufism presented in *Meenaxi* is one that is aesthetic rather than theological.[36] It contains little in the way of the Qurʾān (the controversy notwithstanding) or the *sunnah* (sayings and practices) of the Prophet Muḥammad; there is little sense of a scholarly world or even one of the *pir* (spiritual teacher) and his *murid* (pupil). No Arabic/Islamic calligraphy is shown on screen and no Arabic/Islamic sounds are heard (like the *azaan* (call to prayer) or the recitation of the Qurʾān). No character is shown reading *salah* (formal prayers) and no Islamic stories are embedded in the dialogue or lyrics of the songs. Instead, the motifs, symbols, and metaphors of Sufism are drawn on for their aesthetic qualities. For Husain, Sufism offers an indigenous Indian sociolect through which he captures the delicate (nontheistic) transcendent nature of imagination. As such, *Meenaxi*, though not Islamic, is certainly Islamicate. Husain's indulgence in this paradigm is clear from the numerous examples or references to an Indian Islamicate heritage throughout the film. Nawab's character is an anachronistic persona of a noble of the late nineteenth century, who isn't referred to by name but by an

34. Almond 2007, 119.
35. Almond 2007, 120.
36. And here *Meenaxi* may be contrasted with *Kashf*, which is overtly *Islamic*.

old-fashioned title that harks back to the Mughals. Similarly, Nawab's costume, which consists almost entirely of *sherwanis* (a type of frock coat), not only identifies him as Muslim (as this is a dress traditionally associated with Muslims in the sub-continent) but also with a hitherto gentry of Muslim aristocrats in Mughal India. Husain's use of an Indian Islamicate adds a certain flair and refinement to *Meenaxi* that confers upon it a certain elevated sense of artistic elegance due to its association with the arts of the Mughals and their culture of *adab* (etiquette). Even the architecture of Nawab's home resembles a quasi-*haveli*, the mansions of nobles in pre-independent Indian cities, and of *zamindars* (landowners) in rural areas. This space, due partly to its size, gets transformed for the *mehndi* celebrations, which again is associated with Muslims in India (though also a Hindu custom), while the *qawwali* that is played during it carries Indian Islamicate overtones as of course does the ornate Urdu that Nawab speaks with words like *janab* (sir) and *khala-jaan* (dearest aunt). Finally, food features prominently in the frame narrative, with Nawab shown at one point in the film enjoying a dish of biryani that Meenaxi has prepared. The food (and the biryani specifically) signifies Mughali cuisine and once again therefore an Indian Islamicate context. Bit by bit, Husain impresses upon his audience the Islamicate as a frame of reference for his film.

Instead of seeing Husain's use of Sufism as merely a plundering of the rich traditions of Islam in South Asia, it may be more accurate to see Husain as achieving two distinct outcomes through his appropriation and presentation of the motifs, symbols, and metaphors by which we perceive the presence of Sufism in his film. Firstly, Husain manages to infuse (Sufi) Islam within an Indian Islamicate heritage that grounds Muslims firmly within India itself. Secondly, it aestheticizes Muslim traditions, customs, beliefs, and practices in opposition to their politicization, presenting Muslims as cultural citizens and not merely political subjects or denizens within an Indian state. By this sleight of hand the film attempts to rehabilitate Muslims within an Indian imaginary.

DIRTY PICTURE AND THE "PURITY" OF SUFISM

A song that illustrates my point and all the more so because it comes from Milan Luthria's critically acclaimed *Dirty Picture* (2011), is Vishal-Shekhar's *Mera Ishq Sufiyana*. The film is based loosely on the life and career of South Indian dancer and actress Vijayalakshmi Vadlapati (screen name, Silk Smitha) who was best known for her erotic dance numbers and playing vamp roles. True to its title, the film is daring and characterizes a creative shift in Bollywood. To find a Sufi song in such a film may first seem inappropriate and out of place, leading one to think its presence is merely commercial and/or part of that idea of trivialization that Ananya Jahanara Kabir, Manuel, and others have noted.[37] However, it is precisely because of this that its presence is not necessarily debased or undermined. Rather, the Sufi song offsets the reflexively witty narrative that is certainly salacious and seedy but ironically so.

Amidst so much sex and sexual innuendo in *Dirty Picture*, the song, *Mera Ishq Sufiyana* provides a certain elegance and authenticity otherwise missing in the superficial glitz and kitschy glamor of South India's film industry during the 1980's, when the film is set. The scene that immediately precedes the song sets up the potential of the Sufi dream sequence to single-handedly offset the film's (playfully engaged) titillating idiom.

Disowned by the very people who exploited her in their invention of her as a "star," Silk is left alone and without any friends during the second half of the film. At this point, the character of Abraham enters Silk's life as an unexpected and unlikely lover, given his strong aversion to her throughout. But this love affair is very different from all the others Silk has been involved in, mostly because when Abraham's initial animosity gives way to his latent attraction, he sees her for who she is: a broken character whose vulnerability comes from her own strength. Silk is vulnerable because her power is premised on her sexuality, which, as the film presents it, is a currency within a hetronormative-patriarchal system. As a visionary director, Abraham wants to create meaningful cinema and this positions him as an outsider in an industry dominated by formulas and commercialism. Silk too is an outsider; she is related to no famous personalities, cannot speak English, is uneducated, and comes from a rural backwater. Both Silk and Abraham therefore are outsiders and this lends the love that grows between them a uniqueness absent from all the prurient love affairs shown on screen. True to form though, this love is not of the sanitized variety stereotypical of many run-of-the-mill Bollywood films; it is one characterized by a fiercely frank appraisal of characters and their realities. Silk is not suddenly transformed into a bashful virginal character but remains the promiscuous temptress. The attraction between her and Abraham however, still manages to appear more than simply libidinal and this is largely because of the song *Mera Ishq Sufiyana,* and the dialogue that precedes it.

Not hiding her reality, Silk replies to Abraham's question regarding ever having fallen in love, by saying, "Of the type that leads you to bed? Many times. Of the type that makes you sleepless out of excitement and joy? Never." Abraham then looks at her more intensely and asks in whispered

37. Kabir 2003, Manuel 2008.

tones, "How many people have touched you?" Matching his whispered tone, she replies: "Many have touched me, but few have touched *me*." This tender moment splits Silk into two selves: one that is public and profane, continually exploited and used for vicarious pleasures; and another that is private, hidden, lost even. It is the second that momentarily appears sacred and pure. The *sufiyana* song that follows this short exchange does not debase the Sufi tradition necessarily, but appears as a way of conferring authenticity and meaning on a love that stands out of all the carnal pleasures that congregate around Silk as a signifier. What is more, the fact that Sufism and its motifs, symbols, and metaphors are mobilized to this end, suggests that the place of Sufism in the cinematic imaginary is as a paradigm of ultimate spiritual purity used to express nuance and meaningful sentiment. Far from being trivialized, an Indian Islamicate heritage in Hindi cinema could be read as offering an alternative emotional register by which Indian Muslims and Indian Islam are foregrounded.

The aesthetic then emerges as a key vehicle in Hindi cinema through which Islam, Muslims and an Indian Islamicate heritage finds expression in that "common Indian public culture" that Dwyer has written about.[38] Here the motifs, symbols, and metaphors of Sufism offer an alternative spiritual idiolect to cinematic imaginary. Sufi-Islam and its emphasis on devotion rather than the law lends it well to be used as a paradigm of ultimate spiritual purity.

But is the aesthetic merely a vehicle and therefore expendable when new aesthetic conventions emerge? Is this current confluence within Hindi cinema of the aesthetics of Hindi films and an Indian Islam/Islamicate heritage indeed a fad? Not necessarily. Hindi films have always drawn on Indian Islam and Islamicate traditions and have done so in both narrative and aesthetic form.[39] What I have tried to show is that in Bollywood currently there is an overt aestheticization of Islam, Muslim practices, and an Indian Islamicate heritage. So much so, that even films that have little to do with these often draw on this heritage in their aesthetics simply because it is a normative feature of Hindi cinema and its history (much as it is of India itself).

But whereas earlier films and their portrayal of this cultural heritage presented a vernacular vision of Islam and Muslims as part of Indian culture and constructed that culture as theo-magical with its depiction of miracles and providential plans,[40] cinema more recently has begun to express

38. Dwyer 2010, 134.

39. See, Haider 2014; Bhaskar and Allem 2009; Sarrazin 2013.

40. See *Coolie* (Manmohan Desai, 1983) and *Allah Rakah* (Ketan Desai, 1986) as well as devotionals that were part of the B-grade circuit, such as *Rahim Dil Jallad* (Qamar Narvi, 1985). For more on Muslim devotionals see, Dwyer 2010.

this common public culture as underpinned by a diffused sense of spirituality that is expressed most cogently in an aestheticized mode and taken up most actively through the idiom of Sufism.[41] The causes of this change seem, however, to be more socio-economic than theosophic. Citing Desai as her reference point, Faiza Hirji writes that "observers of Indian film ... have suggested that Bollywood films are increasingly marketed to the affluent diaspora," a shift that has resulted in many changes, one of which is a move away from a vernacular spirituality to one that is aestheticized.[42] A globally aware audience with a growing sense of sophistication, a move from small cinemas to the multiplexes, and the rise of a metropolitan middle class within India are not incidental to this new expression of the religious and the spiritual. The fact that Sufi-*Islam* emerges as a vehicle to further this new aesthetic sensibility produces an aesthetic Muslim modernity which, whether it sets out to or not, helps embed (on a subliminal level if nothing else) Islam as part of India's heritage and its present if not also its future.

WORKS CITED

Adonis. 2005. *Sufism and Surrealism*. Translated by Judith Cumberbatch. London.

Almond, I. 2007. *The New Orientalists: Postmodern Representations of Islam from Foucault to Baudrillard*. London.

Anonymous. 2003. "In conversation with M. F. Husain." June 20. http://www.screenindia.com/fullstory.php?content_id=5966

Anonymous. 2010,"Sufi Influence on Bollywood Music Has Deepened: Abida Parveen." *Journalism of Courage Archive* November 14. http://archive.indianexpress.com/news/sufi-influence-on-bollywood-music-has-deepened-abida-parveen/710994

Anonymous. 2012. "Sufism Losing Value in Commercial Bollywood: Atif Aslam." *The Indian Express* August 31 https://indianexpress.com/article/entertainment/entertainment-others/sufism-losing-value-in-commercial-bollywood-atif-aslam/

Bennett, C. 2005. *Muslims and Modernity*. London.

Bhaskar, I., and Allen, R. 2009. *Islamicate Cultures of Bollywood Cinema*. New Delhi.

van Bruinessen, M. 2009. "Sufism, 'Popular' Islam and the Encounter with Modernity." In *Islam and Modernity: key issues and debates*, edited by K. M. Masud, A. Salvatore, and M. van Bruinessen, 125–57. Edinburgh.

41. See *Sawaariya* (Sanjay Leela Bhansari, 2007), *Anwar* (Manish Jha, 2007), *Kadarnath* (Abhishek Kapoor, 2018), *Rockstar* (Imtiaz Ali, 2011), *Bajrang Bhijaan* (Kabir Khan, 2015).
42. Hirji 2010.

Chittick, W. 1983. *The Sufi Path of Love: The Spiritual Teachings of Rumi*, Albany.
———. 2000. *Sufism: A Short Introduction*. Oxford.
Deshpande, A. 2009. *Class, Power and Consciousness in Indian Cinema and Television*. New Delhi.
Dwye, R. 2010. "I'm Crazy about the Lord: The Muslim Devotional Genre in Hindi Films." *Third Text* 24 (1): 123–34.
Ernst, C. W. 2005. "Ideological and Technological Transformations of Contemporary Sufism." In *Muslim Networks: From Hajj to Hip Hop*, edited by M. Cooke and B. Lawrence, 191–207.
Goyal, S. 2017. "Sukhwinder Says That Bollywood Musicians Don't Know What Sufism Means." *Hindustan Times* April 17. https://www.hindustantimes.com/music/sukhwinder-says-that-bollywood-musicians-don-t-know-what-sufism-means/story-CvvDPdQPir5ve5EAzIriuI.html
Haider, S. 2013. "*Entering the Fold: Muslim* Terrorism on the *Hindi* Screen and India's *Entry into* a Global *Modernity*." In *The Other India*, edited by O. P. Dwivedi, 51–74. Newcastle upon Tyne.
———. 2014, "Shooting Muslims: Looking at Muslims in Bollywood through a Postcolonial Lens." In *Postcolonialism and Islam*, edited by G. Nash, K. Kerr-Koch, and S. Hackett. London.
Hirji, F. 2010. "Change of Pace? Islam and Tradition in Popular Indian Cinema." *South Asian Popular Culture* 6 (1): 57–69.
Hodgson, M. 1974. *The Venture of Islam*. Vol. 1–3. Chicago.
Hogan, P. C. 2011. *Affective Narratology: The Emotional Structure of Stories*. Lincoln.
Kabir, A. J. 2003. "Allegories of Alienation and Politics of Bargaining: Minority Subjectivities in Mani Ratnam's *Dil Se*." *South Asian Popular Culture* 1 (2): 141–59.
Kortu, N. 2017. "Bollywood's Been Dishing Out Faux *Sufiyana* Songs to Us. Here's What's Wrong." *Hindustan Times* April 2. https://www.hindustantimes.com/music/bollywood-s-been-dishing-out-faux-sufiyana-songs-to-us-here-s-what-s-wrong/story-YqlplrTpDh8rPH303PJ3tO.html (accessed 5 July 2018).
Kumar, S. 2004. "Husain Pulls *Meenaxi* Out of Theatres." *The Tribune* April 17. http://www.tribuneindia.com/2004/20040417/nation.htm#8
Manuel, P. 2008. "North Indian Popular Sufi Music in the Age of Hindu and Muslim Fundamentalism." *Ethnomusicology* 52 (3): 378–400.
Metcalf, B. 1982. *Islamic Revival in British India: Deoband? 1860-1900*. Princeton.
Pak-Shiraz, N. 2011. *Shi'i Islam in Iranian Cinema: Religion and Spirituality in Film*. London.

Ramanarayan, G. 2004. "Cinematic Vision: In Conversation with Santosh Sivan." *The Hindu* March 21. http://www.hindu.com/mag/2004/03/21/stories/2004032100370500.htm

——. 2016. *Hussain's Raj: Visions of Empire and Nation.* Mumbai.

Ramaswamy, S. ed. 2011. *Barefoot across the Nation: Maqbool Fida Hussain and the idea of India.* London.

Sardar, Z. 1998. *Postmodernism and the Other: The New Imperialism of Western Culture.* London

Sarrazin, N. 2013. "Devotion or Pleasure? Music and Meaning in Celluloid Performances of *qawwali* in South Asia and the Diaspora." In *Music, Culture and Identity in the Muslim World,* edited by K. Salh. New York.

Schimmel, A. 1975. *Mystical Dimensions of Islam* Chapel Hill, NC.

Smith, M. 1995. *Early Mysticism in the Near and Middle East.* Oxford.

Werbner, P. 2003. *Pilgrims of Love: The Anthropology of Global Sufi Cult.* London.

FILMOGRAPHY

Dirty Picture. Directed by Milan Luthria. India: Balaji Motion Pictures, 2011.

Meenaxi: A Tale of Three Cities. Directed by M. F. Husain. India: Yashraj Films, 2004.

Comedies of Terror: Strategic Offenses and Genre Tactics

Samhita Sunya

A BRIEF SEQUENCE from Hindi-language comedy *Tere Bin Laden: Dead or Alive* (Abhishek Sharma, 2016) shows CIA head David DoSomething and his younger female colleague Junior passing a joint back and forth, in the midst of the following conversation:

> David DoSomething: And you remember the time I busted Saddam Hussain for those imaginary "weapons of mass destruction"?
>
> Junior: That was a great work of fiction!
>
> David DoSomething: Wasn't it? Now whose brain child was that, Junior? Say the name!
>
> Junior: David DoSomething! That's you, Sir!
>
> David DoSomething: Oh yes it is!
>
> Junior: I so wanna blow your trumpet!

The exchange is replete with ostensibly exaggerated depictions of American "DoSomething" machismo and narcissism, the fictitious premises of the War on Terror, and the surreptitious exercise of military power with the nonchalance of taking an illicit hit of marijuana for a momentary, self-gratifying high. That the War on Terror was ever about eradicating Islamist terror unfolds as utterly (and literally) laughable, as the film's comedic genre proclivities and intertexts uncannily and explicitly reproduce an implicit genre demand at the heart of a statist discourse of the US-led War on Terror as well – that is, a suspension of disbelief that vouchsafes the absurd.

In this chapter, I examine three War on Terror comedies (henceforth referred to "terror comedies") from the Global South, all of which reference *Harold and Kumar Escape from Guantanamo Bay* (Jon Hurwitz and Hayden Schlossberg, 2008), the Hollywood stoner-comedy precedent that most prominently inaugurated the genre of terror comedy. All three films that I examine – *Tere Bin Laden* (Abhishek Sharma, 2010), its sequel *Tere Bin Laden: Dead or Alive* (Abhishek Sharma, 2016), and *Road to Kabul* (Brahim Chkiri, 2012) – were box office hits in India and Morocco, respectively. The films' satirical prowess ensues from a cocktail of intertextual references to Hollywood cinema and the War on Terror, rendered from another side of the world –

backstage, as it were – to characterize the War on Terror as a ridiculous farce propped up by thoroughly doctored, fake images of a threatening, Islamist Other.

When, for example, the aforementioned *Tere Bin Laden: Dead or Alive* character David DoSomething masquerades in brownface as fictitious Indian film producer David Chhaddha and accidentally reveals that he is part of the CIA, DoSomething/Chhaddha quickly papers over the slip with the clarification that by CIA he means, of course, Cinema in America. The cover is itself but another slip, satirically suggesting that there is very little difference between the activities of the CIA and those of Hollywood, characterized as partners in the business of producing – and profiteering from – self-serving fictions. The three films' comedic genre proclivities motivate a suspension of disbelief on the part of their audiences, who behold a set of implausibly zany characters and ludicrous storylines. The comedic genre intertexts are ultimately uncanny, as all three films render the War on Terror itself as a similarly bizarre, logic-defying genre of fiction whose coherence depends entirely upon a suspension of disbelief on the part of its proponents.

I begin this chapter with an overview of the abundance of scholarly inquiries that have taken up the question of media and genre vis-à-vis the War on Terror. Noting that US/Hollywood contexts have been the primary arena of inquiry in these scholarly treatments, I move to a discussion of the thoroughly transnational terrain of both Hollywood genres, on the one hand, and the War on Terror, on the other, which are self-consciously interwoven – particularly through invocations of *Harold and Kumar Escape from Guantanamo* – into the narratives and formal strategies of *Road to Kabul* as well as the two *Tere Bin Laden* films. Through intertextual engagements with Hollywood genres, all three films unfold as self-consciously backstage, behind-the-scenes views of the War on Terror from non-US vantage points. The implausible plot elements and caricatured tropes of radical Islamists, US politicians, CIA agents, and a generation of young (stoner) South Asian and Middle Eastern citizens caught in the fray, produce a trenchant satire of the levity with which US-led invasions have ignited catastrophic wars in and beyond Iraq and Afghanistan, the latter premised upon so preposterous a set of justifications as to emerge as a work of farce par excellence.

AUDIO-VISUAL GENRES AND THE WAR ON TERROR

The range of scholarship on genre, audio-visual culture, and the War on Terror is immense. The stakes of this work lie in the characterization of both 9/11 and the War on Terror as being fundamentally constituted by media events and practices, from the spectacular destruction of the twin towers and viral videos of beheadings, to leaked photographs of torture, infrastructures of surveillance, and the widespread use of drones as primary tactics of a US-led war. As Judith Butler, Lisa Parks, and Anjali Nath, among others, have pointed out, however, the flip side of this war of spectacular, mediatized violence is its extraordinary (and in a sense also spectacular) opacity – who/what is the enemy, exactly, and how, and to what end, are these wars in Afghanistan and Iraq, among other locations, being fought?[1] This opacity, as Elisabeth R. Anker insightfully notes, has been overwritten by a US political discourse that offers coherence through a tantalizing script that unfolds along the most conventional structures of classic melodrama:

> A paradigmatic example of melodramatic political discourse is President George W. Bush's speech on the War in Afghanistan at the Pentagon on October 11, 2001. The story that the speech emplotted relied on melodramatic genre conventions – including a narrative of virtue and redemption, heightened affects of pain, detailed explanations of individual suffering, and a sense of overwhelmed victimhood that transmutes virtue into strength – to both unify [US] national identity and authorize a war that had already begun four days prior.[2]

Anker's keen characterization is notable for identifying the naturalization of a set of formulaic, melodramatic narratives as objective facts in a statist political discourse. In this melodrama-as-political-genre, Anker notes, the US is cast as a hapless, virtuous, suffering victim at the hands of an aggressive, evil enemy. The US bravely comes to take the helm of a noble war in the wake of its immensely tragic suffering on 9/11, to bring about justice as its own virtue triumphs over the villainy of a shadowy enemy.

Anker's work thus identifies mainstream US political discourse on the War on Terror as *itself* an exemplar of melodramatic genre conventions, in contrast to the abundance of scholarly accounts that have evaluated representations of the War on Terror across classic and emergent genres that include docudramas, videogame war genres, road movies, horror, and zombie flicks.[3] As this body of scholarship continually highlights the War on Terror as a thoroughly mediatized event, inquiries into the ethics of representation on the one hand, and the ethics of war tactics on the other, start to bleed into one another to the point of interchangeability.

---

1. Butler 2009; Parks 2006; Nath 2014.
2. Anker 2014, 7.
3. Kellner 2009; Bennett 2010; Chung and Diffrient 2015; Seja 2011; McRobert 2012; Bishop 2015; Schulzke 2013.

If, in other words, a mainstream US political discourse justifies the War on Terror through modes of melodrama, then melodrama – or, one could say, surveillance video, drone camera footage, etc – is not merely a mode of representing the War on Terror but in fact a key tactic of its execution.

Most prolific among Anglo-American cinematic engagements with the War on Terror, whether obliquely or directly, are those that resort either to documentary and hybrid docudrama forms, or to popular action genres. Bruce Bennett speculates that "a generic and stylistic turn" towards documentary genres has occurred as a critical response to the spectacular images of violence that have characterized the War on Terror, given documentary genres' degree of gravitas as well as their "abiding impression of indexicality or immediacy."[4] In an analysis that brackets documentary responses to the War on Terror to focus on popular action genres, Klaus Dodds takes up a somewhat defensive position in recuperating the potential for critical reflections in genres other than that of "documentary, which ha[s] arguably explored the dark countours of the the war on terror more convincingly."[5] Dodds concludes that while a series of Hollywood action thrillers certainly privilege and frequently justify the violence perpetrated by the US in the course of the War on Terror, they still do open up important spaces for critique. Dodds means this in quite a literal sense, as he notes that spatial elements of the mise-en-scene across Hollywood action thrillers unveil labyrinthine networks of hidden and public spaces alike that bolster the War on Terror's relentless campaigns of torture and violence by the US military and intelligence, both domestically and overseas.

Crucially, Dodds acknowledges that melodrama underlies the narrative proclivities of the action-thriller genre, alongside its spectacle-driven formulae. Dodds notes that melodrama "is used routinely to stake out moral oppositions, suspenseful races or tense movements, emotional intensification and sensational endings," and that this structure of binary moral oppositions certainly does limit – though it does not necessary cannibalize – the films' spaces for critiques in action-thriller genres that depict the War on Terror.[6] Dodds' identification of the limited, binary character of melodramatic formations, and Anker's identification of melodrama as a political discourse that underlies the War on Terror, both constitute primary nodes of satire in the *Tere Bin Laden* films as well as *Road to Kabul*.

The films portray the Islamist "enemy" as comprised of caricatured, small fringe groups of doddering, hotheaded buffoons in their respective

4. Bennett 2010, 210.
5. Dodds 2008, 1622.
6. Dodds 2008, 1624.

countries, whose arsenal for violence is utterly incommensurate with that of the US military. In addition, the films depict US government, military, and intelligence officials to be completely aware of their role in spinning narratives that clinch the buy-in of a public who believes in a very "real" threat, which is all but. In several layers and from many perspectives, the films exaggerate the inability of ordinary citizens around the world to distinguish fact from fiction, especially as both are mediated by images. By deflating the linchpin of the melodrama that has underlain the political terms and representational discourse of the War on Terror – that is, the threat of the evil Islamist, terroristic other – satire recasts the War on Terror as a US-scripted farce, upon a geopolitical theatre of the absurd.

HAROLD AND KUMAR GO ABROAD

Among cinematic genres that have approached 9/11 and the War on Terror, comedy has been less prominent. As Shilpa Davé notes, the 2008 release of *Harold and Kumar Escape from Guantanamo* and its tremendous success at the box office was exceptional in this regard.[7] Her insightful analysis shows how genre elements of the stoner comedy as well as road movie enable and circumscribe the film's critiques of racial profiling, detention, and torture. Davé keenly argues that the film's comedic elements effectively draw attention to the simultaneous invisibility and post-9/11 visibility of Asian Americans in US discourses of race. She notes, however, that its critiques of racial profiling, torture, detention are dulled by its ultimate investment in (re)establishing Harold and Kumar as normative American stoners – for example, as Americans who are *not* marked by cultural difference in any respect, their superficial appearance of difference notwithstanding.

Davé pointedly notes that the film, in place of sharper critiques of torture, detention, and the US-led invasions of Iraq and Afghanistan occasioned by the war on terror, instead lampoons the paranoia of white Americans for their fear of terrorists as well as the foolishness of agents in torture and detention programs, who erroneously nab Harold and Kumar instead of *actual*, foreign, Arab-speaking terrorists. It is in this manner that the stoner comedy genre works to avow a melting-pot vision for Asian Americans, wherein Asian Americans like Harold and Kumar are neither undesirable nor threatening precisely because they are – despite their appearance of difference – fully normative, unaccented, young, stoner Americans.

Even as both *Tere Bin Laden* films and *Road to Kabul* invoke *Harold and Kumar Escape from Guantanamo* as a popular comedic precedent and Hollywood

7. Davé 2013.

intertext, their critiques of racial profiling and the War on Terror emanate from non-US spaces and perspectives that are, in turn, addressed to non-US audiences. The films are far less susceptible to pressures of responding to a widespread post-9/11 US discourse of citizenship and belonging, which has repeatedly and visibly cast doubt upon the American-ness and patriotism of Arab Americans, Muslim Americans, and South Asian Americans. Instead, the films forward a satire that ultimately shows the War on Terror *on the whole* to be absurd – rather than merely its propensity to mistakenly suspect and detain a pair like Harold and Kumar, whose normative Americanness and harmlessness couldn't be any more obvious.

Road to Kabul not only references *Harold and Kumar Escape from Guantanamo* through its mise-en-scene and genre elements of both the stoner comedy and road movie, but also invokes a longer genealogy of Anglo-American cinema-cum-military engagements with the Middle East through its title. *Road to Kabul* makes a self-conscious, titular reference to David Butler's 1942 classic Hollywood comedy *Road to Morocco*, which, according to Jack Shaheen, "is probably one of the most stereotypical films ever to come out of Hollywood."[8] In addition, *Road to Kabul*'s fictional plot about a group of young Moroccans who take a road trip across Afghanistan in search of their friend, only to find themselves constantly running from both Afghan, Taliban-esque militants and US military and intelligence officials, gestures towards the true-story subject of British filmmaker Michael Winterbottom's 2006 *Road to Guantánamo*. Winterbottom's film concerns the 2001 detainment of three British citizens of South Asian heritage, who in October of that year had taken a road trip to Afghanistan from Pakistan, where they had traveled to attend a friend's wedding. The three were captured and eventually transferred by the US military to Guantánamo Bay. They were detained, interrogated, and tortured there as suspected enemy combatants, before their 2004 release sans any charge.[9]

The main characters in *Road to Kabul* are four young men who form a friendly gang of idle stoners, though the context for their idleness is not merely their love of marijuana, but that of widespread difficulties in finding employment. The stoner genre is thus connected to an issue that would have been resonant among disaffected youth in other Arab contexts as well, with unemployment surfacing as a major contributor to the Arab Spring uprisings that began in 2010, just two years prior to *Road to Kabul*'s release.[10] As the young men dream about leaving Morocco, the Netherlands,

8. Blair 2010.
9. McGuinness 2006.
10. Said 2016.

renowned for its marijuana-friendly laws, is aptly invoked as their holy grail within the stoner comedy genre. The men cite financial obstacles that stand in the way, in addition to the difficulties of acquiring a European visa with an Arab passport. When presented with a chance to pay a middleman who advertises himself as a visa broker, the gang pools a large sum of money for at least one of them to be able to leave. Hmida becomes the lucky one who gets this opportunity.

It is by chance, through a newscast that plays in a bar, that the men see their beloved friend mouthing "save me" at the camera, in the background of a live broadcast from war-torn Afghanistan. The gang discovers that they have been scammed by Ouchen, a con artist who sent Hmida off with an Afghan visa instead of a Dutch one. The threesome, joined by Hmida's frantic mother, resolves to embark upon a trip to find and retrieve their friend, holding Ouchen responsible and forcing him to come along. Aside from the citations of both stoner and road movie genres, one of the most explicit invocations of *Harold and Kumar Escape from Guantanamo* occurs when the men are in Afghanistan and naively don orange jumpsuits, sold to them by a street vendor as highly fashionable items. A still from this moment of the film, featuring the four men in the iconic orange uniforms of non-compliant Guantánamo detainees, came to circulate as the film's poster in yet another citation of *Harold and Kumar Escape from Guantánamo*, which was advertised with a similar image of its eponymous duo in orange jumpsuits.

Like the young men in *Road to Kabul* who dream about a future that is bigger, better, and elsewhere, Ali Hassan, the protagonist of *Tere Bin Laden*, is a starry-eyed reporter for Danka TV, a small-time fictional Pakistani channel. Ali obsessively fantasizes about going to the US and making it big, though when he gets his chance to travel to the US, his hopes are dashed when he is ejected from the flight because several white passengers panic that he is a hijacker. The scene aboard the plane in the early moments of *Tere Bin Laden* imitates an early scene from *Harold and Kumar Escape from Guantanamo* that sets the plot in motion, in which paranoid white passengers panic that Kumar is a terrorist and mis-hear his confession that he has a *bomb* instead of a *bong*, after Kumar is caught for the nonviolent infraction of attempting to use his smoking contraption onboard the aircraft.

Through unmistakable citations of *Harold and Kumar Escape from Guantanamo*, the films *Road to Kabul* and *Tere Bin Laden* not only nod towards their Hollywood terror comedy predecessor, but also interweave a self-aware, meta-cinematic commentary that illuminates the power of the US in producing fictional images – about itself, and about the rest of the world – that circulate as truth. In *Tere Bin Laden*, Ali remains so smitten with Hollywood-induced fantasies of the US despite being blacklisted as a potential terrorist after the plane debacle. He is so desperate for a windfall that will enable him to purchase a counterfeit passport and identity to travel to the US, and when he comes across a chicken farmer named Noora who bears striking resemblance to Osama bin Laden, he sees his ticket to the US. Unbeknownst to Noora, who thinks that he is being interviewed about his prize-winning rooster Sikander, Ali recruits camera assistant Gul, makeup artist Zoya, communist radio jockey and mimicry expert Comrade Qureishi (who is lured with the promise that he will get to curse the US to his heart's content), and bookish writer Latif to prepare, script, and dub a fake, new tape of Osama bin Laden threating the US yet again. Ali's plan, to anonymously ransom the tape, works. However, as a new round of bombings of Afghanistan begin in response, Qureishi is furious and accuses Ali of having blood on his hands. The CIA gets closer and closer to nabbing the gang, and the resolution occurs through a mutual agreement between the CIA head – who is motived by a bounty – and Ali's entourage, to produce another (fake) tape in which bin Laden declares his change of heart and asks for a ceasefire.

The absurdly farcical plot of *Tere Bin Laden* depicts the War on Terror and the American Dream as two sides of the same (propaganda) coin, both structured by the circulation of (scripted, staged) images. The initial fake Osama bin Laden tape is a problem, but only because its agenda – that is, Ali's scheme – is not one that emerges from US interests. When the CIA head realizes that the tape is a fake, their course of action is not to publicize the truth, but to justify a ceasefire with another fake tape that is produced through a collaboration between a CIA agent and Ali's gang. The sequel, *Tere Bin Laden: Dead or Alive,* opens by self-referentially showing the entirety of the first film to have been a Bollywood hit. The characters in the sequel are ostensibly the actors in the first film, who are now themselves, and they go by their actual names.

The endless, layered self-referential mise-en-abyme that blurs the boundaries between fiction and reality, original and copy, satirically comments upon the ubiquity of manipulated images, to the extent audiences (that is, us) cannot distinguish between facts and forgeries, even when the latter are so patently outrageous. The suspension of disbelief that is generically motivated by comedic genre elements and intertexts, in other words, is diagnosed as the mechanism by which the War on Terror garners legitimacy, however unreasonable. This critique breaks through what Davé insightfully identifies as the limits of *Harold and Kumar Escape from Guantanamo,* wherein an instance of misreading and racially profiling Harold and Kumar as terrorists motivates the "comedy of terrors," rather than the outlandishly exaggerated misrepresentations of US victimhood at the hands of an evil Islamist Other, which has underpinned the discourse of the War on Terror.

BEHIND THE SCENES

With the opening of *Tere Bin Laden: Dead or Alive*, the audience is pulled into an ostensibly behind-the-scenes, backstage view of the actors in the wake of *Tere Bin Laden*'s success. Like the first film, the sequel literalizes its construction of a backstage view of the War on Terror through a conflation of the overseas violence that is out of view and beyond the frame of US borders, with processes of film production (art direction, costumes and makeup, scriptwriting, lighting, shooting, editing, and dubbing) that are not apparent through the hallmark Hollywood effect of continuity editing. While Ali Zafar makes a guest appearance as himself, in playing a star with an overinflated ego in the wake of *Tere Bin Laden*'s success, the main character of the sequel is Sharma, a caricature of a young, idealistic cinephile with lofty dreams of becoming a Hollywood director via Bollywood. Sharma runs away to Bombay in search of a chance to follow his dream and break away from the family business of running a small sweet shop.

Tere Bin Laden: Dead or Alive's comedy unravels as a behind-the-scenes tug of war for Osama bin Laden lookalike Paddi, as Sharma (Bollywood), the US government/CIA head David DoSomething (Hollywood), and a buffoonish Pakistani militant leader named Khalili each hope to use Paddi to stage very different kinds of footage of Osama bin Laden for their own ends, following the 2011 breaking news of his death at the hands of the US military within the film. The sequel portrays an aggressive, warmongering, and ambitious US President Barack Obama under pressure to provide proof of Osama bin Laden's killing, after the military has failed to record the killing in the euphoria of their trigger-happy drunkenness. David DoSomething approaches Paddi in brownface as Hollywood producer David Chhaddha, intending to have Paddi killed on set in order to circulate the recording as proof of bin Laden's killing on President Obama's behalf. But Paddi insists that he will only act if the film is directed by Sharma, who envisions a melodramatic, Bollywood action film of Osama bin Laden's capture and killing called *Tora Bora Nights*. At the same time, the bumbling Khalili hopes to capture Paddi and the other cast and crew of *Tere Bin Laden* (and its sequel being filmed within the film) in order produce a tape that discredits the US military's account by showing Osama bin Laden to be alive and well.

In this behind-the-scenes comedy, the War on Terror is shown to be a tug of war over images that are staged and concocted as indices of supposedly real events. The levity with which the US approaches war as mere sport is satirized by a scene that unfolds in a CIA quarter, as David DoSomething takes over a console that is outfitted as if it is a videogame, with the title *Game of Drones*. DoSomething enthusiastically uses the controls to fire at figures on the screen, and parallel editing shows the simultaneous chaos among Khalili's ragtag group of desert-dwelling militants panicking, as they run amuck while attempting to duck the aerial strikes. When Daaga, a diminutive, baby-faced militant, releases a herd of livestock and uses the herd as cover to escape, DoSomething throws his hands up, frustrated that he cannot strike the herd for fear of angering PETA, and the console screen tauntingly flashes "Game Over."

The *Game of Drones* sequence comedically draws attention to issues that are much more grave – the hypermediation of the War on Terror that numbs the scale of killing, torture, and maiming by drones and other remotely controlled weapons; the disproportionate use of force by the US military against enemies that are quite poorly armed; and the complete disregard for the humanity of populations in war-torn areas of Iraq, Afghanistan, and Pakistan – among other locations – not only on the part of the US military, but also on the part of the public. DoSomething is shown to be carefree over any backlash for killing people, though he halts the drone strikes for fear of backlash from PETA when a herd of livestock passes across the screen. The added joke, of course, is on the efficacy of PETA's well-known, sensationalist tactics that court controversy as a way of gaining added publicity and media coverage for their causes.

In *Tere Bin Laden: Dead or Alive*, even President Obama is portrayed as a gun-toting, trigger-happy maniac backstage (that is, in a reality that is painstakingly hidden from view), in contrast to his public-facing performance as a suave, level-headed, cerebral, president with considerable restraint. In *Road to Kabul*, too, the US president makes a brief appearance, though the president in the latter film is a George W. Bush-like, Anglo figure, who is lampooned for his indiscriminate, irrational warmongering and poor sense of geography. Having just landed in Kabul, he keeps referring to his location as "Baghdad," and when he is corrected, he is confused and asks whether they are in the midst of a war in Kabul as well. The wry satire points to the tenuous links between the bombings of Afghanistan in retaliation for the attacks of 9/11, and the invasions of Iraq for its as-yet-nowhere-to-be-found weapons of mass destruction. The films point to the War on Terror as being waged upon far-fetched, fanciful tales – like the rumor that Osama bin Laden was hidden away in Afghanistan; the fairytale about Afghan princesses locked up in that ever-oppressive torture chamber known as "the burqa"; and the evil, mustachioed Saddam stockpiling that three-letter word that the US needed to wrest from his tyrannical grip certainly not *oil*, but WMD, of course.

PROJECTIONS OF THE RADICALIZED OTHER

In his reading of *Tere Bin Laden*, Jitinder Gill notes that the film takes up the topic of religious extremism and "provides insights that go beyond the acrimonious binary polemics that frame any debate about this issue." Gill notes that the film's title is a pun that could either mean the "Without you, Laden" in a pining, romantic sense; or "Your Bin Laden." The dual registers of this title point to the indispensability of Bin Laden for various agenda, and the different versions of Bin Laden for these various agenda – that is, "your" Bin Laden versus "my" Bin Laden. Gill concludes:

> The film aims to show that associations founded on political convenience are transitory and lacking any moral validity; Osama bin Laden, who was a valued ally of the CIA when he fought the Soviet army in the eighties, became America's biggest enemy twenty years later. The same man whom contemporary Americans perceive as an incarnation of evil is revered as a freedom fighter and martyr by some followers of Islam. By projecting a stance that interrogates various versions of Osama bin Laden, the film tries to undercut each of them.[11]

I hope to show that the *Tere Bin Laden* films not only demonstrate the invalidity of each ideological version of Bin Laden, as either a heroic martyr for extremists or a patently evil enemy of the US that had supported him as an ally in earlier decades; but also are highly self-aware in mobilizing comedic genre elements to highlight the role of images in rallying a call to arms, however absurd and far-fetched both the image as well as its corollary narrative. In other words, the films do not merely show that there is a discrepancy between bin-Laden-the-hero-of-extremists and bin-Laden-the-enemy-of-America, but show bin Laden – and the figure of the Islamist extremist in general – to be a ridiculous prop that motivates the outlandishly farcical drama that we know as the US-led War on Terror.

Especially in the sequel, *Tere Bin Laden: Dead or Alive*, the Islamist extremists are caricatured as a bedraggled, foolish bunch whose antics include a terror Olympics complete with a suicide bombing competition in which martyrdom becomes the prize for the lucky terrorist whose suicide vest actually manages to explode. Such a comedic caricature highlights the disproportionate military power of the US armed forces, whose drones, aerial

11. Gil 2013, 152

jets, missiles, and sprawling infrastructures of satellite and surveillance technology are juxtaposed with a ragtag group whose homemade suicide vests are more than likely to not work properly. In addition, the armed forces seem to target this bunch for mere sport, rather than any sense that they actually pose a threat. Furthermore, in a tongue-in-cheek manner, the visual appearance of the leader, Khalili, constitutes a tacit caricature of a Hindu guru-godman.

It is in the middle of watching a retrospective of bin Laden's all-time best videos – in the derelict theatre with popcorn, no less! – that Khalili, the leader, becomes incensed by a mistakenly-included clip from *Tere Bin Laden*, in which Paddi-as-Noora plays their revered leader. At the same time, Khalili is so taken with Paddi's resemblance to bin Laden that he plans to kidnap the cast and crew to record and sell a (fake) tape that will scare the world into believing that bin Laden is yet alive. But when the moment of confrontation comes, the American military easily waves Khalili out of the way by writing him a hefty check in exchange for leaving Paddi be. The central conflict of the War on Terror is shown to be that of maintaining its own, absurd, fictional storyline that entirely depends upon the fantastic projection of the Islamist Other as a foreboding enough enemy by which the US can remain an equally fantastic, top-notch, good guy/action hero.

At the end of *Road to Kabul*, too, the US-led War on Terror is unveiled as wholly belonging to the theater of the bizarre, when the gang of friends is taken to the big boss referred to as "ben Kaddour." His name revered by the militants and feared by the Americans, ben Kaddour, like bin Laden, is described as dwelling in a secret hideout in Afghanistan. When the fearful group of Moroccan friends is escorted to this big boss towards the end of the film, they instantly recognize ben Kaddour as Said Bey, a well-known Moroccan actor who plays himself playing ben Kaddour in the film. Stunned, Said Bey explains that he was out of work as an actor and that although he auditioned and was hopeful about many other parts, the only role he managed to get was that of playing the bearded ben Kaddour for the Americans. Said Bey admits that he remains confounded by the nature of the drama in which he has been cast – that is, the War on Terror – as he wryly notes that they are all mere puppets who have been cast in various parts, as the US has turned the world into its stage. In this manner, across the *Tere Bin Laden* films and *Road to Kabul*, the Global South is revealed as a mere set and its people, mere dispensable extras, in the production of an absurd, ongoing, violent farce that has been thoroughly scripted by the US and continuously projected under the moniker of the "War on Terror" for almost two decades, with no foreseeable end anywhere in sight.

Works Cited

Anker, E. 2014. *Orgies of Feeling: Melodrama and the Politics of Freedom*. Durham.

Bennett, B. 2010. "Framing Terror: Cinema, Docudrama and the 'War on Terror.'" *Studies in Documentary Film* 4 (3): 209–25.

Bishop, K. 2015. "The New American Zombie Gothic: Road Trips, Globalisation, and the War on Terror." *Gothic Studies* 17 (2): 42–56.

Blair, E. 2010. "'Sex And The City' Cast Abu Dhabi As The City? Really?" *NPR*, May 22. http://www.npr.org/templates/story/story.php?storyId=127054238.

Butler, J. 2009. *Frames of War: When Is Life Grievable?* New York.

Chung, H. S., and D. S. Diffrient. 2015. *Movie Migrations: Transnational Genre Flows and South Korean Cinema*. New Brunswick.

Davé, S. 2013. *Indian Accents: Brown Voice and Racial Performance in American Television and Film*. Champaign.

Dodds, K. 2008. "Hollywood and the Popular Geopolitics of the War on Terror." *Third World Quarterly* 29 (8): 1621–37.

Gill, J. 2013. "Tere bin Laden": 'Islamic Terror' Revised, *SPECS journal of art and culture* 5: 140–55.

Kellner, D. M. 2009. *Cinema Wars: Hollywood Film and Politics in the Bush-Cheney Era*. First edition. Chichester.

McGuinness, D. 2006. "Guantanamo Film Re-Opens Debate." *BBC News*, February 15. http://news.bbc.co.uk/2/hi/entertainment/4715474.stm.

McRobert, N. 2012. "'Shoot Everything That Moves': Post-Millennial Zombie Cinema and the War on Terror." *Textus*, no. 3.

Nath, A. 2014. "Beyond the Public Eye: On FOIA Documents and the Visual Politics of Redaction." *Cultural Studies ↔ Critical Methodologies* 14 (1): 21–28.

Parks, L. 2006. "Planet Patrol: Satellite Imaging, Acts of Knowledge, and Global Security." In *Rethinking Global Security: Media, Popular Culture, and the "War on Terror,"* edited by A. Martin and P. Petro, 132–50. New Brunswick.

Said, M. 2016. "Arab Youth Employment in the Wake of the Global Financial Crisis." In *Young Generation Awakening: Economics, Society, and Policy on the Eve of the Arab Spring*, edited by E. A. Sayre and T. M. Yousef, 50–71. Oxford.

Schulzke, M. 2013. "The Virtual War on Terror: Counterterrorism Narratives in Video Games." *New Political Science* 35 (4): 586–603.

Seja, N. 2011. "No Laughing Matter? Comedy and the Politics of the Terrorist/Victim." *Continuum* 25 (2): 227–37.

Cinema of Misrecognition:
Islam, Gender, and the Terrorist In
Contemporary Indonesian Film

Alicia Izharuddin

INTRODUCTION

Globalization of screen cultures and religio-political discourses has produced a dynamic media ecosystem of representations of Islam and Muslims. Indonesia's rich cinematic culture reflects this heady confluence and requires us to ask questions on the political and ethical consequences of this global moment; what happens to images of Islam and Muslims created by Muslim filmmakers at the margins of the global geopolitical order, in the case of this essay, Indonesia? What is the global import of such films produced by Muslim filmmakers in the post 9/11 age? What frameworks of understanding inform the narrative trope of Muslims misrecognized as terrorists in the global media domain of representations?

Although well-known as the nation with the largest Muslim population, Indonesia is situated both geographically and geopolitically at the periphery of the global politics of Islam and contemporary debates on terrorism. It has undergone fissuring crises in the twentieth century yet emerged a compelling democratic experiment at the turn of the present century.[1] Until recently, Indonesia fostered a reputation for religious moderation and pluralism with a leadership that responds to homegrown terrorism.[2] To explain its long-vaunted moderate virtues, the conception of "Islam" in Indonesia has been described as "syncretic" and "dynamic," born out of peaceful interactions with Buddhism and Hinduism, though the latter faith traditions were phased out from much of the archipelago by the fifteenth century.[3] State denial of Islam as political ideology under the New Order (1966–1998) ensured that it was limited to social development. Veiling in schools was banned until 1991. When Suharto resigned in 1998 taking the New Order with him, the pressure cooker valve of Islamic aspirations was released. The theater of Islamic power struggles ensued and upon its stage came the Is-

---

1. Horowitz 2013, 30–48.
2. Abuza 2006, 38–60; 67–75.
3. Rickels 1981, 7–8.

lamic film, a genre that promotes the moral transformation of its audiences through Islamic symbolism and teachings,[4] in reinvigorated form.

There is a strong consensus that film and media have been irreversibly transformed by the terrorist attacks in the United States on September 11, 2001. Questions concerning the nation, security, terrorism, and cultural anxiety pervade cinematic narratives in response to the global shifts of that historic day. For scholars in film and media studies, new frameworks and methodologies of investigation are necessary to keep up with the ever-changing institutional and technological interfaces of politics, media, and the military.[5] Likely to be a response to Western representations of Muslims as terrorists, filmmakers in majority Muslim societies outside the Middle East and South Asia have been producing filmic narratives to counter, subvert, and come to terms with the rise of terrorism within their own national boundaries.[6] In the films discussed in this essay, the reconfigured Indonesian nation is engaged, and at times forced to confront, a post-9/11 world where Muslims in Indonesia are thrust into the bigger picture of global Islam.

This essay seeks to unravel the gendered and racialized underpinnings of misrecognizing Islam and Muslims, particularly the designation of the Indonesian man as terrorist and public anxiety with the niqab. These two tropes align with common constructions of "good" and "bad" Islam in various global contexts.[7] In Indonesian cinema, "bad" Islam is expressed as a religious and cultural ideology belonging to a foreign "Other" and opposed to the construction of Indonesian national identity.[8] Mis-reading and misrecognition characterize the distorted conceptualization of Muslim-as-terrorist in airport security procedures, failed visa applications to the US, and outright hostility towards individuals from entire swathes of the Middle East and South Asia. Mistaking the Muslim *Indonesian* man and woman for a terrorist, however, is a narrative device deployed not by Western Islamophobic discourse but as a means of narrating the Self. The party wrongly characterizing the Muslim Indonesian is simply reading by appearance and "imprisoning someone in a false, distorted and reduced mode of being,"[9] often with certainty and authority. It then becomes the

---

4. See Izharuddin 2017.

5. Rich 2004, 109–11; Slocum 2011, 183–91.

6. See Martin 2007.

7. Evelyn Alsultany's *Arabs and Muslims in the Media: Race and Representation After 9/11* (2012) systematically dissects the construction of "good" and "bad" Arabs and Muslims in US media culture.

8. Izharuddin 2015, 397–412

9. Taylor 1994, 25.

prerogative of the misrecognized to remedy the terms of mutual engagement. Because to be misrecognized, as Nancy Fraser argues,

> ... is not simply to be thought ill of, looked down on, or devalued in others' conscious attitudes or mental beliefs. It is rather to be denied the status of full partner in social interaction and prevented from participating as a peer in social life – not as a consequence of a distributive inequality (such as failing to receive one's fair share of resources or "primary goods"), but rather as a consequence of institutionalized patterns of interpretation and evaluation that constitute one as comparatively unworthy of respect or esteem. When such patterns of disrespect and disesteem are institutionalized, for example, in law, social welfare, medicine, and/or popular culture, they impede parity of participation, just as surely do distributive inequities.[10]

As an important trope in the genre, misrecognition is found in narrative alongside its correction, the demonstration of the Muslim Indonesian's worth and authenticity in a world remapped by 9/11. To underline the significance of *one-way* misrecognition in the self-construction narratives of the Islamic film genre defined above, one will need to compare it with the *mutual* misrecognition between the west and terrorists in "real life" discourses of terrorism.[11] Western governments and terrorists may easily misrecognize each other as different despite sharing a similar binary worldview of unending war, morality, and justice, of good versus evil. Both accuse each other of "remaking the world" in the other's image and wreaking havoc in their respective wakes. Not coincidentally, both claim to have God on their side.[12]

The narrative of "good" Indonesian Islam in the Islamic film genre reflects the gendered wellspring of religious commodification, a preserve mainly of affluent middle-class Muslim Indonesians after decades of suppression under General Suharto's New Order on Islamic symbols in the public sphere.[13] As a medium that caters primarily to urban middle-class Indonesians, the Islamic film genre dovetails with cultural shifts that signal the activation of a consumerist Muslim identity. Nonetheless, it is a genre that critiques, albeit from a privileged lens, extravagant affluence and socioeconomic inequality between Muslims in Indonesia as a threat to piety. However, the activation of Muslim middle-class consciousness is marked by

10. Fraser 1995, 68–94
11. Saniotis 2006
12. See Lincoln 2003, 19–32.
13. Fealy 2008, 29–31; Heryanto 2011, 61–62; Sasono 2010, 48.

antagonism and deep ambivalences about Arab culture and debates about the authenticity of Indonesian Islam.[14]

The accentuation of Indonesian Islam and Muslim as fundamentally different from Arabs and the trope of religious authenticity represent a new preoccupation in the Islamic film genre, one that has been inflected greatly by the discourse of global geopolitics post-911 and terrorism. However, it is a preoccupation that, paradoxically, serves to obscure the centuries-long historical influences of Arab cultures seen as central to the expansion of Islamic teachings in the archipelago. The new anti-Arab sentiments that percolate contemporary Islamic films in Indonesia signals a departure from the unproblematic embrace of Arab-style attire worn by nationalist and Islamic figures of the past. Ambivalence about "Arabization" is selective; there is little debate about replacing the language of the Qur'ān with the local vernaculars. The heterogeneity in Indonesian perception of "Arab" culture and its peoples is made more nuanced by experiencing the Arab world itself through pilgrimage and employment. Entrenching Indonesia's lack of power and influence in the age of globalization is the pattern of gendered migration to the Arabian Peninsula.[15]

In the selected films made between 2008 and 2015 examined in this essay, "Islam" is constructed as a cross-cultural politics between Muslims in Indonesia, the Middle East, and "the West." It participates in the politics of margin and center, near and far, self and Other. In these films, Muslims from Indonesia are affected by "far away" events like 9/11 and enter into the world as pious pilgrims on a journey of constructing the self. In particular is the typology of Muslim women and men marked unambiguously as "good," peaceful, productive Muslims. Violent events implicating acts of terrorism during the post-Suharto years would trigger existential soul searching and redefinition of Indonesian Islam, none more than the Bali bombings in 2002 that took more than 200 lives.

A recuperation of "Islam" from its extreme interpretations took place in a national crisis traced to an Islamic boarding school in a rural Javanese village where nine Muslim members of the terrorist organization Jemaah Islamiyah plotted and carried out the mass murder in Bali in October 2002. Notwithstanding the uncompromising legal repercussions of terrorism in Indonesia (three of the Bali bombers have been sentenced to death), it bears mentioning that the censure against terrorism in the Indonesian media culture is less straightforward than it first seems. Although state and religious leaders condemn acts of terrorism in the name of Islam and filmmakers have mobilized the cinematic medium to convey the message

14. Lücking and Eliyanah 2017, 103.
15. Diederich 2005, 129.

of national cohesion against extremist violence, some films about terrorism have been banned in Indonesia. The 2011 documentary film featuring penetrating interviews with the convicted Bali bombers, *Prison and Paradise* by Daniel Rudi Haryanto, failed to obtain a Censorship Certificate (STLS) from the Indonesian Film Censorship Board, which prohibits the public viewing of the film. Similarly, the 2016 documentary film, *Jihad Selfie* by Noor Huda Ismail, a journalist and former schoolmate of one of the Bali bombers, was pulled from screenings in Jakarta for being a security risk. The incongruously-named *Jihad Selfie*, hinting at the role of social media in the recruitment of soldiers into transnational terrorist organizations, follows the journey of young Indonesian men from their humble beginnings as students in Islamic boarding schools to gaining further education abroad before arriving in the Islamic State (ISIS) in Iraq and Syria where the glory of jihad and martyrdom awaits them. Like in many films made after 9/11 elsewhere, there is a tendency to "humanize" terrorists and would-be terrorists[16] to sketch a portrait of radicalization, to explain and ultimately to establish and understand their motivations. Far from an uncritical documentation of radicalized young lives, the film ends with an emphatic call for Indonesians to turn away from transnational terrorism and re-integrate into their own society.

In this essay, I seek to examine the ways in which Indonesian cinema enters the transnational discourse about Islamist terrorism. In doing so, I develop a conceptual framework that emphasizes the politics of representation in the production of these films. By adopting Rey Chow's "film as ethnography" I argue that films become both ethnography and autobiography when the filmmaker, protagonists, and audiences, in their encounter with "foreign Arab" culture and "the West," recreate the world in their own images. The dual strategies of ethnography and autobiography are necessary for Indonesian filmmakers in their own struggles to define the authenticity of Indonesian Islam and Muslims. Such strategies cohere with the politics of cultural recognition by historically disadvantaged and misunderstood groups. As Nancy Fraser observed, the politics of recognition predominates the post-socialist ideological landscape as the basis for claiming justice. It calls assumptions of "universality" into question, for failing to acknowledge that standards of universality privilege dominant members of society and violently exclude others. Thus, the politics of recognition foregrounds aspects of marginalized identity whether it is gender, race, or religion over one's other overlapping identities to be recognized for approval and rights.

---

16. Martin 2007.

The Contemporary Islamic Film Genre as Ethnography and Autobiography

Filmmakers in Indonesia in the early 2000s create and deploy the cinematic image as a means of articulating something about "Islam." Their films would fall within the generic rubric of the "Islamic film," a genre that is conceived through a polemical and aesthetic articulation on homegrown Islamist extremism, suicide bombing, women's status within Islam, and inter-faith relations. The exponential rise and success of films with Islamic themes from 2008 onwards have been strongly attributed to the processes of Islamization in the public sphere, processes that transform the meaning of Islam in its commodified and popular expressions. The Islamic film is, however, more than a narrative-driven genre about spiritual struggle and redemption. It is conveyed as a transparent medium for proselytization (*dakwah*) through its considered incorporation of Qur'anic passages and Islamic iconography to guide its Muslim protagonists and audiences to be "better" Muslims.[17] As a highly lucrative venture that suffers little from criticisms of profiteering from Islam, the genre is careful to maintain its ethical integrity through the hiring of pious Muslim actors, halal financing of films, consultation with high-profile muftis, and filming practices that are organized around the crew's religious obligations.[18]Other than for *dakwah*, the representation of Muslims in contemporary Indonesian cinema mobilizes aims that fall into two broad themes: as contemplative material for Indonesian viewers and as filmic emissary to the outside world. In the former, local audiences are presented with a vision of religious aspiration with clearly defined boundaries of the nation and its ideology of diversity. In the latter, Indonesian Muslims are projected outwards into the global flux (sometimes read as chaos to the order of the nation) constrained by Islamophobia and religious racism. With reference to the latter, I would like to argue that Indonesian cinema's representation of Islam and Muslims is a form of "new ethnography" or "auto-ethnography" as a means of remedying the injury of misrecognition. "Old" ethnography is comprised of hegemonic "Western" anthropologists studying distant exotic cultures. Critical rejection of colonial discourses along with the crisis in representation have reformed "old" approaches to ethnography, upending the West's unquestioned authority to interpret other cultures.[19] "New ethnography" involves that which is performed by those "who were previously ethnographized and who have,

17. Sasono 2013, 47.
18. Izharuddin 2017, 51; Imanda 2012, 94.
19. Clifford 1986, 8–9.

in the postcolonial age, taken up the active task of ethnographizing their own cultures."[20] This is not to say that "new" ethnography has completely supplanted the "old" but rather to suggest that critical reflections on the relations of knowledge production have altogether redefined ethnography. Such redefinitions operate within continuing power inequalities especially with respect to anthropology's repositioning of its "objects" of study.

Total epistemological subversion of the deadlock in anthropology being unfeasible in the present time, Rey Chow proposes a rethinking of visuality to reclaim the former object of ethnography's subjectivity. Here, the postcolonial subject's position is necessarily one of "to-be-looked-at-ness," whereby she is both object and subject of the ethnographic gaze and pays tribute to the reflexive turn in anthropology. "To-be-looked-at-ness" is derived from Laura Mulvey's theory of the male gaze,[21] whereby women are not only the object of the gaze but themselves see through a masculinized gaze. The construction of the female as both object and subject of the gaze is echoed in John Berger's dictum, whereby "men act and women appear. Men look at women. Women look at themselves being looked at."[22] Here "to-be-looked-at-ness" and the formerly ethnographized are brought together in parallel. Even as subjects who are doing the looking, the past and present experience of being the object of the gaze does not dissipate and lives on especially in cross-cultural representation. And it is in cross-cultural representation that auto-ethnography, the ethnography of the self, becomes the viable project for formerly ethnographized subjects to partake. As a metaphor for contemporary Islamic films in Indonesia, ethnography reconfigures the meanings that fix "us" and "them" in the global discourse on terrorism.[23]

The metaphor of ethnography is especially enhanced in the post-9/11 age as the genre negotiates national boundaries and religious identity in a more dangerous world for Muslims. That the genre is compelled into weaving an ethnography of the nation as self from global discourses gives it the authority of autobiography. The story of the nation bears characteristics of narratives of the self and the autobiography in which watershed historical events define its character and identity. Simply more than a retrospective of "life as lived" in past tense prose, the autobiography is, as Jerome Bruner argues, about the presentation of "exceptionality" in the narrative of the self performed, incidentally, in the "present tense."[24] Marked as exceptional by the narrator, the turning points of a nation are so because they individualize

20. Chow 2010, 152.
21. Mulvey 1997, 442.
22. Berger 2008, 47.
23. Said 2006, https://www.thenation.com/article/essential-terrorist/.
24. Bruner 2001, 29.

and distinguish its identity from others. The conscious marking off of events – like the misrecognition of Indonesian Muslims as terrorists and extremists – is necessary in the narrative of Indonesian difference and authenticity.

Indonesian autobiographical writings by the feminist campaigner Raden Ajeng Kartini, Marxist anti-colonial nationalist Tan Malaka, novelist Hamka, and poet Sitor Situmorang are examples of the canonical power invested in the narrative of the self as sutured to the Indonesian nation and its ideals. Writing their life stories offers autobiographers not only the advantage of interpreting their historical and cultural circumstances but also to establish for readers the presuppositions of the narrator's self-knowledge.[25] The structure of these modern autobiographies, with their emphasis on the narrator's personal struggles and vision for the nation, is intended with strong affinity and a didactic purpose for the Indonesian reader. This is because, as C. W. Watson has observed, "autobiographical narratives in Indonesia all to a degree position themselves in relation to the evolution of the nation."[26] The publicness and intentions of an autobiography, its presuppositions about oneself, how it relates to others and circumstances of the times, inevitably makes the narrator an inter-subjective Self rather than an autonomous one. These defining characteristics of the autobiography in which "the constructed Self and its agentive powers become [...] the gravitational center of the world" constitute a kind of "world-making"[27] that the Islamic film genre seeks to achieve. To maintain the integrity of the Self and its allies at the center of world-making, it is inevitable to distinguish oneself from an out-group whose role it is to define the qualities of the in-group.

THE TURNING POINT

In Europe, Britain, and the United States where acts of terrorism have been committed by Muslim men, political leaders are quick to assert that the perpetrators were not "real" Muslims. It is a rhetorical strategy that serves to sever the stubborn link between Islam and terrorism and emphasize instead that such acts are ideological outliers against the current of majority belief. In Indonesia, the subject of terrorism is confronted with a more subdued discourse of Islamic authenticity. For clerics and filmmakers, Muslim men and women seduced by radicalization have misunderstood the peaceful message of Islam, taking instead a hardline literalist interpretation of jihad. The traditionalist Muslim organization Nahdlahtul Ulama, which sees itself as a global player in the geopolitical discourse on Islam, promotes a simi-

25. Bruner 1995, 162.
26. Watson 2000, 15.
27. Bruner 2001, 35.

lar view. Its message of celebrating the pluralism and indigeneity of Islamic practice is a counternarrative to the supremacy of Middle Eastern Islam. However, it risks essentializing Arab cultural influences as Other, denying the long history of Arab migration to the archipelago and reproducing Javanese hegemony over other cultural groups.

The Indonesian Islamic film genre is motivated by these dilemmas that yoke the question of being Muslim in the global age of terrorism together with a contemplation on the meaning of Islam in Indonesia. Using a familiar premise – Indonesian Islam is peaceful and at peace with modernity and diversity – the genre re-appropriates the global negative stereotype of Muslims and constructs a vision of the "good" Indonesian Muslim based on existing cultural references to idealized behavior. The discursive formations that distinguish *halus* (refined) as opposed to *kasar* (coarse) that cut across behavior, social etiquette and material culture inform contemporary definitions of "good" Indonesian Muslim masculinity. Seen as central concepts in the aristocratic Javanese worldview, *halus* is all that is urbane, polished, and restrained in contrast to the disorderly, rough, racist and barbaric, which are registered as *kasar*.[28] The binary oppositions of *halus* and *kasar* rehearsed in representations of the Indonesian Muslim man and his Arab male counterpart, who abuses women and looks down on Indonesians, stand as a recurring trope in the Islamic film genre. These Indonesian characteristics of idealized behavior can be confounding for non-Indonesians, resulting in misrecognition. In 2003, the Australian media was confronted with the culturally inscrutable facial expressions of the convicted Bali bomber Amrozi bin Nurhasyim, who smiled and raised his thumbs as his death penalty was announced. Amrozi's seemingly cheerful demeanor no doubt infuriated the world but it elided the fact that the smile carries a multitude of meanings in Indonesian culture. A man who guards his emotions to remain polite may actually be shy, anxious, embarrassed, and afraid.[29]

The misrecognition of Muslim women in face-veils, niqab or burqa has a long tradition. They are (mis)-represented as an Orientalist mystery, a body that denies access to the colonial gaze.[30] In contemporary visual culture, the woman cloaked in the burqa is entirely dehumanized as objects, even as black rubbish bags ready to be disposed of, as depicted in the 2011 German International Human Rights campaign.[31] Sometimes, the headgear becomes

28. Geertz 1960, 232.
29. Saniotis 2006.
30. Alloula 1986, 14.
31. "Muslim Women and Their White Saviors," *Sociological Images*, 6 May 2011, https://thesocietypages.org/socimages/2011/05/06/muslim-women-and-their-white-saviors/

an unintentional trompe-l'œil, as in the photograph featuring black seats that look eerily like a group of women wearing the burqa (Figure 1). A Norwegian anti-immigration group used the image in 2017 to express their fear and xenophobic views on Muslim immigration. Not realizing that they were actually bus seats rather than women the group was roundly ridiculed for their anti-Islamic misrecognition-turned-delusion. Thus, being mistaken for an object, being oppressed, and a terrorist became a turning point for Muslims after 9/11, which led to the intense foregrounding of Muslim identity and claims in the public sphere.

Figure 1. "Terrifying" bus seats

Fear of misrecognition pulls a niqabi from the brink of possible death in the Indonesian film *Khalifah* (2011) directed by Nurman Hakim. Unlike the more romanticized representation of the face veil in Indonesian cinema during this period, *Khalifah* situates the face veil within the gendered discourses of xenophobia and national security. The face veil may be exotic and even romantic in the Middle East, but in Indonesia, it inspires fear and suspicion. From the outset of the film, the eponymous female character adopts the niqab at her Indonesian husband's behest. As a salesman he travels frequently from Saudi Arabia bringing home imported goods, both material and ideological. Working-class and unworldly, Khalifah is the embodiment of the combined dangers of extremism, terrorism, and female passivity that ensnare Indonesian women. Khalifah gradually loses her personal and economic identity in scenes where the niqab is constructed in diametric opposition to putative Indonesian femininity: unveiled and in Western-style clothing. She risks losing her job as a hairdresser after she imposes limits on physical interactions with non-Muslim women who visit her salon. When she discovers in the news that male terrorists disguised as Muslim women in the niqab have been gunned down by the police, she learns that misrecognition is fatal and hastily removes the niqab. *Khalifah* is a moral parable in which women's bodies are re-inscribed as a site of cultural anxiety and the protagonists are vulnerable to the fatal whims of misrecognition.

Portrayals of masculinities demonstrate greater moral and cultural complexities as distinctions are made not simply between Indonesian Muslim man and his Arab Other, but are played off against other typologies of Indonesian Muslim masculinities constructed through class and intra-faith narratives.[32][33] Like *Khalifah*, we see a similar misrecognition of Muslim men in *3 Doa 3 Cinta* (*3 Prayers 3 Loves*, Nurman Hakim, 2008) and *Syahadat Cinta* (*Vow of Love*, Gunawan Punggaru, 2008), where the central male characters are wrongly imprisoned for participating in terrorist activities. As products of the Islamic boarding school system, by the 2000s misunderstood as the hotbed of terrorism, the men must suffer shame and betrayal before rehabilitating into recognizably "good" Muslims through prayer and heterosexual marriage. For the young men in *3 Prayers 3 Loves*, directed also by Nurman Hakim who was determined to remedy noxious stereotypes of Islamic boarding school students,[34] the collapse of the World Trade Center twin towers in New York is a faraway event witnessed on television. The event marks the beginning of their collision with the global geopolitical enterprise of the so-called War on Terror. But the foreign threat of Orientalist Arab culture and its contemporary association with extremism is felt closer to home with egregious consequences. In one scene in the film, the wearing of turbans during Islamic prayer is ridiculed (Figure 2), foreshadowing the humiliated male character's descent to a suicide bombing attempt. In these films, the West recedes from view as a totem against which Indonesian Islam is defined. Minor Western (read: American) characters do not pose a direct threat to the lives of Indonesian Muslims, even going as far as being benevolent figures who help alleviate their hardship. First regarded with suspicion by the most religiously zealous of the young men, a wealthy American man in *3 Prayers 3 Loves* is eventually transformed into his personal

---

32. Izharuddin 2017, 143.

33. See Hoesterey and Clark (2012) for further discussion on controversies in Indonesian Islamic films that implicate images of men.

34. Hoestery and Clark 2012, 220.

savior when he assists in paying the young man's ailing parent's hospital bills. By contrast, Arab Islam threatens to eclipse local iterations of Islam in the everyday and is not redeemed through character transformation.

Figure 2 Ridiculed for wearing the turban and lacking
authenticity. Scene from *3 Prayers 3 Loves*

Indonesian men are also at risk of being victims of misrecognition when they are abroad in other Muslim societies. In the 2014 film *Haji Backpacker*, directed by Danial Rifky, the titular character Mada is a morally wayward young Indonesian man turned fugitive when he is suspected of murder in Bangkok. His turning point occurs when he is mistaken for an Israeli spy in Pakistan and violently interrogated. Mada's Indonesian passport provides insufficient evidence of his identity, whose contents are made more suspicious by exit stamps that document multiple short trips across Asia. His only way of proving his Muslim identity is by reading the Qur'ān, which impresses and gains the praise of being a "good Muslim" by his interrogator. The violence of misrecognition reforms him and he makes a journey to Mecca following this dramatic event. Mada's travel to the holy city is facilitated by a luxury yacht owned by an Arab man, although he rides as a deckhand who is paid to clean the vehicle. Here, in a geographical location far removed from his homeland, an Indonesian Muslim man gains conditional respect from other Muslims. For the men in these films, misrecognition traumatically interrupts their personal lives but provides an opportunity to strengthen their spiritual resolve, a turning point to enter the protective fold of the nation. In the scenes explained above, the discourse of misrecognition produces particular kinds of Muslims, bodies, and articulations. *Haji Backpacker* belongs to a small cluster of films that, through the portrayal of Indonesian Muslims interacting with other Muslims and individuals of different faiths abroad, casts the "Indonesian Muslim" perspective of the world that invites a participation in "global experiences of belonging, discrimination, and identity formation."[35]

CONCLUSION:

As a medium for claiming authenticity, the Indonesian Islamic film genre is a gendered and racialized site of power and ideological struggle. At this juncture one wonders about the ethical potential of the Islamic film as a contemplative medium for tolerance, diversity, and empowerment.[36] As Sonja van Wichelen[37] has observed, public debates about Islam in Indonesia are typically funneled down a narrow and often reductive framework of judgment and control. The limitations on the breadth and complexity of representation notwithstanding, it is fair to say that the world-remaking tendencies of the contemporary Islamic film genre perform "recognition as remedies [that] sometimes presuppose an underlying conception of redistribution."[38] Redistribution here is one of signification, rather than an economic one that Fraser promotes, in the global circuit of images of Islam and Muslims. The typologies of Muslim women and men that the genre sets against each other, through the device and epistemological logic of ethnography and autobiography, participate in the claims that the friendly face of *Islam Nusantara* (or the local Indonesian way of being Muslim) is just as authentic as Arabian Islam and may even be superior.

As ethnography, the Islamic film genre behaves as a mediator between systems of cultures. It establishes some alliances with other Muslim cultures regarded as civilized as itself and tells a story about the Indonesian nation and Islam as Self in opposition to Arab culture. Although the effect is a kind of world-making, or re-making in its image, it is not one hermetically

35. Barker 2017.
36. Interestingly, films about interfaith relations in Indonesia that have been widely hailed as cultural touchstones for tolerance and diversity have attracted censure from authorities and extremist groups. Hanung Bramantyo's 2011 multi-narrative film *Tanda Tanya* (Question Mark), which features a Muslim church bomber fueled by anti-Christian sentiment is one such case in point.
37. Wichelen 2009, 79.
38. Fraser 1995, 73.

sealed from the rapidly changing global mediascape. Instead, the world-remaking effects of the Islamic film genre is a dialogical textual production in interaction with screen cultures and religious politics on the ground and beyond. Representational strategies used in the Islamic film genre gain particular urgency at this present moment of rising conservatism in Indonesia, characterized by co-optation by mainstream politics of extremist groups and leaders. However, due to institutional barriers to filmmaking that addresses Islamist radicalism and the understandable reluctance of filmmakers to portray local iterations of extremism, it is no wonder they turn instead to caricatures of Arabs as a convenient foil to *Islam Nusantara.*

The global inequalities that form the relations between Indonesia and the wider world to whom it speaks are re-asserted in the racism, "religious" and otherwise, and the exploitation of Indonesian workers in the Middle East. Antipathy and outrage against the sexual violence and modern-day slavery of Indonesian female domestic workers in the Arabian Peninsula strike as the main affective tenor in discourses on Indonesians finding fortune in the Middle East.[39] The Islamic film genre functions as a discursive space for recuperating Muslim masculinity and femininity in the post-9/11 world when the redefinition of Indonesian Islam and the nation is at stake. Its world-making capacities adhere to a simple framework that obscures indigenous origins of extremism and oppression, simplifies the complexities that drive young Indonesians to radicalism, and draws homogenizing conclusions about cultural out-groups that are seen in absolute opposition to Indonesia and its Muslim population.

Works Cited

Alloula, M. 1986. *The Colonial Harem.* Minneapolis: University of Minnesota Press.

Barker, Thomas. 2017. "Travels and Travails: Cosmopolitan Muslims in Indonesian Cinema." *Cinema Poetica.* 27 May 2017. https://cinemapoetica.com/travels-and-travails-cosmopolitan-muslims-in-indonesian-cinema/ Accessed 25 March 2020.

Berger, J. 2008. *Ways of Seeing.* London: Penguin.

Bruner, J. 1995. "The Autobiographical Process." *Current Sociology* 43 (2): 161–77.

———. 2001. "Self-Making and World-Making." In *Narrative and Identity: Studies in Autobiography, Self and Culture,* edited by J. Brockmeier and D. A. Carbaugh, 25–37. Amsterdam and Philadelphia: John Benjamins Publishing Company.

39. Silvey 2004.

Chow, R. 2010. *The Rey Chow Reader*. Edited by P. Bowman. New York, Chichester: Columbia University Press.

Clifford, J. 1986. "Partial Truths." In *Writing Culture: The Poetics and Politics of Ethnography*, edited by James Clifford and George E. Marcus, 1–26. Berkeley: University of California Press.

Diederich, M. 2005. "Indonesians in Saudi Arabia: Religious and Economic Connections." In *Transnational Connections and the Arab Gulf*, edited by M. Al-Rasheed, 142–60. London: Routledge.

Fealy, G. 2008. "Consuming Islam: Commodified Religion and Aspirational Pietism in Contemporary Indonesia." In *Expressing Islam: Religious Life and Politics in Indonesia*, edited by G. Fealy and S. White, 15–39. Singapore: Institute of Southeast Asian Studies.

Fraser, N. 1995. "From Redistribution to Recognition? Dilemmas of Justice in a 'Post-Socialist' Age." *New Left Review* 212:68–94

Geertz, C. 1960. *The Religion of Java*. London: The Free Press of Glencoe.

Heryanto, A. 2008. "Pop Culture and Competing Identities." In *Popular Culture in Indonesia: Fluid Identities in Post-Authoritarian Politics*, edited by A. Heryanto, 11–46. London: Routledge.

Hoesterey, J. B., and M. Clark. 2012. "Film Islami: Gender, Piety and Pop Culture in Post-Authoritarian Indonesia." *Asian Studies Review* 36 (2): 207–26.

Imanda, T. 2012. "Independent Versus Mainstream Islamic Cinema in Indonesia: Religion Using the Market or Vice Versa?" In *Southeast Asian Independent Cinema*, edited by T. Baumgartel, 89–104. Hong Kong: Hong Kong University Press.

Izharuddin, A. 2015. "The Muslim Woman in Indonesian Cinema and the Face Veil as Other." *Indonesia and the Malay World.* 43 (127): 397–412.

———. 2017. *Gender and Islam in Indonesian Cinema*. Singapore: Palgrave Macmillan.

Lücking, M., and E. Eliyanah. 2017. "Images of Authentic Muslim Selves: Gendered Moralities and Constructions of Arab Others in Contemporary Indonesia." *Social Sciences* 6 (3): 103.

Martin, E. 2007. "The Global Phenomenon of 'Humanizing' Terrorism in Literature and Cinema." *CLC Web: Comparative Literature and Culture*, 9 (1): 12.

Mulvey, L. 1997. "Visual Pleasure and Narrative Cinema." In *Feminisms: An Anthology of Literary Theory and Criticism*, edited by R. Warhol and D. P. Herndl, 438–48. New Brunswick and New Jersey: Rutgers University Press.

Rich, B. B. 2004. "After the Fall: Cinema Studies Post-9/11." *Cinema Journal* 43 (2): 108–15.

Riddell, P. G. 2001. "Arab Migrants and Islamization in the Malay World during the Colonial Period." *Indonesia and the Malay World* 28 (84): 113–28.

Said, E. 2006. "The Essential Terrorist." *The Nation*. https://www.thenation.com/article/essential-terrorist/

Saniotis, A. 2006. "Why is Amrozi Smiling?: 'Misrecognition' and the Politics of Terror." *Borderlands*. Volume 5, no. 2.

Sasono, E. 2010. "Islamic-Themed Films in Contemporary Indonesia: Commodified Religion or Islamization?" *Asian Cinema Journal* 21 (2): 48–68.

———. 2013. "Islamic Revivalism and Religious Piety in Indonesian Cinema." In *Performance, Popular Culture, and Piety in Muslim Southeast Asia*, edited by T. P. Daniels, 45–75. London: Palgrave Macmillan.

Silvey, R. 2004. "Transnational Migration and the Gender Politics of Scale: Indonesian Domestic Workers in Saudi Arabia." *Singapore Journal of Tropical Geography* 25 (2): 141–55.

Slocum, D. 2011. "9/11 Film and Media Scholarship." *Cinema Journal* 51 (1): 181–93.

Taylor, C. 1994. *Multiculturalism*. New Jersey: Princeton University Press

Watson, C. W. 2000. *Of Self and Nation: Autobiography and the Representation of Modern Indonesia*. Honolulu: University of Hawaii Press.

Wichelen, S. 2009. "Formations of Public Piety: New Veiling, the Body, and the Citizen-Subject in Contemporary Indonesia." In *The Body in Asia*, edited by B. S. Turner and Z. Yangwen, 75–96. New York and Oxford: Berghahn Books.

Debating Polygamy in Indonesian Cinema

Thomas Barker

INTRODUCTION

Scholar of Indonesian Islamic television Inaya Rakhmani argues that since the late 1990s, the inclusion of Islamic content in commercial television programming has led to a mainstreaming of Islam.[1] By this she means that Islamic practices and beliefs circulate in a commercial media space, away from the direct domain of Islamic authorities and scholars. What emerges is a combination of faith and market forces that produces new forms of pop culture containing new representations of an Islamic life. That is to say, the inclusion of Islamic content in commercial pop culture is not simply the commodification of Islam, but that representations of Islam become open to variation and subject to debate.[2] Whilst Rakhmani's work focuses on television, and in particular local soap opera (*sinetron*), which is a widely watched genre on free-to-air broadcast television, a similar phenomenon is seen in feature film where many of the same producers operate.

Drawing on Rakhmani's work, and a growing body of scholarship on Islamic pop culture, this chapter discusses the presentation of polygamy in a number of recent Islamic films. Following on previous discussions of polygamy in *Berbagi Suami* (*Love for Share*, Nia Dinata, 2006) and *Ayat-Ayat Cinta* (*Verses of Love*, Hanung Bramantyo, 2008),[3] this chapter analyzes the recent feature film *Surga yang Tak Dirindukan* (*A Paradise Not Longed For*, Kuntz Agus, 2015) a romantic drama with a central plot line involving polygamy. Whereas the public debate about polygamy often demands either a pro or anti position, this chapter details and analyzes the nuances and complexity of the competing discourses that the films present as preferable alternatives to polygamy. *A Paradise Not Longed For*, I will argue, is able to frame its unfavorable presentation of polygamy through the deployment of a melodramatic love-triangle and by contrasting polygamy with a competing and preferable discourse of monogamous romance and family-building. Presented in this way, the film's message is packaged in a palatable form for mainstream audiences, which in part explains the film's box-office success

1. Rakhmani 2012; 2016.
2. Sasono 2010.
3. Kurnia 2009; Paramaditha 2010; Heryanto 2008.

and points to the ways in which a soft critique of polygamy appears on the cinema screen.

THE ISLAMIC TURN

Over the past two decades a revival of Islamic faith has been observed in the proliferation of Islamic symbols, practices, and beliefs across a broad range of sites in Indonesian daily life.[4] This revival contrasts with the three decades of New Order governance from 1966 to 1998 under which Islam was subject to state control and public life was secularized. Although the majority religion of Indonesia, under the New Order Islam was confined largely to rituals and routines, and subordinate to the prevailing state discourses of order, development, and modernization. Political Islam and Islamic groups were seen as a threat by the New Order regime and it moved to neutralize them through political party amalgamation and by encouraging the two largest Muslim organizations – Nahdlatul Ulama (NU) and Muhammadiyah – to concentrate on social development including health, welfare, and education programs. In line with New Order ideology, the leading Muslim intellectual of the New Order era Nurcholish Madjid famously declared in 1970, "Islam yes, Islamic parties no!"[5]

Islam was not excluded from being represented in pop culture such as music and films, but it tended to be mundane, moralizing, or preachy.[6] Characters were nominally or incidentally Muslim, and their faith was rarely a central part of their identity or motivation. Female characters rarely wore the headscarf (*jilbab* or *hijab*), and if they did wear a headscarf it was loose with hair visible (*kerudung*).[7] Popular *dangdut* singer Rhoma Irama used his music, and later his film roles, to moralize to audiences about the evils of drinking, sex, and gambling, and embodied the victory of righteousness over sin. Looking back over this period, Asrul Sani commented that "our films have been trying to replace the role of the *kiai*" suggesting that Islamic films of the New Order period were largely doctrinal in their presentation of Islam.[8]

Over the 1980s and 1990s however beliefs about the practice of Islam were beginning to change under influence from developments in the Islamic world, including the Muslim Brotherhood in Egypt, the Iranian Revolution, and other Salafist movements.[9] Understanding of piety was shifting towards

4. Heryanto 2008; Hoesterey and Clark 2012.
5. Bourchier and Hadiz 2014, 88.
6. Sasono 2010.
7. Paramaditha 2010.
8. Sani 2000.
9. Roy 2004; Machmudi 2008.

a much more holistic conception or "way of life" and not just in rituals and obligations such as Friday prayer or giving of alms (*zakat*). Followers of this new piety movement prioritize Islam as a source of personal identity and live their faith through consumption choices, social habits, fashion, and other symbolic markers. Many observers have noticed the increase in the number of women wearing the *jilbab* or *hijab* in school and on university campuses, reflecting a growing desire by young Muslim women to embody their faith through their clothing.[10]

Reflective of these trends was the increased Islamization of lifestyle and entertainment media over the 1990s,[11] with the 1998 *sinetron Doaku Harapanku* (*My Prayers My Hopes*) a precursor to the new wave of Islamic television programming.[12] Broadcast nationally on RCTI and produced by the large commercial Multivision Plus (owned by Raam Punjabi) production house, *My Prayers My Hopes* began as a Ramadhan serial but ran for a total of two years. Although following a typical melodramatic narrative involving a loving husband, a beleaguered wife, and a meddling mother-in-law, the characters seek solace in their faith and invoke Islam in their actions and decisions. For commercial producers like Raam Punjabi, this turn to Islamic content was profitable but it also marked the beginning of what Inaya Rakhmani has called the "mainstreaming of Islam" through television.[13] Many other religiously-themed formats followed, including drama, variety shows, and self-help sermons led by new celebrity tele-preachers. Television producers tapped into a growing desire to see aspects of Islamic faith and practices incorporated much more into mainstream entertainment to fulfil the call to *dakwah* (proselytization, propagation).

In cinema, Islamic content emerged later as many of the new generation of young filmmakers who emerged after 1998 were not religiously inclined and much more focused on trying to attract an urban, secular audience of teenagers much like themselves. Hanung Bramantyo for example who has become one of the key Islamic filmmakers started out making very different films. Although he came from a Muhammadiyah family in Yogyakarta, his faith was not at the forefront of his identity as a filmmaker. However, a confluence of events, including an offer from MD Pictures to be the director of *Verses of Love*, propelled him into the forefront of the new wave of Islam-themed cinema. Islam-themed films discuss everyday topics of love and marriage, with many based on popular Islamic literature by authors such as Asma Nadia and Habiburrahman El Shirazy, and biopics based on

10. Nef-Saluz 2007.
11. Pamungkas 2015.
12. Rakhmani 2012; 2014.
13. Rakhmani 2014; 2016.

the life of famous Muslims such as *Sang Pencerah* (*The Enlightener*, Hanung Bramantyo, 2010) about the founder of Muhammadiyah, Ahmad Dahlan, or *Hijrah Cinta* (*Love Emigration*, Indra Gunawan, 2014) about popular preacher Jefri Al Buchori. Many producers and filmmakers have tried to capitalize on this market segment and have developed a new subgenre often labelled *film Islami*.[14]

Due to the more progressive nature of the filmmaking community and its creative inclinations, Islamic films have not been shy in engaging controversies and issues within Islam and its practice in Indonesia. More activist filmmakers have used the form to raise critical questions including around radicalism (*3 Doa 3 Cinta* [*3 Prayers 3 Loves*, Nurman Hakim, 2006]), veiling (*Khalifah* [Nurman Hakim, 2011]), women's education in Islamic schools (*Perempuan Berkalung Sorban* [*Woman in a Turban*, Hanung Bramantyo, 2009]), and multiculturalism (*Tanda Tanya* [*Question Mark*, Hanung Bramantyo, 2011]) amongst others. For example, Bramantyo's *Question Mark* portrays a multiplicity of everyday characters: one who has converted from Islam to Christianity; a veiled woman who works in a Chinese-owned pork noodle restaurant; a Muslim assigned to guard a Christian church during Easter; and an out-of-work Muslim actor who plays Jesus in the church's nativity play. When *Question Mark* was released in the cinemas it was protested by conservative Islamists and a subsequent television broadcast had to be cancelled due to protests. Whilst it is relatively easy to provoke such groups to protest, more broadly these films signal a willingness on the part of filmmakers to engage with prominent issues and problems relating to the practice of faith in Indonesia and to contribute to a larger public discourse around Islam and religion more broadly.

THE ISSUE OF POLYGAMY

Alongside the wearing of the headscarf (*hijab*) and conversion (*muallaf*), polygamy is one of the most hotly discussed issues in contemporary Indonesian Islam today. Whereas conversion or wearing the headscarf are largely seen as matters of individual choice,[15] polygamy not only involves more than one person but challenges prevailing norms around the institutions of marriage and the family. Both marriage and family-life are idealized within normative political and religious discourse in Indonesia and within the broader heteronormative ideology tied to nation building.[16] Yet due to the proliferation of voices and positioning in Indonesian Islam

14. Hoesterey and Clark 2012; Izharuddin 2016.
15. E.g. Randello 2017.
16. Boellstorff 2004, 470.

over the past two decades, arguments for polygamy have become more visible in traditional and new media such as websites, television shows, and in
magazines even if they represent a minority view.[17]

During the New Order, the state introduced restrictions on the practice
of polygamy within the broader effort to codify and regulate marriage.
According to Khoiruddin Nasution, the 1974 Marriage Law was introduced
to provide greater protections to women and to promote marriage as a
monogamous union, especially for civil servants and government employees.[18]
Although provoked by women's rights activists, the 1974 Marriage Law also
contributed to the state's gender ideology by regulating family life and
gender roles in the interests of male-led nation building. Under the 1974 law
polygamy is allowed but "restricted" in that it can only be practiced under
certain conditions and follow strict procedures.[19] In reality, though, the
law was not strictly enforced, and so polygamy did not disappear, although
official numbers were reduced.[20] According to Nasution,[21] this policy of
"restricted" polygamy put Indonesia on a par with many other Muslim
countries, but after 1998 the Marriage Law was amended, first in 2000 to
remove the restrictions on civil servants and state officials, and then later
it "loosened or dropped legal restrictions on polygamy [...] to accommodate
Islamic demands."[22]

Polygamy returned to public debate in the 2000s as previously repressed
communities or practices were able to be more open and self-promoting.
Progressive voices and feminist movements have been prominent,[23] but
many conservative and religious movements have emerged and gained
significant traction if not publicity.[24] Advocates of polygamy found a new
voice in Puspo Wardoyo, a successful fried chicken restaurant entrepreneur,
who attributed his success and expansion of his outlets to his ability to take
more than one wife.[25] In 2003, he organized the Polygamy Awards and invited prominent polygamists and their wives to a lavish ceremony in Jakarta.
Guests included vice president Hamzah Haz and celebrity preacher Aa Gym.[26]
Despite being met with some protests,[27] the Polygamy Awards marked a

17. Brenner 2011.
18. Nasution 2008.
19. Nasution 2008, 209–10.
20. Nurmila and Bennett 2016, 72.
21. Nasution 2008.
22. van Wichelen 2009, 175.
23. van Wichelen 2009.
24. Suryakusuma 2017.
25. van Wichelen 2009.
26. Brenner 2006.
27. Hoesterey and Clark 2012, 212.

growing willingness by advocates of polygamy to be more public about their marriages, and to use the media to promote and justify the practice.

Yet promoting polygamy could also hurt reputation and popularity, as seen in the case of Aa Gym, a popular Islamic evangelist who had built a successful Islamic advice enterprise that included seminars, publishing, and talk shows. Aa Gym had attracted an active and dedicated following, especially amongst women who liked his style of address and mode of teaching. However, when Aa Gym took a second wife in 2006, many of his hitherto dedicated followers and customers turned their backs on him and condemned his actions.[28] Many felt that his actions contradicted his own teachings and sympathized with his first wife, who they felt was being side-lined or victimized. Despite the emergence of Islamic celebrity preachers, polygamy has a variety of opinion and it cannot be said that all Muslims, even those who subscribe to new forms of preaching and *dakwah*, automatically support polygamy. Opinions about polygamy are filtered by other discourses around faith and consistency, and social norms of marriage.

Arguments justifying polygamy often cite Qur'ānic scripture and examples from the life of the prophet Muhammad. Most cited is verse 4:3 from Surah An-Nisa in the Qur'ān which in part states "you may marry whichever [other] women seem good to you, two, three, or four." *Hadith* reports about Muhammad's life are also used as a justification, since after the death of his first wife, Khadijah bint Khuwaylid, Muhammad married another eleven women. In addition, proponents of polygamy draw on the *fiqh* (jurisprudence) and "the symbolic importance of the Qur'ānic passage that allows it [polygamy]."[29] Other social and moral reasons are also given to justify polygamy, such as regulating men's "excess of sexual potency" through marriage rather than committing adultery or visiting prostitutes.[30] In some arguments, polygamy is necessary because there are more men than women in the world and because of the rise of "female singleness" due to women choosing careers over family.[31]

Opponents of polygamy use similar sources of evidence to establish their opposition to the practice, including "contextualization of the verses, contradictory verses, and strict conditions."[32] Surah An-Nisa is not a carte blanche endorsement of polygamy but provides conditions, including who a man can marry and under what circumstances: the verse is preceded by the following "If you fear that you will not deal fairly with orphan girls,..."

28. Hoesterey 2008, 96.
29. Lev 1996, 193.
30. van Wichelen 2009, 177.
31. van Wichelen 2009.
32. van Wichelen 2009, 184.

and continues "If you fear that you cannot be equitable [to them], then marry only one, or your slave(s): that is more likely to make you avoid bias" (Qur'ān 4:3). Verse 129 adds that "You will never be able to treat your wives with equal fairness, however much you may desire to do so..." These verses raise the issue of fairness, suggesting that it is difficult to be just dealing with respective wives. Further, others cite the different social and economic conditions between now and when the prophet Muhammad was alive arguing that polygamy is no longer necessary in the modern world.[33] In actual practice, many opponents argue that polygamy is practiced for less than noble purposes and that pro-polygamy arguments are self-serving, misogynist readings by men.[34]

Whilst the fairness argument is important to those opposed to the practice of polygamy – and it forms a part of the three films under consideration – I want to offer another source of opposition to polygamy. For many young Muslim Indonesians, polygamy may be allowed by scripture, but it comes into conflict with modern ideas of monogamous romantic love which proliferate in contemporary Indonesian pop culture. Prevailing normative discourse supports romantic love leading to monogamous marriage as an ideal outcome and life goal. This is often presented within the romantic ideal of finding one's "soulmate" (*jodoh*), namely that there is one person "out there" with whom we are matched and destined to fall in love with and marry. A *jodoh* is singular and exclusive. In this framework, polygamy is an archaic, even sleazy, practice. As consumers of pop culture young Indonesian audiences are intimately familiar with the ideals of monogamous romantic love and this shapes their expectations and desires in their own lives. In this combination of what Heryanto calls "piety and pleasure" romantic monogamous love between soulmates trumps polygamy.[35]

POLYGAMY IN FILM

Three recent Indonesian films stand out for their engagement with polygamy: *Love for Share* (2006), *Verses of Love* (2008), and *A Paradise Not Longed For* (2015). Both *Verses of Love* and *A Paradise Not Longed For* are based on popular novels of the same title. By comparing these three films I want to argue that *A Paradise Not Longed For* differs from the other two films in the way that it critiques polygamy. All three films can be read as anti-polygamy, but in *A Paradise Not Longed For* we find the clearest use of romance and monogamy as an alternative to polygamy.

33. Nurmila 2009.
34. Suryakusuma 2017; Brenner 2006.
35. Heryanto 2011.

Love for Share is a three-story omnibus that advocates a clear anti-polygamy position by director-producer Nia Dinata, a globally-savvy feminist filmmaker. Nia Dinata heads the Kalyana Shira Foundation, a film production company that has produced a number of commercial features as well as activist-minded films such as *Perempuan Punya Cerita* (*Chants of Lotus*, Nia Dinata, Lasja Fauzia, Upi Avianto, Fatimah Tobing Rony, 2007), *Conspiracy of Silence* (Ucu Agustin, 2010), and *Batik, Our Love Story* (Nia Dinata, 2011). Within the Indonesian film industry, Kalyana Shira is known as a progressive, independent organization which takes on social issues, especially around women's rights, in the films they sponsor. *Love for Share* was in part funded by the Ford Foundation, and was screened overseas at festivals, including the Tribeca Film Festival in 2006, and has been celebrated internationally by Western feminists and academics for its feminist commentary on Islam and portrayal of polygamy as a destructive practice.[36] When released domestically the film was praised but had little traction with local audiences.

Love for Share tells three stories of women who are victimized by polygamous marriages across a cross-section of Indonesian society with variations in wealth and class position, autonomy, self-determination, and agency within the polygamous households. As Novi Kurnia has argued in her analysis of the film, *Love for Share* presents a diverse range of women's perspectives and is therefore an intervention in the typically male-dominated discourse around polygamy. The film shows polygamy to be at the initiative of the men, often through duplicity or secrecy, such that the women are often times unaware that the man they are marrying or have married has other spouses. Kurnia describes the approach taken by the filmmaker Nia Dinata as "soft" and operating "within the limits and prohibitions of Indonesian film and religious culture."[37]

Verses of Love (2008) was the first of the new Islamic pop films, recording a phenomenal audience of 3.7 million and breaking the longstanding record held by the secular love story *Eiffel... I'm in Love* (Nasri Cheppy, 2003). Prior to directing *Verses of Love* (2008), Hanung Bramantyo had not expressed any prior intention of directing a *film Islami* and the popularity of *Verses of Love* caught him and many others by surprise. Set in Egypt, *Verses of Love* is the love story of Indonesian student Fahri who is studious, popular, handsome, and thus a paradigm of a new kind of Indonesian Islamic masculinity.[38] Despite being the object of affection of a number of women around him, Fahri marries the beautiful veiled Turkish-German woman, Aisha. But when he is accused of rape and arrested, he must also marry the Coptic Christian Maria

---

36. Kurnia, 2009; Imanjaya, 2009.
37. Kurnia 2009, 54.
38. Hoesterey and Clark 2012.

in order to secure her testimony. Maria had fallen unconscious after she was hit by a car and her coma is partially a result of her unrequited love for Fahri. When Fahri marries her, she wakes up, and her subsequent court testimony exonerates Fahri. For the film, Fahri's decision to take a second wife is not only a humanitarian decision but accords with Maria's own desire for Islam shown in scenes of her trying on the headscarf and learning passages of the Qurʾān to impress Fahri, who is the object of her affections.[39] Maria's marriage and thus conversion to Islam signals a triumphant moment.

Nevertheless, Ariel Heryanto has argued that the polygamous marriage portrayed in *Verses of Love* is in fact more troubled than celebratory, describing the film as "anti-polygamy."[40] Book author El Shirazy was reportedly displeased with the presentation of polygamy in the film, as it differed from his intentions. Compared to the original book where Maria dies soon after marriage, the film extends the period of the polygamy, dramatizing the difficulties of a polygamous marriage.[41] Aisha and Maria are shown to be jealous of each other while competing for Fahri's attention as Fahri struggles to accord each wife a fair amount of affection and care. After Maria dies from her health complications, the final scene of the film shows Fahri and Aisha walking hand in hand across a sand dune accompanied by a posthumous voiceover of Maria saying, "God willing, you have found your soulmate now Fahri."[42] By allowing Aisha and Fahri to continue as a monogamous couple, the reminder of *jodoh* becomes important in the way in which the film asserts monogamous partnership over polygamous marriage. Even if *Verses of Love* is read as pro-polygamy, Hoerstery and Clark argue that the character of Fahri "valorize[s] an alternative Muslim masculinity that aspires to be loving and gentle, but decidedly not hypermasculine or patriarchal"[43] and that his decision to take a second wife was in response to an "emergency situation."[44]

A PARADISE NOT LONGED FOR

A Paradise Not Longed For follows the wave of romantic Islamic films begun by *Verses of Love* and on its domestic release during Lebaran (Eid al-Fitr) was seen by 1.5 million people, making it the top film of 2015. Although directed by relative newcomer Kuntz Agus, *A Paradise Not Longed* For continues the collaboration between production company MD Pictures and Hanung

39. Paramaditha 2010.
40. Heryanto 2014, 56.
41. Brenner 2011.
42. "Insya Allah kamu berdapat jodoh kamu Fahri."
43. Hoerstery and Clark 2012, 213.
44. Brenner 2011, 227.

Bramantyo who co-produced. The paradise in the title evokes the religious concept of a posthumous heaven as reward for one's earthly religiosity and piety, but in the film has a more contextual meaning. *Paradise* here refers to the marriage between the main characters, Pras and Arini. When Arini discovers that Pras has a second wife – Meirose – she accuses him of abandoning the "paradise" of their married life that they had worked to build together.

A Paradise Not Longed For establishes the marriage between Arini and Pras as perfect and founded on mutual attraction and romantic love. They meet one day by chance when Pras helps an injured boy back to the Islamic school where Arini teaches. He sees her nurturing side and Arini recognizes Pras' caring nature. With the blessing and encouragement of her parents, Arini and Pras marry in a simple Javanese wedding ceremony, beginning their married life together, which grows to include a house, two cars, and a daughter, Nadia. Pras establishes an architecture firm with his two university friends, Amran and Hartono, and their business grows. There is a kind of equilibrium created and the couple lead a perfectly stable, happy, prosperous, and comfortable middle-class lifestyle replete with modern amenities, and beautiful surroundings. This will be upset when Pras secretly marries Meirose one day when he is out of town on an assignment.

Pras' marriage to Meirose comes by way of an accident and his desire to preserve life, rather than out of lust or hatred for Arini. While driving on a winding road one day, Pras rescues a woman in a wedding dress who has crashed her car after driving recklessly. He rushes her to the hospital where the doctors inform Pras that the woman is pregnant and requires a Caesarean section. Even though he's not the legal husband or father, Pras assents to the operation and she successfully gives birth to a baby boy, whom Pras names Akbar. Although she recovers, Meirose disappears from her bed and Pras then finds her on the roof of the hospital contemplating suicide. In order to save her, Pras promises to marry her and take care of her son. His altruism is motivated by having lost his own mother when he was a boy – which is shown in a pre-title daydream sequence. With the impromptu marriage completed, Pras is left in a dilemma, and having failed to reach Arini earlier, decides not to tell her about Meirose. Instead, Pras keeps his marriage secret and sets Meirose up in her own house so she can raise and care for Akbar. Over time though, what began as an act of altruism for Pras becomes more difficult to maintain as he increasingly becomes conflicted. Meirose begins to seduce Pras by cooking for him and when he gives her religious material, by asking him to teach her personally.

As Arini becomes increasingly suspicious about Pras' activities outside the home she discovers a pharmacy receipt in his possession which she discovers is for Meirose and Akbar. She acquires the address and encounters Meirose and learns of her husband's duplicity. This discovery is additionally devastating for her since her father had also kept a secret second wife unbeknownst to her, which her mother had endured silently for many years. Moreover, when proposing to his daughter, Pras had promised her father that he would never hurt Arini. Yet this discovery reveals to Arini that even Pras is no better than other men. Arini feels betrayed and heartbroken, and there is a lot of sympathy created around her position as the aggrieved wife who had placed her trust in a "good" man.

Despite her anger and disappointment, Arini provides the solution to the polygamy problem. Taking advice and inspiration from her own mother to be "sabar dan ikhlas" (patient and sincere), she proposes for Meirose to visit their house and stay the night. This is precipitated by Pras struggling to fulfil a promise he made to Nadia to attend her puppetry show when Akbar falls sick and Pras decides to stay with Meirose. When Pras calls Arini to tell her he cannot come, Arini is able to dispense advice over the phone about Akbar's sickness, freeing up Pras to attend the show and not disappoint Nadia. Arini's actions not only resolve the emotional conflict of the plot but establish the relative hierarchy between the two wives, showing Arini to be the more maternal and magnanimous woman. After being accepted into their house later that night, Meirose feels inadequate compared to Arini and decides to leave, entrusting Akbar to the care of Arini and Pras to be a younger brother to Nadia. She leaves a video message to both Arini and Pras saying that she has to leave so that she does not interfere with their family.

While there are similarities with *Verses of Love*, *A Paradise Not Longed For* plays up the theme of fairness through the Arini-Pras-Meirose love triangle. In a classic love-triangle melodrama the multiple affections generate conflict that are resolved when the monogamous couple emerge triumphant at the end of the film. By relying on this established trope in Indonesian melodrama the problems of polygamy can be mentally related to the problems of a love-triangle without generating too much resistance or awareness towards the polygamy itself. This provides "cover" for the filmmakers to subtly critique polygamy. *A Paradise Not Longed For* sets up an idealized romantic marriage before showing how it can be ruined by a second wife, even if she is married out of altruism and not lust. In this way, *A Paradise Not Longed For* is similar to *Verses of Love*, by showing how polygamy is a troubled and difficult configuration. *A Paradise Not Longed For* remains within mainstream concepts of love and romance but uses them to advance a critique of polygamy.

Key to *A Paradise Not Longed For*'s problematization of polygamy are the women characters, especially Arini. As to be expected Arini gets jealous, but her subsequent response is to turn to her faith in order to strengthen her resolve and position as the first and therefore rightful wife. Here the film is playing on romantic ideas of love and devotion that by not giving up on her husband, by rising above the pettiness of the situation, and by seeking solace and strength in faith, she can win back her husband, thus restoring the perfect marriage that they had beforehand. At the same time, she becomes competitive and asserts her needs, thereby creating an untenable situation for Pras, who can no longer be fair to her. Arini does not seek to annul the marriage, rather her actions are consistent with a contextualized response to the situation she is in. *A Paradise Not Longed For*'s presentation of love and romance remains firmly within the normative mainstream concept of romance leading to monogamous, happy marriage. Within this configuration, polygamy is "illogical."

CONCLUSION

Taking the three films that represent polygamy in Indonesian cinema – *Love for Share*, *Verses of Love*, and *A Paradise Not Longed For* – Indonesian filmmakers have generally made films that can be described as "anti-polygamy." This can be attributed to the progressive politics of Indonesia's current crop of filmmakers. However, the way in which polygamy is presented shapes the argument of the film and can also impact its reception. *Love for Share* adopts an activist perspective on the practice of polygamy by showing polygamous marriages as based on deceit and suffering. *Verses of Love* and *A Paradise Not Longed For*, on the other hand, adopt mainstream tropes of romance and self-actualization showing polygamy to be unfair and causing conflict. In *A Paradise Not Longed For* a clear comparison between polygamy and monogamy is drawn, showing monogamy to be practically and morally superior.

For the mainstream audience in Indonesia, there is still a preference for normative ideals of romantic love, leading to a monogamous marriage and a comfortable household. If pop culture is a dream factory, then monogamous love and marriage are the dream of the mainstream audience of Indonesia today. This clashes with the more "conservative" belief from more traditionalist Islamic groups and individuals who advocate for the normalization of Islamic cultural and legal practices such as compulsory *hijab*, gender segregation, banning alcohol, and the full legalization of polygamy. In between is a generation sensitive to the requirements of their religion, and who aspire to normative life goals, but wanting modern forms of love that include romance, material wealth, and stable family life. To them, polygamy is incompatible with these ideals.

WORKS CITED

Bourchier, K., and V. Hadiz, eds. 2014. *Indonesian Politics and Society: A Reader*. London and New York.

Boellstorff, T. 2004. "The Emergence of Political Homophobia in Indonesia: Masculinity and National Belonging." *Ethnos* 69 (4): 445-64.

Brenner, S. 2006. "Democracy, Polygamy, and Women in Post-'Reformasi' Indonesia." *Social Analysis: The International Journal of Social and Cultural Practice* 50 (1): 164-70.

———. 2011. "Holy Matrimony? The Print Politics of Polygamy in Indonesia." In *Islam and Popular Culture in Indonesia and Malaysia*, edited by Andrew N. Weintraub, 212-34. London.

Diani, H., and Y. T. Suwarni. 2006. "Cleric Aa Gym Rekindles Polygamy Debate." *The Jakarta Post*, December 4.

Fealy, G. 2007. "Consuming Islam: Commodified Religion and Aspirational Pietism in Contemporary Indonesia." In *Expressing Islam: Religious Life and Politics in Indonesia*, edited by G. Fealy and S. White, 15-39. Singapore.

Heryanto, A. 2011. "Upgraded Piety and Pleasure: The New Middle Class and Islam in Indonesian Popular Culture." In *Islam and Popular Culture in Indonesia and Malaysia*, edited by A. N. Weintraub, 60-82. Abingdon and New York.

———. 2014. *Identity and Pleasure: The Politics of Indonesian Screen Culture*. Singapore.

Hoesterey, J. B. 2008. "Marketing Morality: The Rise, Fall and Rebranding of Aa Gym." In *Expressing Islam: Religious Life and Politics in Indonesia* edited by G. Fealy and S. White, 95-112. Singapore.

Hoesterey, J. B., and M. Clark. 2012. "Film Islami: Gender, Piety and Pop Culture in Post-Authoritarian Indonesia." *Asian Studies Review* 36 (2): 207-26.

Imanjaya, E. 2009. "The Curious Cases of Salma, Siti, and Ming: Representations of Indonesia's Polygamous Life in 'Love for Share.'" *Jump Cut: A Review of Contemporary Media* 51.

Izharuddin, A. 2016. *Gender and Islam in Indonesian Cinema*. London.

Kurnia, N. 2009. "Berbagi Suami (Love for Share): The Discourse of Polygamy in a Recent Indonesian Film." *Intersections: Gender and Sexuality in Asia and the Pacific* 19.

Lev, D. S. 1996. "On the Other Hand?'" In *Fantasizing the Feminine in Indonesia*, edited by L. J. Sears, 191-206. Durham and London.

Machmudi, Y. 2008. *Islamising Indonesia: The Rise of Jemaah Tarbiyah and the Prosperous Justice Party (PKS)*. Canberra.

Nasution, K. 2008. "Polygamy in Indonesian Islamic Family Law." *Shariah Journal* 16 (2): 207-22.

Nurmila, N. 2009. *Women, Islam and Everyday Life: Renegotiating Polygamy in Indonesia*. London and New York.

Nurmila, N., and L. R. Bennett. 2016. "The Sexual Politics of Polygamy in Indonesian Marriages." In *Sex and Sexualities in Contemporary Indonesia: Sexual Politics, Health, Diversity, and Representations*, edited by L. R. Bennett and S. G. Davies, 69-87. London and New York.

Pamungkas, A. S. 2015. "The Dakwah Media in Post Suharto Indonesia: From Politics of Identity to Popular Culture." Ph.D dissertation, Berlin: Humboldt-Universität zu Berlin.

Paramaditha, I. 2010. "Passing and Conversion Narratives: Ayat-Ayat Cinta and Muslim Performativity in Contemporary Indonesia." *Asian Cinema* 21 (2): 69-90.

Rakhmani, I. 2016. *Mainstreaming Islam in Indonesia: Television, Identity & the Middle Class*. New York.

———. 2014. "Mainstream Islam: Television Industry Practice and Trends in Indonesian sinetron." *Asian Journal of Social Science* 42:435-66.

Randello, T. 2017. "Hijab: A Personal Choice." *The Jakarta Post*, February 21. http://www.thejakartapost.com/life/2017/02/21/hijab-a-personal-choice.html.

Roy, O. 2004. *Globalized Islam: The Search for a New Ummah*. New York.

Sani, A. 2000. "Asrul Sani: Films Can Never Replace the Function of 'Kiais'," *Tempo*, 12 November.

Sasono, E. 2010. "Islamic-Themed Films in Contemporary Indonesia: Commodified Religion or Islamization?" *Asian Cinema* 21 (2), 48–68.

Suryakusuma, J. 2017. "Reinterpreting Islam: First the female clerics, now the feminists." *The Jakarta Post*. May 31. https://www.thejakartapost.com/academia/2017/05/31/reinterpreting-islam-first-the-female-clerics-now-the-feminists.html.

van Wichelen, S. 2009. "Polygamy Talk and the Politics of Feminism: Contestations over Masculinity in a New Muslim Indonesia." *Journal of International Women's Studies* 11 (1), 173-88.

Philippine Muslim Women on Screen:
From Sheltered Daughters to Revolutionaries[1]

Vivienne SM. Angeles
La Salle University

FILIPINO FILMMAKERS have produced more films on Muslims than on any other minority group in the Philippines. Films about Muslims usually focused on men, who were often presented as villains who disrupt social order in southern Philippines. In the 1980s, Filipino films started to portray Muslim men as heroes – albeit still demonstrating some negative stereotypes of being traitors, violent and quick to anger in parts of the films.[2] Muslim women were never the protagonists in earlier films, and their roles as wives, caring mothers, and sheltered daughters were secondary[3] if not marginal to the story.

This essay examines the evolving representation of Philippine Muslim women on film, from sheltered females to women exercising their agency and fulfilling multiple roles outside the home. This changing representation is dictated by the nature of Christian-Muslim relations in the Philippines, and the emergence of independent filmmakers who are motivated by their experiences in southern Philippines. In spite of this evolution and depiction of expanded roles of women, however, the films also retain, to some extent, traditional notions of women's subordination to men, who continue to be heads of households, decision makers, and pillars of the home. The films *Brides of Sulu* (John Nelson, 1934/1937)[4] *Zamboanga* (Eduardo De Castro, 1937), *Badjao* (Lamberto V. Avellana, 1957), *Perlas ng Silangan* (*Pearl of the Orient*, Pablo Santiago, 1969), *Bagong Buwan* (*New Moon*, Marilou Diaz-Abaya, 2001), *Limbunan* (*Bridal Quarters*, Teng Mangansakan, 2010), *Sheika* (Arnel Mardoquio, 2010), *Ang Paglalakbay ng Mga Bituin sa Gabing Madilim* (*Journey of the Stars in the Dark Night*, Arnel Mardoquio, 2012), and *Daughters of the Three-*

---

1. I thank Teng Mangansakan and Arnel Mardoquio for sharing their respective films and insights.

2. For example see *The Real Glory* (Henry Hathaway, 1939), *Muslim Magnum .357* (Ronwaldo Reyes, 1986), *Mistah: Mga Mandirigma* (*Mistah: Warriors,* Bebong Osorio, 1994). See Angeles 2016.

3. *Brides of Sulu* (1934), *Pearl of the Orient* (1986), *Badjao* (1957).

4. The film dates the copyright to 1934 but the blurb on the DVD cover mentions 1937 under the director's name.

Tailed Banner (Teng Mangansakan, 2016) present Muslim women and reveal this development. Directors of these films engage in a form of communication that invites the viewer to a sense of place, to the cultural traditions and challenges faced by a people long marginalized by colonial Islamophobia that continues to affect Muslim-Christian relations in the Philippines in contemporary times.[5]

To demonstrate the changes in the portrayal of Philippine Muslim women, the films are presented chronologically and placed in the social and political contexts in which they were produced and viewed. The subjects of the films are Moros, born Muslims who trace their lineage to pre-colonial families in the islands of Mindanao and Sulu in southern Philippines. They are both a religious and an ethnic minority[6] whose views on gender are dictated by their interpretation of Islam and traditions. The Spanish and American colonizers called them Moros (Moors) in a derogatory way but in the early 1970s, the Moro National Liberation Front, the largest Muslim secessionist movement in the country at the time, transcoded[7] the term "Moro" and re-appropriated it to refer to their courage, bravery, heroism, and independence. For this essay, I use the term Moro women because it is the specific cohort, albeit of different ethnic affiliations within the larger Philippine Muslim community, presented in the films.

THE "OTHER" IN PHILIPPINE FILMS

Muslims constitute 5.6 per cent of the more than 100 million population of the Philippines.[8] As a people who profess a different religion from the Spanish-enforced Christianity,[9] and who belong to ethnic tribes that were largely untouched by colonial cultural impositions, Muslims became the "other" in Philippine society, conforming to Plate's view of otherness as "that which resides outside the margins of the dominant cultural representations, outside the social-symbolic order."[10] This "othering" was exacerbated by two other causes: first, the insular nature of the country's geography, which provided physical isolation of Moros in the southern islands of Mindanao and Sulu, and second, colonial literature that depicts Muslims in negative

---

5. See Gowing 1979.

6. Philippine Muslims belong to different ethnic tribes: Maranao, Maguindanao, Tausug, Molbog, Jama Mapun, Kalibogan, Sangil, Yakan, Palawani, Kalagan, Iranun and Badjao.

7. Hall 1997.

8. The 2018 World Bank figures showed the Philippine population at 106,651,922. See https://data.worldbank.org/indicator/SP.POP.TOTL?locations.

9. The 2010 Census figures indicate that there are 74.2 million Roman Catholics and 5.1 million Muslims in the Philippines. Philippine Statistics Authority 2015.

10. Plate 1999, 4.

terms,[11] which in turn became the basis of early Philippine history school books. Such depictions influenced the way Filipino Christians thought about Muslims. Muslim women, as portrayed in films, demonstrate a "double otherness": first, as part of the Moro other, and second, as women in a male-dominated society.

The changing representation of Philippine Muslim women has been influenced by the pattern of Christian-Muslim perception of each other as well as what the director intends to achieve in his film. As Margaret Miles claims, films arise in and respond to concrete historical circumstances and at the same time endeavor to make the viewers see what the director wants to communicate.[12] Hall's view of language as one of the media through which thoughts, ideas, and feelings are represented in film is also relevant to this study, since words and the moving image complement each other in the production of meaning.[13] This study also deals with the issue of gender, which is socially constructed and intersects with other socially constructed categories like race, class[14] and ethnicity[15] which, in turn, help shape the different aspects of the Moro women's experiences.

MORO WOMEN IN EARLY FILMS

Films on Moros have been part of Philippine film history since its early years. Two films, *Tarhata* (Jose Domingo Badilla)[16] and *Moro Pirates* (José Nepomuceno), made in 1931, were among the seventy-five silent films produced in the Philippines from 1912 to 1933. Current film archivists contend that clips from these two movies were incorporated into the early sound movies, *Brides of Sulu* and *Zamboanga*.[17] Two Americans, George Harris and Eddie Tait, produced both films for the American market and cosmopolitan audiences in the Philippines.[18] *Brides of Sulu* was shown in the United States and Frank Capra was reported to have admired the film, saying it was "beautiful regardless of conditions."[19] Both films play upon the exoticism of a people and emphasize their differences from the rest of the country and the United States. The narrator of *Brides of Sulu* underscores

11. See for example Montero y Vidal 1886.
12. Miles 1966, 11.
13. Hall 1997.
14. Lorbell and Farrell 1991.
15. Gopaldas 2013; Crenshaw 1991.
16. There are two other films entitled *Tarhata,* one produced in 1941 and the other in 1957. Both are unavailable for this study.
17. San Diego 2011.
18. Buenconsejo 2013.
19. Rawitsch 2015, 211.

that the Sulu group of islands is "500 miles from Manila and 500 years behind the march of civilization." The foreword to *Zamboanga* repeats this notion of backwardness, saying:

> Ages back, in the vigorous morning of history, men seeking women raided and robbed one another's homes, islands, even countries. Women were fair game and the hunt a deadly sport. Then, civilization tempered man's barbarism and the day of women raiders passed. Only in a few far, distant and untraveled places does the barbaric custom still survive.

The film then moves on to the "distant and untraveled place," the Sulu islands, with the narration highlighting the differences between the Moros, the Christianized Filipinos, and the rest of humanity.

In *Zamboanga*, a scene shows Hadji Rasul declaring to his wives that they all tire him and he wants a "new, young, and beautiful wife." He offers marriage to Minda Mora, the granddaughter of the Datu[20] but she rebuffs him because she is in love with someone else. As if to demonstrate what the foreword to the film says about "women raiders," Hadji Rasul and his men raid the community and take Minda Mora forcibly. Danoa, Minda Mora's lover, joins the grandfather's followers as they pursue Hadji Rasul. A clash of bladed weapons and spears ensue, Danoa is reunited with Minda Mora and they are married, following Muslim and local Moro traditions. The scene with Hadji Rasul and the wives and the abduction of Minda Mora portray women like commodities at man's disposal.

Brides of Sulu's promotional materials tout the film as "forbidden love in a lost civilization" with the wide-eyed Datu and the daughter's lover both holding barongs, a multi-purpose bladed weapon popularly used in Sulu, but a weapon that non-Muslims associate with the Moro *juramentados*.[21] Forbidden love, because it is between a Tausug Moro woman and a Badjao[22] man and as the film's foreword says, "the hatred of the 'Mohammedan' Moro for the unbeliever is not fiction."

Although the foreword describes the film as a simple love story, the narration and the scenes appear to emphasize the complexities of a people prone to raiding, taking women by force, and fighting non-Muslims.

---

20. *Datu* is a title for a chieftain who is part of the ruling structure, with territorial jurisdiction under the Sultan.

21. *Juramentados* were Muslims who committed ritual suicide as a response to colonialism. See Majul 1972, "Appendix B."

22. Although Badjaos are now included in the thirteen Muslim tribes, they were classified as pagans in pre-colonial times.

In *Zamboanga*, the right of the father, Datu Tambuyong, to arrange the marriage of his daughter, Benita, to a man of his choice, prompts the latter to run away with her non-Muslim pearl-diver commoner lover, Assan, and sail to an uninhabited island. They are, however, captured by the father's "Moro warriors" and brought back home, but Benita insists on marrying Assan. The Datu relents after Assan undergoes trials to prove his worth, converts to Islam, and promises to serve Benita's people. They are married, following Muslim and local customs, one of which involves Benita sitting on a pile of cushions that are turned by attendants several times to symbolize that "she will obey her new lord and master." Aside from Benita, who stands out as the daughter of the Datu and hence, member of the local aristocracy, the women in the film are vendors, dance performers, and spectators. Benita is the exceptional Moro woman who defies her father's decision, marries her lover, but submits to the ritual that symbolizes her subservience to the new husband.

 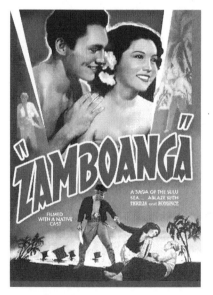

World War II and the Japanese occupation from 1942 to 1945 interrupted American colonization of the Philippines. The Japanese took over the film industry, producing mainly propaganda films linked to their war aims.[23] There is only one film on the Moros from the 1940s, *Tarhata* (Manuel Silos), about a Moro princess who falls in love with a Christian soldier.

23. Del Mundo 1999, 34.

POST-COLONIAL FILMS

Badjao (1957) is considered a classic in Philippine film history. Hassan, a Bad-jao, meets and falls in love with Datu Tahil's niece, Bala Amai. Datu Tahil would allow the marriage only if Hassan converts to Islam, gives up his Bad-jao identity (as the Datu considers the Badjao to be an inferior tribe) and lives as a Tausug. Hassan does as required but finds it difficult to live among a people that does not really accept him and who create difficult situations, including acts of violence (burning their home). Hassan's selfless act of turn-ing his back on his ethnic identity and living among the Tausugs reaches its limits when he realizes that his acceptance is contingent upon his providing precious blue pearls to Datu Tahil. Hassan confronts Datu Tahil and decides to return to his people. While Bala Amai is a key character in the film as a woman belonging to the local aristocracy who dared to fall in love with a man coming from a tribe they consider inferior, she is not a participant in family decision-making and is absent in the confrontation between her husband and her uncle. She is the silent witness to the conflict between her family and husband. Bala Amai tells her husband: "I will go wherever you go. I forced you to live with my people. That was my mistake. As a wife, it is my duty to serve and cherish you. I will go wherever you go." Bala Amai, who broke away from the conventions of marrying within the tribe, and who owned up to her uncle's demands on Hassan as her mistake, emerges as the dutiful wife who surrenders her agency and subordinates herself to Hassan's decision. Any discussion on courses of action they should take as husband and wife in response to the actions of the Datu and his men against them is glaringly absent. Except for Bala Amai, women are missing in the film and Bala Amai herself is submerged in the tension among the male characters, thus underscoring the stereotypical notion of Moro women subordinate to the men.

Pearl of the Orient (1969) is the story of Amid, a Moro prisoner in a Spanish ship, who escapes, then falls in love with Dayang Mahalina, the daughter of a Sultan. When a lady-in-waiting advises Dayang Mahalina to reciprocate the love of Amid, the latter asks: "why do we have to talk about it when in our culture we do not choose whom to marry?" Amid, however, has to undergo tests to prove his worth in a contest with Datu Hamid, another admirer of Dayang Mahalina. Amid bests the others and the Sultan declares him not just the rightful winner of the contest but also of his daughter. Here, Dayang Mahalina is the prize awarded to the brave Moro. It so happens that she also has feelings for Amid, which she could not show in conformity with Moro expectations of its women. If Datu Hamid had won the contest, Dayang Mahalina would have had to marry him.

In 1972, President Ferdinand Marcos declared martial law in the Philippines. One of the reasons for the declaration was the existence of the Moro National Liberation Front (MNLF), a secessionist movement whose goal was to establish an independent Islamic state in southern Philippines. As a way to appease Muslims, the martial law government launched programs of accommodation for Muslim minorities and started emphasizing that Islam is part of Philippine heritage and Muslims are ethnic minorities who happen to profess Islam. The government programs included recognizing Muslim holidays, revising school textbooks to include Muslims in more favorable light, creating an Institute of Islamic Studies, and bringing about an environment that encourages and nurtures culture and religious pluralism. The government information office produced films to publicize these programs. In 1996, the government and the MNLF signed a peace agreement but the conflicts continue on, involving other Muslim groups.

THE 2000S AND INDIE FILMS ON MOROS

The 2000s witnessed the growth of independent films in the Philippines. By indie films, I refer to films made outside of the major studios, usually low-budgeted and distributed independently. With access to affordable means of film production[24] and the support of government institutions like the National Commission for Culture and Arts, which awards grants and sponsors film festivals, individuals and groups are encouraged to participate in the process of cultural production.

The films on Moros for this time period are mostly indie films, starting with *New Moon* (2001). The film is set against the Philippine military's bombing of the Moro Islamic Liberation Front (MILF)[25] camps on orders of president Joseph Estrada in 2000. The deaths, destruction, and displacement extended beyond the camps and affected both Christians and Muslims in the area. *New Moon* explores the issues of war and peace, their causes and effects, through family discussions and is centered on two brothers, Ahmad, a physician, and Musa, a commander of the MILF. However, Ahmad's wife, Fatima, and his mother, Bai Farida, play critical roles, involved in the discussions on issues plaguing Mindanao and its people, and offering their positions on the conflict situation and the need for peace. In spite of the tragedy that killed their only son, Fatima assists Ahmad as he tends to the wounded and lead people as they move constantly to escape the ravages of war. Even if the roles of Fatima and Bai Farida appear to be secondary, they

24. Gancio 2015.
25. The MILF was a splinter group of the Moro National Liberation Front and also sought to establish an Islamic state.

have a prominent presence as the scenes shift from war scenes to brothers' discussions. Most of the characters are women, wives and mothers, who, together with their children are in constant motion, moving to safer places.

The advent of digital films democratized filmmaking in the Philippines, with young Moros now writing, directing and producing their own films. In 2010, Teng Mangansakan, a Moro filmmaker and journalist who attended the University of Iowa International Writing Workshop, released his first feature film, *Bridal Quarters*. The story centers on seventeen-year-old Ayesha, and her arranged marriage. She questions the practice but accepts it as the dutiful daughter, who although interested in someone else, is bound by familial obligations and traditions. Ayesha's father assigns her aunt Farida to be in charge of bridal preparations, which include isolation from the public a month before the wedding.

The film also addresses the issue of polygamy. Ayesha's mother, hurt by her husband's having taken a second wife, is more pained by what people would say about her husband's having chosen a Christian woman. She counsels Ayesha that "perhaps part of being a woman is to accept our fate, in the belief that Allah will reward our suffering in the hereafter. Pray to Allah that you would learn to love Hussein (the intended groom). In that way, you will bear the burden with grace." Farida, the aunt, counsels Ayesha to forget her own feelings, think of family honor, and endure whatever comes. Farida speaks from her own experience of subverting family wishes when she insisted that she would marry her Christian lover in spite of strong family objections. A family member killed her lover, thus leaving Farida with the burden of guilt – that if she had respected the objections of the family, her lover would still be alive. Farida represents the past, Ayesha the present, and Saripa, Ayesha's younger sister who questions traditions and vows that she would never agree to an arranged marriage, the future. The film ends with Ayesha dressed as a bride ready for the wedding ceremony and assisted by the women in the family. A slow-moving film, it is interspersed with scenes of Mindanao, as the director also intended to showcase the peaceful place that is often interrupted by war.

Arnel Mardoquio's *Sheika* (2010) is about a Tausug widow, Sheika, and her sons Modin and Alfad. They move to Davao, a Christian-dominated city, to escape the armed conflict in her hometown, Jolo, where her husband was killed. Fearful of possible Christian-Muslim tension in Davao, they cover up their Muslim identity, change their names to Shei, Dindin, and Sorsoy, respectively, and pretend they are from another region of the country. All three take whatever jobs they can as they struggle to make a living. In the process, Dindin is recruited to monitor potential assassination targets of the Davao

Death Squad (DDS). The DDS is a group of motorcycle vigilantes who are paid to kill drug users, dealers, and petty criminals.[26] The brothers eventually become drug users themselves, and Dindin also witnesses the setting up of a murder by the DDS. The DDS kills both brothers. Mired in poverty, alone in the city without resources to give her sons a decent burial, Shei pushes her sons' bodies over the bridge. Shei later discovers the contact information of DDS members in Dindin's cell phone and decides to hunt for her sons' killers herself. She finds Asul, who had a hand in her sons' deaths, but fails to stab him and ends up being shot by Asul in the head. Shei survives, but repeated tragedy causes her to have a mental breakdown and she ends up in a mental hospital. While there, she unexpectedly receives loving care from Gary, a janitor in the hospital. However, after a period of unrequited affection from Shei, Gary eventually rapes her, resulting in new pregnancy. Gary is jailed for his transgression but before he dies in prison, he writes Shei to ask for forgiveness. The last scene shows Shei, already recovered from her mental breakdown, with her daughter visiting Gary's grave. She tells her daughter that he is an old friend. This film underscores maternal love and sacrifice and ends with renewal, this time with a young daughter.

Mardoquio's other film centered on Moro women is *The Journey of the Stars in the Dark Night*. It is a political film narrating the journey of Amrayda and Fatima to protect Faidal, whose parents were killed by government troops aided by US marines. Before the parents were attacked, the mother, Armina, sent Faidal, off to escape with a backpack filled with ransom money. Amrayda and Fatima, revolutionaries themselves, are becoming weary of the war but forego their plans to go to Zamboanga in order to help the boy escape because he is being pursued by government troops for the ransom money. Lovers themselves, Amrayda realizes that she is now the guardian of Faidal and her relationship with Fatima can not continue. With the help of Bapa Indo, another revolutionary, they sail out in the evening on a small boat, but the pursuing government forces kill all of them. Faidal's parents were revolutionaries who turned to kidnapping for ransom, against the advice of Bapa Indo. The film distances the revolutionaries from the kidnapping, which is being pursued by the Abu Sayyaf group in Mindanao, Sulu, and Basilan. This portrayal of women is a departure from previous films. The women are revolutionaries involved in the secessionist movement, making decisions, pursuing dangerous tasks, and being in a relationship frowned upon by the community. This film acknowledges the role of women in the revolution, a subject that has been ignored both in literature and previous films on Moros.

26. Reyes 2016.

Among the latest films on Moros, released in 2016, is Mangansakan's *Daughters of the Three-Tailed Banner*, an adaptation of the first part of a two-part book, *moro2morrow*. It presents two stories of Moro women, one in the country and the other in the city. The film opens with women mourning the loss of the last male member of the family, who died as a *mujaheedin*, a fighter in the secessionist movement. The matriarch decides to look for suitable husbands for the two eligible women in the family. One of them, Tonina, is single but unbeknownst to the family, is pregnant by a cousin who also died in the war. Tonina is torn between leaving the village and heading to the city. Nora, a transgender woman known to the family as Abdulghafar, returns home to claim her share of family resources but her sister tells her that she has lost all her privileges when she decided to be an "unnatural woman." Another member of the family, Sophia, is schizophrenic but is the witness to everything going on. Since she is a "mad" woman, her stories are seen as products of her madness, even if true. Pregnancy out of wedlock, being transgender, and being schizophrenic are outside of the strict family norms and in Philippine Muslim society, such "afflictions" are viewed as shameful to the family. Tonina's "sin", however, is redeemed when, after deciding to stay in the village, she gives birth to a boy, to the joy of the family matriarch who sees the baby as the guarantor of family continuity. In spite of the women being able to run the household and fend for themselves, the idea of having a male member of the family is still critical for Tonina's family. The matriarch's concern for continuity of the family line, and the need for a male in the household, draw attention to the persistence of ideas on primacy of a man in the household and in society.

The other story in *Daughters of the Three-Tailed Banner* centers on Aida, a Moro who left the village to work as an Overseas Filipino Worker (OFW) in Kuwait. Upon arrival in the city, on the first leg of the trip abroad, she found out that the recruiter swindled her so she could not proceed to Kuwait. This is a story shared by many Filipinos since the country launched an overseas employment program in the 1970s to help solve the unemployment crisis in the country. Unscrupulous recruiters preyed on Filipinos desperate for employment, in spite of government regulations enforced by the Philippine Overseas Employment Administration. Ashamed to return home and face family members who helped finance her aborted project, she stays in the city, pretending to be in Kuwait. We learn about her family only through phone calls, which she always ends abruptly. She even speaks some Arabic to make her family think that an Arab boss is present. Many Filipinos can empathize with Aida's story as a woman seeking employment overseas and being swindled. While Aida's being a Moro makes her an "other," she is, however, like the thousands of Filipinos who seek overseas employment in order to help their families.

The village and the city as juxtaposed in the film demonstrate the contrasts in the lives of women. The city provides economic opportunities but at the same time, poses a threat of social and economic exploitation, as experienced by Aida. In the country, conservatism and strict moral rules reign but in the case of Nora, who has spent much time in the city, it is not a hindrance to her return.

CONCLUSION

The representation of Moro women in Philippine cinema is evolving. While earlier films produced during the colonial period portrayed Moro women as love interests and daughters of the local aristocracy and subordinated to the men, in more recent films, like *Sheika* and *Daughters of the Three-Tailed Banner*, women like Tonina, Sheika, Nora, and Aida are making their own choices, exercising their individual autonomy and agency. In some instances, however, as in *Bridal Quarters*, Ayesha questions traditional practices but accepts her father's authority, her mother's and aunt's counsel on arranging her marriage and choosing her husband. She does this hoping that in the end God will reward her for being a dutiful daughter. Just as important is family honor, which is at stake if she refuses the arrangement.

It is in *Journey of the Stars Under the Dark Night* that Moro women as revolutionaries are introduced to Philippine cinema. Armina, Amrayda, and Fatimah are all involved in the movement that seeks autonomy if not independence for the Bangsamoro (Moro nation). In *Bridal Quarters* and *Daughters of the Three-Tailed Banner*, there is talk of the proposed bill creating the new autonomous government and hopes for a better future. That bill failed to pass the Philippine congress but in 2018, President Rodrigo Duterte signed the Bangsamoro Organic Law, creating the new Bangsamoro Autonomous Region.[27]

The films surveyed respond to concrete historical circumstances of Muslims in Mindanao and reveal the spectrum of gender roles from those of long ago to new responsibilities that respond to contemporary situations and family needs. Both the director and the viewer bring their respective social, racial, and class locations in presenting a story on the one hand and in interpreting the meanings.[28] For director Mangansakan, his focus on women is inspired by the women who surrounded him while he was growing up – his maternal grandmother who, as matriarch of the clan, was a central

27. Anonymous 2016.
28. Miles 1966, 11.

figure in his personal development. Mangansakan claims that he explores the spectrum of women from powerlessness, vulnerable members of society to independent, strong-willed individuals. The stories in Mangansakan's films in this study are told from the perspective of women. He is from the Moro culture of Mindanao, hence, he includes some of that culture's traditions in his films. Director Mardoquio also lived in Mindanao, and has been affected by the situation of Muslims and their sufferings caused by the war. He admires "women activists as they have become more assertive and articulate in seeking empowerment for the Bangsamoro people of Mindanao."[29]

Overall, the representation of Moro women has evolved in these films, especially with the works of Mangansakan and Mardoquio presenting the narratives through women's perspectives, and highlighting the tension between tradition and women's agency.

WORKS CITED

Angeles, V. 2010. "Moros in the Media and Beyond: Representations of Philippine Muslims." *Contemporary Islam* 4:29-53.

——. 2016. "Philippine Muslims on Screen: From Villains to Heroes." *Journal of Religion & Film* 20, no.1. http://digitalcommons.unomaha.edu/jrf/vol20/iss1/6.

Anonymous. 2015. "House Failure to Pass Bangsamoro Law." *Asia Journal,* December 23. http://asianjournal.com/editorial/house-failure-to-pass-bangsamoro-basic-law/.

Anonymous. 2016. "Congress Adjourns, Fails to Pass BBL." *Philippine Daily Inquirer,* February 4. http://newsinfo.inquirer.net/761319/congress-adjourns-fails-to-pass-bbl.

Anonymous. 2017. "Emancipated Cinema: A Conversation with Lav Diaz." MUBI, April 20. https://www.youtube.com/watch?v=Eyc8nrIOWvE.

Bautista, A. 2015. *A History of Philippine Cinema.* National Commission for Culture and the Arts. April 15. https://ncca.gov.ph/about-ncca-3/subcommissions/subcommission-on-the-arts-sca/cinema/history-of-philippine-cinema/.

Buenconsejo, J. 2013. "Orientalism in the Narrative, Music and Myth of Amok in the 1937 Film Zamboanga." *Plaridel: A Philippine Journal of Communications, Media and Society* 10 (1): 30-49.

Crenshaw, K. 1991. "Mapping the Margins: Intersectionality, Identity Politics, and Violence against Women of Color." *Stanford Law Review* 43

---

29. Arnel Mardoquio, email message to author, March 30, 2017.

(6):1241-99.

Del Mundo, C. A. 1998. *Native Resistance: Philippine Cinema and Colonialism 1898-1941*. Manila.

———. 1999. "Philippine Cinema: a Historical Overview." *Asian Cinema* 10 (2): 29-66.

Diaz-Abaya, M. 2000. "The Making of Bagong Buwan: Dreaming of a Zone of Peace." *Philippine Daily Inquirer*, January 2.

Gancio, M. C. 2015. "Philippine Contemporary Regional Cinema: A Narrative Analysis of Regional Filmmakers' Accounts on the Re-emergence of Regional Films in the 21st Century." MA Thesis, University of the Philippines, 2015.

Gopaldas, A. 2013. "Intersectionality 101." *Journal of Public Policy & Marketing* 32:90-94.

Hall, S. 1997. *Representation: Cultural Representations and the Signifying Process*. London.

Lapena, C. G. 2011. "Is Silent Pic 'Bride of Sulu' Pinoy or Kano?" GMA News, April 27. https://www.gmanetwork.com/news/lifestyle/artandculture/230766/is-silent-flick-brides-of-sulu-pinoy-or-kano/story.

Lorber, J. and S. Farrell, eds. 1991. *Social Construction of Gender*. Newbury Park.

Majul, C. A. 1973. *Muslims in the Philippines*. Quezon City.

Miles, M. 1996. *Seeing and Believing: Religion and Values in the Movies*. Boston.

Montero y Vidal, J. 1886. *El archipelago Filipinas y las islas Marianas, Carolinas y Palao*. Madrid.

Nocum, A. 2001. "GMA stops military operations vs. MNLF," Philippine Daily Inquirer, February 21.

Philippine Statistics Authority. 2015. "2015 Philippine Statistical Yearbook." https://psa.gov.ph/sites/default/files/2015%20PSY%20PDF.pdf.

Plate, B. S. and D. Jaspers, eds. 1999. *Imag(in)ing Otherness: Filmic Visions of Living Together*. Atlanta.

Rawitsch, E. 2015. *Frank Capra's Eastern Horizons: American Identity and the Cinema of International Relations*. London.

Reyes, R. 2016. "Philippine Priests Lays Bare Existence of Davao Death Squads." *Union of Catholic Asian News (UCAN)*, April 22. https://www.ucanews.com/news/filipino-priest-lays-bare-existence-of-davao-death-squad/75844.

Rushling, G. J. 1903. "Interview with President McKinley." *The Christian Advocate*. https://docplayer.net/48717032-Interview-with-president-william-mckinley-by-general-james-rusling-january-22-1903.html.

San Diego, B. 2011. "Archivists Claim Two Silent Films 'Pirated' by US." *Philippine Daily Inquirer*, August 26. http://entertainment.inquirer.net/11043/archivists-reclaim-2-silent-ph-films-'pirated'-by-us-film-fest-opens-friday.